THE
GEOGRAPHIC BACKGROUND
OF
GREEK & ROMAN HISTORY

THE
GEOGRAPHIC BACKGROUND
OF
GREEK & ROMAN HISTORY

BY

M. CARY, D.LITT. OXON.

FORMERLY PROFESSOR OF ANCIENT HISTORY
AT THE UNIVERSITY OF LONDON

GREENWOOD PRESS, PUBLISHERS
WESTPORT, CONNECTICUT

Library of Congress Cataloging in Publication Data

Cary, M. (Max), 1881-1958.
    The geographic background of Greek & Roman history.

    Reprint. Originally published: Oxford : Clarendon
Press, 1949.
    Bibliography: p.
    Includes index.
    1. Classical geography. I. Title. II. Title: The
geographic background of Greek and Roman history.
DE29.C35 1981   938   81-7170
ISBN 0-313-23187-7 (lib. bdg.)   AACR2

This reprint has been authorized by the Oxford University
Press for sale throughout the world.

Reprinted in 1981 by Greenwood Press
A division of Congressional Information Service, Inc.
88 Post Road West, Westport, Connecticut 06881

Printed in the United States of America

10 9 8 7 6 5 4 3 2 1

PREFACE

IN this book I have endeavoured to make a fresh contribution to a subject whose importance is now generally recognized, the influence of geographic environment on human history, in a study of this influence on the world of ancient Greece and Rome. So far as I am aware, no attempt has yet been made to pursue this theme in a comprehensive way, except in Professor Ellen Semple's excellent book, *The Geography of the Mediterranean Region*, and the scope of her work does not extend beyond this region to those outlying countries which also figured in Greek and Roman history. A new survey of the entire subject in relation to the ancient Greeks and Romans may therefore be opportune.

My general indebtedness to previous writers is set forth in the bibliography at the end of the book. Of the authors therein mentioned, I am specially beholden to D. G. Hogarth, R. W. Lyde, Sir J. L. Myres, H. Nissen, A. Philippson, and Miss E. C. Semple. I also wish to put on record my obligation to T. Frank and his team of contributors to the *Economic Survey of Rome*, to M. Rostovtzeff, and to W. W. Tarn, from whose works I have derived much information and guidance.

My interest in anthropo-geography dates back to my under-graduate days, when I divagated from my authorized reading-list and devoured H. T. Buckle's *History of Civilization*. It has more recently been re-animated by A. J. Toynbee's challenging *Study of History*.

I gratefully acknowledge the assistance which I have received from my friend and former colleague, Miss M. S. Drower, M.B.E., who has read over my chapters on the Near East and has contributed valuable criticisms and suggestions.

I may state in advance my answer to two minor questions of geographical method which have obtruded themselves upon me. (1) A writer describing geographic features which remain discern-ible at the present day, but doing so in reference to past history, will almost inevitably find his pen slipping to and fro between the present and the past tenses. In my opinion such inconsistency is more than pardonable. Rigid uniformity in the use of a single tense may in such a case lead to inaccuracy or ambiguity of statement. Therefore the soundest rule is to select in each instance whichever tense is most appropriate to the particular context. (2) I have made no attempt to observe minute exactitude in the matter of measurements. Extreme accuracy may be essential in mathematical geography and in topographical studies over a narrow field, but in a general descriptive treatise the air of scientific precision thus conveyed is otiose and may be delusive. In particular, I have usually expressed the heights of mountain peaks and passes in round numbers. Approximate statements seem to me all the more preferable in this case, as there still exists much discrepancy in the figures given by modern and even by recent writers.

References to Strabo have been made according to the pages of the standard edition by Casaubon.

M. C.

CONTENTS

LIST OF MAPS

I. THE MEDITERRANEAN AREA

§ 1. GEOGRAPHIC UNITY

THE ancient Greeks and Romans made history in all the three continents of the Old World, and penetrated far into the interior regions of Europe and of Asia. But the principal scene of their activity was on the rims of continents rather than at the centres of the land masses. Their civilization was essentially a product of the Mediterranean area, and the Mediterranean Sea was *mare nostrum* to them in a double sense—a political possession, but also a great formative influence.

The Mediterranean area has a homogeneous character which manifests itself in various common attributes of its constituent lands. The climate of its component countries, though subject of course to local variations, conforms on the whole to the same general type. 'Mediterranean climate', in consequence, has become a technical term which geographers apply to analogous conditions in divers other parts of the globe—southern California, central Chile, Cape Province, and South Australia. All these districts resemble the Mediterranean area in their latitude (*c.* 40° N. or S.), and in fronting westward upon a wide ocean; but only in the Mediterranean zone does its peculiar climate extend far inland from the ocean face. The climate of Moscow is radically different from that of London, but between Cadiz and Beirut the weather undergoes no fundamental change.

Again, in their geological structure the Mediterranean countries are mostly of one piece. Broadly speaking, the Mediterranean area as now constituted was the product of a vast upheaval in the Tertiary Age, which created a framework of heavily folded mountains round a deeply sunken trough.[1] Originating in the same up-thrust, Mt. Lebanon resembles the Sierra Nevada in its tectonic forms, and the French Riviera is reproduced in the Crimean coast.

Furthermore, as a natural result of likeness in climate and structure, the Mediterranean lands are clad in a similar distinctive type of vegetation. The Mount of Olives near Jerusalem has many a counterpart in Sicily and the Balearic Isles, and the 'maquis' of Corsica is also spread widely over Greece.

---

[1] Within this trough the Mediterranean Sea as a continuous piece of water was not formed until a comparatively recent period.

Lastly, the Mediterranean border regions, while sharing a common sea front, are marked off sharply from their hinterlands by an almost unbroken ring of mountains and deserts. The centrifugal pressure which created the Mediterranean valley built up its mountain faces into high walls, backed by more gently shelving ramps on their continental sides. By way of exit from the Mediterranean area, Nature has provided only a few commodious passages; if we do not avail ourselves of these, we must 'go over the top' or risk famine in a no-man's-land.

§ 2. CLIMATE

A preliminary question here arises: Was the Mediterranean climate, as we know it, already prevalent in Greek and Roman times, or is it the product of some later transformation? Climatic changes in prehistoric times, but at an age not vastly removed from Greek and Roman antiquity, have been proved on geological and archaeological evidence.[1] In the fifth and fourth millenniums B.C. North Africa and Mesopotamia were not isolated fringes of fertile land bordering on a wide desert tract; they formed part of a continuous belt of cultivable country enjoying a moderate but regular rainfall. Again, a variety of evidence, which will be referred to in subsequent chapters, places it beyond doubt that at the beginnings of Greek and Roman history several of the Mediterranean lands carried a denser cover of forest than at the present time, and this difference implies a heavier rainfall in preceding ages than the Mediterranean lands now receive.[2]

Occasional data from Greek and Latin authors have also been pressed into service as testimony for a shift of climate since the time of their writing. The principal witness is Livy, who repeatedly records winter blizzards and prolonged summer rains in central Italy.[3] Proof of a change in weather has also been sought in the earlier incidence of harvest time in modern Greece and Italy, as compared with that of classical antiquity.[4] Lastly, considerable areas in the interior of Asia which were cultivable at the beginning of the Christian era have since fallen prey to desicca-

[1] V. G. Childe, *The Most Ancient East*, ch. 2.
[2] C. E. P. Brooks, *The Evolution of Climate*; J. L. Myres, *Who were the Greeks?*, p. 6.
[3] H. Nissen, *Italische Landeskunde*, i, pp. 395 ff. Cf. Appian, *Bell. Civ.* i. 87. 1 (an intensely cold winter in 83–2 B.C.).
[4] Nissen, i, pp. 399–400; P. Groebe, in Drumann–Groebe, *Geschichte Roms*, ii, pp. 743–4.

tion (pp. 165, 189 n.). This process, it is sometimes argued, did
not stop short at the Mediterranean border.

If these reasonings hold good, the climate of the Mediterranean
area in Greek and Roman times was wetter and cooler, and more
akin to that of central Europe than to that of Mediterranean lands
at the present day. But the evidence adduced is far from con-
clusive. It is not certain how far the desiccation of the Asian
continent in the last two thousand years has been due to natural
causes, and to what extent it is the result of human failure—the
rack and ruin of raids and invasions, or the slow deterioration
of an era of bad government; and in any case a change of climate
in Asia, if such there has been, does not prove a shift of weather
in Mediterranean longitudes. The reason why the date of harvest
now falls earlier in certain Mediterranean lands may be found in
the introduction of better methods of cultivation or the use of
more quickly maturing seeds, rather than in a new cycle of milder
winters and more torrid summers.[1] And the weather records
culled from Livy and other ancient authors may actually be used
to prove the stability of the Mediterranean climate: the reason
why ancient writers reported certain hard winters or wet summers was presumably because these were the reverse of normal.
Finally, a comparison of the modern lines of isocarps (drawn
through the most northerly points at which certain plants, e.g.
figs and dates, will bear fruit) with those which can be deduced
from ancient writers (especially from Theophrastus) shows a
remarkable coincidence between them;[2] and this is an important
consideration, for the fig and date are highly sensitive to any
change of climate. Hence according to one recent estimate the
temperature of the Mediterranean area, and indeed of the whole
northern temperate zone, has not varied by one degree Fahrenheit
in the past thousand years.[3] Local variations of climate in particular regions of this area need not of course be ruled out;
indeed the extensive deforestation of certain Mediterranean
lands since ancient times renders it probable that in such districts the climate is now more extreme and the summer drought
more severe. But it may be assumed that the Mediterranean
climate on the whole has remained unchanged since Greek and
Roman times.

[1] The northward extension of the Canadian wheat belt in recent years has been
largely due to the establishment of new strains by Sir Rowland Biffen, which
require ten days less to mature.
[2] A. Jardé, Les Céréales dans l'antiquité grecque, p. 66.
[3] S. F. Markham, Climate and the Energy of Nations, p. 23.

The determining factors of climate—latitude and the local distribution of land and water—combine in Mediterranean lands to produce a peculiar and distinctive cycle of weather. In the winter the Mediterranean area, which extends, roughly, from lat. 30° to 45°, lies in the path of the westerly gales which are then prevalent over the Atlantic between lats. 30° and 60°. Mt. Atlas and the Spanish plateau partly intercept these ocean winds, but the Straits of Gibraltar and the funnel between the Pyrenees and the Cévennes provide them with regular 'cyclone tracks' into the Mediterranean basin. This basin, moreover, is a prolific source of home-made cyclones, by reason of the disparity of temperature between its heat-retaining waters and the chilled hinterlands, which causes an influx of air from the adjacent continents. The wind-eddies which are thus formed, like the swirl of emptied water round a bath-sink, originate most frequently in certain cyclone centres, such as the Gulf of Lions, the region of the Lipari Islands, the Adriatic, and the seas round Cyprus, but every part of the Mediterranean comes within their reach. Under the joint influence of these intrusive and indigenous disturbances the Mediterranean winter is a season of frequent high winds which sometimes freshen into sharp squalls and change direction rapidly.[1]

The resultant churning of the air induces a heavy rainfall, rising to maxima in October and March, but copious in every winter month. The downpours are particularly heavy where steep mountain faces force the air-currents upward into a more chilly atmospheric stratum and so wring out of them an additional supply of 'orographic' rain. Of the 30 inches of mean annual rainfall in the Mediterranean area, more than 20 are precipitated in the winter months; while the total annual supply is less than that of England, the winter quota is somewhat higher. But the rain-clouds do not brood over the land, as in more northerly climes; they empty themselves in sharp cascades rather than in reluctant drizzles, and they do not leave a trail of mist or fog behind them. For all its boisterousness the Mediterranean winter is also a season of blue skies and clear sunshine. Its occasional north winds, blowing from a frozen continent, bite shrewdly even in a sunny spell, and in wet weather they smother the uplands in snow. But in calm weather even the midwinter sun strikes with the force of an April sun in England; in the coastlands the rain

[1] For some lively descriptions of sudden gusts from all quarters of heaven see Homer, *Odyssey* v. 291 ff., and x. 46 ff. (unloosening of the bag of Aeolus).

rarely turns into snow, and the snow never lies long.[1] The average winter temperature of the Mediterranean lowland regions is considerably higher than that of the English plain. The mean January temperature of London (a relatively warm winter resort for its latitude) is 38°; at Rome it rises to 45°, at Athens to 48°, at Palermo to 50°, and at Malaga to 60°. The Mediterranean lands, as a whole, are free from that continuous cold whose numbing effects have never been adequately counteracted until the advent of efficient modern methods of artificial heating.[2] But the chief advantage which the Mediterranean winter holds over those of more northerly regions lies in its longer spells of bright weather; though often wet and wild, it is never a period of settled gloom.

In summer the Mediterranean area passes under the sway of the north-easterly trade winds which then set in from the middle latitudes towards the sub-tropical zone. In Mediterranean longitudes this northerly current is intensified by a strong inward draught towards the Sahara, which from April to September sucks in the surrounding air like an immense natural furnace. Originating in the Eurasian land-mass, the predominant wind of the Mediterranean summer contains little moisture, and as it passes from cooler to hotter regions such water as it carries is evaporated more rapidly than local cloud-forming eddies can condense it. Apart from occasional trails of feathery cirrus, the Mediterranean summer sky is usually swept clear for a sun whose midday rays beat down almost vertically.[3] During the dog-days the thermometer readings of the Mediterranean area rise almost to a tropical level. In London (the hot spot of England) the mean July temperature is 62°; at Rome it is 76°, and 80° at Athens; in a few districts it goes up to 90°. In comparison with the ground temperature, it is true, the prevailing northerly wind is cool, and in the coastal districts the sea breezes that spring up in the afternoon dispel the midday's oven heat. In any case, the dryness of the atmosphere robs it of that enervating effect which saps human energy in regions of humid heat. The most adverse feature of the Mediterranean climate lies not in its high temperature so much as in its prolonged and regular drought. Apart from an

[1] The rapidity of change between rain and sunshine in the Mediterranean winter explains the ascendancy of the sky-god Zeus or Jupiter in the Greek and Roman pantheon.
[2] Markham, op. cit., p. 41.
[3] Hence to the Greeks and Romans the sun-god was the 'all-seeing' one. But the machine-like precision with which he plied his summer course did not suggest that he could regulate the weather like the 'cloud-packing' Zeus or Jupiter.

occasional thunderstorm, most of the Mediterranean lands are bereft of summer rain for a period that may extend over several months.

In its general climate the Mediterranean area is not a lotus land. Its winters are rougher and less balmy than seductive weather reports from its small and rare coastal strips of the Riviera type would indicate. The summer temperature rises above the level most conducive to high vitality; glare and dust are trying to weak constitutions;[1] and occasional visitations (mostly in spring time) by a torrid blast from the African desert[2] bring severe if passing discomfort. Yet it is not without reason that Mediterranean folk count themselves among Nature's favourites in the matter of climate. They enjoy an optimum annual mean of temperature[3] and of rainfall,[4] and their ratio of sunshine, which generally exceeds 2,000 hours in the year,[5] errs if at all on the side of over-measure. Some features of its winter climate, which on first impression might seem deterrent, its brisk winds and quick variations of temperature, reinvigorate body and mind after the summer's set fair weather.[6] Above all, the clear, crisp, and luminous air of the Mediterranean region provides a stimulus such as few other parts of the world can offer.

It is therefore no mere accident that the Mediterranean area has been one of the world's most continuous centres of civilization. The Mediterranean lands have indeed passed through more than one Dark Age; but the cause of these periods of Decline and Fall should be sought in political and social failures rather than in the slings and arrows of untoward natural conditions.

[1] The effect of prolonged exposure to unquenched ultra-violet rays from the clear Mediterranean sky may also be deleterious in the case of Nordic new-comers, whose pink skins do not readily absorb a short-wave radiation. (For the same reason some British settlers fail to become acclimatized in Kenya and South Africa.)

[2] This wind is known as the 'Notia' in Greece, the 'Scirocco' in Italy (the *plumbeus Auster* of Horace), and the 'Leveche' in Spain. It resembles the Föhn of Switzerland in being a fall-wind whose temperature is raised in the descent to a denser atmospheric stratum. In addition, it is laden with sand like a 'desert storm'. Fortunately it never lasts long.

[3] 59° in Italy, 63° in Greece. The English mean of 50° lies at the lower end of the optimum range.

[4] 30 inches: about the same as in England.

[5] 2,400 hours at Rome, 2,750 at Madrid (1,300–1,400 hours at London, c. 1,650 at Worthing).

[6] It is partly because of its vigorous air circulation that the Mediterranean climate is classified by Ellsworth Huntington (*Civilisation and Climate*), together with that of other wind-swept regions (e.g. the borderlands of the central North Atlantic and New Zealand), as one of the world's best.

§ 3. STRUCTURE

The great telluric displacement which scooped out the central Mediterranean trough and upraised the lands around it did not wholly obliterate the older geological strata, whose hard crusts protrude here and there in massive blocks amid the newer formations. These remnants of a former continent comprise the Spanish *meseta* or tableland, Sardinia and Corsica, part of Tuscany, the toe of Italy, the Rhodope chain in the Balkan peninsula, and central Lydia. But the older land-mass has been partly drowned by the fissure of the Mediterranean Sea, and partly overlaid by the upthrust of new strata from the centre of the basin towards its periphery. The framework of folded mountains which was thus built round the Mediterranean was subsequently twisted by transverse stresses, or fractured by local subsidences, so as to produce a complicated pattern of discontinuous chains. In its western section it has taken the shape of a broken coil whose fragments include the Pyrenees, the southern rim of the Alps, the Apennines, the Atlas range, and Sierra Nevada. In the eastern Mediterranean area it streaks out from the tangled knot of the Dalmatian Alps in three divergent and re-converging strands, (1) the main Balkan range and the Crimean mountains, (2) the highlands of Albania, of the Chalcidic peninsula, and of northern Asia Minor, (3) Mts. Pindus and Oeta, the coastal range of southern Asia Minor, and Mt. Taurus. These three loops run out into the neighbouring chains of Mt. Caucasus, the Armenian massif, and Mt. Anti-Taurus.

The earth-movement which thus remodelled the face of the Mediterranean region took place in a relatively recent geological age. Indeed it is even now not wholly spent, for the Mediterranean land still 'works'. The catastrophic earthquakes and volcanic eruptions which have punctuated its natural history have been the convulsive flings of an earth-Titan whose uneasy limbs have not yet come to full rest. Upheavals and subsidences in the Mediterranean sea-bed have caused many a rise and fall in the water-level and altered the contours of the coastline.[1]

The older formations of the Mediterranean lands are mostly composed of granite protruding in massive blocks. The overlying cap of younger rock consists predominantly of limestone,

---

[1] A settlement off the coast of Egypt has submerged a system of moles near the island of Pharos in which some scholars have seen the handiwork of craftsmen from Minoan Crete. G. Jondet, in *Mémoires présentés à l'Institut Égyptologique*, 1916 (quoted by A. J. Evans, *The Palace of Minos*, i, pp. 292–7).

with pockets of sandstone and schist in its interstices. The limestone is generally of a hard-faced variety which is liable to be
fissured by internal strains, but resists disintegration on its surface;[1] and the Mediterranean climate provides neither the sharp
frosts nor the humid heat which speed up the process of erosion.
The Mediterranean mountains accordingly show little sign of
weathering: they stand out in bold relief and rise in sharp cliffs
rather than in gentle ramps. Their cleanly chiselled shapes, seen
through a lucid atmosphere, lend a peculiar charm to Mediterranean scenery. The same rugged contours mark the drowned
landscape of the Mediterranean Sea, whose floor as a rule sinks
rapidly from the coastline and at some points collapses into a
sheer abyss.[2]

§ 4. MINERAL RESOURCES

The natural resources of the Mediterranean area were almost
sufficient to meet the relatively modest requirements of an ancient
civilization, but they are by no means in lavish supply, and their
successful exploitation demands hard work and settled conditions
of life.

The most abundant source of mineral wealth in the Mediterranean lands consists in their building-material. The prevailing limestone formations provide an inexhaustible quarry of rock
whose texture is not too refractory to the mason's chisel but hard
enough to withstand rapid weathering. On the other hand the
coal measures are neither extensive nor well distributed, and the
flow of mineral oil is a mere trickle. Coal of good quality is now
mined in Spain, in Asia Minor, and in north-west Africa, but
the total Mediterranean output falls far short of modern requirements. This deficiency, it is true, was not felt in the Greek and
Roman world, whose modest needs of fuel were satisfied with the
use of timber and charcoal. Theophrastus knew of 'a black stone
that burnt' and served to feed the local forges[3] (the lignite of Elis
in western Peloponnesus), but the other Mediterranean coal
deposits apparently remained undiscovered and undesired.

The wealth of the Mediterranean lands in metals is likewise
insufficient for modern requirements. Some of its minefields

---

[1] Limestone is soluble in water charged with carbon dioxide and therefore undergoes erosion by rivers containing decomposed organic matter; it cracks under severe
mechanical stresses; but is far less subject than schists and sandstones to the influence of the daily weather.

[2] The depth of water to the east of Sardinia slightly exceeds 2,000 fathoms; to
the west of Crete it is a little short of 2,500 fathoms.

[3] *De lapidibus*, § 16.

were already exhausted in ancient times. Among others, the silver-mines of Laurium (p. 76) and the goldfields of Mt. Pangaeus (p. 294) ceased to be productive before the Christian era; and the goldfields in particular had a merry rather than a long life, for they consisted mostly of surface deposits which were speedily scooped up by prospectors in a 'Klondyke rush'. But the deficit was continually made good from new sources of supply, and the occasional acute shortages of bullion which were reflected in the heavy depreciation of coinage from certain Greek and Roman mints may usually be traced to political disturbances, resulting in an interruption of supplies, rather than to a failure at their source. The most important metals, copper and iron, were relatively plentiful in the Mediterranean lands, and most of the available ores were easily reducible—an important consideration in days when the processes of extraction were still for the most part rough and ready.[1] The only permanent deficiency in the common metals was in tin, the supplies of which had mainly to be derived from western Spain and Britain.[2]

§ 5. SEA PRODUCTS

The Mediterranean Sea is a vast storehouse of the most essential of all minerals, common salt. Its saline content is unusually high, because the evaporation of its waters under relentless summer suns is not fully compensated by the inflow of the rivers;[3] and the shallow lagoons which fringe its coast at certain points form natural salt-pans. The Mediterranean salt trade at the present day supplies the world's markets in competition with the traffic in English rock-salt; in ancient times it was probably the earliest material of regular indigenous commerce. A lesser mineral product consists in the coral beds near Naples and Hyères (on the French Riviera); the coral beads were formerly exported as far afield as central Europe and India.[4]

The gate of Gibraltar has a sill of hard rock at a depth of 1,200 feet below water-level which has the effect of a gigantic natural

[1] See especially O. Davies, *Roman Mines in Europe*, where it is shown that many of the lesser minefields were already being worked in Roman times.

[2] On the quest for Atlantic tin see M. Cary, *Journal of Hellenic Studies*, 1924, pp. 166 ff.

[3] One reason why the water of the Mediterranean is clear and of a rich blue colour is because it is well impregnated with salt, which has the property of precipitating the earthy matters discharged by rivers.

[4] J. Déchelette, *Manuel d'archéologie préhistorique*, 2nd ed., iii, pp. 363–5; E. H. Warmington, *The Commerce between the Roman Empire and India*, pp. 263–4.

lock and almost converts the Mediterranean Sea into a self-contained lake. Though an inward current through the Straits compensates the Mediterranean for its net loss of water by evaporation, it is not sufficient in volume to counteract another solar effect, the warming up of the water to the highest temperature of all seas in the temperate zone: whereas the temperature of the Atlantic bottom is 37°, that of the Mediterranean floor is 55°. Because of its permeating warmth, the Mediterranean is a favourite haunt of the more rudimentary and delicate marine animals (cockles and mussels), whose food value as *frutti di mare* has always been appreciated by its coastal population.[1] But as a fishing-ground the Mediterranean cannot compare with the northern and north-central Atlantic. It lacks the shallow spawning-grounds, such as the Dogger Bank and the Newfoundland shoals, which are necessary for the mass-production of fish, and the warmth of its waters is an actual deterrent to several species of the highest food value, such as the cod, the sole, and the herring. Since the Middle Ages there has been a regular import trade in fish from Atlantic to Mediterranean countries, and even in ancient times (when inland populations, being under no religious obligation to include fish in their diet, were not regular consumers), fishing-grounds outside the Mediterranean, the Black Sea and the Gulf of St. Vincent, had to be laid under contribution.

On the other hand, certain small species of fish, such as the anchovy and the sardine, thrive in the Mediterranean. Of the larger invertebrates, the cuttle-fish to this day remains a familiar sight of Greek markets. But by far the most important contribution of the Mediterranean to food-supply is derived from the tunny, a large fish weighing sometimes over 300 lb., which makes an annual migration across the entire length of the sea and appears at certain places off the coast in enormous numbers.[2] At these points the fishing industry was mainly concentrated in ancient times and became the staple occupation of the neighbouring towns. As the migration season fell due, watchers would be stationed in towers to announce the arrival of the shoals,[3] and stationary nets

---

[1] For this reason the Mediterranean is also a natural museum of biology. Of Aristotle's studies in animal life, his descriptions of marine species have the highest value; and nowadays the aquarium at Naples is one of the chief centres of marine research.

[2] As the migration route of the tunnies begins at the Straits of Gibraltar, their spawning-grounds are generally assumed to be in the Atlantic.

[3] Theocritus, iii. 26; Oppian, *Halieutica*, iii. 637; Dittenberger, *Sylloge Inscriptionum Graecarum* (3rd ed.), 1000, l. 12: οἱ μισθωσάμενοι τὴν σκοπὴν ἐπὶ Ναυτίλεωι. (On the island of Cos.)

would be put out to intercept them on their regular track.[1] The numerous salt-pans along the Mediterranean coast also facilitated the growth of a secondary fish-pickling industry which made a substantial contribution to the larders of the poorer households.[2] For the tables of the well-to-do the same industry prepared anchovy sauce, which was a favourite material for seasoning.

The Mediterranean Sea is rich in two lesser forms of animal life which also played a part in the ancient economy. The sponge-beds of the Aegean Sea and the Bay of Tripoli are the chief source of supply for modern Europe;[3] the ancient Greek and Roman world was already drawing upon them. But in ancient times a far more important industry was based on the beds of the purple molluscs which frequented some of the shallow bays of the Mediterranean coast. The dye which could be produced from these animalculae ranged over a large variety of colours. The juice of the purple-mussel was either purple in the modern sense, or vermilion, according to its species; and a series of artificial hues from violet to blue could be extracted from it in the boiling-vat.[4] The purple dyes had a special advantage over the vegetable colouring matters on which the ancient world chiefly depended, in that they were naturally fast and did not need to be treated with alum or other fixatives.

§ 6. PLANT LIFE

The plant life of the Mediterranean lands owes its distinctive features in large measure to their peculiar climate and structure. The climate favours a vigorous vegetation by reason of its open winters, which do not wholly suspend the growth of plants or the cultivation of the soil; and the long hours of summer sunshine ensure the perfect maturing of field and orchard produce. But the distribution of the rainfall is less opportune than in Atlantic Europe, where it is evenly spread over the entire year, or in continental Europe, where the summers are wetter than the winters. The Mediterranean climate is prodigal of its water-supply while the plants take their winter rest, and turns it off at the season when their sap flows strong and their need of drink is greatest. Moreover the incidence of the summer rain varies considerably

[1] Open-sea trawling did not need to be practised. The Mediterranean fisheries were therefore not such important schools of navigation as those of the North Sea have been since the Middle Ages.
[2] Tubs with sprats in brine are still a familiar sight in the Greek food-markets.
[3] The modern sponge-diving industry is almost entirely in Greek hands.
[4] H. Blümner, *Technologie und Terminologie der Gewerbe und Künste der Griechen und Römer*, i, ch. 4.

from year to year: one season may produce ten inches, the next may yield no more than three or four;[1] and part of the summer precipitation is in the form of torrential but fleeting downpours (usually to the accompaniment of thunder and lightning), which fill the river beds but do not soak deeply into the earth. The remainder of the summer's scanty store of rain is largely dissipated by evaporation, which lowers the water-level in the soil from month to month.[2]

The productiveness of the Mediterranean lands is further diminished by their mountainous character, and this to an even greater degree than a casual glance at the map might suggest. The Mediterranean mountains have not yet been weathered into rounded forms; they stand out in sharp relief, and their flanks often do not admit of tillage, even though Mediterranean cultivators have always been experts at driving their ploughs *en corniche* along a steep declivity. Furthermore, the mountains fulfil but poorly their function of storing the winter's rain and snow. With rare exceptions, they fail to attain the line of permanent snow in Mediterranean latitudes (*c.* 10,000 feet).[3] By April or May only the higher summits are still decked with white caps, the lesser heights are merely braided with silver streaks; by midsummer even the taller peaks stand bare.

Among the predominant limestone formations such part of the rain or melted snow as is not washed down to the sea in torrential spates does not percolate slowly through the subsoil, but is absorbed through cracks and sink-holes in the mountain-sides into subterranean caverns. Here and there these underground waters meet with a substratum of clay or other impervious material and are forced back to the surface, where they break out in springs. The head-springs of the river Timavus in Venetia and of the Clitumnus in Umbria set the pens of ancient writers flowing by their impetuous gush;[4] but neither of these is more prolific than that of the Sorgues in Provence, whose output is at the rate of nearly 500 cubic feet per second. These springs are of

---

[1] This irregularity of the summer rainfall is an embarrassing feature of other dry regions such as Australia and west-central North America.

[2] Even in England the summer rains of a normal season merely replace the water lost by evaporation.

[3] Apart from the marginal chains of Alps and Pyrenees, the only mountain chain of Mediterranean Europe which overtops the 10,000-foot line is the Sierra Nevada.

[4] The Timavus: Vergil, *Aeneid* i. 244–6; Strabo, p. 214. The Clitumnus: Pliny the Younger, *Letters*, viii. 8. A submarine spring off the coast of Argolis spouted up through the sea surface (Pausanias, viii. 7. 2); another supplied the Phoenician city of Aradus with drinking-water drawn up through a siphon (Strabo, p. 754).

fundamental importance for the settlement and cultivation of Mediterranean lands. In their immediate neighbourhood they create oases of rich vegetation; farther afield they supply water for irrigation, or to feed the aqueducts of near and distant cities. But they do not compensate in full for the general dryness of the subsoil.

The value of the Mediterranean rivers for purposes of water storage is also limited. After the downpours of winter, and following upon occasional thunderstorms, they break into a sudden spate as they receive the spill-water from the mountains, and hastily carry off the flood into the sea;[1] in summer the lesser streams dwindle to a mere trickle or dry up altogether.

In the upland regions the dearth of water is less noticeable at the higher levels, where 'orographic' rain, due to the cooling of ascending air currents, is scattered in occasional showers during every month of summer, and cloud caps on the peaks often spread a protective blanket. The drought is also less rigorous in the protrusive formations of softer rock (mostly sandstone and schist), and in the pockets of sedimentary marl and light clay amid the mountain folds. Everywhere else the layer of humus is usually thin and interspersed with outcrops of bare rock. The fertile areas are mostly to be found among the piedmont terraces, which are often well supplied with springs, and in the lowland plains, which lend themselves best to irrigation and are enriched with detritus from the rivers in flood time (the finest and most easily cultivable silt being deposited near the river mouths). This sedimentation, to be sure, is not an unmixed benefit, for as the rate of flow becomes more sluggish at the end of their course, the rivers tend to obstruct themselves with their own detritus, and tongues of fenland are formed around their stagnating waters. But, except at periods when disordered political conditions have stayed his hand, the Mediterranean cultivator has usually been prompt to cut new channels to drain off the overflow.

These natural conditions have imposed a distinctive régime of plant life and of cultivation in Mediterranean lands. In a climate of hot summers and of winters not consistently cold, the zone of vegetation ascends to 6,000–7,000 feet, and cultivation is possible up to 5,000 feet. But the distribution of plants is determined mainly by the relative abundance of water in the hot season. At a height of 3,000 feet and above, where the summers are relatively

[1] In the winter campaign of 1943–4 the Italian rivers sometimes carried off the temporary bridges of the allied forces into the bargain.

cool and damp, the vegetation takes on the same character as on the European continent. Thick copses of deciduous trees, especially of oaks and Spanish chestnuts,[1] clothe the lower ranges of the mountain sides, while beeches and conifers ascend the higher levels up to the limits of tree growth. Where the soil is not deep enough to give a foothold to trees the mountains are carpeted with patches of short matted grass, resembling the summer pastures of Switzerland. In some sheltered pockets cereals will grow up to a height of 4,000–5,000 feet.[2]

In an intermediate zone, extending roughly from 1,500 to 3,000 feet, the full effect of the summer drought manifests itself. The natural tree-growth is here confined in the main to sparse straggles of pinewood; the typical vegetation of this tract consists of evergreen bush and scrub, ranging from dwarf holm-oaks, laurels, and junipers down to gorse and thyme and acanthus. These 'bad lands' are not wholly unproductive. Their shrub vegetation decks itself with a profusion of brightly coloured and strongly scented flowers, which attract myriads of bees and support an extensive perfume industry.[3] But no amount of human effort can convert the 'maquis' area into cultivable land.

The soil of the lowlands, consisting mostly of light clays and marls, is rich in plant food and easy to work. Wherever the supply of water is adequate, these lands can support a rich and even a luxuriant vegetation.[4] Of the principal field plants, the various members of the cereal family do not find Mediterranean conditions uniformly congenial. Oats, which thrive best in a cool and damp summer, are hardly cultivated in southerly latitudes. Maize (an American plant) and rice thrive in those limited areas where ground water is abundant. Wheat and barley find the spring rainfall insufficient to induce a profuse growth and are less prolific than in France or England;[5] but they mature rapidly under the summer sun and are ready for cutting before the soil is dried out.

[1] The horse-chestnut was unknown to the Greeks and Romans. It was introduced into Europe by the Turks.

[2] The author has observed maize cobs on a threshing-floor near Bassae in Arcadia, at an altitude of at least 4,000 feet.

[3] The choicest scents of the Avenue de l'Opéra at Paris are distilled from the flowers of the Provençal uplands. The agave and cactus, now a common sight of Greece and Sicily, are American importations.

[4] The contrast between the various vegetation zones can be most readily observed from the railway which winds round Mt. Etna between Catania and Taormina, with a summit point of 3,250 feet.

[5] No figures are available for computing the average yield; but 18 bushels per acre was considered to be well above the normal (p. 144). The present English yield is about 35 bushels per acre.

These two species therefore formed the staple crops of Greek and Roman agriculture.

The choicest produce of the Mediterranean soil is to be found in the orchard areas, where long hours of baking sunshine draw out the fruit's full flavour. The indigenous European species, the apple, plum, and (more especially) the pear, and even more the natives of the Near East, the cherry, apricot, and peach, yield excellent crops. All these varieties, however, are restricted to regions with a generous water-supply. The really characteristic fruit plants of the Mediterranean are the fig, the olive, and the vine. These species develop long tap-roots (that of the olive can thrust down to 10–12 feet), and thus reach water-level in the sub-soil even in the driest of summers. The vine, which ripens in September, and the olive, which is not ready for picking before November, benefit by the continued sunshine of the early autumn;[1] and the olive comes to no harm in the relatively mild winters of the lowlands, although, being a shivery plant, it is seldom to be found above the 2,000-foot level.

In the Mediterranean lowlands permanent pasture can be established only in the fenlands and river-meadows, or in artificial irrigation fields. The spring and the autumn rains produce a flush of grass, and the autumn herbage maintains a slow growth during the winter; but in summer the grazing-grounds, save in a few favoured areas, are parched and withered.

Naturally it is the garden country of the lowlands which attracts the attention of most visitors to the Mediterranean area, and it is this which has spread the illusion, prevalent in more northerly climes, that the Mediterranean is a region of exuberant natural riches. But if account be taken also of the large tracts above the 1,500-foot level which produce nothing but bush or scrub or wiry grass, it will appear that its average of fertility falls below that of the more favoured countries of central and northern Europe, such as France and England. If its productivity in ancient times nevertheless surpassed that of adjacent lands, the difference should rather be credited to the superior technique of the Mediterranean cultivators, itself largely a product of the more orderly social conditions of the Mediterranean world.

§ 7. Land-work

(i) *Tillage.* However deficient Greek and Roman cultivators might be in their knowledge of plant chemistry and biology, and

[1] The change to winter conditions does not as a rule take place until mid-October.

in their mechanical apparatus, they had learnt by empirical methods how to adapt their methods of cultivation to the peculiar conditions of the Mediterranean area. Various details of their procedure which on first impression might seem inept have been proved serviceable in the light of modern experience in other countries where deficiency of water imposes similar problems and restrictions (e.g. central U.S.A. west of the Mississippi, western Argentine, northern and western South Africa, and the interior of Australia).[1]

In the cultivation of the principal cereal plants, wheat and barley, the basic feature of the Greek and Roman system was a two-year shift, under which any given piece of land was left fallow in one year and cropped in the following season. A similar technique of 'dry farming' is now observed in countries where the average annual rainfall is less than 18 inches. The principle of maintaining the land's fertility by a judicious rotation of crops was not unknown to the ancients: experiments were made in annual cropping, and in some specially favoured districts several harvests might be taken from one plot in the same year.[2] But the practice of stinting the crops could be justified on the ground that it conserved the water-supply in the subsoil. In the fallow year the land would be opened up by repeated ploughing. Thus Varro prescribed one operation in spring (when the fields had partly dried after the winter rains), another in early summer (before the soil had become hard-baked), and a third in the early autumn (after the new rains had again made the ground friable).[3] By this continuous stirring of the soil the upper layer was kept loose and rough, so as to check the formation of pores and consequent rise of the water to the surface by capillary attraction. The ploughs in ordinary use were shallow and did not cut deeper than four inches.[4] Improving landlords made experiments with heavier ploughshares, but these exposed the loosened humus to the risk of erosion by wind in summer and to washing out in winter.[5]

[1] See especially the valuable observations by Miss E. C. Semple, in *The Geography of the Mediterranean Region*, part iii.

[2] Vergil, *Georgics* i. 71–83; Varro, *De re rustica* i. 44. 3. In a lease drawn up on behalf of the Attic deme of Dyaleis the tenant was required to sow one third of his land with cereals, and to plant another third with vegetables. (Michel, *Recueil des inscriptions grecques*, 1357, ll. 22–3.) For an example of two crops in one year, see Theophrastus, *De Causis Plantarum* iii. 20. 7. For a treble harvest in Campania, see p. 134.   [3] Varro, i. 30, 32, 33. Cf. Columella, *De re rustica* ii. 4.

[4] The deep-cutting ploughs which were used in ancient Britain (p. 267) were well suited to its stiff clay soil and its almost dust-free summers.

[5] For similar reasons the traditional tillage of the powdery loess lands of northern

The regular season for sowing, both wheat and barley, was autumn. In Attica the Great Eleusinian Mysteries, which marked the first stage in the life-history of the grain crop, were held in September, and in Italy the Saturnalia, which celebrated the completion of the sowing, fell in December. During the relatively mild winter a start could thus be made with the germination of the seed, and there would be no danger of its displacement in the heavy thaw that follows a deep frost.[1] The seed was set in rows by means of rotary drills or, more commonly, was raked into line after broadcasting by hand. This alinement would enable the field workers to pass between the rows after the sprouting of the grain (in February or March) and to hoe the soil, thus keeping it clear of weeds and conserving its water under a roughened surface.[2] After the ripening of the grain the usual practice was to cut the stalks near the head, so as to leave a residue of high-standing stubble to serve as winter feed for peregrinating flocks (pp. 18–19). Threshing was generally done by means of sticks or the hooves of oxen. Some enterprising landlords had recourse to time-saving devices, wheeled reaping-machines with revolving arms for cutting the haulms—rude prototypes of the modern McCormick,[3] and threshing-sledges with spiky stones set under the boards.[4] But in the set fair weather of a Mediterranean harvest-tide there was no such need of hurry as in a catchy English August; leisurely methods and primitive implements therefore held their own.

(ii) *Grazing*. The methods of the Greek and Roman pastoral industry were in a large measure determined by the dearth of water in the summer season. For the pasturing of horses and cows—high-cropping animals that require long, lush grass—the fenlands and natural river meadows were of very limited range. Enterprising graziers supplemented them by irrigation;[5] to improve or re-create their artificial meadows some landlords periodically ploughed them up, thus aerating and cleaning the soil and

and central China, by means of shallow ploughs or hand-hoes, should not be condemned off-hand.

[1] In Russia and central North America grain is mostly spring-sown. In England wheat is usually sown in autumn, and barley (a more shallow-rooted species) in spring.

[2] The modern practice of hoe-cultivation for beets, turnips, and potatoes has been derived from the traditional methods of Mediterranean tillage.

[3] Pliny, *Naturalis Historia* xviii, § 296.

[4] Varro, i. 52. 1 ('plostellum Punicum').

[5] Vergil, *Eclogues* iii. 111. Cato (*De re rustica*, ch. 9) strongly recommends the creation of artificial meadows, 'if you have the water'.

conserving its water-supply.[1] The provision of natural herbage
was eked out with cultivated fodder-plants, the cytisus shrub with
its clover-like leaves, and the *herba Medica*, which under the
name of alfalfa forms the basis of the pastoral industry in the
dry regions of the modern world. The 'medic herb' was specially
valued because its long roots could find water on ordinary tillage
land; under careful cultivation it might yield six mows in one
season.[2] Even so, green fodder remained scarce, and the stock
of cows and horses was relatively small. The place of the horse
as a farm worker was taken by oxen, who were fed on barley and
leguminous plants from the arable lands or, if the supplies of
these failed, on the leaves of trees;[3] and for milk-production the
Greeks and Romans made large use of sheep and goats, as their
successors in Mediterranean lands continue to do.

Sheep and goats, indeed, have always been the principal grazing
animals of the Mediterranean area; in addition to milk, they
have been Mediterranean man's principal purveyors of clothing-
material.[4] The goats are omnivorous to a fault: they do much
damage by browsing on the shoots of shrubs and trees, thus
assisting in the evil work of deforestation, and it is as much in
view of them as of human pilferers that Mediterranean orchards
are habitually enclosed in walls of dry stone.[5] But because of
their capacity to make the most of all available grazing they have
ever been the favourite animals of the Mediterranean crofter.[6]
Sheep not only thrive on the short and wiry grass of the poorer
pastures, but can be moved continuously from one feeding-ground
to another. Their nomadic habits have been exploited in all ages
of Mediterranean history by graziers who drive them to and fro
between a summer and a winter station. For the summer season
the flocks ascend into the mountains, where pasturage is available
long after it has dried up in the plains (p. 14); at the coming of

[1] This process is well described by Columella (ii. 18), and also recommended
by Pliny (xviii, § 259). It anticipated the modern English system of 'leys' or
temporary grazings.

[2] Columella, ii. 11; Pliny, xviii, §§ 144–8.

[3] Cato, 30, 60. The slow gait of the ox, and the long time which he consequently
took in ploughing the crop-lands, mattered little to Greek and Roman cultivators,
who had the whole fallow year in which to prepare the seed-beds.

[4] Pliny (xxxiii, § 135) records the case of a Roman landowner who possessed
257,000 sheep and goats (as against a mere 3,600 yoke of oxen). It is estimated that
in modern Greece there are more than ten times as many sheep, and more than
eight times as many goats, as there are horned cattle.

[5] On the depredations of goats see Eupolis, fragment 14 (Kock).

[6] Vergil's eulogy of the goat (*Georgics* iii. 305–21) reflects the point of view of the
smallholder.

winter they return to the lowlands, where they feed on the stubble and on the self-sown rough herbage of the fallow fields, and spend the nights in the open without risk of frostbite. At the present day the system of 'transhumance' or alternating pasturage is still practised on a large scale by the Vlach shepherds of northern and central Greece.[1] In ancient times it attained its highest development in Italy after the Roman conquest, when the Roman Peace rendered it possible to organize mass-migration along certain recognized cattle drifts (*calles*), and flocks might make a double annual journey between the Samnite highlands and the plains of Apulia.[2]

The system of 'transhumance' saved the Greek and Roman graziers the expense of steadings and forage crops during the winter. On the other hand, it deprived the cultivators in the plains of their principal source of manure in summer when the sheep, instead of being folded near the crop land, browsed on the mountain-sides. To make up for the loss full use was made of green manure; some landlords raised leguminous crops in order to plough them in as fertilizers.[3] Even so, it is doubtful whether they restored to the land as much plant-food as they withdrew; but the theory that the land was becoming exhausted in ancient times, though already familiar to Roman writers on agriculture, rests on no cogent evidence.[4]

(iii) *Plantations.* Ever since Homer described with evident delight the gardens of Alcinous, and abhorred the sea as 'so much surface lost to vineyards',[5] and Varro gave a cry of joy at the thought that Italy had become 'one great orchard',[6] the fruit-grower has held pride of place among Mediterranean land-workers. Special encouragement was given by ancient governments to planters;[7] special clauses were inserted in leases to

[1] N. G. L. Hammond, *Annual of the British School of Athens*, xxxii (1931–2), p. 140. Transhumance is also practised in modern Italy and Spain and southern France, and in the region of the central Rockies. In France and Italy the migration is now partly effected in railway trucks (A. Grenier, *Mélanges d'archéologie et d'histoire*, 1905, pp. 295–328).

[2] Varro, ii. 1. 16; H. F. Pelham, *Essays*, pp. 300 ff.

[3] The evidence is collected in Semple, op. cit., ch. xv. The growing of leguminous crops for soil-enrichment (by stimulating the activities of certain beneficial bacteria) has now become a regular practice of scientific agriculture.

[4] This theory was combated in ancient times by Columella (i, ch. 1), and recently by M. Rostovtzeff, *Social and Economic History of the Roman Empire*, pp. 329–30.

[5] *Odyssey* vii. 112 ff.; πόντος ἀτρύγετος, *passim*.

[6] i. 2. 6.

[7] e.g. by the Ptolemies in Egypt, and by Hadrian in north-west Africa (remissions of taxation).

ensure good cultivation by them,[1] special immunities were accorded in war conventions for the preservation of fruit-trees;[2] and gardens received a special measure of irrigation-water.

The vine and the olive in particular were the favourites of the ancient Mediterranean fruit garden. Originating in the East, they had reached Crete and had been passed on thence to the Greek mainland in prehistoric times; Greek colonists acclimatized them in Italy and Gaul, and the Romans transplanted them to Spain and north Africa. The cultivation of vines or olives was often combined, as it still is nowadays, with the raising of cereal crops, by planting on the crop lands in widely spaced rows. No other branch of ancient land work was studied more closely by the agronomists,[3] and none other was more carefully adapted to the prevailing natural conditions.

In Mediterranean lands the vines need not be confined to the southward facing slopes; they will ripen fully in the plains and even on the northern sides of hills. Indeed the chief danger is not that the grapes should remain sour, but that they should shrivel through excess of sunshine. To avert this risk it has been a custom of Italian planters, ancient and modern, to train their vines up living trees, such as elms and poplars, instead of tying them to stakes; the foliage of the trees will then be pruned so as to temper sunshine with shade in due degree. Greek planters used stakes or let the vines trail along the ground, but to mitigate the sun's glare they would now and then raise clouds of dust— an ancient counterpart to the present orchardist's smoke-screen. Where the subsoil was dry, ancient planters cut irrigation trenches for the vines and pruned away the side roots so as to induce deep growth in the tap root.

The drying of grapes for raisins is an easy process in the strong October sun of the Mediterranean area; and the problem of keeping wine through the summer heat could be readily solved by cellaring it in the natural caves that abound in the Mediterranean limestone formations.

The olive is even more a typically Mediterranean plant than the vine. Its sensitiveness to frost, it is true, banishes it from regions of relatively cold winters—from high tablelands and from plains shut off by coastal ranges from warm sea winds. At

[1] *Inscriptiones Graecae*, xiv. 645, ll. 112–13.
[2] Thucydides, ii. 72. 3. (King Archidamus at Plataea.)
[3] Particular attention is paid to viticulture in the surviving works *De re rustica*. See Columella, bks. iii–v, and Vergil, *Georgics* ii. 1–419, with the commentary by R. Billiard, *L'Agriculture dans l'antiquité d'après les Géorgiques de Virgile*, chs. 8–11.

best it is of slow growth, requiring some thirty years to attain full productivity, and it is uneven in its yield from season to season. But it is so well adapted to the Mediterranean climate that, once planted out, it requires little attention. Its picking season falls at a time when all other harvests have been gathered: the berries for table consumption are culled in October and November, those held back for pulping and pressing in late autumn. The produce of the olive, moreover, is particularly suited to the needs of Mediterranean people. Its best quality of oil serves as an alternative to butter, for it keeps better in the hot season, and in ancient times its inferior brands were the best available substitute for mineral oil in lamps.

Though the olive is a drought-resisting tree, it needs to be well spaced out for full production, so as to have an adequate range of ground water. Ancient orchardmen were well aware of this requirement, for they usually exceeded by a long way the minimum distance of 9 feet between tree and tree as set forth in the laws of Solon.[1] Columella prescribed an interval of not less than 25 × 25 feet, or of 40 × 60 feet, if crops were to be grown between the rows.[2] In the semi-desert zone of southern Tunisia Roman planters increased the gap to 75 feet each way.[3] The sowing of wheat between the rows was specially suitable to olive orchards; the trees, whose foliage is short and slim, did not stint the wheat of sunlight, and the wheat drew its water-supply from a different ground-level.

Because of its slow rate of growth, the olive requires ordered social conditions, for few will plant it who cannot look forward to reaping its fruits at a somewhat remote date. The Greeks judged well when they chose the olive branch as a symbol of peace, and Athena, the patron of patient craftsmanship, as the tree's protecting deity; and it is no mere accident that the greatest extension of olive culture over Mediterranean lands belonged to the age of the Roman Peace. The olive remains the chief memorial of Greek and Roman civilization on the Mediterranean country-side, whether it is viewed in mass-plantations, as in the plain of Crisa below Delphi and on the long fringe of Apulian coastland between Foggia and Brindisi, or in isolated clumps on the banked-up earth of many a hill-side terrace.

(iv) *The 'monsoon' plants.* Certain favoured regions of the Medi-

[1] Plutarch, *Solon* xxiii, § 7.   [2] v. 9.
[3] Modern French colonists have redeemed the southern Tunisian steppe from a long period of unproductiveness by replanting it on the Roman pattern.

terranean area which enjoy a more than usually mild winter and lend themselves to intensive irrigation are well adapted for growing plants derived from the monsoon regions of India: rice, sugar-cane, the cotton shrub, and the various species of citrus-trees. All of these were acclimatized on a large scale in the Middle Ages under Saracen influence, and until the eighteenth century Europe obtained most of its sugar and cotton (to say nothing of oranges and lemons) from the Mediterranean lands. Cotton had become known to the Greeks by the time of Herodotus, sugar and rice in the Hellenistic age, yet it is doubtful whether any of these plants was established by them on Mediterranean soil, with the exception of cotton, which was being grown in Egypt by the second century A.D., but not on such a scale as to become a familiar object, and a bitter citron which had no food value.[1] The date-palm was transplanted from Mesopotamia to the Mediterranean border and became familiar in Greece and Italy as a garden tree. Its fruit can be made to ripen under irrigation in regions of torrid summer, such as south-eastern Spain and southern Tunisia; but in the ancient Mediterranean world the only edible dates came almost solely from Tunisia, and these, though sweet, were 'evanescent'.[2]

(v) *Forestry*. In addition to the palm, the Greeks and Romans propagated the Oriental plane (a native of Persia) in the Mediterranean countries. The Romans went further and made a beginning of introducing landscape trees into the continent of Europe: they extended the range of the plane-tree as far north as the English Channel.[3] But while they took an intelligent interest in decorative and shade-giving trees, they displayed culpable negligence in the preservation of their forests, despite their large requirements of timber for house-construction, shipbuilding, and charcoal-burning. From the preceding age of heavier rainfall (p. 2) they had inherited a copious natural growth of forest, so that they were able to meet their needs of material by drawing upon their stored-up capital without troubling to replace it by fresh plantation, or to protect the self-sown saplings against the depredations of goats. By the fourth century B.C. the Athenians had laid bare the flanks of the Attic border ranges,[4] but they could make up the loss by importation from the north Aegean area

---

[1] On the monsoon plants see especially E. H. Warmington, *The Commerce between the Roman Empire and India*, pp. 208–19. Cotton-trees in Egypt: Pollux, vii. 75.

[2] Pliny, xiii, § 26.   [3] Ibid. xii, § 6.

[4] Plato, *Critias*, III B, C.

(pp. 41, 76).[1] By the end of the Republican era the Romans had similarly stripped Italy, but they could still lay Corsica and north-west Africa under contribution. But this improvised procedure laid up trouble for future generations. Once the régime of dry summers had established itself in the Mediterranean lands the natural re-growth of the forest trees was retarded, and in denuded areas the heavy winter rains might carry off the original coating of humus before the new saplings could bind it with their roots.[2] In the Mediterranean uplands many a hill-side which once was richly wooded is now clad in a sorry mantle of maquis, or stands completely bare; and where vanished forests no longer temper the summer sun or absorb the rains of winter, the climate, though probably maintaining its former mean annual temperature and rainfall, has almost certainly become more extreme in its seasonal variations.

§ 8. THE MEDITERRANEAN LANDSCAPE

The typical vegetation of the Mediterranean lands has a distinctive effect upon the Mediterranean landscape. In the garden areas, especially where ornamental trees have been planted, the scenery may suggest an earthly paradise. But this appearance is delusive. Outside the regions of artificial landscape the characteristic evergreen plants of the Mediterranean make no such appeal to the eye as the shapely deciduous trees of more northerly countries. None of them are of tall stature or spread their leaves proudly, and their foliage is more adapted to water-conservation than to decorative display. In order not to offer a purchase to hot ground-winds the leaves are slight and of simple shape; for protection against ultra-violet rays they are of sombre hue; and to prevent evaporation they are coated with a waxy film which deadens the colour tones. Still less can the sparse and fugitive patches of grass compare with the rich lawns of lands with summer rain. The charm of the Mediterranean landscape lies rather in the bold and endlessly varied structure of its mountains, showing up clear-cut against a luminous background, in the intricate interplay of land and water on the coastline, and in the deep translucent colouring of sea and sky.[3] The landscape of the Medi-

---

[1] On the ancient supplies of timber, especially for naval purposes, see A. C. Johnson, *Transactions of the American Philological Association*, 1927, pp. 199 ff.

[2] In some modern re-afforesting operations round Athens it has been found necessary to blast holes into the rock so as to provide a safe bedding for the saplings.

[3] Appreciation of Mediterranean scenery formerly found its chief expression in

terranean can be as stimulating and exhilarating as its climate, but in general it lacks the rich restfulness of England's meadowland and parkland, and it does not strike the same note of deep contentment.

§ 9. FAUNA

The Mediterranean fauna differs but little from that of the European continent and has undergone no important change since Greek and Roman times. The forest cover which Greeks and Romans inherited from the prehistoric age was a natural preserve for large game such as lions, bears, wolves, and boars, so that Homer's heroes had abundant opportunity for dangerous forms of the chase. In the remoter and wilder mountain tracts, such as Mts. Atlas and Taurus, the stock of fierce carnivora remained sufficient to provide for the beast-hunts of imperial Rome; and it was probably from Mauretania that the Carthaginians derived their war-elephants. But in historic times, wherever maquis gained on jungle, the big beasts of prey grew scarce or vanished. Though boar-hunting never died out, the really typical field-sport of a Roman gentleman under the empire was hare-coursing. In 480 B.C. the camels in Xerxes' army were attacked by lions in the forests of Macedonia, but this is the last record of this species running wild in Europe.[1]

North Africa from Tripoli to Suez is infested with dangerous reptiles,[2] but the snakes of Mediterranean Europe and the Near East are for the most part harmless. In Greece it was popularly believed that snakes were incarnations of dead men,[3] and the tamer species were sometimes even accepted as house-mates.

Of the disease-carrying animals, one species of insect has made a large and wicked contribution to Mediterranean history—the anopheles mosquito, which harbours the germ of malaria. The mosquito breeds in the stagnant pools of river deltas and in the shallow lakes of mountain valleys. Malaria has desolated tracts of the Mediterranean region which once were closely populated, e.g. the coasts of Latium and Albania and the Boeotian inland. Whether this scourge was of more than sporadic incidence in ancient times remains a moot point. The disease had certainly

Latin literature (A. Geikie, *The Love of Nature among the Romans*). Ancient writers bestowed their praise more especially on the quieter and tamer landscapes.

[1] Herodotus, VII. 125. The bear and wolf played a far lesser part in Greek and Roman folk-lore than in that of northern and eastern Europe.

[2] For a gruesome description of them see Lucan, *Pharsalia*, ix. 700–889.

[3] On snakes in Greek religion see especially Miss J. E. Harrison, *Prolegomena to the Study of Greek Religion*.

made its entry by then into the Mediterranean world,[1] but whether it became endemic over any large area is uncertain. On other grounds besides those of disease-prevention the draining of stagnant waters is a function of any well-ordered society, and emissory channels for certain waterlogged areas of Greece and Italy, which incidentally would have washed away the lairs of the anopheles, were undoubtedly cut in ancient times.[2] Whether the bickerings that distracted Greek and Roman society from time to time, or the mere apathy which social disorder may leave in its trail, ever sufficed to give the mosquito a start that could not be overtaken, is still an unsolved problem.

A pleasing feature of the Mediterranean world is the quantity and variety of its bird life. In addition to the birds of passage who migrate annually between the European and the African continents, many native or imported species are to be found there. These permanent residents have ample means of subsistence, for the maquis is rich in berries, and the ground supplies of food are not sealed up in winter by hard frost, nor covered up under a blanket of snow; and in taking the air the birds need have little fear of fog, their worst enemy. The attention which the Greeks and Romans bestowed on birds, whether as professional interpreters of their flight in the art of divination, or as disinterested students of natural life, finds its explanation in the richness of their field of observation.[3]

§ 9. COMMUNICATIONS

(i) *The Mediterranean Sea.* The sea which gives its name to the Mediterranean area is the largest ocean-inlet on the globe, extending over a length of 2,330 miles from Gibraltar to Port Said, i.e. as far as from Ireland to Newfoundland. Even before the opening of the Suez Canal it was the chief focus of sea communication between East and West; and ever since the invention of sea-going vessels it has been one of the world's busiest avenues of inter-coastal traffic, and one of its chief schools of navigation.[4]

[1] The evidence has been collected by W. H. S. Jones (*Malaria: a Neglected Factor in the History of Greece and Rome*).

[2] The desiccation of Lake Copaïs in recent times (p. 71) has redeemed Boeotia from its bad reputation as a fever-haunt.

[3] On the birds of Homer, see a delightful essay by J. M. Boraston, *Journ. Hell. Stud.*, 1911, pp. 216 ff.

[4] In the later Middle Ages Italian seamen introduced the compass to the West and constructed the first scientific charts. In the Age of Discovery Italian navigators not only made some of the principal voyages but trained the explorers of other countries.

As a school of navigation the Mediterranean Sea can teach hard lessons. In winter it is a cyclone-track and a cyclone-factory (p. 4); at this season it is frequently swept by gales which freshen up at short notice and change direction rapidly. The capriciousness of the winds and the irregular conformation of the coasts give rise to baffling cross-seas and eddies; and if the billows of the Mediterranean never soar to the heights of the Atlantic rollers, neither do they move with the rollers' regular rhythm: height for height, they are the more dangerous because of their incalculable onset. As an inland sea in a mountain setting the Mediterranean is also exposed to sudden gusts that swoop in winter and early spring from the chilled coastal ranges on to the warmer sea-surface. A notorious example of these fall-winds is the Bora of the eastern Adriatic; but other such harpies may pounce on mariners from any high coast.

For these reasons 'the seas were closed' to the ancient Greeks and Italians in winter, in the sense that regular sailings were suspended, and short crossings only were attempted as occasion might offer.[1] The dangers that attended those who sailed out of season might be illustrated from Caesar's narrow escape on an attempted winter crossing of the Adriatic,[2] and from St. Paul's shipwreck on Malta in the late autumn.[3]

But once the winter cyclones have blown themselves out, the Mediterranean waters pass over into the régime of a trade-wind with a constant direction from a northerly or north-easterly point, before which sailing-vessels can run safely and speedily. Occasionally the summer wind freshens up to gale force, and at all times the square-rigged vessels of the ancient world had difficulty in beating up against it.[4] But at night-time it renders down regularly; and at many points of the coast a brisk alternate play of land and sea breezes, arising from different rates in the rise and fall of temperature on land and on sea, will temporarily counteract the prevailing wind and allow those who are quick off the mark to steal a march upon it.[5]

A feature of the Mediterranean Sea which is partly a hindrance

[1] The 'close season' was reckoned from 10 November to 10 March (Vegetius, *Epitome rei militaris* iv. 39). In the Middle Ages it ran from 1 November to 1 March.

[2] Suetonius, *Divus Iulius* 58, § 2; Plutarch, *Caesar* 38, § 3.

[3] *Acts of the Apostles*, ch. 27.

[4] The triangular 'lateen' sail, now universal in the Mediterranean, was introduced by the Saracens.

[5] A night breeze helps sailers up the Dardanelles in summer-time.

but mainly a help to navigation is the feeble action of its tides. The sill at the Gibraltar Gates (p. 9) intercepts the ocean tides and breaks their force, so that they become wholly dissipated in the open water beyond C. Palos (at the south-east corner of Spain), and regain force only in a few outlying sea-funnels, such as the upper Adriatic. In general the tidal range of the Mediterranean does not exceed twenty inches.

The lack of brisk tidal movement in the Mediterranean entails this disadvantage, that its coasts do not receive a daily scouring, and that in consequence the earthy detritus of the rivers, which is concentrated by precipitation on meeting salt-water, is not washed away regularly, but accumulates in mud banks across the river mouths. A notorious example of such an obstruction in ancient times was the bar formed from the silt of the Tiber, which eventually threatened to put the city of Rome under blockade and so compelled the emperor Claudius to make a new cut for the discharge of the river;[1] and several cases of harbours being definitely ruined by silting will be mentioned in subsequent chapters. Consequently the chief emporia of the Mediterranean, instead of being located at river estuaries, like those of Atlantic Europe, are situated at a distance from them. This rule holds good of Barcelona, Marseille, Genoa, Naples, Trieste, Piraeus, and Alexandria, or of their ancient equivalents.[2] In ancient times tidal inertia also diminished the value of the more deeply recessed harbours, in that sailing-vessels might have difficulty in clearing such stations in calm weather without an ebb tide to assist them.[3]

On the other hand, the slightness of the tidal flow relieves Mediterranean seamen of the problems and dangers of a shifting water-line. They need not wait for flood-water before entering port, nor construct high sea-walls and docks with lock-gates. A constant water-level also facilitates beaching, and this was an important consideration in the days of wooden hulls, for in the warm Mediterranean waters these will soon become foul under constant immersion.[4]

[1] Strabo, p. 231; Suetonius, *Claudius* 20, § 3.

[2] By the time of Augustus lighthouses had been erected at the mouths of some rivers (e.g. the Rhône—Strabo, p. 184), but many of the river exits probably remained unlighted.

[3] A. E. Zimmern, *The Greek Commonwealth*, pp. 30–1. It was perhaps on this account that Smyrna was eclipsed by Ephesus in ancient times.

[4] The Athenian ships in the Sicilian Expedition were largely rendered unfit for lack of beaching facilities (Thucydides, vii. 12. 3). Greek ship-builders preferred pine-wood, not fully seasoned, to oak for their ribs and planking, because its sap kept the hulls comparatively clean. Oak was used for the keels only.

By its action in cutting off the waters of the Mediterranean from those of the Atlantic, the ledge of rock at the Straits of Gibraltar also prevents the formation of strong currents, such as the thermal difference between the Sea and the Ocean waters would otherwise set up. A shallow under-current from the Atlantic induces a weak surface movement along the African and Syrian coasts, and intermittent local streams may flow in narrow waters under the stress of strong winds. At two points, in the Straits of Messina and in the Euripus channel between Euboea and the Greek main-land, the play of currents is complicated by converging but unsynchronized tides. In the Euripus a rising tide and a wind-driven current in one of the funnels, and a receding tide in the other, may combine to induce a veritable mill-race of seven or eight knots. In the Straits of Messina the divergent pulls of a mid-stream current, which sometimes rises to four knots, and of two coastal counter-streams causes local eddies of sufficient force to draw small vessels into their whirl (though not to engulf them).[1] But these two danger zones are marine curiosities. The general rule is that ships may drift at leisure on a Mediterranean current, but need not fear to be carried away.

A hydrographic map of the Mediterranean will show occasional straight flat stretches of sedimentary coast with a shallow approach. But its contours are for the most part the product of a land-collapse, whose lines of breakage have been subsequently warped and notched by the impact of storm-sped waves on outcrops of softer rock between the limestone buttresses. At many points accordingly the coast is as steeply scarped as the mountains of the inland, so as to present a sea face of formidable cliffs. But as a rule the water-line extends across a slope rather than along a precipice, thus providing conveniently shelving strands for running aground, and a sufficient depth of water up to the land-ing-point. Moreover, the innumerable bays and gulfs into which subsidence and erosion have scooped out the coast provide an endless variety of natural harbours. At some points an intrusive sea has flooded a river valley or an inland subsidence-trough, so as to form deep land-locked inlets such as the Gulfs of Actium and Corinth. At others it has not merely lapped round a mountain spur but has undercut it, thus carving out a T-shaped or 'anvil' projection and two back-to-back harbours, either of which will provide in turn a sure shelter from the prevailing wind of the

[1] The Charybdis of Homer was identified with an eddy near Messina which Strabo describes with a little pardonable exaggeration (p. 268).

moment. Occasionally the mordant sea-water has ended by saw-
ing off the protruding neck and has converted the anvil-table into
an offshore island, and the result is a single harbour with a natural
breakwater across its face. The Greeks and Romans often improved upon the natural harbourage by means of moles and
jetties, but their purpose in this was mainly to provide space for
wharves or to secure the port entrances against enemy raids.[1]

But the chief allurement of the Mediterranean Sea is to be
found in its good conditions of visibility and the wealth of landmarks which it offers. In the winter season low cloud and driving
rain may blur the field of sight, but fogs that blot it out altogether
are rare. In summer the guiding lights of sun and stars are
seldom dimmed, and in the dry air distant objects stand out con-
spicuously. Mainland chains or island peaks will show up at
ranges extending to 100 miles, thus enabling ships to hold an almost
straight course over long routes without losing sight of land.
Before the coast of France disappears from his view a seaman
will descry the tall shoulder of Mt. Cinto in north-west Corsica;
with Sardinia still in sight, he will make out the islands that fringe
the northern coast of Tunisia. Proceeding from Gibraltar and
following the African coast to C. Bon at the apex of Tunisia, he
will then catch sight of Mt. San Giuliano (ancient Eryx) in
western Sicily; having cleared the heel of Italy, he will observe
the bold outline of the Epirote coast; from the southern tip of
Greece he may pick his way to Asia Minor through the Greek
archipelago, or he may take a more southerly course with the
Cretan peak of Mt. Ida in constant view. Navigation in the
Mediterranean is therefore not far different from the journey of
a landsman along a well-defined route, and Homer spoke aptly
of the sea's 'liquid lanes'. Lacking the compass and the sextant,
ancient wayfarers could nevertheless traverse the Mediterranean
in all directions without being 'at sea'.

(ii) *The border countries.* Intercourse by land within the Mediterranean area is relatively difficult. In many regions it is beset
and circumscribed by close-set barriers of mountains, most of
which, having been erected by a rolling-up movement of the
earth, present a steep escarpment on at least one of their faces.
Faultings and subsidences within the mountain systems have
indented them with passes of relatively low altitude, and rivers
have carved erosion valleys across them. But these valleys are

[1] On ancient harbour installations see K. Lehmann-Hartleben, 'Die antiken
Hafenanlagen' (*Klio*, Beiheft XIV, 1923).

mostly narrow and tortuous, and any pass rising to 3,000–4,000 feet is liable to be snowbound for part of the year. The Mediterranean rivers, moreover, are more of a hindrance than a help to travel. Most of them have a torrentially rapid fall in their upper reaches, and in their lower courses they are ill suited to navigation on account of their inconstant water-level.[1] Few of them attain great width, yet even the smaller streams may lack convenient crossing-points. Where the rivers pass over a limestone slab, they usually cut their bed into a deep trough,[2] and in the coastal plains they are apt to meander through marshy deltas. On soft and level ground Roman engineers were active in amending natural waterways by cutting artificial channels, but they could not force a passage through a ledge of rock, save at prohibitive cost.

In the ancient Mediterranean world, therefore, rapid communication by land was possible only where all-weather roads and bridges had been provided. These were eventually constructed in every Mediterranean country by the Romans, but even the Romans shirked the task of 'shaving' the gradients in mountain districts, so that their roads were at some points inconveniently steep for vehicular traffic. In an age when horse-collars were unknown and horseshoes had not yet passed into common use,[3] the steepness of the ramps rendered the long-distance haulage of heavy merchandise almost impossible. The transport of goods by land was mostly effected by pack-animals; in the movement of ponderous or bulky commodities the sea routes inevitably played the major part. On these grounds we may doubt whether in ancient times a 'law of isthmuses' was in general operation, according to which trading vessels would not make a continuous voyage round a peninsula or far-flung promontory, but would discharge their cargo at the promontory neck, from which point the merchandise would be conveyed overland for re-embarkation in another hold at the opposite side of the isthmus.[4] Undeniable instances of such breaking of bulk can

[1] For the same reason water-mills were uncommon in the Greek and Roman world, though their principle was understood. Blümner, op. cit. i, pp. 45–9; M. Rostovtzeff, *Social and Economic History of the Hellenistic World*, iii, p. 1645 (a mill at Venafrum); A. W. Parsons, *Hesperia*, v, pp. 70 ff. (another at late-Roman Athens).

[2] These deep-cut river beds were a serious obstacle to the allied troops in the Battle of Italy as they advanced along the west coast south of Naples, and along the Adriatic coast north of C. Garganus.

[3] G. Méautis, *Revue des études anciennes*, 1934, p. 88.

[4] For this law see V. Bérard, *Les Phéniciens et l'Odyssée*, i, pp. 68 ff. (criticized by A. E. Zimmern, *The Greek Commonwealth*, pp. 317–18 n.).

be adduced, but only in special cases where the sea route involved a large detour (p. 82) or was infested by pirates or privateers, or where the intervening isthmus was low-lying all the way.

On the other hand, the Mediterranean lands have, in historical times at least, been generally clear of dense forest, such as rendered large tracts of the European continent almost impassable until late in the Middle Ages. Alike in their plantations and in their natural timber standings, the trees are sufficiently spaced out to give a relatively easy passage. Even so, communications within the Mediterranean lands could never be easy without the helping hand of man.

§ 10. Society and Politics

The pervasive influence of Mediterranean geography on the Greeks and Romans is illustrated in numerous features of their social and political life.

The Mediterranean climate makes for an open-air existence. Where summer heat is tempered by the play of breezes, and winter chill by a clear sun, life out of doors is pleasant over the greater part of the year. This open-air habit found expression in the plans of Greek and Roman houses, for those whose owners could afford the necessary ground space were usually laid out round one or more courts[1]—a practice which survives in the less 'Europeanized' regions of the Mediterranean. In the cities shady recesses from the summer sun and the winter downpours are almost a necessity. The streets of Mediterranean towns have therefore from time immemorial been made as narrow as is consistent with traffic requirements, the side-alleys on hill sites often being mere staircases of the 'Clovelly' type; and the Greek and Roman architects who planned 'show' streets in the major cities made a point of lining them with porticoes and colonnades. In the streets and open squares of the towns rich and poor alike met their friends, spent their leisure, and transacted much of their business;[2] and they sought their entertainment in unroofed theatres and arenas (the concert halls alone being covered over). For political affairs it was not only the massed Popular Assemblies that met in the open. The Areopagus at Athens held session in a porch (the *Stoa Basilike*), and the Dicasteries in open courts (in

[1] The 'court' style of mansion was already prevalent in prehistoric Crete.
[2] At Rome the 'city' men forgathered, not in a Bourse or Royal Exchange, but *ad Ianum*, i.e., by an arch in an open place. Nowadays the open-air cafés of Mediterranean towns are recognized resorts for business talks.

the literal sense); at Rome magistrates set up their tribunals in
the Forum or one of its adjacent porticoes.[1]

With these open-air habits went a readiness of social contacts
and a general use of intercourse that made every Greek or Roman
town into an informal club. Though aristocratic personages
might be accompanied on their outings by an escort of retainers,
to save themselves from too intimate a contact with the common
folk, they did not withdraw themselves from its gaze, but courted
it in their public appearances. A similar tradition of affability, or
at least of accessibility, was observed by political leaders; even
kings and tyrants obeyed the law of *civilitas*, and it was not until
the third century of the Christian era that Roman emperors
accepted the Oriental custom of mysterious seclusion in the
recesses of a palace.

The density of settlement in Mediterranean lands is regulated
to a large degree by one of their determinant features, the general
scarcity of natural water-supplies in summer. The Anglo-Saxon
'tun', with its population of one hundred persons or less, could
not be reproduced here, except in the pockets of softer rock where
the winter rains percolated more evenly through the subsoil, so
as to provide an easily tapped store of water. On the more usual
limestone formations the irregular distribution of water neces-
sitated a closer aggregation near the infrequent water-points—
at a river-side or, most commonly, in the neighbourhood of a
spring. Here substantial and closely built villages, with populations of 500 persons or over, would be formed, and under favourable conditions the villages would grow into towns with several
thousand inhabitants. Though political and economic factors
must also be invoked to explain the genesis and the siting of
ancient Mediterranean cities (pp. 48 ff., 110), the primary factor
of water-supply usually determined the growth of the villages
which were the nuclei of the towns.[2]

The habits of communal solidarity which life in compact
settlements everywhere engenders were reinforced in Mediterranean lands by the need of joint action in the matter of water
regulation—the provision of drainage canals for the winter floods
and, more especially, the equitable rationing of supplies for

[1] Eventually, however, the Roman officials withdrew more and more into the
basilicae or covered halls which sprang up especially since the time of Caesar.

[2] J. L. Myres, *Mediterranean Culture*, pp. 13–14. It has been observed by A.
Philippson (*Der Peloponnes*, pp. 585–6) that in modern Peloponnesus the population of villages varies from 150 to 600, according as they stand on the softer or the
harder rock-formations.

irrigation. To this extent life on the Mediterranean country-side provided a schooling for the more intensive co-operation of the members of a city-state.

But if natural conditions in Mediterranean lands made for communal co-operation, they did not favour agrarian communism. This form of organization is most compatible with a pastoral economy. But under Mediterranean conditions the prevailing type of land-work consisted of tillage and orchard cultivation. In these occupations, and especially in the tending of gardens, success must largely depend on the individual's devotion to his particular plot, and (in the absence of any highly organized machinery of state) this could be best assured by the institution of personal property.

Yet the natural economy of the Mediterranean lands did not play into the hands of capitalist exploitation. The generally broken and tumbled surface of the country did not favour the consolidation of plots into large units like the Bonanza farms of the American Middle West; consequently the savings in production costs that result from operations on a big scale could not be realized, save in abnormal districts. Least of all could standardization and the processes of mass-production be introduced into the numerous corners and pockets where garden cultivation was practised, for here individual skill and attention prevailed over organization.[1] The absorption of small property into the ownership of wealthy landlords, which was a recurrent feature of Greek and (more especially) of Roman history, was due in the main to political and social rather than to strictly economic causes. On the one hand, the exigencies of military service, which called the peasant away from his plot and might leave it untended for long periods, continual devastation by invaders (as in the later days of the Roman empire), and the lure of 'bread and circuses' in the cities, were so many inducements for the small owner to sell out; on the other hand, the social prestige and (in some states) the political privileges that accrued to landed property, and the general lack of other safe objects of investment, turned every moneyed person into an eager buyer. Even so, concentration of ownership did not necessarily entail the merging of small units of cultivation into *latifundia*. Having regard to the conditions

---

[1] This applied particularly to labour in the vineyards. The olive orchards required less intensive cultivation but more expensive machinery in the form of oil-presses. For this reason, and because of the olive-tree's slow rate of growth, which withheld the hope of a speedy return on labour expended, capital played a larger part in its exploitation.

imposed by Nature, some wealthy landlords made their purchases
in small and scattered parcels, and those who consolidated their
holdings into compact blocks not infrequently let them out in
small lots, instead of applying organized methods of capitalist
exploitation.[1] The only branch of land work which gave any
decisive advantage to operations on a large scale was 'transhumance' pasturing, for under proper organization hardly any
more labour was required for the tending and droving of large
herds than of small ones. Whatever the method of ownership,
la petite culture remained the normal practice in ancient land-
work.

Another natural feature of the Mediterranean lands which left
its mark on Greek and Roman history was the more or less abrupt
transition from the cultivated lowlands to the maquis and the
summer pasture of the upper zones, and the consequent segrega-
tion of the husbandman from the herdsman. From this dissociation natural enmities sprang up in the ancient world, such as
still obtain between Fellahin and Bedouin in the Near East. For
the mobile and armed herdsman it was a constant temptation to
supplement his scant living by raiding the plains, and to rid himself of this recurrent nuisance the lowlander had to organize his
resources of greater man-power. The feud between Mountain
and Plain runs like a red thread through early Roman history,
culminating in the hard-fought and critical Samnite wars; and
mindful of their early tradition as guardians of the Italian lowlands, the Romans subsequently pacified large tracts of provincial
land by the drastic method of *deductio in plana* of unruly upland
populations.[2] Yet the practice of 'transhumance', entailing a
voluntary *deductio in plana* for herdsmen in the winter season,
and a bargaining about the regular use of grazing-spaces in the
lowlands, tended to overlay ancient feuds with emergent under-
standings, and the drovers' codes which Roman lawyers drew
up for Italian pasturages confirmed the Roman soldiers' work of
pacification. The need for highlanders to import salt for themselves and their herds also laid the foundations of friendly traffic
between Mountain and Plain, and the Via Salaria, which led from
the salt-pans of Ostia through Rome to the Sabine mountains,
was as much a path of peace as an invasion track.

[1] On this point see especially G. Salvioli, *Le Capitalisme dans le monde antique*,
ch. 4.
[2] C. Jullian, *Histoire de la Gaule*, iv, pp. 74–5; C. H. V. Sutherland, *The Romans
in Spain*, p. 135; Rostovtzeff, *Roman Empire*, p. 222 (Dalmatia).

A more potent inducement to peace, however, was the intensive cultivation of olive and vine in Mediterranean lands. Tillers of the crop-land had periods of rest in their calendar, during which they could afford to take a holiday in the form of a campaign against some neighbouring state: even though the battle should go against them and their crops should suffer ravage, the damage was no greater than a year's hard work to follow could repair. But the labour in the vineyards was continuous, and the destruction of an olive-tree might require half a lifetime to make good. It was, therefore, no mere fancy which caused the Greeks and Romans to offer an olive branch as a symbol of peace.[1]

But the most important natural factor in ancient Mediterranean history was the Mediterranean Sea itself. This great water has its dangerous moods, and throughout the ages it has scared some of its border peoples into remaining land-lubbers. But those who have adventured it and mastered its comparatively simple rules of navigation have earned their due reward in economic prosperity or political lordship. The fundamental similarity of the Mediterranean lands has not precluded disparities of detail between them sufficient to render them economically complementary to each other, and so to draw them together into habits of economic co-operation. Some regions were natural granaries, others were ill suited to corn-production but well adapted to produce wine or oil; and the raw materials of industry were variously distributed over the whole area. Thus the inter-Mediterranean traffic in foodstuffs and textiles, in ceramics and metal-ware, grew to be of basic importance for the material civilization of Greece and Rome; but the mass-movement of staple commodities would have been impossible without the commodious highway of the Mediterranean Sea.

This sea was equally indispensable as a connecting link between the members of any comprehensive political union. The importance of naval power in the Mediterranean as an instrument of empire may be illustrated from each successive thalassocracy of ancient times, from the Minoan, the Athenian, the Ptolemaic, and the Roman lordship of the seas.[2] The part played by road

[1] Fortunately the wood of the olive is exceedingly tough. The demolition parties of an invading army, unless inured to lumber-work, might blister their hands severely before their axes had cut deep.

[2] The importance of naval power as an instrument of empire was clearly understood by the Athenian writer known as the 'Old Oligarch' (*Constitution of Athens*, ch. ii, §§ 1–8). For a more general survey see J. H. Rose, *The Mediterranean in the Ancient World*.

communications in holding the Roman empire together should not be overlooked, but it was, above all, the Mediterranean Sea that enabled it to coalesce into an organic unity, for it alone could render possible that frequency of intercourse among its constituent parts which made them 'members of one another'.[1] Seconded by wise Roman statesmanship, the natural uniting force of the Mediterranean Sea allowed the scattered populations of its borderland to achieve a cultural *bloc* which has ever since been a major factor in world civilization.

[1] For this reason too Polybius could write that under Roman rule Mediterranean history had become 'organic'—σωματοειδής (i. 3. 4).

II. GREECE. GENERAL

§ 1. CLIMATE

THE term 'Greece' is here taken to denote the southern projection of the Balkan Peninsula, reckoned from Epirus and Thessaly, together with the Ionian Isles and the isles of the Aegean Sea, in all an area of *c*. 30,000 square miles.

This territory may be regarded as the most typical of Mediterranean regions, for it exhibits most of the Mediterranean characteristics with peculiar distinctness. Its climate adheres closely to the Mediterranean norm of boisterous but bright winters and set fair summers. The winter rainfall is heavy everywhere, and on the western coastlands it rises to 40 inches; and when Boreas blows, he breaks in with a biting blast from the Russian steppes. Yet between the bouts of rough weather there are 'halcyon days'—a term applied by the ancient Greeks to a fine spell that usually sets in at the turn of the year, when the kingfisher (ἀλκυών) was supposed to build his nest on the sea's calm surface. During these interludes a clear sky, a warm sun, and a flickering breeze combine to counterfeit an English May. Even Boreas is more suggestive of March than of December: he may herald himself with flurries of snow, but presently he will sweep the clouds away and, still blowing strong, will keep the sky open for a clear, hard sun. At Athens the Popular Assembly and the Jury Courts held frequent open-air meetings throughout the winter, and the chief dramatic festival, at which thousands of spectators sat all day in an unroofed theatre, was held in March. But the playgoers of later days were no doubt grateful when King Attalus I of Pergamum built them an adjacent portico to which they might retire during the not unusual squalls of rain.

In summer the rainfall gives out, but for an occasional thunderstorm, during a period that varies from two months in the northern districts to four months in Peloponnesus. Not even the western coastlands, which are drenched in winter, escape the summer drought.[1] The glare of the summer sun, reverberating from the white limestone surfaces of the mountain-sides, is almost blinding, and in districts which are cut off from cooling breezes its heat equals that of the tropics: in the Thessalian basin Larissa

---

[1] The mean summer rainfall in Greece is no more than 7 per cent. of the year's total.

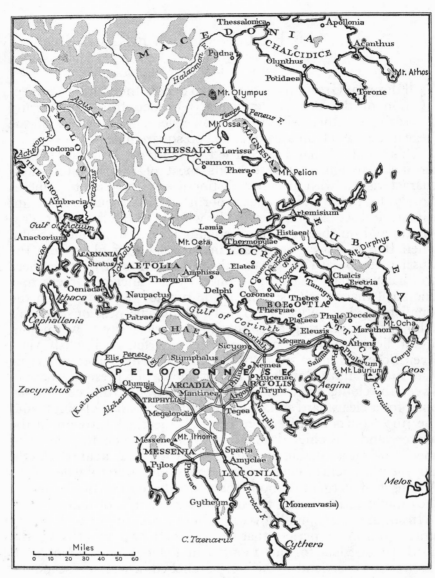

GREECE

has a mean July temperature of 90°, thus sharing with Seville the highest summer readings of Mediterranean Europe. But the greater part of Greece benefits by the summer 'trade-winds' that sweep across the Aegean Sea with peculiar vehemence, so much so that in some of the islands they prevent tree-growth on the northern slopes.[1] And the play of alternate land and sea breezes reinforces the effect of the etesians. The sea breezes that spring up in the early afternoon effectually temper the torrid noontide heat, and after nightfall, when the etesians die down and the air becomes stale, the land breeze restores its circulation.

If, following the practice of the ancient Greeks,[2] we consider the influence of the world's climates upon the health and temperament of its peoples, we shall find that the Greek climate is by no means of the restful 'Riviera' type. For persons of a nervous disposition it is over-stimulating, and herein we may discover part cause of that contentiousness of disposition which has always been the besetting fault of the Greek people. But for those of normal constitution it is a tonic that tautens the fibres of body and mind.[3] Its action is heightened by the vivifying effect of Greek scenery. In the Greek landscape the predominant colours, the dull green of its foliage and the hard grey-white of its limestone formations, strike somewhat cold. But the infinite variety in the structure of the mountains, whose every rib and fold reveals itself in sharp relief, and the ever-changing pattern of an interweaving land and sea, provide a perpetual challenge to the attention of those who can take in line and form. Greece, therefore, is a natural home of artists,[4] and of thinkers who do not shut their eyes to the world. But its history is a reminder that only under the influence of a special political and social stimulus could Nature's gifts produce their full effect in human achievement.

§ 2. STRUCTURE

That Greece was the product of an epoch of storm and stress in a not far remote geological period is revealed by continued volcanic activity and frequent earth tremors within its territory.

---

[1] Conversely, the summer season at Corfu, which is unusually calm, was a severe trial to the British troops stationed there in the first half of the nineteenth century.

[2] Herodotus, ix. 122; Hippocrates, *De Aëribus*, ch. 24.

[3] It is notable that a high proportion of the famous men of Greek antiquity approached or exceeded the span of threescore and ten years.

[4] It is no mere accident that ancient Greece was more famous for its sculptors than for its painters. The Greek landscape is conducive to visualizing in three dimensions.

The Lemnian volcano, Mt. Mosychlos, is now quiescent, but wisps of smoke from its crater warned the ancient Greeks that in its hollows the forge of Hephaestus was aglow. Strangely enough, Greek tradition did not preserve the record of an explosion, of date *c.* 1700 B.C., which transformed a one-time circular island into the small archipelago of Thera and its satellites, now clustering round a deep sea-channel formed by the crater's submersion.[1] The general instability of the Greek lands was anciently symbolized by the god Poseidon, who not only swayed the sea waves but rocked the none too solid earth. A series of seismic shocks in Crete during the second millennium B.C. was probably the reason for successive reconstructions of the palace of Cnossus.[2] In historic times two notable earthquakes caused havoc at Sparta (464 B.C.) and Rhodes (227 B.C.). These major disasters were the more violent convulsions of an eternally unquiet earth. In 373 B.C. Poseidon varied his procedure by launching a tidal wave which completely engulfed the Achaean towns of Helice and Bura.[3]

In Greece the vast folding-up process, by which the general mountain system of the Mediterranean area was created, was followed by partial collapses, to which the land and the adjoining seas largely owe their present conformation. The principal product of this compensatory sagging movement was the Aegean Sea, whose islands are the emerging peaks of a drowned plateau.[4] On the Greek mainland the sinuous but regular lines of the fold-ridges were fractured at many points, and the pattern of mountain and plain was cut across with troughs of sunken highland and intrusive arms of the sea. No other country of the Mediterranean presents a more tumbled surface than Greece: it is estimated that not much more than 20 per cent. of the land is level.[5]

The texture of the Greek mountains is of the usual Mediterranean material. Though softer sub-strata of schist and sandstone lie open to view here and there, they are for the most part sheathed with a layer of hard limestone, which has produced its usual effects of bold scenery, scanty soil-formation, and ill-

---

[1] Later eruptions, extending to recent times, have built up their lava cones into new islets.

[2] On the earthquakes, ancient and modern, in Crete, see A. J. Evans, *The Palace of Minos*, ii, pp. 313–25; iv, pp. 988–92.

[3] Diodorus, xv. 48. 3.

[4] Herodotus wrote better than he knew when he compared the towns of Egypt as they protruded from the Nile flood with the isles of the Aegean (ii. 97. 1).

[5] A. Struck, *Zur Landeskunde von Griechenland*, p. 167 (3¼ million acres out of 16 million).

regulated water-supply. Though Mt. Olympus only just falls
short of 10,000 feet, few other peaks overtop 8,000; their capacity
to hold snow in storage is therefore limited.

§ 3. VEGETATION

The climate, the relief, and the rock-formation of Greece
combine to deck it out with a typical Mediterranean vegetation,
but at the same time to stunt its growth and to spread it out
unevenly. In the lower ranges of the mountain zone tracts of
deciduous forest (predominantly of beech) are still to be found.
The flanks of Pelion and Ossa, whose woodlands excited the
admiration of ancient travellers,[1] are well clad even now; the
range of Pindus and the Arcadian highlands are still well stocked
with timber. In ancient times various regions, which the lumber-
man's axe, the charcoal-burner's kiln, and the crofter's goat have
since laid bare, or have made over to maquis, were well covered
withtrees. In Minoan days cypress beams with a width of sixteen
inches were felled on the mountains of Crete,[2] and Homer's
Greece was well furnished with coverts for big game. Though
the forest cover of Cithaeron and Parnes had been mostly stripped
by the time of Plato,[3] boars could still be hunted there in the age
of the Antonines.[4] The plain of Mantinea, now lying wide open,
once carried an oak wood which could be described as a 'sea of
trees' ($\pi\epsilon\lambda\alpha\gamma\sigma$).[5] Yet, even so, by the fifth century B.C. the timber
standings of the Greek homeland no longer covered the needs of
its inhabitants, and the importation of foreign-grown lumber had
become a staple branch of commerce.[6]

The intermediate zone of bush and scrub extends far down
the hill-sides and leaves scant room for pockets of arable and
orchard land, not exceeding 25 per cent. of the total acreage,
in the intermontane plains. The productive area of Greece has
indeed been utilized to the utmost by its husbandmen, ancient
and modern, who have terraced the hill-sides to the upper limit
of cultivation and have laboured incessantly to clear the soil of

[1] Pseudo-Dicaearchus, ii, § 1 (C. Müller, *Geographici Graeci Minores*, i, p. 106).
[2] J. L. Myres, *Who were the Greeks?*, p. 6.
[3] *Critias* 111 B, C.
[4] Pausanias, i. 32. 7. Pausanias' description of Greece may be held to reflect the
conditions of his own day; there is no need to assume that it was derived from some
earlier author (J. G. Frazer, *Pausanias and other Greek Sketches*, pp. 112 ff.).
[5] Pausanias, viii. 11. 1, 10.
[6] A. C. Johnson, *Transactions of the American Philological Association*, 1927,
pp. 199–209.

its perennial crop of stones. Moreover, its choicest patches of
orchard country are of such fertility as to raise Greece to the
rank of a food-exporting region. Its wine and oil were probably
the staple products for its oversea trade in the Minoan and
Mycenaean ages; in historic times, and especially in the Hellenistic period, they certainly commanded a wide market. At
the present day the export of raisins and currants (the latter a
species of grape which was not cultivated in ancient times) goes
a long way to balance the Greek trade budget. But in many parts
of Greece the arable surface is so restricted that the raising of
cereals is almost reduced to the scale of a garden operation;[1]
and the stony nature of the soil compels the cultivation of barley
in preference to wheat, whose long roots cannot find accommodation in it. The wheat consumed in Greece through the ages has
mostly been of foreign growth, and to this day it remains the
principal import commodity.

The legend of the Elysian Fields (reserved for the Blest in
after-life) is an ancient illustration of the scarcity value of water-
meadow and lush grass in Greek lands. The grazing industry of
Greece would be insignificant but for its large stock of goats and
sheep.[2] The goats find their sustenance in the scrub land, and as
unauthorized intruders on the forest preserves. The sheep are
driven to and fro between mountain and plain; at the present
day 'transhumance' plays an important part in the Pindus regions,
where the Vlach shepherds form a distinctive section of the
population.

§ 4. MINERAL RESOURCES

Greece's chief store of mineral wealth consists in her ample
supplies of good building-stone and in several rich veins of marble.
Of her coloured marbles the only varieties to be extensively
quarried in ancient days were the white-and-green *cipollino* of
Carystus in Euboea, which had a vogue under the Roman
emperors, and the *verde antico* of Atrax in north Thessaly, which
may still be admired in the panellings of St. Sophia at Constantinople. The finest of the white marbles, which were in
double demand for building and for sculpture, were mostly produced in the Cyclades and in Attica. The Attic source was Mt.
Pentelicus, a long and shapely ridge adjoining the eastern coast

---

[1] Grain is often grown in Greece between rows of olives.
[2] The proportion of sheep and goats to horned cattle has recently been estimated
as 45 and 33 to 4.

but in full view of Athens, which supplied the blocks for the
temples on the Acropolis and for the statuary of Phidias.[1] The
Pentelic marble had a smooth grain; its surface strata were flecked
with iron rust, but its inner layers were of pure white colour. In
the general estimation of the ancient Greeks it did not rank quite
as high as the marble of Paros, which had a slightly coarser grain
but unequalled translucency, and was therefore the favourite
material of sculptors.

Another industrial material with which Greece was well supplied was potter's clay, derived from sedimentary deposits in
river-beds. The best qualities contained the right proportion of
fine grit to prevent either cracking or shrinkage in the potter's
kiln, and were sufficiently free from lime to resist crumbling.
The finest ceramic ware of ancient Greece was the product of a
long-established craft tradition working on a perfectly suitable
material.[2]

Greece possesses a varied supply of metals, mostly dispersed
in small pockets.[3] The chief concentrations formerly were in the
copper mines of Euboea and the silver deposits of Laurium in
Attica (p. 76). Most of the ancient minefields are now exhausted,[4]
but some of the available sources of metal were never worked
in days of old. With their crude methods of iron-smelting the
ancient Greeks could not have successfully reduced the poorer
and refractory ores; consequently they relied in the main on their
beds of hematite,[5] or on imported iron from the high-grade deposits of northern Asia Minor (p. 157).

The small fields of lignite now under operation in Euboea were
unknown to the ancients; and a 'black combustible stone' that
was to be found in Elis,[6] and was there used to feed the local
forges, remained a curiosity. The tar wells of Zacynthus,[7] the
pumice deposits of Thera, and the emery of Naxos (used as an
abrasive in gem-cutting) were formerly under exploitation; but
the obsidian of Melos, a bottle-green stone with a sharp edge,

[1] The Pentelic quarries have again been brought under exploitation by a British
company (Marmor Ltd.).
[2] Miss G. M. A. Richter, *The Craft of Athenian Pottery*.
[3] For details see C. Neumann and J. Partsch, *Geographie von Griechenland*.
[4] The tailings at Laurium are being worked over by modern companies.
[5] The hematite deposits of Laurium were not exploited in ancient times (O.
Davies, *Roman Mines*, p. 248). Their neglect was presumably due to the superior
attractions of the silver mines.
[6] Theophrastus, *De Lapidibus*, § 16.
[7] Herodotus, iv. 195. 2. These wells were a natural wonder in the historian's
eyes.

which had furnished the Aegean area with cutting implements in the Early Minoan age, passed into oblivion with the coming of bronze.

§ 5. External Communications

The ancient Greeks, who believed that their country was well favoured in the matter of climate, could not but admit that 'poverty shared board with it, and would not be denied'.[1] No other gift of Nature could wholly compensate for the sheer deficiency of cultivable soil, which maintained literally a *res angusta domi*. The point at which all the productive land was taken up came early in Greek history, and henceforth the need to find alternative means of subsistence has never ceased to be pressing. To this urgent problem the ancient Greeks discovered two valid solutions, oversea trade and emigration; and they applied these remedies to such good effect that they secured for themselves a sufficient margin of wealth and leisure to serve as a seed-bed of their high civilization. The history of ancient Greece was therefore determined in large measure by its external communications.

On the landward side the frontier of Greece is dominated by no such impressive barrier as the Alps or Pyrenees; yet it is cut off from the European continent no less effectively than Italy or Spain. Its continental approach is blocked by a continuous arch of elevated land, rising in Mt. Olympus to little short of 10,000 feet. Two notches in the ridge to the west of Olympus give access to Thessaly at a height of 3,000 feet (the Petra and Volustana passes); but from their starting-points at Petra and Phylace in Macedonia to their junction at Oloösson in Thessaly these tracks provide rough going all the way. In 169 B.C. a Roman army forced the Petra pass in the reverse direction, but reached Macedonia in such an exhausted condition as to be unfit for battle.[2] At the coastal end of the Olympus range the vale of Tempe (p. 62) affords an entrance on level ground, but it narrows into a gorge of barely 150 feet. In 336 B.C. Alexander, at the head of a flying column, turned the pass by scaling Mt. Ossa, its southern flank, but this scramble was an alpinist's *tour de force*, and was accomplished only by cutting steps in the face of the cliff.[3] On other occasions when the pass of Tempe was carried the defence was caught unready, and the invaders simply marched through.[4] At the north-western end the mountain barrier is less con-

---

[1] Herodotus, vii. 102. 1 : τῇ Ἑλλάδι πενίη αἰεί κοτε σύντροφός ἐστι.
[2] Livy, xliv, chs. 2–5.   [3] Polyaenus, iv. 3. 23.
[4] So Xerxes in 480 and the Galatians in 279 B.C.

tinuous, but the approach across the western Balkan highlands is through a labyrinth of deeply sunk valleys (p. 57). From Albania the Zygos pass, which follows the valley of the river Aoüs, provides access to Thessaly (p. 57), but the Klisura ravine at its entrance offers a formidable obstacle.[1] The north-western frontier, therefore, gave as good security as the Olympus range.

In the epochs of disintegration that preceded and followed the age of ancient Greek civilization the northern entrances of Greece gave passage to barbarian intruders, to the Dorians at the close of the second millennium B.C. and to the Slavs after A.D. 600, either of whom in turn stole through a disorganized defence.[2] But in the intervening centuries, save on rare occasions, they refused admission to invaders from the mainland and thus left the Greeks free to devote their energies to expansion overseas.

While Greece is almost closed to the European continent it lies wide open on its sea fronts. The territory of the Greek main-land is one-third that of Italy and one-sixth that of the Spanish peninsula, yet its coastline (2,600 miles) is longer than that of the two larger peninsulas (Italy 2,150 miles, Spain and Portugal 2,300 miles). No point of Central Greece lies farther than 40 miles from the sea, and none in Peloponnesus is distant more than 32 miles.

The seas that encompass Greece are as typically Mediterranean as the Greek lands themselves. In winter-time the southern Adriatic is a storm-centre with an irregular play of currents; and the north Aegean is infested until late in spring with a gusty north wind resembling the mistral of the Gulf of Lions.[3] Occa-sional fall-winds may swoop down from any coastal range: their force and frequency off Cape Malea at the south-eastern tip of Peloponnesus gave this headland a particularly bad reputation. Long stretches of the seaboard are lined with sheer cliff. On opposite sides of Greece the coasts of Epirus and of Thessaly are almost continuously iron-bound, and the Thessalian coast, which lies exposed to the strong north-easterly trade-winds of summer as well as to the northerly gales of winter, is dangerous at all

[1] In 198 B.C. the Roman general Flamininus by-passed the Aoüs gorge by a mountain track, but in doing this he was assisted by a local traitor (F. W. Walbank, *Philip V of Macedon*, pp. 149–52). In winter 1940–1 the Italian invaders of Greece were stopped dead at the Klisura position.

[2] On the coming of the Dorians see N. G. L. Hammond, *Annual of the British School at Athens*, xxxii (1931–2), pp. 139–47.

[3] It was such a wind that wrecked the Persian fleet under Mardonius in 492 B.C. (Herodotus, vi. 44. 2). On its danger to modern shipping see S. Casson, *Macedonia, Thrace and Illyria*, pp. 36–7.

seasons.[1] In summer the force of the etesians in the Aegean Sea compelled Greek merchantmen to sail by a carefully constructed time-table: if they were bound for a cruise in the Black Sea they would have to make the Dardanelles before the end of spring. The handicap imposed upon the Athenians by the summer trade-winds blowing in the teeth of their north-bound expeditionary forces repeatedly allowed Philip of Macedon to steal a march upon them and needed to be carefully considered in Demosthenes' counter-strategy.[2]

The surrounding seas accordingly remained closed to all Greeks in winter and to some Greeks at almost any season. The Thessalians and Boeotians always remained landsmen, and Hesiod did not consider the Aegean really safe except for fifty days after the summer solstice.[3] Apart from the Corinthians and Megarians, none of the Peloponnesians or of the other peoples grouped round the Corinthian Gulf plied a regular oversea trade. Even the island populations have not been seafarers continuously: at the present day the inhabitants of the Archipelago confine themselves in the main to inshore fishing operations.

But the Greek seas also offer in full measure the compensating advantages of Mediterranean navigation. The intricate inter-mixture of earth and water induces a peculiarly strong play of land and sea breezes, of which ancient seamen knew how to take full advantage.[4] Though some of the coasts run straight and sheer like sea-walls, innumerable gulfs and inlets lie between them, and shelter is provided at many points by headlands and offshore isles. Above all, no other expanse of water is distinguished by a clearer atmosphere or a greater profusion of landmarks than the Aegean Sea. In its northern region the peaks of Athos and Samothrace can hardly be lost out of sight. The Parthenon may be descried from the citadel of Corinth; from Mt. Dirphys in Euboea Athos is discernible; and from another Euboean height, Mt. Ocha, the view extends across the Aegean to Chios. An observer on the promontory of Sunium at the tip of Attica may take in at a glance the cluster of the Cyclades as far as Melos, as though he were

[1] The thank-offerings which the Athenians made to Boreas after the havoc suffered by the Persian armada off C. Sepias in 480 (Herodotus, vii. 188–90) suggests that he blew on this occasion with exceptional violence. But in any summer the wind off this coast may reach gale force.

[2] *Philippic I*, §§ 31–2; *De Chersoneso*, §§ 14–17.

[3] *Works and Days*, ll. 663 ff.

[4] Thus in the 'Battle of the Corinthian Gulf' the Athenian admiral Phormio correctly calculated that the early morning land-breeze would throw the ill-trained Peloponnesian crews into disarray (Thucydides, ii. 84. 3).

reading a map, and from Melos the central range of Crete shows in clear outline. Navigation in the Aegean is thus reduced to the simplicity of a ferry service.

The inhabitants of Greece have therefore never been able to disregard for long the call of the sea. The earliest illustrations of sea-going ships, constructed with keel and ribs, are preserved on seal-stones from the Aegean islands that date back to the third or second millennium B.C.,[1] and the earliest recorded lordship of the seas is that which was exercised by the Minoan rulers of prehistoric Crete. The continental invaders of Greece who closed its prehistoric period were soon lured on to naval adventure, as were its Albanian immigrants in the eighteenth and nineteenth centuries. In the first millennium B.C. the Greek seaman was a familiar figure over all the eastern and part of the western Mediterranean, and with the rebirth of Greece in the nineteenth century its flag has become a common sight in these waters. The history of ancient Greece is largely a record of successive thalassocracies, and Greek civilization was mainly the product of cities with a seafaring tradition.

§ 6. INTERNAL COMMUNICATIONS

On the other hand, the obstacles to easy travel within the Greek mainland are even greater than a mere glance at the map, showing its high relief, would suggest. The irregular strike of the mountain system leaves no room for long corridors running parallel to well-defined ranges. In Greece cross-country journeys in almost any direction are like trips on a switchback railway, and since many of the mountain passes are at a height of 3,000 feet or over, they are snow-bound for at least part of the winter. Of the Greek rivers only a few of the larger ones, such as the Acheloüs and the Thessalian Peneus, are navigable over short stretches during a brief part of the year. In winter the streams are often in spate, yet 'all-the-year-round' (ἀέναοι) water-courses are the exception. In summer their dry beds would offer a natural roadway, were they not encumbered with boulders. In the limestone regions, moreover, the rivers often begin their course in a deep gorge, and some of them end it by disappearing bodily down a 'swallow-hole' or natural tunnel (καταβόθρα), where their beds have cracked wide open or a rift has been formed in a hill-side.

In modern times the difficulties of travel in Greece have been

[1] A. J. Evans, *The Palace of Minos*, ii, pp. 239–45.

greatly reduced by road-construction. The roughly paved mule-tracks of the Turkish era still render good service in the remoter regions, and the principal towns are now linked up with coach services on a tarmac surface. In prehistoric days the lords of Cnossus and Mycenae made a beginning of constructing metalled roads (pp. 88, 96); but their successors in the city-state age hardly went beyond the paving of short avenues to some important centres of religious pilgrimage such as Delphi and Eleusis. The political disunity of the city-state period, itself in part a result of the natural fragmentation of Greece, prevented the several cities from remedying Nature's shortcomings by a common policy of road-building on a national scale.[1]

§ 7. THE GREEK CITY-STATES

The influence of the geography of Greece on its politics is plainly discernible in the development of the Greek cities, which gave rise to the typical Greek states of ancient times.

The primary unit of settlement in Greece, as in most Mediterranean lands, was a village, situated in the arable or orchard land at one of the none too frequent points where a river or spring provided a perennial supply of water.[2] This type of habitation, being well adapted to its natural surroundings, endured throughout ancient times. In some regions of Greece, such as Aetolia and Arcadia, the greater part of the population lived in villages until the fourth century B.C., and in later centuries a partial reversion to this method of grouping took place.

Yet already in the third millennium B.C. larger aggregates of dwellings, to which the name of 'city' is more appropriate, came into being on Greek soil, and about 800 B.C. a more general shift of population into close-built towns set in. Henceforth the city became the prevalent place of habitation among the Greeks, and the city-state their normal political unit.

The earliest known towns in Greek lands, dating back to the Early Minoan age (before 2100 B.C.), arose in eastern Crete at

---

[1] The improvement in communications which even a rudimentary integration of small states may bring about may be illustrated from the remarkable achievements of cantonal road-construction (the Axenstrasse along the Lake of Lucerne, the Devil's Bridge across the Reuss near Andermatt, and the track across the Gemmi pass), undertaken in the eighteenth and early nineteenth centuries by the loosely federated Swiss cantons of that period.

[2] J. L. Myres, *Mediterranean Culture*, pp. 13–14. Temporary hut-villages (καλύβια) are set up nowadays by the shepherds at the water-points near the summer grazing-grounds. The fact that on Greek soil the village was prior to the city was duly observed by Aristotle (*Politics*, i. 1. 7).

the sites of Gournia, Mallia, Mochlos, and Palaiokastro. It is a common feature of these towns that they stood close to the sea, or right at the water's edge, on level ground or on the lower slope of a hill. The palace town of Cnossus in central Crete, lying some four miles inland, was ensconced in a fold between two slight rises, and the settlement of Phylakopi on the island of Melos was situated almost flush with the sea. Of the Minoan palaces Phaestus in southern Crete alone occupied a dominant position, astride of a tall mountain spur. The sites of the Minoan towns in general were evidently chosen for their commercial advantages and in disregard of military considerations; they demonstrate as effectually as the absence of fortifications around them that the people of prehistoric Crete were seafarers and traders rather than warriors.

But the prehistoric cities of the Greek mainland tell a different story. Mycenae occupied the crown of a hill near the watershed between the Argive and the Corinthian plains. Amyclae, the predecessor of Sparta, stood on an isolated bluff above the Eurotas valley, and Pylos (close to the historic site of like name) was perched on the top of a flat hill.[1] Orchomenus in Boeotia was built on a tongue of land at a river confluence, in a position that was also characteristic of many ancient Italian towns. These sites combine with the massive fortifications at Mycenae to prove that the function of the early mainland towns was to fend off invaders or to hold down a conquered country-side. At all these fortresses the citadel was the nucleus of the settlement, and any habitations at its foot were accretions.

The cities which were founded after 800 B.C. conformed more closely to the Mycenaean than to the Minoan pattern in the choice of their sites. One general characteristic of the early Greek towns was that they stood at some distance from the coast even when, as in the case of Athens, Corinth, and Argos, a favourable situation on the seaboard was at hand. A less acute observer than Thucydides could have drawn the conclusion that their primary purpose was not to give access to the sea, but to keep the visiting sea-folk (mostly pirates in those unrestful days) at arm's length.[2] Another almost unvarying feature of these cities was that they stood on elevated ground. The most favoured type of site was a

---

[1] K. Kourouniotis and C. W. Blegen, *American Journal of Archaeology*, 1939, pp. 557–76. Similarly, the Achaean and Dorian immigrants into Crete occupied new hill-top sites in preference to the open towns of their Minoan predecessors (E. Kirsten, *Die Antike*, 1938, pp. 311–19).

[2] Thucydides, i. 7.

E

mountain spur or slope ascending suddenly from a plain and surmounted by an abrupt outcrop of sheer rock; the dwelling-houses and the market-place (ἄστυ) would occupy the shelving ground, and the citadel (πόλις in the exact sense)[1] would be up-reared on the high bluff.

The two classic examples of cities thus sited were Athens and Corinth. The citadel of Athens, which took the place of an older Mycenaean fortress, stood on an isolated hill, recessed to a distance of some four miles from the Attic coast, and rising 300–400 feet above the lower town, with an almost vertical drop on all sides except the west;[2] the ἄστυ, which eventually enveloped the πόλις on all sides, first grew up near the ramp leading up to the citadel.[3] The ἄστυ of Corinth was built on a platform at the summit of a gentle rise from the Corinthian Gulf, and at a distance of 1½ miles from it. The choice of site was partly determined by the powerful spring of Pirene, which still discharges into a Roman well-house, and partly by a neighbouring peak, the citadel hill or Acrocorinth, which towers nearly 2,000 feet above sea-level and commands the approaches to the Gulf (p. 82).

On the Greek islands the Minoan tradition of open settlements near sea-level was also abandoned, as the inhabitants moved away from the water's edge and established their new towns on higher ground under a steep citadel-rock. Their choice of emplacements on the island of Rhodes was particularly significant. Avoiding the northern tip, which offers a natural harbour commanding the passage between the Aegean and Levantine Seas (p. 101), they betook themselves to remoter sites at Ialysus and Lindus, which were indifferently placed for traffic but possessed high-towering citadels. By way of exception, Delos occupied an almost level piece of ground near the coast; but its sanctity was a sufficient citadel.

Individual Greek towns, while conforming to the general pattern of πόλις and ἄστυ, naturally showed many variations of detail in their sites. Argos, Messene, and Pharsalus had two citadel-hills; at Thebes the fortress of Cadmeia occupied the upper end of a uniformly shelving slope; Sicyon stood, in Italian fashion,

---

[1] The primary sense of the word πόλις is preserved in official Attic inscriptions, where it refers specially to the Acropolis (e.g. in Tod, *Greek Historical Inscriptions*, 51A l. 4, B l. 13).

[2] Water for the citadel was supplied by a spring, the Clepsydra, which issued from the north slope and was included in the fortifications by means of an outwork (E. A. Gardner, *Ancient Athens*, pp. 23–5).

[3] Gardner, op. cit., pp. 88 ff.

on a high tongue of land between two rivers. By way of contrast
to the general rule, a few cities occupied sites which had little or
no defensive value, but were mainly chosen as natural centres of
communications. Sparta, Megalopolis, and Larissa lay by river-
sides on mounds which raised them above flood-level yet left
them easily accessible on all sides; Piraeus spread from the water's
edge over a low hill. But Piraeus was protected by the Athenian
navy; and the three inland towns were, or strove to be, capital
cities whose first requisite would be, not security against attack,
but power to strike out quickly in all directions. Counterparts
to the sites of Sparta, Megalopolis, and Larissa are to be found,
significantly enough, among many Roman colonies.

The Greeks who set up colonies overseas in the eighth and
following centuries followed similar principles in their choice of
town sites, for they could not always reckon on a friendly welcome. Following the practice of the earlier Phoenician colonists,
they established themselves on off-shore islands, as at Mytilene,
at Cyzicus, at Platea (the predecessor of Cyrene), at Emporiae,
at Pithecussae (modern Ischia, at the entrance of the Bay of
Naples).[1]

Failing an island, they would select the head of a peninsula (as
at Sinope and Syracuse), or its neck (as at Potidaea and Cardia).
Settling on the mainland, they would give preference to a stretch
of coast adjoined by a protective ridge or bluff. In some cases
the colonists made a progression from an island or peninsula to
an adjacent continent. From Pithecussae they moved to Cumae
and fortified a steep bluff overlooking the Campanian plain; from
Platea they advanced ten miles inland to Cyrene and built their
ἄστυ under a two-peaked acropolis.

The siting of the Greek cities, whether in the Greek homeland
or in the colonial areas, thus bears out Thucydides' observation
that their primary purpose was to give security. Instances that
confirm this rule *ex contrario* may be supplied from later ages,
when altered political conditions brought with them new methods
of settlement. In the Hellenistic period, when the Greeks established themselves as conquerors all over the Near East, they
could make a free choice of sites for their new foundations, and
accordingly had less regard for their defensibility. When the

---

[1] Phoenician settlements: Thucydides vi. 1. 6. Gades is a good example.
Mytilene: Strabo, p. 617. Cyzicus: id., p. 575. Platea: Herodotus, iv. 151–3.
Emporiae: a good description in Strabo, p. 160. Pithecussae: id., pp. 247–8.
The islands at Gades and Mytilene were eventually united to the adjacent land
by sedimentation.

Roman Peace brought general security to the Greek homeland, the population partly reverted to habitation in open villages.[1] In the thirteenth and following centuries, when the break-down of the Byzantine Peace again rendered the seas unsafe, the inhabitants of the Aegean islands scampered to the hill-tops;[2] but in the nineteenth century, when freedom also brought with it more ordered conditions, they have again descended towards the water's edge.

But if security was the primary purpose of most Greek cities, economic considerations also played a part in the choice of their sites. Almost invariably they were located within a pocket of fertile land, or closely adjacent to it. The pervasive intermixture of mountain and plain in the Greek lands gave its people a plentiful choice of natural fortresses, isolated bluffs or projecting spurs, that lay within easy reach of the cultivable area. Therefore the cities attracted within their walls not only the craftsmen and traders but the literally 'suburban' land-workers, who would set up their dwellings inside the urban area. The towns were therefore not mere islands in a wide expanse of open country, but they dominated the small patches of cultivable land which lay as it were at their feet; and this geographical ascendancy was readily translated into political supremacy. Thus, whereas in the Middle Ages the territorial rulers were the political overlords of the towns and granted them at most a charter of communal independence, the Greek cities absorbed the adjacent country-side within their own authority and ruled it from a single centre, so that one word (πόλις) sufficed to denote both 'city' and 'state'. That peculiar institution, the Greek city-state, had its roots in the geographic conformation of the Greek lands.[3]

§ 8. Greek Warfare[4]

The control which the geography of Greece exercised over ancient Greek methods of warfare, though not so rigorous as

[1] J. A. O. Larsen in Frank, *Economic Survey of Ancient Rome*, iv, pp. 471–2. Larsen points out that this was not a symptom of absolute depopulation. For similar conditions in Roman Sicily, cf. V. Scramuzza, op. cit. iii, p. 368.

[2] Thus Kastro lies well above the ancient city of Melos, and Santorin above the ancient city of Thera.

[3] On the Greek city-state in relation to Greek geography, see especially V. Ehrenberg, *Aspects of the Ancient World*, ch. 3, and F. E. Adcock, *Cambridge Ancient History*, iii, ch. 26.

[4] On this subject in relation to Greek geography see also G. B. Grundy, *Thucydides and the History of his Age*, chs. 9–14; A. W. Gomme, *A Historical Commentary on Thucydides*, i, pp. 10–21.

might have been expected, is none the less easily discernible in the history of operations both by land and by sea.

The tactics and equipment of Greek armies were never completely adapted to the natural exigencies of campaigning in Greek lands. The flanks of the Greek mountain-sides, besides being steep and rugged, are rendered doubly difficult by thickets of tough and prickly scrub in the maquis area, and by masses of loose scree, alternating with smooth but slippery slabs, on the bare patches of the hill-sides. Neither is there much opportunity for shock tactics and mass-manœuvring on the scanty tracts of level ground, for these are largely beset with vineyards and olive-groves enclosed with intersecting stone walls. On the Greek country-side, accordingly, light-armed and unencumbered troops would always appear to have held an advantage over heavily accoutred ones, and skirmishing operations to have been more suitable to the terrain than set battles in close formation. Indeed the history of modern Greek warfare entirely bears out this supposition. The victories gained by the Greek insurgents in the War of Independence were obtained by guerrilla tactics derived from the 'klephts' or brigands who used to infest the mountains of the border regions. The astonishing successes of the Greeks in the winter campaign of 1940–1 were in large measure due to the fact that they were specially trained and equipped for mountain warfare and conducted their operations so far as possible over difficult ground.

On those rare occasions when ancient Greek states put their trust in their light-armed contingents the result was the same. The victories of the Aetolians over the Athenian forces under Demosthenes in 426 B.C., and of the Athenian 'light brigade' under Iphicrates over the Spartan 'heavies' at Corinth in 390 B.C., have received due recognition; but they were less significant than the extraordinary running fight in which the Aetolians recovered Delphi from the Galatians and drove the invaders out of Greece in headlong rout (winter 279–278),[1] or the uphill scramble by which Antigonus Doson's 'Alpini' climbed to victory at Sellasia (222).[2] None the less, ever since the seventh century B.C. the standard Greek infantryman, the 'hoplite', was burdened with a heavy suit of armour and was trained to manœuvre and fight in elbow-to-elbow formation; the light-armed troops as a rule were ill trained and rendered merely auxiliary services. It is

[1] Pausanias, x. 22–3; W. W. Tarn, *Antigonos Gonatas*, pp. 156–7.
[2] Polybius, ii. 68.

difficult to explain this paradox except on the ground of a blind military tradition, derived from some early successes in the seventh and sixth centuries, and especially from the fascination of the Greek hoplite triumphs at Marathon and Plataea.[1]

On the other hand, the Greeks simply conformed to the conditions which geography laid upon them when they put their trust in infantry rather than in mounted troops, whose part they limited to flank-guarding and pursuit after battle. The only cities that made fuller use of their horsemen were those of Thessaly and (to a lesser degree) of Boeotia; even after the days of Alexander, whose cavalry won the day for him in the plains of Asia, the Greeks of the homeland set little store by their mounted forces. Thessaly and Boeotia had sufficient meadowland to rear a strong breed of horses and enough open country for cavalry evolutions. In other parts of Greece the horses were not sufficiently big-boned for shock tactics,[2] and room was lacking for cavalry actions on any large scale.

In ancient Greek land-warfare active operations were confined, with adequate reason, to the months of summer. Although the Greek winters are for the most part open, and the occasional frosts are never so severe as perforce to drive troops under cover, yet the snow in the uplands may hinder movement across the mountains, and in the plain the land may be flooded, or at any rate mud-bound, by the winter rains. Under such conditions, and in the absence of all-weather roads, Greek hoplites would easily be reduced to immobility, and even light-armed forces, such as those of the Persians in 480 B.C., would be confined to winter-quarters, if only because they could not keep themselves supplied in the field. When Epaminondas made a successful winter march across the Arcadian plateau in 370–369 B.C.[3] he accomplished an unusual *tour de force*, and the winter campaigns of Philip II of Macedon nonplussed his Greek adversaries.[4] So well was it understood that in Greek warfare winter was a close season, that mercenary forces would bargain for a holiday at this time of the year.[5]

Geographical conditions also exerted an indirect effect upon

---

[1] Gomme, op. cit., p. 14, concludes that the failure to develop guerrilla tactics was due to social and economic rather than to military reasons.

[2] The legs of the horsemen on the Parthenon frieze dangle well below their horses' slender barrels.

[3] Xenophon, *Hellenica*, vi. 5. 20.

[4] Demosthenes, *Philippic I*, § 31; *III*, § 50.

[5] G. T. Griffith, *Mercenaries of the Hellenistic World*, p. 283.

Greek methods of campaigning. Since Greece was by nature a country of small holdings, its cultivation was mainly in the hands of a peasantry who tilled the soil with their own hands (αὐτουργοί). These 'self-workers' might have time for a diversion before the corn harvest, or between harvest and vintage, but they could not afford to absent themselves from their homesteads for the entire duration of summer. Inter-city warfare therefore tended to resolve itself into holiday-time campaigns between neighbours, and states that were called upon to wage a protracted war against a distant enemy might have trouble in keeping their forces together. Appraising the chances of Athens in the Peloponnesian War, Pericles took into account this handicap to an effective occupation of Attica by the Peloponnesians, and the event confirmed his calculations.[1] The increased use of mercenary troops in the warfare of the fourth century was no doubt due in large measure to this same disability of peasant conscript forces.[2]

In Greek lands the advantage which the defenders have always held in siege warfare, until the invention of modern artillery, was reinforced by the strong situation of most Greek towns, which might frustrate the approach of an investing force close up to the walls and restrict its chances of successful attack to one or two presumably well-guarded sectors.[3] The weakness of Greek siege-craft, combined with the shortness of the campaigning season, goes far to explain the habitual indecisiveness of inter-city warfare; and these conditions derived to a great extent from geographic factors.

In most of the major wars of Greek history, before the coming of the Romans (the Persian and Peloponnesian, the Corinthian, and the Lamian Wars), the decision came, not by land, but by sea. This was entirely in accord with the basic facts of Greek geography, for the intrusive fingers of the sea within the loosely compacted body of the Greek lands gave to the naval arm a reach such as it possessed nowhere else in the Mediterranean area.

The lesson of the importance of sea-power was probably first learnt by that characteristic and almost perennial product of Mediterranean life, the pirate, to whom the Mediterranean Sea offered itself as a natural hunting-ground. Innumerable creeks and coves furnished him with his secret bases; half-hidden

[1] Thucydides, i. 141. 7; iii. 15. 2.

[2] As a part-alternative to mercenary recruitment, Demosthenes advocated the employment of short-service conscripts in relays (*Philippic I*, § 21).

[3] It is significant that the *Poliorcetica* of Aeneas Tacticus are largely taken up with petty stratagems whose object is to catch the defenders napping.

channels between the islands, the side-alleys to the 'wet lanes' (as Homer well described them) of sea traffic, provided him with unsuspected action-stations; and a knowledge of local sea and land breezes gave him a start on his victims.[1]

The most effective answer to the corsair's cutter was the state's man-of-war. Specialized warships were therefore produced early in Greek history, and their standard type, the trireme or three-bank galley, became a powerful instrument alike of police and of policy.[2] The trireme, to be sure, was not a good sea-going craft; and it was ill suited to the boisterous and incalculable conditions of the Mediterranean winter. Consequently it was an axiom of Greek warfare that operations on sea as on land should terminate with the end of summer. In addition, the cruising range of the trireme was severely limited by the narrowness of its dimensions in relation to the crew which it carried.[3] But in the relatively smooth seas of the Mediterranean summer it could, under expert handling, attain a high speed and a considerable manœuvring power, and in beating up against adverse etesians its oarage could supplement its canvas. Its incapacity for long continuous voyages mattered relatively little in waters where land was never far distant, or where outlying bases could be made available by naval power. For these reasons galleys of Greek type continued in use in Mediterranean naval wars until the advent of modern artillery. The first great naval battle of modern times, fought in 1571 at Lepanto (ancient Naupactus, in the Gulf of Corinth), was waged with vessels not essentially different from those with which the Athenian admiral Phormio won a victory in those same waters in 429 B.C.[4]

---

[1] H. A. Ormerod, *Piracy in the Ancient World*, ch. 1.

[2] The reputed date of the first trireme was *c.* 700 B.C. (Thucydides, i. 13. 3). On the build of the trireme and the disposition of its oars, see A. Köster, *Das antike Seewesen*.

[3] A. W. Gomme, *Journ. Hell. Stud.*, 1933, pp. 16–24. On the hardships suffered by a crew which could not land in order to obtain food or sleep, see [Demosthenes,] l. 22.

[4] In 1690 the French admiral Tourville collected a squadron of galleys for his abortive invasion of England.

III. GREECE. REGIONAL

THE most outstanding feature of ancient Greek politics was the invincible separatism of its several cities and cantons, which was in part at least a result of the geographic fragmentation of the country. The history of ancient Greece was therefore to a large extent the history of its particular districts, and a full understanding of it requires some knowledge of the natural features of these constituent parts.

§ 1. EPIRUS

This borderland had no important political contacts with the rest of Greece, except in the reign of its most famous king, Pyrrhus; indeed before the Hellenistic period it was a debatable point whether its people should be reckoned within the Greek nation. Its political detachment has a valid explanation in its geographical seclusion. The coast of Epirus is iron-bound in almost its entire length and does not possess a single good harbour. On its eastern boundary the striated chain of Mt. Pindus, with a summit elevation of 8,000 feet, shuts it off solidly from Thessaly. The Zygos pass, forming the watershed between the two largest rivers of Greece, the Acheloüs and the Peneus, is relatively easy, despite its altitude of 5,500 feet, for it rises and falls in a continuous slope on either side. But the remaining adits to Thessaly are exceedingly laborious, for to the south of the Zygos pass the Pindus ridge splits into several chains, which have to be surmounted in succession by those travelling across the grain of the country.[1] These lesser passes may have played a part in the migrations of the Achaeans and Dorians in prehistoric days,[2] but in subsequent centuries they carried little traffic.

The interior of Epirus is sundered into separate compartments by an intricate system of ridges towering over deeply sunk valleys. The gorge of the river Acheron was so profound, and so massively screened from the rays of the sun, that in the imagination of the Greeks it served as the gateway to the underworld. Consequently

[1] A. Philippson, *Thessalien und Epirus*. For a description of the Zygos pass see pp. 174–93.

[2] For the migrations of the Achaeans see W. Leaf, *Homer and History*, p. 51 (the Tymphrestus pass into the Spercheus valley); for those of the Dorians, see N. G. L. Hammond, *Annual of the British School of Athens*, xxxii (1931–2), pp. 131–79.

the land was subdivided politically into fourteen cantons (ἔθνη), and during the greater part of Epirote history the cantons had no connecting link save a loose federation of the three main territorial groups, the Chaones, Molossi, and Thesproti.

In its complicated mountain pattern Epirus bears a resemblance to the rest of Greece, but in its climate it displays a marked difference. Not only is its total rainfall (40 inches, rising to 52 inches at Jannina) well above the Greek average, but it is spread more evenly over the seasons (as also happens in the neighbouring Balkan lands—p. 294), and the summer drought is broken by frequent thunderstorms. Hence, although the ancient oak-groves at Dodona have disappeared, many surviving patches of deciduous forest attest the country's former richness in timber. Furthermore, Epirus could carry an abundance of cattle in its well-watered and well-drained valleys; the yield of its kine was so high as to stimulate the imagination of ancient writers,[1] and in spite of the seclusion of Epirus from the world markets the Roman financier Atticus thought it worth while to organize its ranching industry on a large scale.[2] A particularly good tract of land surrounded Lake Pambotis in the territory of the Molossi (a mountain tarn formed by the choking of a kata-bothra at the valley bottom). From this luxuriant plain, more-over, a comparatively easy road followed the line of the river Aratthus past Ambracia to the Gulf of Actium.[3] Molossia was therefore the rallying-point of Epirus. Its cantonal dynasty pro-vided the line of kings which united the entire country in the fourth and third centuries; in modern times its chief city, Jannina, has been the capital of a would-be emperor (Ali Pasha) and an early seat of the renascent Hellenic culture. But it is significant that Pyrrhus removed his capital from the interior to Ambracia, so as to have readier access to the outer worlds which he sought to conquer.

§ 2. ACARNANIA

The principal territory between the Gulf of Actium and the Corinthian Gulf was Acarnania, a limestone plateau with a typical Greek climate and maquis vegetation. On its landward side Acarnania drops sharply towards the Acheloüs valley, except

---

[1] According to Aristotle (*Historia Animalium* iii. 21) Epirote milch-cows yielded up to 9 gallons a day. The present record stands at *c*. 3,000 gallons a year (P. Smith, *Daily Telegraph*, 10 Oct. 1946), and a yield above 2,000 gallons is considered excellent.

[2] Varro, *Res rustica*, bk. ii, *passim*.

[3] Hammond, op. cit., pp. 146–7, 171.

in the neighbourhood of Stratus, where the river passes through a stretch of level land and offers an easy crossing. In addition, a corridor skirting the east bank of the Gulf of Actium gives good communications with Ambracia.[1] A cluster of small harbours lines the western coast, but the mouth of the Acheloüs is obstructed with an archipelago of mud flats.[2] To the north of Acarnania the Gulf of Actium opens out with a wide expanse of sheltered water. This roomy recess was well suited to serve as a winter station for Antony's armada in 32–31 B.C.; but the sinuosities of its entrance channel detracted from its value as a commercial harbour, and most of the transit trade that might have accrued to it was intercepted by the Ionian Isles. Acarnania therefore remained an almost self-contained territory. Like Epirus, it was a loose federation of cantons, with its capital at Stratus, the natural centre of communications.

§ 3. THE IONIAN ISLES

The number of the Ionian islands is in continuous danger of reduction by the attachment of Leucas[3] to the mainland. The shallow channel that separates it from Acarnania is liable at any time to be sealed by a tongue of wind-borne detritus from the island's chalk cliffs. From the days of the Corinthian tyrant Cypselus this tongue has had to be repeatedly cut, or deflected by sea walls, in order to keep the fairway open.

To a traveller approaching Greece from France or Italy the Ionian islands convey a delusive first impression of the country's fertility. They receive the highest rainfall of all Greek lands (54 inches at Corcyra), and its uneven distribution—for in summer the rain fails almost completely—is of comparatively small account, for the greater part of the winter downfall is absorbed in the rich subsoil which has been formed by the weathering of soft outcropping rock. Their orchard land therefore produces a surplus of wine and oil for export. An additional importance attaches to the two terminal islands of the chain, which serve as connecting links between Greece and Italy. Zacynthus attracted

[1] Hence the ephemeral importance of the Amphilochian border tribe behind the Gulf of Actium in the early stages of the Peloponnesian War.

[2] A good description of the silting process is given by Thucydides (ii. 102. 2–4).

[3] Leucas was an island in the days of Homer, and was again made into one by Cypselus (Strabo, p. 452). At the time of the Peloponnesian War a bar had formed across the channel (Thucydides, iii. 81. 1). For a fuller discussion see O. Maull, in Pauly-Wissowa, *Real-encyclopädie der Klassischen Altertumswissenschaft*, s.v. Leukas.

the attention of the Athenians in the fifth and fourth centuries, possibly as a port of call on the open-sea route to Sicily; in a later age it became a stage on the Venetian voyages round Peloponnesus.

But this island has usually been by-passed for the benefit of its northern rival, Corcyra, which has a more commanding position for trade than any other part of western Greece. Corcyra is the natural starting-point for ships sailing up the Adriatic or putting across to Italy, for on its eastern face it possesses a good harbour of the 'anvil' type, formed by the protrusive spur of a citadel hill, and it lies closest of all Greek lands to Italy, which at this point is only forty-five miles distant.

The situation of Corcyra as the focal point of travel between Greece and western Europe has been the chief determinant in its variegated history. Realizing its potential importance as a general entrepôt for western commerce, Corcyra in ancient times refused to be tied to the apron-strings of its mother city Corinth, and in the interests of free trade sought to avoid entangling alliances. But without the aid of the other Corinthian colonies in north-west Greece, which were content to be 'exploitation areas' of their possessive mother state, it could at best only maintain a precarious independence. After two brief and reluctant attachments to Athens in the fifth and fourth centuries it became in Hellenistic times a shuttlecock between rival dynasts in Macedonia or Sicily, bent on securing for themselves the entrance to the Adriatic. Its importance as the gateway of the Adriatic was subsequently emphasized by its long affiliation to Venice, and by the competition of Britain and France for its possession during the Napoleonic Wars. In the Roman era, and again in recent times, its other function as the point of entry into Greece for travellers from the west has been the more predominant one.

§ 4. AETOLIA

The fact that the Aetolian people for a long time remained in a backward condition and never quite shook off their habits of barbarism has created the impression that they lived in a particularly wild country. As a matter of fact Aetolia possesses several good tracts of arable alluvium, and abundant water-storage in its chain of lakes.[1] But its plains were segmented by a series of ridges extending from west to east, and its outer communications were equally obstructed by border ranges. From its north-eastern

[1] See the description of the Aetolian lowlands in W. J. Woodhouse, *Aetolia*. These regions now grow large tobacco crops.

frontier a relatively easy pass to the south of Mt. Tymphrestus gave access to the Spercheus valley and the Malian Gulf; but the more northerly passes into Thessaly were more arduous, and Mt. Corax, rising to nearly 8,000 feet, interposed a formidable barrier between Aetolia and western Locris. A Roman army which attempted to invade Aetolia in 189 B.C. was severely tried by the difficulties of its passage;[1] and the grandiose scheme of the Athenian general Demosthenes in 426 B.C., to force his way across Aetolia and Locris into Boeotia,[2] would no doubt have broken down at this same position, if the Aetolians had allowed him to proceed thus far. The eastern half of the Aetolian sea-board was isolated by a coastal range, and its western portion was rendered worthless by silting and lagoon-formation, the work of a current which carried detritus from the Acheloüs towards the Corinthian Gulf.[3]

For a long time, accordingly, the Aetolians shared the seclusion of the Epirotes and Acarnanians from the general current of Greek life, and remained dissociated into three cantons which co-operated only in times of invasion. The centralized federation which they created about the time of Alexander was a geographic *tour de force*; its seat of government at Thermum was a sanctuary without a natural-grown city around it, and when the Aetolian League acquired a fleet, it had to borrow the Locrian port of Naupactus to house it. *A fortiori* the extended Aetolian League of the third and second centuries, which reached out to Acarnania and Malis and thus spanned central Greece from Adriatic to Aegean, ran counter to natural lines of communication. The League, in fact, resembled the original Swiss Confederacy in being a military rather than a political and economic association,[4] and its chief cohesive agency was its excellent army of light troops, the most agile in all Greek lands.

§ 5. THESSALY

This district is a box-like compartment with an almost level floor and four upright sides. The rim of its enfolding mountains was formerly all but complete, and the water which the river

---

[1] Livy, xxxvi. 30. 3.   [2] Thucydides, iii. 95. 1.

[3] Mesolonghi, situate between the sea and a lagoon, came into existence as a medieval place of refuge (W. M. Leake, *Travels in Northern Greece*, i, p. 113).

[4] It was acutely pointed out by E. A. Freeman (*History of Federal Government*, i, pp. 271–2) that the Aetolian League could not develop after the manner of the Swiss Confederacy, because it could not incorporate within itself natural centres of commerce like Bern and Zürich in the Swiss lands.

Peneus with its fan-like array of tributaries brought down from
Mt. Pindus had no natural outlet. The accumulated flood eventually cut a gap by erosion through the eastern mountain wall and
was drained off into the sea.[1] In historical times a cluster of small
lakes survived from the parent pool, and the Peneus required

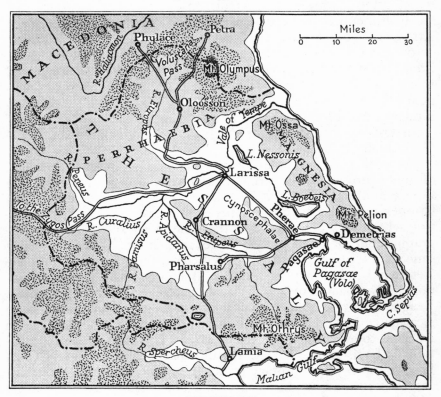

THESSALY

embankments to prevent fresh inundations;[2] but the floor of the
pool dried out so as to form the broadest and richest plain of
Greece. The deep alluvial loam of Thessaly was ideally suited
for wheat production: at the present day the yield rises to forty-
four bushels per acre.[3] In addition, the valley of the Peneus provided the largest expanse of meadowland in Greece, and the
flanks of the mountains were well clad with fruit and timber

[1] Herodotus (vii. 129. 4) shrewdly but incorrectly guessed that the gap in the
sea-wall was due to an earthquake.
[2] Strabo, p. 441.
[3] A. Jardé, *Les Céréales dans l'antiquité grecque*, p. 69, n. 6.

trees.[1] The Thessalians could well afford to be such hearty eaters that their rich fare aroused the envious disdain of other Greeks. But they had to pay a price for Nature's indulgence to them. The high rim which contains Thessaly on all sides imposes upon it a continental climate with extremes of temperature. The torridity of the summer heat is aggravated by occasional fall-winds from Mt. Pindus which become superheated by compression in the denser atmosphere of the plain. In mid-winter spells of calm weather are accompanied by a 'cold inversion', when a gravitational sinking of the heaviest and coldest air causes severe frost in the valleys. Consequently the only part of Thessaly where olives can thrive is round the Gulf of Volo (ancient Pagasae), where sea winds temper the inland chill.

The encompassing mountain wall has the further effect of isolating Thessaly more or less on all sides. The efficacy of the barriers by which the Olympus and Pindus ranges seclude Thessaly from Macedonia and north-western Greece has already been observed (pp. 44–5). Similarly the coastal ridge of Ossa and Pelion denies it access to the Aegean Sea. On its southern border, however, the lower and flatter chain of Mt. Othrys (5,750 feet) has a correspondingly easy pass by way of Lamia into the Spercheus valley; and between the ridges of Othrys and Pelion a break in the high ground has given the sea an inlet into Thessaly, while from Volo, at the head of the gulf to which it gives its name, a low col gives ready access into the interior. Thus situated, Thessaly was not in frequent contact with the rest of Greece, and until the fourth century B.C. it remained a 'backward area'. But its seclusion was less complete than that of north-western Greece, and its vicinity to two such powerful states as Thebes and Macedon drew it now and then into their gravitational field, so that its affairs became interwoven with the history of Greece in general.

The distinctive natural conditions of Thessaly gave a peculiar turn to its political development. Its open champaign land favoured the consolidation of holdings into large estates, and its self-contained economy retarded the growth of urban life, for such cities as sprang up in it remained mere strongholds or small market towns. Political power accordingly was retained in the hands of the large landowners. The water-meadows of the Peneus basin also contributed to the ascendancy of this class by nurturing a large breed of horse which furnished the best cavalry of all

[1] Ps.-Dicaearchus, ii, § 1.

Greece and gave the mounted nobles complete mastery of the unencumbered plains.[1] Long after the rest of Greece had established the supremacy of town over country Thessaly was being ruled by a Greek counterpart of the rural chivalry in medieval Europe.

The interior plain of Thessaly was unbroken by any difficult ground except a low diagonal ridge (rising to 2,500 feet), whose rounded contours were no serious hindrance to communications. No other district of Greece was better fitted by nature to become the seat of a single territorial state. Yet the Thessalians scarcely progressed beyond the cantonal stage of development until the fourth century, and were not associated in a durable political union until the age of foreign overlordship under Macedon and Rome. This paradox may be partly explained by the country's compact frontiers, which for some centuries protected it against foreign pressure, so that no 'challenge' constrained the cities to weld themselves into a resistant mass. In the fourth century, it is true, the entire country was forced into a fleeting union by the city of Pherae, which had benefited by the recent growth of an export trade in grain by way of the Gulf of Volo, for which it was the natural collecting centre, and had thus acquired a preponderant political power.[2] But before they could consolidate their dominion the rulers of Pherae were tripped up by Thebes and Macedon, which made a belated but decisive entry into Thessalian politics. Thus Thessaly, which by virtue of its wealth and man-power was a potential leader of Greece and was indeed cast for that part by Jason of Pherae (c. 370 B.C.), ended its political history as a puppet federation under Macedonian or Roman control.

This control the kings of Macedon exercised by a dual line of communications. In addition to the entrance by the vale of Tempe they used the sea-route to the Gulf of Volo, at the head of which they reared the fortress of Demetrias, embracing and surmounting the old harbour town of Pagasae,[3] to serve as one of the 'Fetters of Greece'.

§ 6. THE SPERCHEUS VALLEY

A miniature counterpart of the Thessalian plain extends between the southern border of Thessaly and the ridge of Mt. Oeta in central Greece. Here the river Spercheus has built up a fertile

[1] Alexander's charger Bucephalus was of Thessalian breed.
[2] H. D. Westlake, *Thessaly in the Fourth Century* B.C., pp. 48–9.
[3] F. Stählin, E. Meyer, und A. Heidner, *Pagasai und Demetrias*.

alluvial valley, and has considerably extended it since ancient times.[1] But this plain at best did not provide room for a populous state, and its territory was divided between two diminutive states, Aeniania at the head of the valley, and Malis at its coastal end.

The only political significance of the valley therefore lay in its position as a land of passage. In prehistoric times it may have given the immigrant Achaeans their earliest access to the Aegean Sea;[2] and in Hellenistic days it provided the Aetolian League with an outlet to the same waters (p. 61). But this avenue was of limited usefulness, for the sea-arm into which the Spercheus debouches, the Gulf of Malis, is rendered too shallow for shipping by the river's sedimentation on a high sea-floor. The pan-Hellenic importance of the Spercheus valley derived from the fact that it provided the only convenient land link between Thessaly and central Greece, and that it guarded the entrance to the Pass of Thermopylae and its associated passes.

The Pass of Thermopylae is a corridor extending for some five miles between Mt. Oeta (7,200 feet) and the Malian Gulf, with two narrow 'gates' at either end, and a middle 'gate' which in Herodotus' time left room for a single carriage-way.[3] The mountain-side, though not sheer cliff, was too steep and too thickly covered with scrub to permit of any orderly advance by a military body. So far as is known, the pass was never forced in ancient times by a frontal attack, but it was repeatedly turned.

In 317 B.C. Cassander outmanœuvred Polyperchon, who barred his return from central Greece to Thessaly, by crossing the Malian Gulf in an improvised fleet of boats and rafts.[4] But this marine outflanking of the pass (which, like any other 'beach landing', would need very careful planning and timing) was unique of its kind. The usual circumventing route was by a track in the steeply ascending canyon of a small mountain stream, the Asopus.[5] The entrance of this gorge has the appearance of a

---

[1] The Pass of Thermopylae is now lined with a fringe of fen-land, and the road from the Pass to Lamia takes a course which in ancient days would have required a journey by boat.

[2] Leaf, *Homer and History*, p. 51.

[3] Herodotus, vii. 198–200; G. B. Grundy, *The Great Persian War*, pp. 277–91. The mound near the eastern gate, where Leonidas made his last stand (Herodotus, vii. 225. 2), was at some distance from the barrage wall previously built by the Phocians. (M. Marinatos, quoted by Mrs. E. Blegen, *American Journal of Archaeology*, 1939, pp. 699–700.)

[4] Diodorus, xix. 35. 2–3.

[5] A good modern road zigzags up the cliff on the right flank; the railway skirts the opposite cliff in a series of galleries.

blind alley,[1] and it is not surprising that Xerxes should have failed to recognize it as a by-pass until a Greek traitor offered to show him the way round. In 480 B.C. the approach to the ravine was apparently not barred by any artificial defence, but in 426 B.C. the Spartans built the fortress of Heraclea beneath the Trachinian Cliff, a projecting bastion on the left bank of the

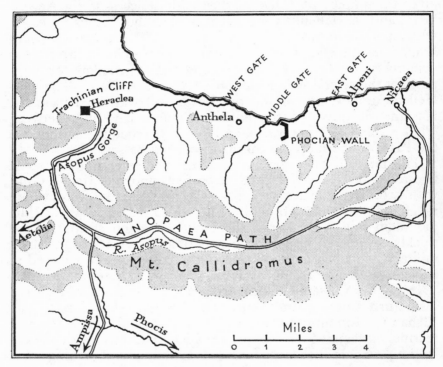

THERMOPYLAE

stream,[2] so as to take ascending parties in flank. The defile ascended between cliffs 700–900 feet high, which at one point gave it a passage of only 20 feet.

From the upper end of the ravine there was a choice of routes: (1) A sheep-track across the southern shoulder of Mt. Oeta which gave a surreptitious entrance into Aetolia. One section of the invading Galatians stole along this path in 279 B.C.[3] (2) A comparatively easy road which led to the head-waters of the Cephissus

[1] See the photograph in Grundy, op. cit., between pp. 260 and 261.
[2] Thucydides, iii. 92. 6; Y. Béquignon, *La Vallée du Spercheios*, pp. 243–60.
[3] Pausanias, x. 22. 2–3.

and followed the river valley across Doris and Phocis into Boeotia. This avenue into central Greece was used by Philip of Macedon in 339 B.C., when the Thebans barred his advance through the Pass of Thermopylae.[1] (3) From Cytinium in the upper Cephissus valley another convenient road diverged past the western flank of Mt. Parnassus to Amphissa and reached the Corinthian Gulf at Crisa. The Spartans explored this alternative northward road from Peloponnesus in 457 B.C., and in 426 B.C. they established it as a line of communications to Heraclea and Thessaly.[2] (4) The mountain path of Anopaea, nearly 20 miles in length, which undulated across the shoulder of Mt. Callidromus to a height of 3,500 feet and ended in a steep descent to the rear of the Pass of Thermopylae.[3] An invading force might easily lose this track amid the enveloping forest,[4] and in any case should have been stopped dead near its summit. Yet Persians, Galatians, and Romans in turn caught the defence napping and cleared both the Asopus gorge and the Anopaea track without serious opposition.[5]

§ 7. LOCRIS

Eastward of Oeta the mountain massif of central Greece divides into two parallel ranges; the northern range skirts the Euboean channel, while the southern one follows the line of the Corinthian Gulf. Either of these ridges leaves room for a sequence of narrow coastal plains, and between them the valley of the Cephissus opens out into a wide and fertile basin. The two coastal strips and the intermontane valley constituted three separate states.

The small pockets of lowland that front on the Euboean Channel formed the territory of eastern or Opuntian Locris. Like Achaea, which occupied a similar position in Peloponnesus, eastern Locris appears to have been a federal state.[6] Its total area of cultivable land was inconsiderable, and its sea trade was

[1] Didymus, *Commentary on Demosthenes* (ed. Diels and Schubart), col. x, ll. 37 ff. Philip captured Cytinium *en route*. This gives the direction of his march.

[2] Thucydides, i. 107. 2; iii. 92. 6; Diodorus, xiv. 38. 4, 82. 10 (395 B.C.). A military road was built along this line in 1917 to supply the British Expeditionary Force at Salonika and again rendered service in the spring campaign of 1941.

[3] Grundy, op. cit., pp. 301–3.

[4] This happened to Cato's flying column in 191 B.C. (Plutarch, *Cato Major*, xiii. 2).

[5] Galatians: Pausanias, x. 22. 11 (in a day-time mist). Romans: Livy, xxxvi. 18. 6 (by a night surprise).

[6] Ancient authors habitually designed the state as οἱ Λόκροι, not οἱ 'Οπούντιοι (after the principal town, Opus). In the fifth and fourth centuries several of the towns struck their own money, but after 338 B.C. a federal coinage was put into circulation (B. V. Head, *Historia Numorum* (2nd ed.), pp. 336–7).

insignificant, for whatever traffic went by the Euboean back-water was mostly in the hands of the Chalcidians (p. 74). From the standpoint of Hellenic history, eastern Locris resembled the Spercheus valley in being a land of passage. It contained the main road which, emerging from Thermopylae, skirted the coast until it found a gap to the west of Mt. Cnemis and gained the valley of the Cephissus at Elatea.[1]

Western or Ozolian Locris, the counterpart of Ozolian Locris on the Corinthian Gulf, had a coast-line extending from the Gulf of Crisa to the bottleneck of the Corinthian Gulf, where the town of Naupactus stood like a miniature Gibraltar. But the rest of its sea-front was almost wholly iron-bound, and apart from some petty piracy[2] the Ozolian Locrians took little interest in seafaring, so little indeed that in the fifth century they left Naupactus in the hands of the Athenians, who realized its strategic value in their warfare against Corinth. The seclusion of western Locris from the rest of Greece was almost as complete as that of its neighbour, Aetolia, and the civilization of its people remained equally backward.[3] But on its eastern margin it included part of the fertile plain of Crisa, and of the cross-road from the Corinthian Gulf to Thermopylae (p. 67). The town of Amphissa, lying astride of this route, therefore played its part in the general history of Greece.

§ 8. PHOCIS

The middle plain of the Cephissus and a corresponding stretch of seaboard on the Corinthian Gulf, east of the Gulf of Crisa, constituted the territory of Phocis. But for the eastern portion of the plain of Crisa, which belonged to it, the seaboard of this district is of little value, and the real heart of Phocis was the Cephissus valley, where most of its small cities were perched on opposite spurs of the Callidromus and Parnassus ranges. Its federal capital was situated near Daulis, where a road from the lower end of the valley forked into two branches, the one cutting

---

[1] By capturing Elatea in 339 B.C. Philip cut off the land retreat of the Thebans àt Thermopylae. The Frankish overlords of Greece after the Fourth Crusade built an important roadside fortress at Boudonitza, in a more westerly and more difficult gap through the coastal range.

[2] See M. N. Tod, *Greek Historical Inscriptions*, no. 34, for a set of rules by which two small Ozolian communities, Oeanthea and Chaleum, sought to impart a gentlemanly tone to their depredations.

[3] Thucydides (i. 5. 5) noted as a survival of primitive barbarism the habit of wearing armour which the Ozolians of his day shared with the Aetolians and Acarnanians.

It is not known whether the western Locrians formed a federal state.

across the Cephissus to Elatea, and the other skirting the southern flank of Parnassus in the direction of Delphi and Crisa.[1]

But the history of Phocis turned less on its own confederacy than on the single city of Delphi, which might be described as in it but not of it. Situated on a narrow ledge under the south-western flank of Mt. Parnassus (8,200 feet), and separated from the plain of Crisa by a steep declivity of 2,000 feet, Delphi was not a natural focus of traffic; and its easiest communications were westward to Amphissa rather than eastward to the Cephissus valley, the road to which was a difficult one, running *en corniche* along the southern slope of Parnassus.[2] The financial importance which eventually accrued to it was an after-effect of its fame as an oracular seat, and its detachment from the Phocian federation as an extra-territorial 'Vatican city' (a status conferred upon it *c.* 585 B.C. by a coalition of interested Greek cities) did justice to its geographical position. Delphi was essentially a place of 'withdrawal', where quiet minds might meditate and crystallize their thoughts at leisure.

§ 9. BOEOTIA

The lower course of the Cephissus is separated from its upper reaches by two spurs projecting from the opposite ranges of Cnemis and Parnassus, which narrow its valley at one point to a quarter of a mile. These spurs mark the frontier between Phocis and Boeotia.

The territory of Boeotia reproduces on a reduced scale some of the special features of Thessaly. It is a river basin encased within a framework of mountains, and its land has been partly redeemed from the bed of a lake (Copaïs). The coastal ranges of central Greece are continued in Mt. Helicon (5,000 feet) on the southern border, and by the low ridge of Mts. Ptoüs and Messapus over against the Euboean Channel; and at the end of their course these ranges throw out the cross-arms of Cithaeron and Parnes, which make such a perfect join as to constitute a continuous barrier.

Lake Copaïs was formed by the Cephissus and some lesser

---

[1] Pausanias, v. 5. 1–3. This was the 'riven road' where Oedipus contended with his father for the right of way.

[2] At its approach to Delphi this road passes under a sheer cliff. It was here that the Persian marauders in 480 B.C. were turned back by a cascade of rocks (Herodotus, viii. 37–9). The rocks may have become accidentally detached by the disintegrating action of the sun.

CENTRAL GREECE

streams, which could not find a permanent outlet into the Euboean Channel, because of the periodic choking of the katabothrae which pierced the sea-wall of Mt. Ptoüs. Under commission from Alexander of Macedon an engineer named Crates partly cleared the emissories and canalized the rivers towards them by means of embankments within the lake;[1] but this task was left incomplete, and it was not until 1883 that the drainage of the lake was resumed by cutting new tunnels.[2]

In ancient times a fluctuating area of the basin lay under water, but the fringes of the inundation land provided a fertile alluvial soil. The southern part of Boeotia, which extended like a low platform under Mts. Cithaeron and Parnes, stood well above flood-level, and the river Asopus which traversed it had an open run to the sea; but it also had a rich and deep soil, and was well watered from the springs of Mt. Helicon.[3] Thus, in spite of its lost acres Boeotia was in ancient days one of the most productive parts of Greece: its arable land yielded a wheat of the highest grade,[4] and the water-meadows along Lake Copaïs sustained an extensive stock-raising industry.[5] Copaïs also provided its lacustrine specialities—eels as a delicacy for the Athenian market, willows for carriage-frames and tires, and reeds for the mouthpieces of the *auloi* or wood-wind instruments with which Boeotian virtuosos carried off the prizes at Greek musical festivals.

But Boeotia, like Thessaly, suffered for Nature's favours. The exhalations of the lake made the Boeotian climate raw in winter and sultry in summer, 'and never kind',[6] and they were no doubt a factor in making the Boeotians slow-witted as compared with their Athenian neighbours. The intrusion of Lake Copaïs into the Boeotian plain also had the effect of disjointing it into a northern and a southern section, with only a narrow connecting corridor between the lake-side and Mt. Helicon.

As a result of this geographic bisection, Boeotia was bedevilled with a political dualism which largely determined its history. Its

---

[1] Strabo, p. 407. J. G. Frazer, *Pausanias and Other Greek Sketches*, pp. 349–55; M. L. Kampanis, *Bulletin de correspondance hellénique*, 1892, pp. 121–37; 1893, pp. 322–42.

[2] The work has now been completed (by a British company). The desiccated lake-bed now grows tobacco.

[3] The abundance of running water at Thebes and at Lebadea is still a source of gratification to modern visitors.

[4] Theophrastus, *Historia Plantarum*, viii. 4. 5.

[5] *British Museum Inscriptions*, no. 158, preserves a record of a grazier who kept 220 head of horses and kine, and 1,000 of sheep and goats, on the territory of Orchomenus. [6] Hesiod, *Works and Days*, l. 640.

largest city, Thebes, dominated the Asopus valley and was also
the focus of the passes that debouch from Mts. Cithaeron and
Parnes, and consequently served as the link between Boeotia and
Attica or Peloponnesus. Since it produced in addition all the
political and military leadership of the country, it had a good
claim to be its capital, and at various periods of the fifth and following centuries it made this claim effective by assuming the directive
part in the Boeotian federal state. Nay more, as a federal union
under Theban guidance Boeotia was not ill qualified to become
the directing power of Greece in general. Its territory was rich
enough to maintain a relatively large man-power (though not
so extensive as to allow room for many large estates), and the
peasantry which formed the backbone of Boeotian society
furnished some of the best military material of Greece; and
it had the further advantage of a central position within the
Greek homeland. But Thebes had a rival in Orchomenus, the
chief city of the Cephissus valley, and though Orchomenus never
succeeded in displacing its competitor it served as a rallying-
point for the separatist tendencies of the lesser Boeotian cities,
and thus hindered the consolidation of Boeotia into a compact
federal state. The ascendancy in Greece which Boeotia enjoyed
in mid-fourth century was therefore but a passing phase, dependent on a wasting asset, the military genius of Epaminondas.

Boeotia also shared with Thessaly and her neighbours in
central Greece the lack of a favourable seaboard. Its only safe
harbour on the Euboean Channel, Aulis, had an awkward
entrance; like the Gulf of Actium, it was more suitable as an
assembly point for an armada such as Agamemnon's than for a
trading station.[1] The western coast was cut off from the interior
by an almost unbroken chain of rough mountain land. The
advantage which Boeotia possessed in fronting on several seas
was therefore delusive.[2] Occasional attempts do indeed appear
to have been made to establish an 'isthmus' route leading from
Thisbe on the Corinthian Gulf by way of Thespiae, Thebes, and
Mycalessus to Aulis. Late Helladic pottery along this track suggests the opening of a sea-to-sea traffic in the Mycenaean age;[3]
and copious finds of black-glaze ware near Mycalessus indicate

[1] W. W. Leaf, *Homer and History*, pp. 100–3. (Leaf hardly does justice here to
the advantages of Aulis as a base for an expeditionary force.)
[2] The maritime advantages which Ephorus (quoted by Strabo, p. 400) claimed
for Boeotia have been subjected to a damaging scrutiny by A. W. Gomme (*Annual
of the British School at Athens*, xviii, pp. 189–210).
[3] W. A. Heurtley, *Annual of the British School at Athens*, xxvi, pp. 38–45.

its renewal in the sixth century.[1] But this transit trade was itself transitory. In the early Hellenistic age the persistence with which Demetrius the Besieger strove to capture Thebes may be taken as evidence that he valued it as a link between his bases at Chalcis and Corinth; but his successors were content to rely on the sea route for their communications. The Boeotians in general shared the aversion of their compatriot Hesiod from the sea, and the attempt of Epaminondas to establish a naval supremacy in the Aegean Sea broke down after a single campaign.

But if Boeotia failed to impose its hegemony upon the rest of Greece, it played a continuous part in Greek history and could not, like Thessaly, withdraw from the general course of Greek affairs. Its central position tended to make it a land of passage, and its framework of mountains was neither high enough nor continuous enough to arrest intercourse. The passes across Mts. Cithaeron and Parnes, not rising above 2,000–3,000 feet,[2] lay open at all seasons, and the gap in the northern frontier between Mts. Parnassus and Cnemis was like that of a door left standing ajar. Boeotia consequently was subject to frequent invasions from north and south, and was grimly nicknamed 'war's dancing-floor.'[3] But it also received the beneficial impact of new ideas and, despite Athenian sneers at Boeotian grossness, it made its due contribution to Greek culture.

§ 10. EUBOEA

Ancient writers guessed, what modern geographers have confirmed, that the island of Euboea was a detached piece of the adjacent mainland.[4] The channel which separates it from Greece proper narrows down near Chalcis to less than 100 yards,[5] and the Euboean mountain chains are evidently prolongations of the main ranges of Thessaly and central Greece: the ridge of Mt. Dirphys resumes that of Mt. Pelion, those of the Euboean Olympus and of Mt. Ocha strike in the same direction as Mts. Ptoüs and Parnes. On the east side of Euboea these chains rise to a considerable height (Dirphys to 5,700 feet), thus forming in

[1] P. N. Ure, *Black-glaze Pottery from Rhitsona in Boeotia.*

[2] The two main passes into Attica, by way of Eleutherae and Oropus, are 2,000 feet, the Phyle pass 2,400 feet; the road from Plataea to Megara rises to 2,800 feet.

[3] Plutarch, *Moralia* 193 E; *Life of Marcellus* xxi, § 2.

[4] Ion of Chios, quoted by Strabo, p. 60.

[5] In 411 B.C. the Boeotians endeavoured to attach Euboea to themselves by building a mole across the channel (Diodorus, xiii. 47. 3–6). Apparently this causeway was soon broken down; a swing-bridge has now taken its place. Bridging operations were formerly facilitated by a reef in mid-channel, now blown away.

the season of northerly winds a lee shore no less dangerous than that of Thessaly. The channel between Euboea and the mainland, known as the Euripus, was notorious for its strong and rapidly veering current (p. 28), but gave complete security from the Aegean gales.

In the Euboean mountain system outcrops of softer rock-formations have produced tracts of rich loam, notably in the north of the island and in the plain of Lelantus, overlooking the Euripus, and have clad the hill-sides with high forest. Moreover, the overplus from Euboea's land found a ready market at Athens, which at times drew heavily on its supplies of cattle, grain, and timber.[1] Its mineral resources included a lode in the territory of Chalcis which produced both copper and iron and no doubt contributed largely to the city's early prosperity.[2] In Roman times both the veins had been worked out, but some compensation was obtained from the vogue which the white-and-green marble of Carystus in the south of the island came to enjoy in the Italian market.

But Euboea derived its most permanent advantage from its position commanding the approach to the Gulf of Volo and the routes between the north Aegean and the Saronic Gulf, and from the safe harbourage on its backwater channel. At the north end of the island the town of Hestiaea (renamed Oreus in the fourth century) combined the benefits of a good hinterland and a station on a trade-route from the Euboean Channel to Thessaly and Macedon, and its possession or alliance was coveted by Athens. But the ancient history of Euboea centred mainly in the towns of Chalcis and Eretria, which shared the produce of the Lelantine plain and the control of the Euripus. In the early days of Greek overseas expansion the twin cities played a prominent part as carriers and colonizers. Their subsequent decline was no doubt due in large measure to the degeneration of their friendly rivalry into an internecine conflict,[3] but partly also to the fact that the channel on which they stood was a commercial as well as a maritime backwater, so far at least as the central and south Aegean sea-routes were concerned, so that their trade was intercepted by the towns of the Saronic Gulf, Aegina, Corinth, and Athens. In Hellenistic times, however, Chalcis and Eretria gained a new importance as intermediate stations by which the kings of Mace-

---

[1] In the later stages of the Peloponnesian War Euboea was 'everything' to Athens (Thucydides, viii. 95. 2). [2] Strabo, p. 447.
[3] On the 'Lelantine War' see A. R. Burn, *Journ. Hell. Stud.*, 1927, pp. 170–7.

don secured their sea communications with Corinth, and Chalcis shared with Corinth and Demetrias (p. 64) the dubious distinction of being one of the three 'Fetters of Greece'.

§ 11. ATTICA

The peninsula of Attica, into which central Greece runs out, is a territory whose natural advantages mark it out as a potential

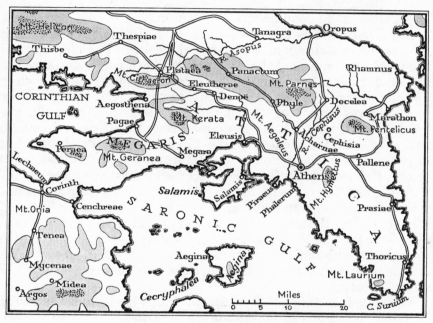

ATTICA AND MEGARIS

centre of a Greek state. In one respect, to be sure, Attica is ill favoured. It is the driest region of Greece, with an annual rainfall of sixteen inches, which barely suffices for the cultivation of wheat. Its mountains are of a hard limestone texture, and of such moderate height as to lose their snow mantles in early spring: the border ranges of Cithaeron and Parnes attain 4,700 feet, and the interior ridges of Hymettus and Pentelicus do not exceed 3,250 and 3,650 feet respectively. The two central plains of the Attic Cephissus (in which Athens lies) and of the Mesogaea (between Hymettus and Pentelicus), and the coastal lowlands of Thria (near Eleusis) and of Marathon,[1] contain small areas of

---

[1] According to Herodotus (vi. 102) the plain of Marathon was good terrain for cavalry. But nowadays at least it is studded with plantations.

richer soil; but Attica as a whole is, in the words of Plato,[1] a 'discarnate skeleton', whose bones show through in large slabs of bare rock. Only one-quarter of Attica is estimated to be cultivable, and part of this is ill suited for anything save the drought-resisting olive-tree. In the fourth century only one-third to one-quarter of the Athenian requirements in cereals was home grown (mostly barley),[2] and from the time of Solon the importation of foreign grain into Attica was a matter of such importance as to require state regulation.

But if Attica was never a forcing-bed of plant life, it was in former times a storehouse of mineral wealth. The clay-beds of the Cephissus supplied the Attic potters with the material of the most extensive export industry in Greek ceramics; and the white marble quarries of Mt. Pentelicus provided the stone for the most famous buildings and statues of Athens.[3] Above all, the south-eastern tip of Attica contained the minefields of Laurium ('alley-town'), the richest in the Greek homeland. In ancient days the hematite and zinc ores of Laurium were left untouched;[4] the lead and silver deposits had become exhausted by the beginning of the Christian era, but in earlier days they were an economic mainstay and an indispensable basis of Athenian finance. The 'boom' of the silver mines, which providentially befell on the eve of the Persian Wars, was probably brought on by an unknown prospector who sank deep shafts across the tenuous upper veins and struck the most prolific lode at the join between two deeper strata of rock.[5]

In relation to the Greek mainland Attica stood in a somewhat eccentric position. Its communications with Boeotia across Mts. Cithaeron and Parnes were not difficult, and this district accordingly became the chief scene of Athenian attempts at overland expansion. In particular, the Athenians maintained almost

[1] Critias III B, C.

[2] A. W. Gomme, *The Population of Athens in the Fifth and Fourth Centuries*, pp. 28–33. The ancient Attic yield of cereals has been estimated at no more than 5–6 bushels per acre (Jardé, op. cit., p. 51). The reason why the wheat-goddess Demeter received special homage in Attica was no doubt because cereals there had a scarcity value.

[3] The blue-grey marble of Mt. Hymettus, which has been much used for revetment in modern Athens, does not appear to have been extensively quarried in ancient times.

[4] The reduction of zinc ore to metallic form, though not beyond the means of ancient technicians (p. 161 n. 5), would seem to have been seldom attempted.

[5] E. Ardaillon, *Les Mines du Laurion*, esp. pp. 14 ff. The prospecting entrepreneur may have been Callias the 'pit-king'—Λακκόπλουτος (M. Cary, *Classical Review*, 1936, p. 55).

unbroken possession of the small town of Oropus, the starting-point of a ferry to Eretria and Chalcis, which lay within easy reach across a spur of Mt. Parnes. On the other hand, Attica was marked off from its western neighbour Megara by the more difficult barrier of Mt. Kerata, which stretches continuously from the Corinthian to the Saronic Gulf and abuts on either coast in a sheer cliff. The only territorial dispute that could reasonably arise between the Athenians and the Megarians turned on the possession of the off-shore island of Salamis. Though actually closer to Megara, Salamis almost inevitably gravitated towards the larger land-mass of Attica. Beyond Megaris a second cross-bolt, Mt. Geranea, double-barred Athenian communications with Peloponnesus, which in consequence normally lay outside the Athenian orbit. The influence of Athens on the Greek main-land was strong and abiding, but it was mainly cultural; her natural lines of economic and political expansion were directed overseas.

In Attica the mountains are not alined continuously along the coast, but leave room for easy landing-places. On its eastern sea-board the Bay of Prasiae probably served as a port in early days, before the growth of Athens had attracted all traffic into the Saronic Gulf;[1] and the Bay of Marathon, protected from the summer north-easters by a long hook at its windward end, pro-vided a capital invasion-beach. On the opposite shore the Bay of Phalerum, where the sea came closest to Athens, was lined with a broad shelving strand and received shelter from the headlands of Colias and Munichia at either end. This commodious beach apparently served all the needs of Athens till *c.* 500 B.C., but after that date the Athenians grew aware of the unique advantages offered by the three deep-water pools ensconced within the adjacent promontory of Munichia. On the southern face of this rocky knobble two circular basins, which served as auxiliary stations for the Athenian navy, were scooped out. The port of Piraeus, wedged in between the re-entrant northern coast of Munichia and a returning curve of the Attic shore, which ter-minated in an outstretched tongue (Eetionea) as in a natural mole, offered ample and secure accommodation within an almost land-locked basin.[2] Girt in with the ring wall of Themistocles and thus made impregnable along its entire sea-face, Munichia became the base and the arsenal of Athenian thalassocracy, and its main

[1] C. T. Seltman, *Athens*, p. 11.
[2] E. A. Gardner, *Ancient Athens*, ch. 14.

harbour, the Piraeus, was equipped to serve as a maritime entre-pôt for half the Mediterranean.[1]

As a centre of naval communications Attica did not share the advantage which Corinth possessed of a double front on an eastern and a western sea. But it was well placed to exercise an ascendancy over the Aegean area. While the islands of the Archipelago were situated at the very hub of the Aegean, their

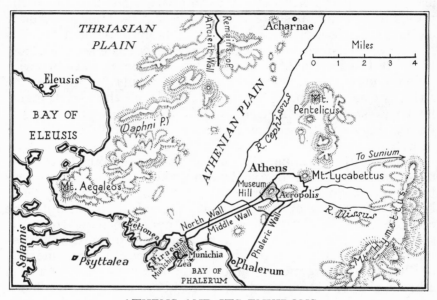

ATHENS AND ITS ENVIRONS

territories and resources were too slight to provide an adequate basis for a dominion over it; and the powerful Greek cities of the opposite Asia Minor coast had a hinterland front which fre-quently drew away their attention. Control over the Aegean was therefore exercised most easily from the Greek homeland; and here Attica held the most commanding position, for the Saronic Gulf on which it formed an intercepting bastion was the natural focusing point for trans-Aegean traffic, and Piraeus was its nearest as well as its safest port of entry.

Attica had another advantage in its possession of a natural capital against which no other site could compete for long. The city of Athens lay within its largest area of cultivable land and

[1] In the last hundred years the Piraeus has again become a general centre for the traffic of the eastern Mediterranean.

was its inevitable centre of communications. It was indeed screened off from the Thriasian plain and Eleusis by Mt. Aegaleus, a low spur projecting from Cithaeron; of all other Attic places, accordingly, Eleusis was able to stand out longest as an independent unit. But a gap between Hymettus and Pentelicus gave Athens easy access to the plains of Mesogaea and Marathon, and to the minefields of Laurium. Finally, the vicinity of Athens to Phalerum and Piraeus assured to it a decisive preponderance in Attica, once its people took to sea-faring. Thus Athens was able at an early stage of its history to establish itself as a seat of central government for the entire country. With an area of some 1,000 square miles at its charge, Athens had indeed to provide additional organs of local administration on the Attic country-side, and it was not until Cleisthenes had established the parish and district governments on a sound basis that centrifugal tendencies within Attica were definitely overcome. But henceforth the resources of Attica were never dissipated between rival centres of power, and the local animosities which distracted the politics of Thessaly and Boeotia did not vitiate the energies of its people. With an undivided Attica at its disposal, Athens commanded a larger man-power and more abundant natural wealth than any other city of the Greek mainland.[1]

If the climate of Greece is to be regarded as the most typically Mediterranean, that of Attica may be considered the most essentially Greek. It is not congenial to invalids, for its summer drought is prolonged, and the dust which vehement north-easters swirl into Athens is a trial for those not of robust health. Yet the quickening and energizing properties of the Greek weather are nowhere more apparent than in Attica. Its crisp and buoyant air, and its translucent sky, against which the Attic landscape stands out clear-cut as in a cameo, combine to nurture keen wits and perceptive minds. If therefore we hold that the choicest gifts of Athens to the world proceeded from her artists and thinkers, we may believe that Nature's highest favour to her was the Attic climate.

§ 12. Aegina

The most determined rival of Athens in the early days of her naval expansion was the island of Aegina, which lies in the Saronic Gulf some twelve miles from the Attic coast, but appears in the lucid Attic atmosphere almost as a 'clot on the eye of

[1] This point is well developed by Freeman, *Federal Government*, i, pp. 122-3.

Piraeus'.[1] On this small and rocky surface was reared a city whose war-fleet held that of Athens at bay, until her antagonist threw the wealth of Laurium into the scales (p. 76) and out-built her, and shared with Athens the palm of victory at Salamis.[2] The Aeginetans were able to make history in this fashion, because they utilized their position of vantage in the centre of the Saronic Gulf, so as to acquire one of the largest carrying trades among Greek cities.[3] History repeated itself in these waters in the eighteenth and early nineteenth centuries, when the Albanian settlers on the islets of Hydra and Spetsai (off the coast of Argolis) gathered a large portion of the Aegean trade into their hands and under the leadership of Constantine Kanares laid the foundations of modern Greek thalassocracy in the War of Independence.[4] But enterprise in oversea trade could not in the long run make up for Aegina's sheer lack of native resources when pitted against the man-power and rising wealth of Athens. Bereft of her war-fleet and her commerce by her successful rival (c. 450 B.C.), Aegina reverted to her original state as an obstruction in the Saronic fairway.

§ 13. Corinth

The Peloponnesus, or 'Island of Pelops', is isolated (or penin-sulated) in more senses than one. The isthmus which joins it to central Greece is not merely narrow—at one point it shrinks to less than four miles—but is crossed by two ridges, Mts. Kerata and Geranea, which leave no room for a road along either coast. The Scironian Rocks in which Mt. Geranea ran out into the Saronic Gulf compelled travellers between Athens and Corinth to pick their way along a track which for six miles ran *en corniche* at a height of 600–700 feet and at points was perilously poised on the edge of a precipice.[5] A safer road was at last provided by the emperor Hadrian;[6] but this could only be achieved by building it outward on a corbelled substructure. The robber Sciron, who in ancient Greek legend hurled wayfarers from the cliff into the water, actually exists in the incorporeal form of a fall-wind which

---

[1] ἡ λήμη τοῦ Πειραιῶς (Plutarch, *Pericles* viii, § 6).

[2] Herodotus, viii. 93. 1.

[3] At Naucratis in Egypt (p. 214) Aegina alone among the cities of Greece proper had a settlement of her own (Herodotus, ii. 178. 3).

[4] We may compare the skippers of Salem, who at this same period made up for the poverty of the New England soil by their trading ventures in transoceanic clippers.

[5] Strabo, p. 391; Frazer, op. cit., pp. 221–3.

[6] Pausanias, i. 44. 6. The modern road and railway have been blasted out of the cliff for long stretches.

blows out to sea in sudden gusts. The track which winds along
the Corinthian Gulf to Boeotia was hardly better. In 378 B.C.
a Spartan force which was caught by a gale while rounding the
headland of Mt. Cithaeron had to scramble to safety on all fours,
abandoning their shields.[1]

Though the Peloponnesus lies close to the main traffic line of
the Mediterranean Sea from east to west, it has never been an
important station for long-distance shipping, except in the days
of the Venetian thalassocracy. The coast is not rich in harbours,
and its southerly outrunners, ending in Capes Taenarum (Mata-
pan) and Malea, are mountainous from end to end. Inside the
peninsula the high ranges of Erymanthus and Cyllene in the
north (c. 7,500 feet), and of Taÿgetus in the south (nearly 8,000
feet), and the confused jumble of the Arcadian highlands, isolate
one district from another. If in despite of its internal barriers
Peloponnesus in ancient times achieved a considerable measure
of political union, the reason is that geographic factors in this
instance were overridden by others of a political and military
order.

At first sight it would seem as if the chief co-ordinating power
of Peloponnesus must have been Corinth, whose geographic
advantages apparently predestined her to a position of leadership.
The least of these gifts of Nature was a strip of fertile land along
the Corinthian Gulf, formed by the sediment from a current
which sets eastward along its southern shore,[2] for in any case
the territory of Corinth was too small to feed a metropolis. A
secondary source of wealth from the Corinthian soil resided in
its beds of white or cream-coloured clay, which fed the most prolific ceramic industry of early Greece.[3] But this branch of manufacture ceased to be a mainstay of Corinth after 500 B.C., when
the Athenian potters captured a large part of the city's export
market.

The chief material asset of Corinth was of course its situation
at the Isthmus, where it controlled the gate of Peloponnesus like
a barbican in front of a medieval city-wall, and at the same time
linked two seas like a miniature Suez or Panama. While the town

---

[1] Xenophon, *Hellenica* v. 4. 17–18.
[2] The fertility of the Corinthian land is rightly emphasized by J. G. O'Neill,
Ancient Corinth, pp. 28–9.
[3] The attribution of the so-called 'Proto-Corinthian' ware, which had a vogue
c. 750–650 B.C., to Corinthian craftsmen has recently been re-confirmed by H. Payne
(*Necrocorinthia*, ch. 4). If this is correct, Corinthian pottery commanded the Greek
export market for over 200 years.

itself lay not far from the narrowest point of the Isthmus, its towering citadel dominated the approach along the Corinthian Gulf and the two main roads from the Peloponnesian interior (by way of Cleonae and of Tenea); and the neighbouring peak of Mt. Onia commanded the eastern adit along the Saronic Gulf. About 450 or 400 B.C. the Corinthians added to the natural strength of this position by constructing a continuous 'Long Wall' from their city to the Corinthian Gulf and a line of forts to the Saronic Gulf.

The strategic value of the Isthmus position was demonstrated again and again in Greek warfare. As a potential line of defence against the Persian invaders in 480–479 B.C. it had an almost fatal fascination for the Peloponnesians.[1] In the 'Corinthian War' of 394–387 B.C. it prevented the Spartans from bursting the bounds of Peloponnesus and re-establishing their authority over the rest of Greece. After its surrender to Philip II in 336 B.C. until its liberation from Philip V in 196 B.C. at the hands of the Romans, Corinth was almost unbrokenly in the possession of the Macedonian kings, and it rendered them good service as the main link in their chain of the 'Fetters of Greece', for it effectually checked collaboration between their enemies within Peloponnesus and outside it. In 146 B.C. it was the last bulwark of Greek independence against the possessive phil-Hellenism of the Romans.[2]

The commercial importance of Corinth was foreshadowed by the trading-post of Korakou on the Corinthian Gulf (west of Lechaeum), which dated back to neolithic times and attained some importance in the Mycenaean age.[3] The advantages of the Isthmus site for trade, it is true, do not seem to have been fully realized until the time of the Corinthian tyrants (c. 650 B.C.). Henceforth, however, Corinth was a dual-harbour town of a unique character, for she now possessed two ports at Lechaeum and Cenchreae, on the Corinthian and Saronic Gulfs respectively, which became focusing-points of west- and east-bound trade in Greek waters. In addition, the city commanded an 'isthmus route' whose advantages were not to be denied. A steamship using the Corinthian Canal (completed in 1893) saves some 150 miles on the voyage from Corfu to Piraeus; an ancient sailing-vessel would have the advantage of avoiding the 'fall-winds' of

[1] For the remains of the substantial fortifications erected at the Isthmus neck in 480 B.C. see J. G. Frazer, *Pausanias' Description of Greece*, v, p. 544.

[2] Pausanias, vii. 16. 3.

[3] C. W. Blegen, *American Journal of Archaeology*, 1920, pp. 1–13.

Cape Malea and the risk of having to beat up against Aegean trade-winds. In ancient times, it is true, the long-cherished and often renewed project of constructing a waterway through the isthmus had to be abandoned, presumably because of the prohibitive cost of cutting through its hard calcareous strata.[1] But a slip-way on which small sea-going craft could be hauled over the neck was in operation from early days (probably from the time of the tyrants), for the isthmus at its narrowest does not rise above 170 feet.

Situated at its principal cross-roads, Corinth was marked out as a potential capital of Greece, and its aptness for this role was enhanced by its central position within the Greek homeland. In fact, it served as the gathering-place of the chief Hellenic congresses of ancient times. It was the rendezvous of the delegates from the patriot states who formed the Greek war-council at the time of Xerxes' invasion, and it was the regular seat of the Hellenic Confederacy of Philip and Alexander of Macedon. The Roman proconsul Flamininus proclaimed the emancipation of Greece from Macedonia at Corinth (196 B.C.), and the Roman governors of the province of Achaea established their court there. The modern kingdom of the Hellenes chose Corinth as its first capital (1832-4).

But the only occasion on which Corinth held any prospect of political ascendancy over Greece in its own right was under its early tyrants, when the despot Periander (c. 600 B.C.) was 'the most powerful man in Europe'.[2] But Periander's preponderance did not survive him. Though always a highly valued subordinate, whether of Sparta in the fifth and fourth centuries or of Macedon in the third, Corinth was a vassal rather than a leader in the political sphere. To this political ineffectiveness one inherent disadvantage in its situation may have contributed. Its commerce was liable to be intercepted by rivals in more outlying positions, Corcyra in western waters, Aegina and Athens at the entrance to the Aegean. But this handicap by no means cancelled the indefeasible benefits of centrality. The main reason for the somewhat self-effacing part which Corinth played in ancient Greek history may be sought in its remarkable penury of outstanding men after the extinction of its tyrant dynasty. Corinth was reputed to contain the most ingenious artificers of Greece,

[1] Such plans were made and partly put into operation by Periander, Demetrius Poliorcetes, Caesar, Caligula, and Nero.
[2] Ed. Meyer, *Geschichte des Altertums*, iii², p. 578.

but with the exception of Timoleon, who displayed his talents in the service of another city, it did not produce (subsequent to Periander) a single political leader of pan-Hellenic rank. Geographic factors count for much in history; but personality is an even greater force.

§ 14. ACHAEA

The Corinthian plain extends westward along the Corinthian Gulf so as to comprise the territory of Sicyon. This city, however, was never merged in the Corinthian state and seemingly had no regular share in its commerce. The material basis of its prosperity and power under its early line of tyrants remains uncertain; but the well-known story of the wooing of Agariste (the daughter of the despot Cleisthenes) suggests that Sicyon temporarily shared with Corinth the trade in western waters, for the provenance of several of the suitors was from north-west Greece or south Italy.[1] In subsequent years Sicyon occupied a position of some importance within the Peloponnesian League, because it stood at the head of two routes across Arcadia which gave the Spartans access to the Corinthian Gulf independently of Corinth's goodwill: a mountain track by way of Orchomenus and Stymphalus, and an easier route through Mantinea and Phlius.[2]

Though Sicyon's most distinguished citizen, Aratus, eventually attached the town to the Achaean League (c. 250 B.C.), until then it stood aloof from Achaea, from which it was separated by an intervening spur of Mt. Cyllene. The Achaean territory, however, is of similar character to that of Sicyon and Corinth, forming part of the same fertile alluvial fringe between the Gulf and the Arcadian mountain front. At the present day Achaea is an important economic asset to Greece, because of its exports of currents and wine; in ancient times it grew flax for the linen industry of its most westerly town, Patrae. But it is narrowly hemmed in by a continuous mountain wall, with a mere backstairs entrance into Arcadia by the gorge of the Erasinus (now traversed by a rack-and-pinion railway). Consequently the Achaeans took hardly any part in Peloponnesian politics until Aratus drew them in. It is strange, however, that they do not seem to have had any active share in the westward trade of Greece.

[1] Herodotus, vi. 127.
[2] The importance of Phlius as a wayside station may help to explain why King Agesilaus made it safe for Sparta by a protracted siege and a political purge (Xenophon, *Hellenica* v. 2–3).

for their open coast offered good landing-places in sheltered water.[1]

In Hellenistic times the earlier local federation of the Achaeans was expanded so as to comprise Arcadia and Argolis, and under Roman protection it eventually took in all Peloponnesus. In view of Achaea's back-to-back position in relation to the rest of Peloponnesus, this extension might seem a geographic *tour de force*; but it was facilitated by the incorporation of Sicyon, which provided easier access to Corinth, Argos, and Megalopolis, the key towns of the enlarged league.

§ 15. ELIS

The district of Elis, consisting of a wide piedmont terrace at the western edge of Arcadia, and of a belt of alluvial coast-land watered by two substantial streams, the Peneus and the Alpheus, might be described as a larger Achaea. In ancient times it shared Achaea's production of flax, as it now participates in the export of currants and wine, but it was chiefly noted for its cattle-pastures, the best in Peloponnesus.[2] At Phea (modern Katakolo) it possessed a moderately good harbour, but most of its coast lay exposed to the weather, and with somewhat better excuse than the Achaeans its people fought shy of the sea.

Unlike the Achaeans, whose 'shoestring' territory was ill suited for political union save on a federal basis, the Eleans had a compact country and a natural centre of communications in the town of Elis, on the margin between piedmont and plain.[3] The entire land was therefore incorporated into the city-state of Elis. But such was the hold of the riant Elean country-side on the local gentry that, contrary to the general Greek custom, they hardly ever came to town.[4] The political pulse of the Elean city-state therefore beat somewhat feebly. An additional reason for its political quietism lay in its possession of the pan-Hellenic sanctuary of Olympia, situated at the point where the Alpheus breaks

[1] In the eighth and seventh centuries the Achaeans founded colonies in south Italy at Sybaris, Croton, and elsewhere. But some of these settlements were purely agrarian, and the commerce of the others was largely with non-Achaean cities. The present-day importance of Patras is partly due to the railway connecting it with Corinth and Athens, of which it has become a passenger outport.

[2] Polybius, iv. 73. 6.

[3] The castle of Glarentza, built by Geoffrey II de Villehardouin as the chief seat of Frankish dominion in the Morea, was a good invasion base for a foreign conqueror, being situated on a bold ridge (Mt. Chelomates) in the central tip of the Elean coast. But its site was too eccentric to serve as the local capital of the small independent state of Elis. [4] Polybius, iv. 73. 7.

out of the hills. With the stewardship of the Olympic games committed to its charge, Elis was inclined to withdraw from the turmoil of Greek politics. But its good lands lay temptingly open to its Arcadian neighbours, and it also was within easy reach of Sparta's strong arm (p. 91). At the price of dependence on Sparta the Eleans purchased a general immunity from Arcadian molestation and obtained leave to enlarge their domain by wresting from the Arcadians the pleasant hill-country of Triphylia on their southern border (c. 455 B.C.).

§ 16. ARCADIA

The boundaries of Arcadia once extended to the western sea by way of the Triphylian corridor. But a fringe of lagoons greatly detracts from the value of the Triphylian coast, and after the seizure of the corridor by the Eleans Arcadia became a purely inland territory.[1] Thus curtailed, it consisted of a highland with gentle declivities and level terraces on its southern and eastern borders, but steeply scarped on its northern and western sides. Its interior was a wild jumble of ridges and troughs, interspersed with land-locked basins which now and then were metamorphosed into lakes by the choking of their katabothrai. The imagination of the ancients was stirred by the precipices that almost encircle Lake Stymphalus, and by the sheer drop of 600 feet by which the Styx hurls its clear waters into a gloomy valley to become the abhorred river of the underworld.[2]

Arcadia's less abrupt slopes are well clad with trees; in ancient times the nuts and mast of its forests provided food for man and beast, and the upland pastures were a breeding-ground for mules —still the best means of transport in the remoter parts of Greece. But its only good crop-lands lay at its southern border in the basin of Mantinea and Tegea, and in the level valley of the upper Alpheus. Arcadia as a whole could ill provide for its population; as in the case of medieval Switzerland, its chief article of export consisted of mercenary soldiers.

Though the Arcadians achieved a temporary political union in the fourth century, their attempts to form an enduring confederacy were impeded by the labyrinthine character of their mountain system, and by the lack of a good site for a federal capital. In Mantinea and Tegea, to be sure, they possessed two

[1] The Arcadian territory might be compared to that of Bolivia after the loss of the Arica–Iquique corridor to Chile.

[2] Frazer, op. cit., pp. 312–15, 324–30.

towns of no mean size, and the importance of these cities was enhanced by their position astride the main road from Sparta to Argos and Corinth. But their situation in relation to the rest of Arcadia was too eccentric to form a convenient place of meeting, and either town neutralized the other in a constant neighbourly feud. Their mutual animosity was probably sustained by recurrent disputes about the regulation of the katabothrai on which the drainage of their territory depended. Should these katabothrai become obstructed, Mantinea, which occupied the lower part of the basin, was liable to suffer from inundation.[1] In the upper valley of the Alpheus Megalopolis stood equally remote from the heart of Arcadia, but it commanded the watershed between the Alpheus and the Eurotas, across which lay the easiest line of communications between Sparta and the rest of Peloponnesus.[2] As a bulwark of Arcadian liberty against Spartan imperialism, Megalopolis became the federal capital soon after its foundation in 369 B.C. In the third century, when most of Arcadia was absorbed into the Achaean League, Megalopolis assumed a similar function as Achaea's sentinel over against Sparta.

§ 17. ARGOLIS

Taken as a whole, Argolis is one of the least favoured parts of Peloponnesus. Its outer coasts are almost continuously rockbound, and although it fronts on the Saronic Gulf it is virtually shut off from that important waterway. Its interior is a tangle of low maquis-clad mountains. But at the head of the Argolic Gulf (the Bay of Nauplia) the uplands make way for a considerable expanse of alluvial plain which is also a centre of communications for Peloponnesus. Like the whole of Argolis, this plain has a low rainfall, and from the time of Homer it was described as 'thirsty' Argos. Yet its western edge is copiously watered by springs fed from the Arcadian katabothrai;[3] indeed the Argive plain, left to itself, would partly degenerate into swamp, but under proper tendance it forms one of the richest irrigation areas of Greece.[4] This part of Argolis therefore could carry a considerable population, and the city of Argos at its centre disposed of a man-power inferior only to that of Corinth among Peloponnesian cities.

[1] For details see W. J. Woodhouse, *King Agis of Sparta*, pp. 27–30.
[2] A little farther down the Alpheus valley the House of Villehardouin built the fortress of Karytaena, which served as a link between the Frankish castles of Glarentza and Mistra (pp. 85 n. 3, 90).
[3] Strabo, p. 371.
[4] In modern times the Argive plain has been used for the cultivation of rice.

The Argive plain also provides the first good landing-place for ships proceeding from Cape Malea along the eastern coast of Greece. At its south-eastern edge the town of Nauplia, protected by the high spur of Mt. Palamidi, affords good shelter from winds sweeping up the gulf; in the eighteenth century it was an important station of the Venetians, and from 1822 to 1833 it served as the capital of New Greece. The value of this sea-front was already recognized in prehistoric days; as the remains of Mycenae, Tiryns, and Midea attest,[1] it was the principal point of entry for the Minoan culture into the Greek mainland. That it was also the base of a prehistoric thalassocracy is suggested by the legendary connexion of the Argive king Danaus with Egypt, by Egyptian records of a Danaan sea-folk,[2] and by the armada which Agamemnon the lord of Mycenae mustered against Troy.[3] In the subsequent age of emigration from Greece to the Aegean and Levantine areas Argos was still a starting-point for over-sea adventure, for it was reputed to be the 'mother city' of several Dorian colonies in Crete, Rhodes, and southern Asia Minor.

But in historic times the Argives turned their backs on the sea and allowed maritime traffic to be diverted to the Saronic Gulf. Their aversion from naval activity was probably due to their pre-occupation with the affairs of Peloponnesus, where they hoped against hope to recover for themselves the previous ascendancy of the lords of Mycenae. From a geographical point of view Argos was not ill fitted to take on this part, for the city lay astride the main artery of Peloponnesian communications from Corinth to southern Arcadia, Laconia, and Messenia. From Corinth an easy saddle-back pass (2,000 feet) leads by way of Cleonae to the Argive plain, on to which it debouches at Mycenae. In pre-historic times the lords of Mycenae reached out across this pass to the Gulf of Corinth, and they established their connexion with Corinth by means of several metalled roads.[4] In later days King Pheidon of Argos resumed control over Corinth. The reason why Argos failed to maintain its hold for long is to be sought in the superior man-power and resources of Corinth rather than in

[1] On Midea see A. W. Persson, *The Royal Tomb of Dendra near Midea.*

[2] On the implications of the legend of Danaus see J. L. Myres, *Who were the Greeks?*, p. 121.

[3] As was pointed out by Thucydides (i. 9. 4), the Trojan War implied a Mycenaean thalassocracy.

[4] On these roads see C. Tsountas and J. A. Manatt, *The Mycenaean Age*, pp. 35–8; M. P. Nilsson, *Homer and Mycenae*, p. 115 (with map).

any difficulty of communications. The connexion with Arcacia was made by means of two gaps in the border range of Mt. Parthenion, the more northerly and commodious one leading to Oenoë and Mantinea, the other one to Hysiae and Tegea. Using one or other of these routes, the Argives repeatedly secured a foothold in Arcadia, and it was no doubt from Mantinea and Tegea, and onward past the site of the future city of Megalopolis, that Pheidon made his famous foray to Olympia. Indeed it might be maintained that the chances of an Argive hegemony in Peloponnesus turned mainly on the prospects of a secure foothold on the basin of Mantinea and Tegea. With this vantage-point in their possession, the Argives cut off Sparta's lines of communication with the Isthmus and were within striking distance of the other main link between south and north Peloponnesus, the Alpheus valley. Their failure to achieve more than a passing alliance with Mantinea or Tegea reduced their role to that of an important makeweight in Peloponnesian politics, but not a potential leader.

§ 18. LACONIA

The two southern districts of Peloponnesus, Laconia and Messenia, resemble Argolis in that they too are framed in a horse-shoe of mountains which present a steep scarp to their outer sea-board and envelop on their inner side a fertile plain fronting on a sea gulf.

Laconia is in one respect one of the most favoured lands of Greece. Its central plain, the valley of the Eurotas, lies snugly ensconced between the chains of Taÿgetus and Parnon and the Arcadian highlands, and it is well watered by an abundance of runnels from Taÿgetus, whose summit (at 8,000 feet) retains its cap of snow until midsummer. At the present day it is covered with olive orchards and orange groves; in ancient times a larger portion of it was given over to tillage, but at any time it could produce food for a considerable population. Laconia therefore does not apply the stimulus of hunger to its people, so as to impel them into commercial enterprise or political adventure, to the same extent as many other parts of Greece.

On the other hand, Laconia is one of the most secluded of Greek territories. The southernmost of the mainland regions, it is almost as far removed from the heart of Greece as Thessaly on the northern margin. It has an easy exit into the Alpheus valley by the head-waters of the Eurotas, but its avenue to the

Isthmus is barred by the Sciritis highland which forms the south-eastern buttress of Arcadia. Its eastern coast offers fair shelter in the Bay of Epidaurus Limera and more especially under the lee of the island of Minoa at its southern end: in the Middle Ages the town of Monemvasia, situated on Minoa, was the centre of the Greek export trade in wine. But from the coast there is no easy passage across Mt. Parnon into the Eurotas valley, and the 'Malmsey' wine of Monemvasia was not produced in Laconia but in the Greek archipelago. On the inner seaboard the Laconian Gulf lies more exposed to the weather than the Gulf of Argolis, and the port of Gytheum has no protection save from a headland of no great reach. Thus geography has marked out Laconia to be a self-contained country, a 'happy land without a history'. But the state of Sparta which occupied it in ancient times was a law unto itself; it defied alike the general customs of Greece and the dictates of Nature, and so left a peculiar mark on Greek history.

In prehistoric times Laconia, albeit the nearest part of the Greek mainland to Crete, was less important than Argolis as a point of entry for the Minoan civilization. In the days of the Dorian invasion the fortress of Amyclae, standing out on a bluff in the central Eurotas valley, held out for a long time against the new-comers and obliged them to make their main settlement at a point some five miles farther up river. With the foundation of Sparta the long paradox of Laconian history begins, for this city stood (or rather straggled) on a site unprotected by Nature, and remained unwalled until c. 200 B.C. Sparta thus was in sharp contrast with the other cities of ancient Greece, as also with its medieval successor Mistra, situated on a lofty spur of Mt. Taÿgetus, where the Frankish invaders of Laconia improved upon Nature with elaborate fortifications.

The expansion of the Spartan state beyond the boundaries of Laconia entailed at its outset another geographic paradox. The Messenian Wars with which the Spartans opened their career of conquest were fought over the top of the highest mountain chain in Peloponnesus, whose shortest and lowest col (the Langada pass, from Mistra to Kalamata) involves a climb through a diffi-cult gorge to a height of 4,500 feet. The bait which lured them across this no-man's-land was another valley which equalled or surpassed that of the Eurotas (p. 92), and its retention became a cardinal article of Spartan policy. But the maintenance of con-trol over an ever-reluctant subject population, across a line of communications which might become impassable in midwinter, imposed a heavy strain upon the Spartans and obliged them to recast their state on a totalitarian basis.[1]

Of the Spartans' subsequent wars of conquest in Peloponnesus too little is known to warrant any detailed geographical comment. But it is significant that after the Messenian Wars their next line of advance was towards Elis, to which they had easy access by way of the Alpheus valley, and that their most critical campaign in the sixth century was fought against Tegea for the possession of Sciritis and the acquisition of a foothold on the main road to Argos and Corinth.[2] The further advance to the Isthmus, which does not appear to have met with strong opposition, was presumably made in the first instance by the comparatively easy route through Mantinea and Phlius (p. 84).

But the Spartans never gained control of the main north-and-south road through Argos, and their remote position at the southern extremity of Peloponnesus added to the difficulties of effective supervision over their dependants. It is true that to some extent they overcame the problem of long lines of communication by their quickness of mobilization and their capacity for forced marches. But not possessing such an instrument of empire as the Roman system of roads, they had to be content with a far less rigorous control over central and northern Peloponnesus than they exercised over their helots in Laconia and Messenia. It is significant that they even allowed some of their dependants in the wilder parts of Arcadia to disturb the Peloponnesian peace by the waging of private warfare.[3] The reason for this policy of non-interference was, no doubt, that Sparta never achieved an effective military penetration into the mountain labyrinth of central and northern Arcadia.

The temporary hegemony which the Spartans acquired over the whole of Greece after the Peloponnesian War ran counter to geographic conditions in an even greater degree. To control the entire Greek homeland from one of its outlying regions was all the more difficult as the Spartans, lacking a good seaboard, possessed scarcely more than a token fleet and had to rely on the

---

[1] Thucydides (iv. 80. 3) points out that the Spartans were constantly preoccupied with standing guard over their helot population. But it was the helots of Messenia who needed most watching, because on geographical grounds they had the best opportunities of rebellion.

[2] Herodotus, i. 66–8.

[3] Xenophon, *Hellenica* v. 4. 36–7. (A war between Clitor and Orchomenus; the Spartans seek to impose an armistice, but not a definite peace settlement.)

contingents of their allies to maintain a precarious thalassocracy. These geographic obstacles to a wider sphere of control may help to explain why the Spartans did not extend their aims to include a permanent pan-Hellenic lordship. While they fought often and hard to uphold their ascendancy in Peloponnesus, which made large but not unbearable demands upon them, they seemingly recognized that a wider Greek dominion would elongate their radius of action to breaking-point. Their fourth-century experiment in a wider imperialism expressed the transitory ambitions of two war-leaders, Lysander and Agesilaus, rather than the set policy of the Spartan people.

§ 19. MESSENIA

The region to the west of Mt. Taÿgetus is in many ways a counterpiece to Laconia. In its outlying parts it is a mountainous waste, and its western seaboard is cut off from the interior by another range of heights. On this coast the Bay of Navarino (ancient Pylos) offers a safe and commodious harbourage, but its lack of a good hinterland deprives it of any commercial advantage, though on two chance occasions it served as a base for war fleets and became the scene of important naval encounters.[1] The inner Gulf of Messenia affords fair shelter at Koroni and Kalamata (ancient Pharae). Koroni was a port of call for the Venetians, and Kalamata now has a considerable export trade in the produce of the Messenian plain. In ancient times, however, the history of Messenia was almost confined to the central plain of the rivers Pamisus and Nedon. This inner lowland is larger and even more prolific than that of the Eurotas, and the lower basin of the Pamisus deserved its ancient name of Macaria ('Land of Bliss').

The central plain was connected at its top end with the Alpheus valley by means of a low pass, and thus had easy access to central Peloponnesus. But its chief political asset was the broad saddle-backed mountain of Ithome, rising sharply at its western edge to a height of 2,500 feet. Well supplied with water from springs, and containing in its inner combe an expanse of good pasture and crop land, it provided an ideal site for a city fortress and a capital for the whole of Messenia.[2] When Demetrius of Pharos

[1] In 425 B.C. the main Peloponnesian fleet was driven aground here and eventually captured by an oncoming Athenian squadron. In A.D. 1827 a Turkish fleet was destroyed in a fortuitous encounter with a British and French force under Admiral Codrington.

[2] The remains of Epaminondas' fortifications show that his wall, which followed the line of the high ground, included a wider area than that of most Greek cities.

suggested to Philip V of Macedon that Mt. Ithome was one of
the two 'horns' which he must seize in order to control all Peloponnesus (the other horn being the citadel of Corinth),[1] he spoke
like an unscrupulous politician and a keen-sighted strategist.
But during the long period of its subjection to Sparta Messenia
was curtained off by its conquerors, who exploited it as a mere
food-farm and hunting-preserve;[2] and after their liberation by
Epaminondas the Messenians were content to cultivate their
garden for themselves.

§ 20. THE GREEK ARCHIPELAGO

The islands now comprised under the term 'Greek Archipelago' form the groups anciently known as the Cyclades (the
northern and central cluster) and the Sporades (the southern
outliers).

When Herodotus sought to give his readers a mental picture
of the Nile valley in flood, he likened it to the isles of the Aegean
Sea.[3] In making this comparison he was scientifically correct,
for the Archipelago is in fact the emergent remnant of a collapsed
and engulfed plateau (p. 40). Consisting wholly of mountain
peaks and flanks, it might be imagined as a mere stoneyard, and
indeed Isocrates described its inhabitants as 'cultivating a rock
garden'.[4] But this remark is misleading. To say nothing of the
volcanic island of Thera, whose lava soil now produces some of
the best Greek wine, many of the islands contain surface strata
of schistous rock which conserves enough of the winter rainfall
for a prosperous *petite culture* of terraced fields and gardens.
Furthermore, the Archipelago comprises a varied store of mineral
wealth. It is true that the obsidian of Melos lost its value with
the coming of the Bronze Age; and the yield of the gold-mines at
Siphnos rendered down after an early 'boom'.[5] But the Siphnian
silver-deposits are still under exploitation,[6] as are also the emery
of Naxos, the pumice of Thera, and the sulphur of Melos. In
ancient days the most lucrative of the island minerals was the
marble of Paros (p. 43).

But the main importance of the Archipelago lay in its central
position within the Aegean Sea. It does not, to be sure, offer a

---

[1] Polybius, vii. 12; Strabo, p. 361.
[2] See the map of Messenia by A. J. Toynbee, *Journ. Hell. Stud.*, 1913, facing
p. 247.
[3] ii. 97. 1.   [4] *Panegyricus*, § 132.   [5] Herodotus, iii. 57.
[6] On Siphnos and Seriphos hematite iron ore is now worked; but we do not
know whether it was mined in antiquity.

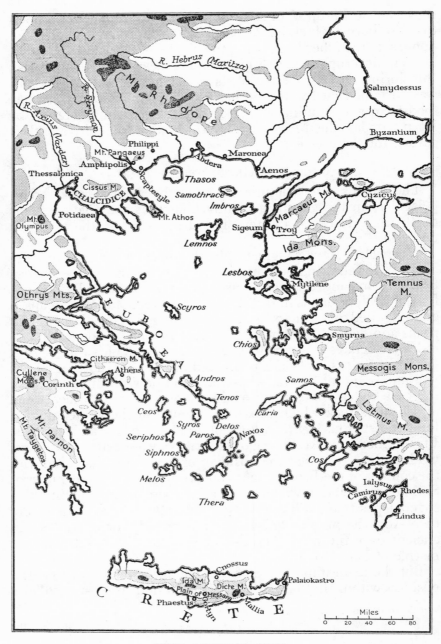

THE AEGEAN AREA

wide choice of good harbours. Melos is scooped out with a
sheltered and capacious basin,[1] and Syros also possesses a safe
port, although in ancient times it was strangely neglected.[2] But
the submerged crater of Thera is too deep for anchorage, and
until it was furnished with artificial breakwaters Delos had
nothing but an open roadstead. Nevertheless sea-going vessels
already plied across the Archipelago in prehistoric times (p. 47);
and when the Aegean Sea became a Greek lake the islands
acquired a permanent value as stepping-stones between Europe
and Asia. In the Hellenistic age, when intercourse between
Greece and the Levantine ports increased apace, their position
as transit stations grew in importance.

The function of the Archipelago as a 'studded lane' across the
Aegean highway is particularly well illustrated by the history of
Delos. This barren and windswept islet was one of the chief
rendezvous for the Greeks of the Aegean area. From early times
it was the meeting-place for the pan-Ionian festival of the Delian
Apollo. After the Persian Wars it played a transient part as a
political capital of the Aegean Greeks banded together in the
Confederacy of Delos. At this period, it is true, it as yet lacked
commercial importance, for the Athenians, who were in effect
the masters of the Confederacy, drew all the long-distance trade
of the Aegean to the Piraeus. In the Hellenistic age, however,
Delos became a focus for traffic between the Greek mainland,
the Black Sea region, and the Levant, and it served as a general
entrepôt for the most important branch of trade in the eastern
Mediterranean, the traffic in grain.[3] The importance of its commerce with the Levant was reflected in the political protectorate
which the Ptolemies exercised over it in the third century and
the Rhodians after 200 B.C. Under the later Roman Republic
Delos enjoyed a fleeting and disreputable prosperity as the chief
receiving centre of the slaves collected in the eastern Mediterranean for transhipment to Italy.[4] The sanctity of Delos as
the reputed birthplace of Apollo no doubt went for something in
its good fortune; but in the main it owed its metropolitan status
to its central position in the Greek world's central sea.

---

[1] British and French frigates used to put in to Melos to shelter from Aegean gales.
[2] Syros first acquired importance as a refuge for displaced persons during the
Greek War of Independence.
[3] W. A. Laidlaw, *History of Delos*, chs. 3–6; on the grain trade, see Rostovtzeff,
Social and Economic History of the Hellenistic World, i, pp. 217 ff., and index, s.v.
Grain.
[4] Strabo, p. 668: Delos was equipped to forward 10,000 slaves in a day.

§ 21. CRETE

Southernmost and largest of the isles of Greece, Crete partakes of the usual mountainous character of Greek lands. Either end of the island is barren and wild, and its western extremity in particular has always lain half desolate. But its central section benefits by natural irrigation from Crete's dominating peak, Mt. Ida (8,000 feet); and the extensive plain of Messara (to the south of Mt. Ida), which is underlain by a limestone of a soft cretaceous variety, is one of the richest in Greece. The huge jars which lined the magazines of the prehistoric palaces of Cnossus and Phaestus were no doubt filled with the wine and oil of the neighbourhood, and the trade of early Crete probably had its origin in the export of its orchard produce. In ancient times, moreover, the Cretan mountains were still well stocked with timber (p. 41); Theophrastus again and again remarked on their grand cypresses.

Crete's isolated position leaves it exposed to the full force of winter and summer winds, and the island is lacking in good natural harbourage. On its northern face Suda Bay provides an excellent naval station, but it lies too far west and away from the centres of production to possess much commercial value. But these disadvantages to the island's trade and seafaring were set off by its surplus production of wine and oil, by its wealth of ship-timber, and above all by its commanding position as the gateway of the Aegean and as a station on the main axis of Mediterranean traffic.[1] It was therefore no mere accident that the prehistoric Cretans were the pioneers of wholesale trade and long-distance sailings in the Mediterranean. For lack of a good central port, the commerce of early Crete long remained dispersed among a number of small towns on the central and eastern seaboard (p. 48). But the ancient legend of King Minos, and the size and splendour of the palace of Cnossus, alike point to an eventual centralization of political power and of economic control (c. 2000 B.C.). This political and commercial unification of Crete could be accomplished the more readily, as the centre of the island was the richest, and the good lands on either side of the central mountain chain could intercommunicate easily by a low pass through which the lords of Cnossus built a metalled road.[2] Thus Nature assisted

[1] In the Second World War the loss of Crete seriously endangered the position of the allied navies in the eastern Mediterranean and virtually shut them off from Greece and the Aegean.

[2] A. J. Evans, *The Palace of Minos*, ii, pp. 60–62.

King Minos to achieve the first thalassocracy in Mediterranean waters and the first highly organized state on European territory. The history of ancient Crete after the fall of Cnossus (*c.* 1400 B.C.) is a long-drawn-out paradox. Its people remained attached to the sea, but not by the wedlock of honest trade: until the final cleaning-up of the Mediterranean by Pompey they kept company with it by the furtive bond of piracy. The chief reason for this change-over from sea-lord to sea-rover may be sought in the chronic disunion and the endless round of local wars between the several independent cities which beset Crete after the disappearance of the Minoan dynasty, causing its people to dissipate their energy in petty turbulence.[1] The contrast between the ordered unity of Minoan days and the political chaos of the historic period is not easy to explain, but a geographical factor probably entered into the causes of it. The two fertile plains on either side of the central ridge are fairly matched in regard to situation and resources. Consequently in historic times Cnossus could not recover its ancient dominion, but found an effective counterpoise in Gortyn, the chief city of the southern lowland;[2] and so long as the principal towns of the island neutralized one another no effective remedy could be found for its political fragmentation.

§ 22. THE OUTER ISLES. THE NORTH AEGEAN

(*a*) *Thasos.* The principal island of the north Aegean, Thasos, is a finely shaped block whose eastern coastal ridge presents a symmetrical façade like that of a Greek temple. Its northerly latitude assures it a somewhat more generous rainfall than the scanty measure which the Archipelago receives; hence it is still well clad with trees, as in the days of Archilochus,[3] and in ancient times it became one of the chief wine-exporting centres of the Aegean.[4] It also contained silver-mines which made its fortune

---

[1] The spirit which animated the Cretans of historic times may be illustrated from the following oath which the people of the small city of Drerus were called upon to swear: 'I shall never be well disposed to the people of Lyttus by any device or contrivance, neither by night nor by day, and I shall strive as far as lies in my power to do ill to the city of Lyttus' (C. Michel, *Recueil d'inscriptions grecques*, 23 A, ll. 37–42).

[2] The palace of Phaestus, which was the prehistoric equivalent of the city of Gortyn, was inferior in size and wealth to Cnossus.

[3] Fr. 18 (Bergk).

[4] For an interesting fourth-century inscription regulating the sale of wine in Thasos see G. Daux, *Bulletin de correspondance hellénique*, 1926, pp. 213 ff.

in the age of the Persian Wars,[1] and from its principal harbour (protected by an off-shore islet against fall-winds from the Thracian coast) it had easy access to the still more lucrative mines of Mt. Pangaeus (p. 294).[1] The Thasians, it is true, were headed off the mainland by the Athenians and Philip of Macedon, but their wine trade still flourished in Hellenistic times.[2]

(b) *Samothrace*. Half-way from Thasos to the Dardanelles the isle of Samothrace rises sheer out of the water to a height of some 5,500 feet. Almost devoid of cultivation, it enjoyed a vogue in the Hellenistic period as the seat of a mystery religion *de mode*, and it has at all times been a main landmark in the north Aegean.[3]

(c) *Lemnos*. Samothrace's southerly neighbour, Lemnos, is much less conspicuous, but has figured more largely in history. At the foot of its extinct volcano lies a plain whose rich lava soil can produce generous crops of wheat.[4] It has the further advantage of a strategic situation commanding the entrance to the Dardanelles, and of a good harbour in Mudra Bay.[5] Lemnos attracted curiously little notice in the early age of Greek colonial expansion; but after the Athenians had become interested in the trade route to the Black Sea they made sure of it by means of a cleruchy, and they contrived to retain almost uninterrupted possession of it until the reign of the Emperor Septimius Severus. Besides safeguarding the Athenian approach to the Black Sea passage it contributed materially to the Athenian food-supply.

§ 23. The Outer Isles. The East Aegean

(a) *Lesbos*. Of the islands adjacent to Asia Minor, Lesbos was large and fertile enough to provide for five towns. Mytilene, by far the largest of the cities, had the advantage of a position on the inshore route along Asia Minor to the Black Sea passage. In spite of its circuitous character this route was of some importance in that it gave shelter from the full force of the etesian winds, which blow strongly down the Dardanelles, and the Bay of Besika

---

[1] Herodotus, vi. 46–7. No traces of ancient gold-mines have been found on Thasos.

[2] A brisk sale of Thasian wine in the Balkan lands is attested by fragments of jars carrying an inscription.

[3] In the *Iliad* (xiii, ll. 10–14) Zeus surveyed the field of Troy from Samothrace. Modern scholars, using contourless maps, have objected that the Gallipoli peninsula would block the view. The error of these *géographes de cabinet* was first exposed by Kinglake, *Eothen*, ch. 4.

[4] It has been estimated that the yield of wheat on Lemnos rose to twenty bushels per acre (Jardé, *Les Céréales*, p. 51).

[5] Mudra Bay served as the naval base for the Gallipoli Expedition in 1915.

(near ancient Sigeum) is still a point of assembly for sailing-vessels waiting for the right opportunity to double Cape Koum Kaleh and enter the Gallipoli channel. Originally built on an off-shore islet, Mytilene was attached to the main island by a process of silting which also provided it with a good 'anvil' harbour.[1] The most significant episode of its history was its early competition with Athens for the control of the approach to the Dardanelles; once this was decided to Mytilene's detriment the city ceased to play such a part in Greek history as its geographic position might appear to have marked out for it.

(b) *Chios.* Described by Homer as 'rocky' ($\pi\alpha\iota\pi\alpha\lambda\delta\epsilon\sigma\sigma\alpha$),[2] Chios is somewhat maligned by this epithet, for its interior at any rate contains rich orchard land. In ancient times it was noted for its figs;[3] at the present day its lentisk groves furnish Greece with its principal liqueur, masticha. Its orchard culture, however, would hardly account for the large number of unfree men who were kept on the island at the time of the Peloponnesian War.[4] We may therefore suspect that its central position along the west coast of Asia Minor favoured its development as a receiving station in the slave-trade before this function was assumed by Delos (p. 95). At the time of the Persian Wars Chios possessed a considerable war-fleet, but it never figured as an important trading-post. It contained no good harbours, and as a terminal station on the transcontinental trade routes of Asia Minor it was eclipsed by the mainland ports of Smyrna and Ephesus.

(c) *Samos.* Albeit a smaller and less fertile island,[5] Samos made a larger contribution to ancient Greek history than Chios or Lesbos. Situated near the junction of the traffic route up and down the coast of Asia Minor and of the main trans-Aegean crossing, it was able to establish trade connexions with the Black Sea and the Levant, and to intercept part of the commerce of Miletus in all these regions. In view of the position of Samos, astride of these several lines of traffic, it is not surprising that its tyrant Polycrates was the first of the Greek arch-pirates who organized sea-roving on a right royal scale. But its black market lasted no longer than Polycrates himself, and indeed at the latest

[1] Strabo, p. 617.
[2] *Odyssey*, iii. 170. Cf. the *Homeric Hymn to Apollo*, l. 172.
[3] In the third century B.C. its wine was exported, together with that of Thasos, to Greek connoisseurs in Egypt (C. C. Edgar, *The Zenon (Cairo) Papyri*, no. 59012).
[4] Thucydides, viii. 40. 2.
[5] Oil was occasionally sent from Samos to Egypt (Edgar, op. cit., no. 59015). But Strabo (p. 637) described the island as $o\dot{v}\kappa\ \epsilon\ddot{v}o\iota\nu os$.

it must have been extinguished by the Pax Atheniensis of the fifth century. Moreover Samos was cut off, like Chios, from the transcontinental trade. Here Miletus and Ephesus had an advantage over the island state, and in the Hellenistic period this priority in the continental markets contributed to the relative decline of Samos. In the third century, however, Samos assumed a new importance as a naval station of the Ptolemies, by means of which they secured their foothold in the Aegean area.

(*d*) *Cos*. This island shared with Rhodes (see below)] and the mainland city of Cnidus an important export trade in wine during the Hellenistic age. This business probably had its most lucrative market in Egypt, whose native liquor could not satisfy the fastidious palates of the wealthier Greek residents. It was probably also in this same period that Cos became the first centre of silk-manufacture in Greek lands. The material for the Coan silks was obtained from a worm which fed on the leaves of the black mulberry, a plant that grows wild in Asia Minor.[1] The location of the industry at Cos was probably due to the mere accident that the difficult art of unwinding the silk threads from the cocoons was first mastered by the women of the island.[2]

§ 24. RHODES

The outlying island of Rhodes is essentially a marginal land, and its history was largely determined by its position on the Aegean frontier. It has a relatively large and fertile territory, and the numerous fragments of jars with official Rhodian stampings which have been found over a widely scattered area of the eastern Mediterranean, and as far west as Sicily, show that in Hellenistic times the island produced a surplus of wine and oil for export. But it does not follow that the entire contents of the jars were home-grown, and it would be quite in keeping with the general economic activity of Rhodes that it should have been a receiving and dispatching centre for other islands and part of Asia Minor.[3] Indeed the historical importance of Rhodes rests mainly on the fact that it was a commercial entrepôt, and for this

[1] The black mulberry also served the needs of the silk industry of medieval Italy until the fifteenth century, when the Chinese white mulberry was introduced. Its silk has a grey or yellow tinge and is of shorter staple than the Chinese article.

[2] The art of unwinding the silk threads was said to have been discovered by a Coan lady named Pamphile (Aristotle, *Historia Animalium* v. 19, p. 551*b*, ll. 13–16; Pliny, xi, § 76). We may recognize in Pamphile the Greek counterpart of Silingi, the traditional founder of the Chinese silk industry.

[3] Rostovtzeff, op. cit. ii, p. 1268. It may be suspected that the Rhodians practised a good deal of *coupage* with different brands of wine.

function it was almost predestined by its position on the main passage-way between the Aegean and the Levantine Seas.

In the days of the Minoan thalassocracy, to be sure, Rhodes does not appear to have been a regular station on the Levantine route; the intercourse of the prehistoric Cretans was with Egypt rather than with Asia, and it is not unlikely that they worked an open-sea route to the Delta.[1] But in the Late Minoan period, when the Greek mainland displaced Crete as a starting-point for naval ventures, Rhodes began to come into its own; the abundance of Late Minoan pottery that has been found on the island was a presage of its future importance as a link between Greece and the Levant.

After 1000 B.C. the trade of Rhodes was mainly directed to Sicily and the western Mediterranean, an area from which it was presently extruded by Corinth and other better-placed competitors. This diversion of traffic may have been due to the general suspension of relations between Greece and the Levant after the Dorian invasion. But after the resumption of contacts between Greece and the Near East in the eighth century the Rhodians left the field to less favourably situated states such as Samos, Miletus, and Aegina. The reason for this apparent lack of enterprise may be sought in the fact that the Greek settlers on the island at first dwelt in dispersion on a number of sites which had been originally selected for their value as strong-points rather than as naval stations (p. 50). Of these towns, Lindus on the east coast and Ialysus near the northern apex achieved a moderate prosperity, but either of them lay too far off the main channel of communications, which naturally passed between the northern tip of the island and the Asiatic mainland. The Rhodians did not rise to the full measure of their opportunities until 408 B.C., when they at last combined to found the city of Rhodes.

The new town of this name was built on a moderately shelving hill of concave shape alongside an open bay. But elaborate harbour works converted this basin into the best-equipped port of the Greek world,[2] and the command which the city exercised over Greece's gate to the Levant gave it a position comparable to that of Byzantium at the other Aegean gate. In the Hellenistic

[1] Natural conditions of navigation in the Levant favour travel in a 'great circle' in an anti-clockwise direction, according to the trend of the prevailing currents (Myres, *Who were the Greeks?*, pp. 220–1). It may be surmised that the early Cretans crossed to Africa, using the heights of Cyrenaica as a landfall, then followed the African coast to the Delta, and returned home by the open-sea route.

[2] Strabo, p. 652.

age, when the Levantine trade acquired a new impetus, the city of Rhodes displaced the Piraeus as the principal clearing-house for the seaborne trade of Greece, and until *c.* 150 B.C. its commercial range probably exceeded that of Alexandria.[1] The attraction which Rhodes now exercised as the general focusing-point of Greek commerce may be illustrated from the fact that it also captured an important share of the traffic with the Black Sea, though this area did not lie within its natural sphere of operations.

After 150 B.C. Rhodes suffered a sharp set-back. Its decline was partly due to the deliberate policy of the Roman Republic in favouring the rival port of Delos at its expense and partly to an unpremeditated blow which the city sustained through the diversion of the Levantine trade from the now impoverished area of Greece and the Aegean to the rapidly expanding markets of Italy. With the establishment of an open-sea route between Italy and Alexandria, Rhodes was once more relegated to a side-alley of commerce.

[1] Rostovtzeff, op. cit. ii, pp. 679 ff.

IV. ITALY. GENERAL

§ 1. CLIMATE

AS defined in the days of Augustus, Italy had an area of *c.* 75,000 square miles; inclusive of Sicily, Sardinia, and Corsica it would have measured *c.* 100,000 square miles.[1]

In its geographic features Italy deviates from the Mediterranean norm to a greater extent than Greece, and for the most part to its own advantage. Its northern half, which until 42 B.C. was officially styled 'Cisalpine Gaul', received this name on ethnic grounds, but might with a fair show of reason have been so called on a geographical consideration alone, for its climate differs but little from that of its trans-Alpine neighbour. This region is partly cut off by its high mountain border from the prevailing westerlies of winter and northerlies of summer. It therefore does not receive its full share of the Mediterranean winter rains, and it experiences calm spells during which the chilled mountain air settles gravitationally on the plains and produces sharp and prolonged frosts. Complete immunity from the north winds is enjoyed only in the 'dead angle' of the Lake District. The mean winter temperature of Venice accordingly falls slightly below that of London, and Turin is considerably colder. In summertime, on the other hand, north Italy does not come permanently under the sway of the dry winds from the Continent, and during calm spells 'convectional' rain falls not infrequently, as the heated air ascending straight from the plains is chilled in the upper altitudes. The total annual rainfall of north Italy is moderate (*c.* 24 inches at Milan), but it is well distributed over the seasons.

The climate of peninsular Italy conforms more closely to the Mediterranean type, with boisterous rain-washed winters, during which the Apennines lie heavily mantled in snow.[2] Occasional hot blasts of a scirocco in spring form the prelude to a summer of deficient rain under the spell of the northerly 'trades'. In Sicily and south Italy the period of drought extends over three to four months, but a regular play of land and sea breezes effectively tempers the heat, which is scarcely more oppressive than that of

---

[1] Sicily covers 9,800 square miles, and Sardinia 9,200.

[2] The Adriatic flank of the Apennines in particular receives heavy snowfalls. These and the winter 'wash-outs' were a serious obstacle to the Allies' advance in the Battle of Italy, 1944–5.

the north. In central Italy the drought is less prolonged: it lasts
two months at Rome, but only one month at Florence.

The praises of the Italian climate were sung by a chorus of
writers, Latin and Greek, who particularly commented on its
temperateness.[1] The air of Italy does not exhilarate to the same
degree as that of Greece, and its sunshine does not possess quite
the same hard brilliance; but its weather is not less genial or
heartening.[2]

2. STRUCTURE

The people of modern Italy receive frequent reminders that
their country is, geologically speaking, still young and restless.
Ancient writers have recorded no such devastating earthquake as
befell Messina in 1908; but Livy again and again mentions tremors
sufficient to cause a passing alarm at Rome,[3] and at Pompeii a
premonitory heave by the giant that lay under Vesuvius neces-
sitated a considerable rebuilding of the town (A.D. 63). A peculiar
feature of Italian tectonics is the long-drawn-out chain of volcanoes which, beginning with Etna, re-emerges in the Lipari
islands and seams the western border of the peninsula from
Campania to Etruria, ending with a few outliers in the Euganean
Hills of Venetia. Most of these fire-mountains had become
quiescent before the foundation of Rome, and the only ones that
were in continuous activity throughout the range of Roman
history were Etna and the Lipari group.[4] Vesuvius in Republican
times was grazed on almost to its summit, but the scorched
appearance of its upper slopes betrayed its past history. In the
words of Strabo: 'Vesuvius is ashy to look at, and it is marked
with funnel-shaped cavities of soot-coloured rock, as though consumed by fire; so one might conjecture that this place was
formerly aflame and contained craters of fire, until the material
to feed it gave out.'[5] Since its re-awakening in A.D. 79 it has been
the most ebullient of Italian volcanoes.[6] Small rises and falls in

---

[1] Varro, De re rustica i. 2; Vergil, Georgics ii. 149 ff.; Pliny, iii. 41, xxxvii. 201
('caeli temperies'). Strabo, p. 286; Dionysius, Antiquitates Romanae i. 37 ('ἀέρα
κεκραμένον ταῖς ὥραις συμμέτρως').

[2] The toughening character of the Italian climate is exemplified in the labor
improbus of the ancient Roman peasant and road-builder, and of the Italian railway-
constructor in various countries of modern Europe.

[3] Thirty-two earthquakes that befell between 461 B.C. and A.D. 394 have been
listed by Nissen, Italische Landeskunde, i, pp. 285–6.

[4] The 'rain of stones' which now and then fell on Rome and was treated as news
by Livy probably had its origin in Stromboli.

[5] p. 247.

[6] A full description of the eruption of Vesuvius is given in the Letters of Pliny

the levels of the coast-line and of lake waters are a reminder that the Italian earth still 'works'.[1]

The predominant formation of the Italian Alps[2] and of the Apennines is a limestone of the usual rigid Mediterranean type; but considerable portions of the northern and central sectors of the Apennines are of softer texture and more intermixed with marl and clay than the mountains of Greece. The greater frequency of rainfall in central and especially in northern Italy is also conducive to more rapid weathering and loam-formation. The Italian mountains, therefore, though partly denuded since ancient days, carry more forest and are better decked with summer pasture than the Greek ones.[3] But the distinctive advantage which Italy possesses over Greece in regard to structure lies in its greater expanse of lowland, and in the exuberant fertility of its two largest plains, the basin of the Po and Adige, and the hinterland of Naples (ancient Campania). Fundamentally the structure and climate of Italy, and consequently its plant life, resemble that of Greece. Here too we meet with the two-year shift on the arable land, the relative scarcity of meadow land, the alternation of summer and winter pastures, and the extensive cultivation of the vine and olive. Compared with France or England, Italy is mountainous and dry and, on the average, not highly productive. But its ancient inhabitants thought of it as a rich country,[4] and Greek visitors from the time of Polybius described its fertility in glowing terms. Of the Greek writers, Dionysius emphasized the balanced excellence of Italy as a cropland and an orchard country, and ended by saying, 'It is full to overflowing of all that is serviceable and gladdens the heart.'[5] Strabo extolled Italy in similar terms: 'It is impossible to do justice in words to its abundance in materials and sustenance for man and beast, and for the excellence of its harvests.'[6]

Italy under Roman rule passed through some serious agri-

---

the Younger (vi. 16). It tallies remarkably well with accounts of the eruption of Tarawera on New Zealand in 1886 (W. Pember Reeves, *New Zealand*, pp. 141–5).

[1] For a rise in the Alban Lake, not due to rain, see Livy, v. 15. 2. At Baiae remains of ancient buildings are visible under the sea.

[2] The Alps consist of a granite core which protrudes in the centre but has been overlaid at the edges with a high cap of limestone.

[3] According to a recent estimate 9·3 per cent. of Greece and 15·7 per cent. of Italy is now forested (E. C. Semple, *The Geography of the Mediterranean Region*, p. 292).

[4] The Latin eulogists of Italy include Vergil (*Georgics* ii. 136–50), Varro (*De re rustica* i. 2), and Pliny (xxxvii. 201).

[5] i. 37.   [6] p. 286.

cultural crises; but these were due to political factors (more especially to the wastage of the peasant population in oversea wars, and their replacement by the servile labour of war-captives) rather than to the niggardliness of the Italian soil. The dependence of Rome on foreign corn also proves nothing against the productive capacity of ancient Italy, for the problem of feeding the capital was mainly one of transport, and the carriage of grain by ship from the provinces proved more convenient than its conveyance from the Italian country-side on donkey-back. At all stages of Roman history land work was the main source of Italy's wealth,[1] and there is no good evidence that the country's eventual decline was due to any widespread impoverishment of the soil.[2]

The relatively high fertility of Italy is the main reason of the large population which it has carried since ancient times, compared with that of other Mediterranean countries. The population of Italy (without the islands) in A.D. 14 has been estimated at 14,000,000.[3] That this high total was not the result of the Roman conquests outside Italy, nay rather was one of its chief contributing causes, may be inferred from the quite disparately large military man-power upon which Rome could draw in 225 B.C. from peninsular Italy alone—770,000 foot and horse.[4]

The industrial resources of Italy are small in comparison with its agricultural wealth. Its only notable minefields in ancient times were the copper and iron beds of Etruria and Elba (p. 125). The marble quarries of Carrara in Liguria are now the world's principal material for statuary; but they do not seem to have been under exploitation before the last days of the Republic. Of the various good limestones for building purposes the most excellent was the 'travertine' from Tibur (Tivoli) near Rome. This variety, which was formed from the deposit of thermal springs, had a pleasing cream colour, and its resistance to weathering may be exemplified from the surviving façade of the Colosseum.[5] But the principal contribution of ancient Rome to architectural tech-

[1] On the relative importance of the revenue derived from the Italian land and from the proceeds of conquest in the days of the later Republic, see T. Frank, *Roman Imperialism*, pp. 292–3.

[2] Ancient Roman landowners, who grumbled about the exhaustion of the soil, were taken to task by Columella, the ablest of the Roman economists, who flatly denied deterioration (see his Preface). Similar conclusions have been reached by Rostovtzeff (*Social and Economic History of the Roman Empire*, pp. 329–30).

[3] T. Frank, *Economic Survey of Rome*, v, p. 1 (based on Augustus's census).

[4] Polybius, ii. 24.

[5] On the building-materials of Rome see T. Frank, *Papers and Monographs of the American Academy at Rome*, vol. iii.

nique, its employment of vaults and arches on a large scale, derived from its possession of an ideal material for the manufacture of concrete, the lava dust (*pozzolana*) of the volcanic soil of western Italy, whose binding properties made a material singularly resistant to strains and stresses.

§ 3. COMMUNICATIONS

Though Italy is not a large country, its disproportionate length (750 miles, exclusive of Sicily) contributes in itself to keep its extremes apart. Herein lies a reason for the long political dissociation between north and south after the end of Roman rule.[1] Moreover communications between either extremity of the country are impeded by the diagonal trend of the Apennines, which consequently cannot be by-passed by following either coast-line. In the northern and central sectors the Apennines are loosely jointed and make room for relatively wide corridors that do not entail hard climbing (mostly *c.* 3,000 feet). But a winter crossing through the deep snow which then lies on the upper levels might become a difficult or even impossible feat.[2] In the south the ranges consolidate into more uniformly high blocks and offer a narrower choice of passes.

The rivers of Italy vary considerably in their capacity for carrying traffic. The larger ones have a sufficiently regular flow to render them navigable for the greater part of the year, and some of the lesser streams which nowadays do not serve as means of communication carried traffic in ancient days.[3] But the numerous water-courses which descend from the Apennines into the Adriatic, and from the Lucanian and Bruttian mountains into the western (or Tyrrhenian) sea, are a positive hindrance to travel. Like the Greek rivers, they cut their beds into deep gullies which intersect the narrow coastal plains at frequent intervals.[4]

The difficulties of internal communication in Italy are not of

[1] A more important contributing factor, however, was the formation of an independent and sovereign Papal Territory which extended from sea to sea and prevented the political integration of Italy before 1870.

[2] Thus Hannibal was beaten back by heavy snow in 218–217 B.C. (Livy, xxi. 58. 3), and Petilius Cerealis' advance on Rome in the late autumn of A.D. 69 was retarded for similar reasons (Tacitus, *Histories* iii. 59. 3).

[3] Among the lesser rivers the Nar (a tributary of the Tiber) and the Sarnus (the river of Pompeii) certainly were navigated in Roman times (Strabo, pp. 227, 247).

[4] In 207 B.C. the retreat of Hasdrubal across the Metaurus was impeded by the abruptness of its banks (Livy, xxvii. 47. 7). In the Battle of Italy the bridging of the Adriatic rivers would have consumed much time but for the invention of the Bailey bridge.

the same order as those which beset the traveller in Greece. Yet they have been sufficient to contribute materially to the political disunity from which Italy has suffered in the Middle Ages and in modern times. Its greater cohesion under Roman rule must be credited in no small degree to the Roman road-engineer, who had a none too easy task in overcoming the obstacles of the Italian country-side.[1]

Italy is cut off from the continent by the highest of Europe's mountain barriers. The Alps, moreover, present their steepest face to Italy, and their highest peaks, with an altitude exceeding 15,000 feet (Mt. Blanc and Mt. Rosa), lie on the Italian frontier. The passes, it is true, cut deep into the ridges and as a rule do not rise higher than 7,000 feet, so that they are mostly free from snow between May and September. On the continental side the approaches to the passes usually ascend by relatively easy gradients and make the barrier appear less formidable than its steep Italian scarp would indicate. For these reasons the Alps form a somewhat treacherous bulwark for Italy, and they have in fact been so often surmounted by hostile armies or intrusive migrants as to give rise to the saying that 'the history of Italy is the history of her invaders'.

This dictum, however, contains even less truth than is to be found in most epigrams. The difficulties of crossing a mountain range in force are to be measured not only by its height but by its width, and the Alps broaden out in some reaches to a massif of 150–80 miles.[2] Moreover many of the passes contain sections which have ceased to be formidable since the Roman or modern engineer drove his road through them, but in their former natural state were difficult or even very dangerous. A piece of one of the St. Bernard passes is described by Strabo in the following terms: 'Part of the road is so narrow as to induce giddiness in foot-travellers and pack-animals that are not accustomed to it (though the native beasts carry their loads in safety). There is no remedy for this, nor for the huge slabs of ice which slide down from above and can cut off an entire convoy or sweep it along with them into the abysses that dip beneath them.'[3] Finally, the wide curve with which the Alps sweep round north Italy gives to its

---

[1] An indirect but important contribution to the unification of modern Italy has been made by the railway engineer.

[2] The sheer magnitude of the Alpine barrier was duly emphasized by Polybius (*ap.* Strabo, pp. 208–9). That width in a mountain chain may be a greater hindrance to communications than height has also been pointed out by G. E. F. Chilver (*Cisalpine Gaul*, pp. 3–4).   [3] p. 204.

defenders the full benefit of operating on inner lines, an advantage which proved of critical importance during the invasion of the Cimbri and Teutones, for it enabled Marius to defeat in detail their combined attack from the west (by the maritime Alps) and the north (by the Brenner or Reschen–Scheideck pass).[1] On the whole, accordingly, the Alps did their duty by Italy while it needed a protective barrier, for in the period before the consolidation of the Roman empire they reduced the number of major invasions to four—those of the Gauls *c.* 390 B.C., of Hannibal in 218 B.C., of Hasdrubal in 207 B.C., and of the Cimbri in 101 B.C. On the other hand, when the Romans went forth to conquer the European continent, their engineers had acquired the knowledge and the resources by which the Alpine barrier could be shorn of its terrors.

Italy's oversea communications are not quite so favourable as its long seaboard might suggest. Its surrounding waters contain three of the chief centres of disturbance in the Mediterranean: the Gulf of Lions, the Lipari Sea, and the Adriatic. Its coasts were described by Strabo as 'harbourless, but for a few big ports,[2] and if this statement is too sweeping, at any rate it holds good of the Adriatic sea-front, which is exposed in almost its entire length to the strong northerlies of that region,[3] and of the central portion of the west coast. These adverse natural conditions may help to explain the paradox that the Romans wrested the lordship of the western Mediterranean from the Carthaginians, and that with Italian crews they won two of the greatest naval actions of ancient times (Ecnomus in 262 B.C. and Naulochus in 36 B.C.), yet they did not institute a regular naval force until the reign of Augustus, and at all times they left the carrying trade of the Mediterranean in other hands.[4] Nevertheless the foreign

---

[1] In A.D. 69 Otho did not take the field in time to prevent the junction of Caecina, marching by way of the Great St. Bernard, and Valens, who entered Italy by one of the western passes.   [2] p. 286.

[3] At Ancona, as its Greek name ("Αγκων) declared, the coast is cupped like an elbow-socket, but its concavity faces northwards, i.e. in the direction where shelter is most required.

[4] After A.D. 800 a new 'challenge' from an oversea enemy (the Saracen corsairs) gave rise to the war flotillas of Pisa and Amalfi, which in turn led on to the armadas of Genoa and Venice. The danger once over, the medieval Italians remained wedded to the sea and became the master mariners and merchants of their age. But here again we meet with a paradox. The improvements in seafaring technique (ampler rigging, accurate coastal charts, and, above all, the mariner's compass), which opened up the oceans and temporarily reduced the Mediterranean to a backwater, were invented by Italian seamen or at any rate introduced by them into Europe.

connexions of Italy were mostly by sea. The southern part of
the peninsula and Sicily lie close to the centre of the Mediterranean waters and possess good harbours at the right places.
Puteoli (the predecessor of Naples) and Syracuse were well situated for the voyage to Africa; Tarentum and Brundisium were
the natural starting-points for Greece and the Levant. In spite
of the disinclination of its people to maritime adventure, Italy
became the centre of ancient Mediterranean traffic, and the great
majority of the immense concourse that congregated in imperial
Rome arrived in it from overseas.

§ 4. POLITICS

In the greater part of Italy climate and geographic structure
sufficiently resemble those of Greece to impose a similar distribution of population. As in Greece, the normal unit of habitation
during the prehistoric area was a built-up village (*vicus*) at a point
of good water-supply. This type of habitation continued prevalent in the Apennine uplands until the end of the Roman
Republic, and the *pagus* (or canton, comprising a small cluster
of villages) endured here for the same length of time as the normal
political unit. But again, as in Greece, urban communities had
begun to make their appearance in prehistoric times,[1] and under
the influences of Greek and Etruscan immigrants, and eventually
of the Romans, the city became the usual form of settlement. In
the selection of sites for their cities the Italians shared the Greek
preference for a piece of rising ground, with a steep crest for a
citadel, and within easy reach of the cultivated land. A favourite
position for Italian towns was a tongue of high ground at a river
confluence; Italian streams, with their more even flow, gave the
added protection of a ditch that did not run dry. But whereas
most of the town sites were chosen, like those of the Greek cities,
for their defensive aptitudes, one important class of Italian settlement, the Roman military colonies, were mainly to be found in
the plains or on piedmont terraces, at river crossings or at the
exits of mountain passes. Like Sparta or Megalopolis in Greece,
they were intended to serve as centres of communication and as
bases for field armies rather than as fortresses and places of refuge.
In Italy the city gave rise to the city-state by a similar process

---

[1] A good example is to be found in the prehistoric city close to the site of the
Roman colony of Bononia (Bologna). See A. Grenier, *Bologne villanovienne et
étrusque.*

to that of Greek political development, and Italian history down
to the establishment of Roman supremacy was in substance that
of its principal towns. On the other hand, the relatively simple
pattern of the Italian map, as compared with the inextricable
confusion of mountain and plain in the Greek lands, was reflected
in a more clear-cut contrast between rival economic and political
interests. In the early annals of Rome the ever recurrent warfare
between the men of the plain and of the uplands runs like a red
thread. This antagonism showed through most plainly in the
Second Samnite War, which was in effect a duel between a
coalition of mountain cantons and an alliance of city-states of
the plain.[1] The sharp division between the long and regular
spine of the Apennines and the extensive coastal lowlands
naturally facilitated a general pairing-off of the peoples of Italy
into two distinct and potentially opposed groups. And the
chances of friction between the two societies were increased by
the system of alternate summer and winter pastures which Nature
imposes upon the grazing-industry of Italy, for this system involved periodic migrations of the flocks between mountain and
plain and could therefore easily give rise to complaints of trespass.
One characteristic consequence of the Roman conquest of Italy
was the institution of a code of drovers' laws and usages to
regulate the seasonal movement of the herds.[2]

The geographical factors which contributed to Rome's supremacy in Italy will be considered in the next chapter (pp. 132–3).

§ 5. WARFARE

The broad resemblance between the geographical conditions
of Greece and those of Italy also shows through in a fundamental similarity of Greek and Roman methods of warfare. In
winter time, even after the appearance of the Roman roads, Italy
was sufficiently mud-bound to prevent any sustained operations
in the open field. The Romans, with all their determination to
wage war as if it were a business and not a sport, recognized this
limitation to the rules of play, and even Hannibal, after some
costly attempts to disregard Nature's time-table, accepted the
usual conditions of seasonal warfare in Italy. The few campaigns
which were conducted in winter were no real exceptions to the

[1] An echo of this antagonism may be discerned in the Italian War of 91–88 B.C.,
in which the insurgents drew their main strength from the Apennine cantons.
[2] Pelham, *Essays*, pp. 300–11.

general rule, for in each case they consisted of nothing more than running down an already defeated enemy.[1]

Large tracts of Italy are sufficiently mountainous and broken to give a clear advantage to light-armed troops over men of the 'hoplite' type. The Romans at first took little heed of this fact, but after some expensive lessons in the highlands of Samnium[2] they learnt to throw out a screen of skirmishers in front of their legions. They also acknowledged the need to adapt their battle-formation to the folds and swellings of the ground by dividing each legion into *manipuli* or companies which could operate independently wherever the terrain required a looser formation. But they adhered to the Greek principle of putting their main trust in the close order of the massed legion. Herein they had better justification than the Greeks, for Italy offered a large expanse of country in which 'steam-roller' tactics were applicable. But by the same token they had less excuse for neglecting their mounted troops; what could be achieved by well-trained force in the open champaign lands of Italy was demonstrated at the Romans' expense by Pyrrhus and Hannibal.

The fore-ordained resemblance between Greek and Roman warfare went one stage farther. In Italy, as in Greece, the natural strength of most of the city sites rendered their reduction by siege an extremely tedious operation. Though we need not believe the tale that the Romans fought a Trojan war of ten years' duration in front of Veii, we need not doubt that the investment of this town strained the Roman war-machine to the utmost;[3] and Hannibal, after beating the Roman armies clean out of the field, could not consummate his victory by the capture of towns.[4] The difficulties of siegecraft in ancient Italy may be part reason why the Romans often gave liberal terms to enemies whom they had defeated in battle.

[1] For example, in 63–62 B.C. (the hunting down of Catiline), 49 B.C. (Caesar's march through Italy), and A.D. 69 (pursuit of the broken Vitellians). On the other hand, severe weather prevented Sulla from keeping the Marians on the run in the winter of 83–82 B.C. (Appian, *Bella Civilia* i. 87. 1).

[2] The lesson was repeated in the mountains of Liguria and the dense forest of the Po basin.

[3] Similarly Sulla, with the resources of Hellenistic siegecraft at his disposal, took two years (82–80 B.C.) to reduce the Etruscan hill-fortress of Volaterrae.

[4] His only important gain by siege, the city of Tarentum, was effected by means of treason.

V. ITALY. REGIONAL

§ 1. CISALPINE GAUL

THE basin of the Po and the Adige, known under the Roman Republic as Cisalpine Gaul, is a territory of almost equal extent to that of Peninsular Italy. As the name 'Cisalpine Gaul' declares, it was the last district of the Italian mainland to become an integral part of the ancient Roman 'Italia'. The reason for this is to be found partly in its mere distance from Rome, and partly in certain geographical features which retarded its development. In consequence of its hard winters (p. 103), the cultivation of the olive is not practised in north Italy, save in a few sheltered regions such as the sub-Alpine border. But the chief distinguishing mark of 'Cisalpine Gaul' is that, in contrast with the rest of Italy, it is embarrassed with a positive over-supply of water.

This excess is not due to the rainfall, which at all seasons is neither scanty nor copious, but to the double allowance of rain-water and melted snow which north Italy draws from the Alps and Apennines; in particular, the summer supply from the Alps is lavish, for the inflow of snow-water from this quarter never ceases.[1] The spates on the Alpine rivers, it is true, are to some extent reduced by the sub-Alpine lakes, which render a useful service in regulating the floods; since their beds have been ground down to a great depth by travelling glaciers—in Lake Como a sounding of 1,345 feet has been taken—their storage capacity is ample. Yet, even so, the over-spill from the Alps is sometimes more than the lakes can hold, and the volume of their effluent streams—especially of the Ticino—may become heavily swollen. In the Po basin the danger of waterlogging is heightened by the continuous building up of the river bed with masses of detritus brought down from the mountains; in the lower part of the valley the river is at all seasons above the level of the plain, and instead of draining the soil would permanently flood it, if left to its own devices.

In prehistoric times, therefore, Cisalpine Gaul was overspread with swamps. The earliest settlers who have left traces of themselves had to erect their dwellings on wooden piles in order to

[1] Since the snow-line in the Alps is no higher than 9,000 feet, many of the peaks wear a permanent cap.

4935

I

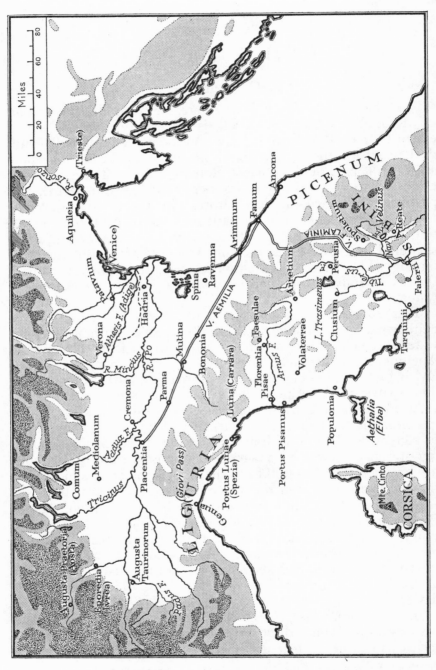

NORTHERN ITALY

keep themselves above flood-level;[1] under Roman rule drainage canals and embankments along the Po in its lower course had to be constructed in order to maintain the land in a habitable condition.[2] Except at points which were convenient as bridge-heads the towns of north Italy were built at a distance from the principal rivers; most of the larger cities, whether of Roman or of later times (Turin, Milan, Brescia, Bergamo, and Verona; or their ancient equivalents) have been strung out along a line of connecting lateral roads of the Roman period, which skirted a shelf of higher ground at the roots of the Alps.

Another hindrance to the early development of Cisalpine Gaul consisted in the dense growth of forest on its humid soil. Before the axe of the Roman woodman had opened up this jungle, more than one Roman army had been ambushed and destroyed in it.[3]

Before the Roman occupation little seems to have been done to groom Cisalpine Gaul out of its primitive uncouthness. But the Roman settlers, by taking in hand the necessary draining and clearing operations,[4] and building roads above flood-level, put another face on the country-side. They left sufficient forest cover to provide for a lumber industry, whose produce was floated down river,[5] and for great herds of mast-fed pigs for the Roman meat market.[6] But they brought the greater part of the plain into cultivation and thus revealed its abundant fertility. The reclaimed polder land consisted of a fat alluvial soil which received a new increment of plant food by sedimentation after each spring flood, and in the rare event of a summer drought it could easily be refreshed by irrigation from the numerous drainage canals.[7]

North Italy in ancient times was not planted with those long lines of white mulberry which are a feature of its modern landscape;[8] it was not yet laid out in rice-fields, and its water-meadows did not give rise to such an extensive dairying and cheese-making industry as at the present day. But its cereal crops, tillering profusely under a good supply of spring rain, astonished visitors from Greece. When Polybius travelled through Cisalpine Gaul he found a positive glut of wheat,[9] and both he

---

[1] E. T. Peet, *The Stone and Bronze Ages in Italy and Sicily*, ch. 13.
[2] Strabo, pp. 212, 217; Pliny, iii. 119.
[3] Livy, xxi. 25. 9; xxiii. 24. 6.   [4] Strabo, p. 217.
[5] Vitruvius, ii. 9. 16.   [6] Polybius, ii. 15. 3; Strabo, p. 218.
[7] Vergil, *Eclogues* iii. III (sluice-gates for the water meadows).
[8] A familiar object of the north Italian roadside, the Lombardy poplar, probably was a later importation from Persia. It is not mentioned by any ancient writer.
[9] ii. 15.1. It is estimated that the price of wheat in Cisalpine Gaul at the time

and Strabo commented on the unfailing harvests of millet (a
bibulous cereal of no great food-value which has now been
replaced by maize). The same Greek couple were also impressed
by the abundance of the vineyards, which did not produce fine
brands but yielded a sufficient barrelage to maintain a considerable export trade to the Danube lands.[1] Lastly, the grazing was
sufficiently varied to produce clips of divers grades, from the
soft wool of the sub-Apennine plain to the hard-wearing upland
materials which supplied the carpet industry of Patavium.[2]

While the levelness of the Cisalpine plain entailed the risk of
waterlogging, it facilitated navigation and road-making, once the
floods had been brought under control. In Roman times the Po,
which descends from Monte Viso in a veritable cascade (with a
drop of 5,000 feet in 20 miles), but has a gentle fall once it has
left the Alps, was navigable as far as Turin;[3] and although the
canal system of north Italy was probably not as extensive as in
the Middle Ages,[4] the water-courses which the Romans cut for
drainage also served for transport.[5]

Under the Roman Republic the development of north Italy
was retarded by one natural disadvantage, in that it was dominated
by the massive citadel of the Alps[6] and was therefore exposed in
its Transpadane zone to raids by the rude mountain tribes who
had the citadel in their keeping. But this brake on its progress
was removed when Augustus incorporated the Alpine lands into
the Roman empire. Indeed north Italy derived a double advantage
from this projection of Roman rule into the European mainland.
It not only gained in security, but it became the centre of communications between Rome and her continental territories.
Henceforth all its geographic advantages came into full play,
and its ranspadane section, which in Caesar's time still passed
for a backward district, became 'the most flourishing side of
Italy'.[7]

of Polybius' travels was one-fifth to one-quarter of the artificially low rates for
grain in the Roman market as fixed by C. Gracchus (H. M. Last, *Cambr. Anc. Hist.*
ix, p. 59).

[1] Strabo, p. 214.
[2] Ibid., p. 218; T. Frank, *Economic Survey*, v, pp. 202–3.
[3] Pliny, iii. 123. In 218 B.C. supplies were conveyed to the Roman army near
Placentia by river (Livy, xxi. 57. 3).
[4] Locks on the canals are first mentioned in the twelfth century.
[5] Strabo, p. 217.
[6] From the summit of an Alpine pass Hannibal seemed to survey Italy 'as from
an acropolis' (Polybius, iii. 54. 2).
[7] Tacitus, *Histories* ii. 17. 2.

Although north Italy forms a distinct geographic unity, it naturally falls into a number of sections which call for separate consideration.

(a) *Piedmont.* The western section, once the 'Land of the Taurini', now known appropriately as 'Piedmont', constitutes a transitional zone between the plain and the mountains. Whereas the ascent from the north Italian lowlands into the Alps is abrupt at all other points, here a broad terrace is inserted in front of the mountain rampart. The land therefore lies well above flood-level, and its soil consists, not of fine alluvial sediment, but of ice-borne detritus of coarser grain. It shares the general fertility of the plains, but is more broken up into separate pockets with bordering tracts of good hill pasture. Its industry, however, is of recent growth, being dependent on its railway connexion with Genoa and the application of hydro-electric power; and in ancient times its mere remoteness from the rest of Italy reduced its importance, until the day when it assumed its historic role as the link between Italy and France.

The Romans took no more than a transient interest in the land of the Taurini until the need to control the passes through the western Alps became apparent to them; and they were slow to recognize this obligation, although Italy's most dangerous invaders, the Gauls and the Carthaginians, found gates of entry here. But after the annexation of Gallia Narbonensis (SE. France) in 120 B.C. they set permanent foot in Piedmont in order to provide a second overland connexion with their new province, in addition to the coastal road through Liguria. Although the easiest passes over the western Alps radiate from Turin—the Col d'Argentière or de Larche (6,500 feet), the Mt. Genèvre (6,200 feet), and the Mt. Cenis (6,800 feet)—the establishment of a Roman colony at Eporedia (Ivrea) in 100 B.C. suggests that their principal line of communications first went by the Little St. Bernard (7,200 feet), which enters the Alps at this point, despite the long and difficult approach to its summit from the Italian side.[1] This choice of route may have been inspired by a temporary interest in some gold-washings near Eporedia, which had caused a gold rush c. 150 B.C. and had attracted the inevitable Roman speculators.[2] When Caesar extended the Roman dominion into central and northern France the Great St. Bernard (8,000 feet) also came into use, and Augustus founded a more

[1] On the western Alpine passes, see also pp. 254–6.
[2] Mommsen, *History of Rome*, iii, pp. 415–16.

advanced station at Augusta Praetoria (Aosta), where the two
St. Bernard routes diverge. But meanwhile one of the more
southerly routes (probably the Mt. Genèvre pass) had been
opened up by Pompey, and under Augustus its starting-point
acquired the status of a colony (Augusta Taurinorum). Thus
Turin entered upon its natural function as a road centre; but its
traffic was military and administrative rather than commercial,
and it could never vie in importance with the more easterly towns
of the north Italian plain.

(b) *Lombardy*. The central portion of Cisalpine Gaul, the
region of the Insubres and Cenomani, modern Lombardy,
played a greater part in Roman history than Piedmont, yet it
did not attain the importance which it has possessed ever since
the Middle Ages. Its slightly shelving plain, composed of fine
alluvial soil, stands sufficiently high to escape the risk of permanent flooding, though it needs to be guarded against spring-
time spates. At Placentia and Cremona it provided the two most
convenient crossing-points of the Po, and it was here that the
Romans established their earliest colonies and road centres.

Besides offering the best gates of entry into the sub-Alpine
lands, Lombardy is also the chief focal point for the passes across
the central Alps. Of these trans-Alpine routes the first to come
into regular use was the one leading up the Adige valley to the
Brenner and Reschen–Scheideck passes (p. 279). From the time
of Augustus and Claudius, when these passes became the main
link with the upper Danube lands, the town of Verona assumed
its historic role as the outer gate of the Lombard plain. On the
other hand, the network of roads that debouch from the Alps upon
Lakes Como and Maggiore (p. 280) was not brought into early
use and was never completed.

The future industrial leadership of Lombardy within Italy was
dimly presaged by the iron manufactures of Comum,[1] whose raw
material was no doubt derived, like that of the cutlers of Milan
and Brescia in later days, from the high-grade ores of Styria
(p. 277).[2] But the silk industry, which was not fully established
before the acclimatization of the white mulberry in the later
Middle Ages (p. 100, n. 1), does not appear to have been introduced into Lombardy in Roman times. For this reason, and

---

[1] Pliny, xxxiv. 144. The good reputation of the ironware of Comum was falsely
ascribed, as usual in such cases, to some special property of its local water.

[2] The 'sword of Noric [i.e. Styrian] steel' was extolled by Horace (*Odes* i. 16.
9–10).

because of the late development of the Como–Maggiore group of passes, whose natural point of convergence is Milan, this city showed no signs of achieving its eventual supremacy among the towns of north Italy until a late stage of Roman history.[1] But in the age of the barbarian invasions, when northern Italy was beset on all sides, Milan was selected as an imperial headquarters, being the most convenient centre for a defensive front that extended along the entire arc of the Alps.

(c) *Venetia.* The country of the Veneti at the eastern end of Cisalpine Gaul underwent a later development than the land of the Insubres and Cenomani, but under the Roman emperors it attained no less a degree of prosperity. Its coastal region, raised barely above sea-level, is liable to a double drenching, by the swollen Alpine streams, and by the Adriatic Sea, whose headwaters rise appreciably on a flood tide. In the days of Strabo its appearance during the season of high water recalled that of Egypt at the time of the Nile's inundation.[2] Until the time when the Romans took in hand the building of dikes and the cutting of drainage channels, much of the land remained uncultivable, and for the time being its only notable product was a strong breed of horses, reared on its extensive fenlands, in which the tyrant Dionysius of Syracuse established a famous stud-farm.[2] Moreover, under the double influence of river sedimentation and tidal drift a chain of mud-banks backed by lagoons was strung out along the sea front, so as to impede access to deep water. Consequently no ancient city of the seaboard attained the position which Venice subsequently held as the link between the eastern Mediterranean and north Italy or the Alpine lands.[3] In the fourth century B.C. the tyrant Dionysius established a colony at Hadria in the Po delta, but this town soon became stranded by a progressive silting which virtually cut it off from the sea: its remains now stand 15 miles from the coast.

But from early days Venetia played an important part as a zone of transit between Italy and the Danube lands, for at its head lie the lowest of all the Alpine cols, the Pontebba, Predil, and Pear Tree passes (with heights of 2,650, 3,800, and 2,800

[1] The modern heavy industry of Milan owes its rise to the import of raw materials from Genoa, and of coal from Germany (by way of the St. Gothard).

[2] Strabo, p. 212.

[3] Venice was originally founded as a place of refuge from the Huns and Avars, because the archipelago of tiny islands on which it was built lay off an inaccessible part of the coast. Its development as a great commercial station was an afterthought and entailed much dredging and embanking.

feet respectively); and the last-named pass is no more than 30 miles in width. In prehistoric times accordingly this was the corridor by which the Terramara and the Villanova folk entered Italy,[1] and in the Age of Migrations it was the doorway by which the Goths and Lombards occupied their new home. The Romans therefore had not long taken possession of Cisalpine Gaul before they established an unusually large colony at Aquileia, the point from which the east Alpine passes branched off, to guard the Venetian plain. From the time of Augustus, when the Romans carried out a reverse invasion of the Danube lands, Aquileia made its own fortune, and that of its neighbour Patavium (Padua), as the starting-point of a brisk overland trade between north Italy and the newly conquered territories. In addition to its own glass cups and jars (the predecessors of the fine Murano ware of modern times), Aquileia forwarded the cloth of Patavium[2] and the wine of the Venetian uplands. Its main stream of traffic went by the Pear Tree pass, which was easy enough to be negotiated by wagons.[3]

(d) *Emiglia*. The southern or sub-Apennine lappet of Cisalpine Gaul, formerly the land of the Boii and Senones, now the province of Emiglia, resembles Venetia in possessing a rich alluvial soil requiring careful drainage, and a partly waterlogged coast-land. Its centres of population were mostly strung out along a ledge of higher ground at the base of the Apennines, and it was on this drier strip of land that the prehistoric culture of Italy attained its climax in the 'Villanova' period (*c*. 1000–600 B.C.).[4] The name 'Villanova' is derived from a village near Bologna, which was the principal seat of this early culture, and it was probably no mere accident that the manufacture of bronze and iron ware on a large scale, which was the distinctive feature of this 'prehistoric Birmingham', had its headquarters in this region. Though the Villanovans probably brought their knowledge of metallurgy from an earlier home in the Danube lands, their supplies of metal, once they had migrated to Italy, would presumably have been derived from a nearer source, and Bologna stands at the entrance of two easy passes across the Apennines into Etruria, formerly the chief mining area of Italy (p. 106).

Although the bronze and iron industries were presently transferred to the neighbourhood of the Etruscan minefields (p. 125),

[1] H. H. Scullard, *History of the Roman World from 753 to 146 B.C.*, pp. 7–9.
[2] On the high prosperity of Patavium, see Strabo, p. 213.
[3] Strabo, p. 207; A. Calderini, *Aquileia*.   [4] Scullard, op. cit., pp. 8–9.

the region of Bologna retained its importance as one of the main points of transit between northern and peninsular Italy. In the period of Etruscan ascendancy (*c.* 550–400 B.C.) it became the sally-port from which the Tuscans overran northern Italy, and their principal city on the northern flank of the Apennines, Felsina, was established on a mountain spur close by the old Villanovan site. Near the mouth of the neighbouring river Renus the Etruscans built the port of Spina, through which they imported masses of fine Greek pottery, now on view in the museums of Bologna and Ferrara. But Spina eventually shared the fate of Hadria (p. 119) and was sealed up with river silt, so that what was once a 'notable Greek city' had shrunk by the time of Augustus into a mere village.[1]

The decay of Spina was no doubt due to neglect of its harbour works by the next inhabitants of Emiglia, the Gauls (after 400 B.C.). During the period of Gallic supremacy in north Italy the Bologna gap served as an avenue for plundering bands to the rich cities of Etruria. When the Romans reversed the movement of invasion and followed up their conquest of north Italy with a peaceful penetration, they founded the colony of Bononia in the plain at the base of the Apennines (on the site of modern Bologna). The location of the Roman settlement indicates that its purpose was to serve as a road-centre rather than a fortress; but it had to share the trans-Apennine traffic with the colony of Ariminum at the tip of the Emiglian plain, where Rome's Great North Road, the Via Flaminia, entered north Italy. The continuation of this road, the Via Aemilia, linked up a chain of Roman colonies extending along the Apennine foot-hills and led on to the Po bridgehead at Placentia. The intermediate stations of Parma and Mutina (Modena) collected the clip from the flocks of the Apennine uplands and became two of Italy's chief clothing centres.

In the reign of Augustus a fresh attempt was made to provide a harbour on the Emiglian coast, to serve as a base for his new Adriatic fleet.[2] Formed out of a lagoon at a distance of two miles from Ravenna, the new port lay sufficiently far south of the Po to escape the worst effects of sedimentation, and a relatively strong tidal scour kept its entrance open for the time being. But its site was so marshy that the city had to be built on piles;[3] and

---

[1] Strabo, p. 214; R. L. Beaumont, *Journ. Hell. Stud.*, 1936, pp. 179–81.
[2] C. G. Starr, *The Roman Imperial Navy*, pp. 21–2; Nissen, op. cit. ii, pp. 250–6.
[3] Strabo, p. 213.

it did not lie altogether clear of the Po's area of discharge, so that in the Middle Ages New Ravenna shared the fate of Hadria and Spina and was wholly cut off from the sea. But in the Age of the Invasions Ravenna's semi-isolation on the land side provided it with a new if undignified function as a hiding-place for unwarlike emperors; in this, and in its pile-construction, it served as a pattern for its eventual successor, Venice.[1]

§ 2. LIGURIA

The rocky coastland in the northern recess of the Tyrrhenian Sea, where the Apennines run out into the Alps, has become, under its modern name of 'Italian Riviera', one of Europe's health and pleasure resorts. But its present-day gardens and palm-alleys are no index of its ancient appearance. Liguria, as this region was formerly called, was the most neglected part of ancient Italy. Apart from a few seaboard pockets of cultivable land, it was a waste of mountains thickly clad with forests, which under a rainfall of fifty inches or more formed an almost impenetrable jungle. This region therefore was mostly left over to its primitive inhabitants, until the Romans acquired an interest in it as a means of approach to two recently conquered territories, Cisalpine Gaul and Spain (*c.* 200 B.C.).

For the embarkation of troops bound for Spain the Romans came to prefer Luna (modern Spezia), a harbour with no commercial hinterland, but providing good shelter in its almost land-locked gulf, to the indifferent Portus Pisanus on the Etruscan coast (p. 124). Farther north the station of Genua was established at the head of a small bay, so as to provide a back-door to Cisalpine Gaul by way of the Giovi pass, the easiest across the Maritime Alps.[2] But as a mercantile harbour Genua in ancient times achieved only local importance, and the difficult up-and-down road connecting it with Etruria and Rome remained subordinate to the more commodious Flaminian and Aemilian Ways (p. 121), which always constituted the main line of communications between Rome and the north.[3]

[1] It is not unlikely that Old Ravenna had also been a city of refuge. According to Strabo (p. 214), Greek colonists from Thessaly had made a settlement there, but to escape molestation by the oncoming Etruscans had left it in the hands of the native Umbrian population, which maintained itself on the site.

[2] The railway through this pass might almost be described as the industrial life-line of Turin.

[3] The road to Genua was not completed until 109 B.C. (Aurelius Victor, *De viris illustribus*, § 72).

The most valuable industrial product of Liguria was the white marble of Carrara, which was in demand at Rome from the last days of the Republic. The forest giants of the interior, some of which attained a diameter of eight feet, furnished timber for Ligurian corsairs and perhaps also for the merchants of Massilia.[1]

§ 3. ETRURIA

Among the various regions of peninsular Italy, Etruria (Tuscany) stood out as the one endowed with the most varied natural resources. It lacked the wide plains of north Italy, but its undulating hill country was mostly cultivable, and its southern tip, falling within the volcanic zone of the peninsula, was highly fertile. In addition, it contained almost the entire mineral wealth of Italy.

The component parts of Etruria, however, were not of equal importance in ancient times. Its northernmost section, the valley of the Arno, which has been the pride of Tuscany since the Middle Ages, was a relatively backward district. Consisting of an almost level plain, it was liable to extensive waterlogging after the spring floods of the Arno—in crossing the valley it took Hannibal four days to draw clear of the inundation area[2]—and so far as our knowledge goes neither Etruscans nor Romans carried out any large embanking or draining operations. Consequently its chief cities, Luca, Pistoria, and Faesulae, lay away from the river at the base of the Apennines. Of the valley towns, Pisa was little more than a station on the coastal road. Florentia was potentially important because of its position near the entrance to three Apennine passes, of which two led to Bononia and one farther south to Faventia (Faenza); yet it occupied an area of only sixty acres, and although its name plainly stamps it as a Roman or Latin foundation, we do not know at what date it came into existence.[3]

In the period of the Etruscan ascendancy in Italy the heart of Tuscany lay in its seaboard district. It was here that the first towns with a distinctively Etruscan civilization were located,[4] and the cities that figure most prominently in early Roman history, Tarquinii and Caere, belonged to this group. The predominance

---

[1] Strabo, p. 222. [2] Livy, xxii. 2.

[3] The choice of dates appears to lie between the middle of the second century or the time of Sulla (Nissen, *Italische Landeskunde*, ii, p. 295).

[4] On the chronology of the Etruscan sites see G. Körte in Pauly-Wissowa, *Real-lexikon der classischen Altertumswissenschaft*, s.v. Etrusker.

of these places in early Etruscan history is not wholly to be explained by their proximity to the sea, for the coast is lacking in good harbours. At the present day it has two serviceable ports, Civita Vecchia and Leghorn (the ancient Centumcellae and

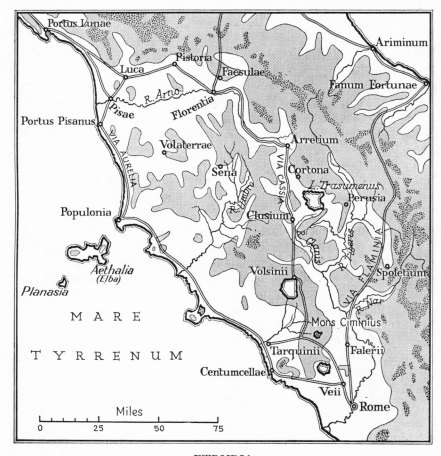

ETRURIA

Portus Pisanus); but Centumcellae remained an insignificant place until the Emperor Trajan provided it with breakwaters, and Portus Pisanus was of transitory importance only in the earlier days of the Spanish wars, when it served as a point of embarkation for Roman troops.[1] None of the early cities of the coastal zone, except Populonia, were situated at the water's edge:

[1] Leghorn was first developed as a port by the Medici rulers of Florence.

they stood back on spurs or ledges of the nearest inland range. The primary attraction of the Etruscan seaboard lay no doubt in the copper-mines near Populonia and Volaterrae and the iron-fields on the opposite island of Elba.[1] If it is true that the Etruscans were immigrants from Asia Minor, we need not doubt that copper and iron were the bait that first drew them to the Tuscan shore. But the more southerly towns of this zone probably owed their early prosperity to the intensive cultivation of the coastal plains. This lowland area, to be sure, needed careful drainage: neglect of its watercourses in the Middle Ages created the ill-famed malarial swamps of the Tuscan coast. But the systematic and efficient manner in which the spill-water was carried off in earlier days is attested by the numerous *cuniculi* or emissory channels which line the south Etruscan seaboard. These were presumably the handiwork of the city-lords of the coastal border, whose princely wealth was probably the fruit of a masterful policy of land-reclamation.[2]

The other most favoured district of ancient Etruria was its eastern border, containing the basins of the Tiber and of its tributary, the Clanis. This region also had its problem of dehydration, for the watershed between the Clanis and the Arno is almost dead level, and both streams emptied their flood-water over it. No final remedy for these inundations was applied in ancient times, for the cities farther down either valley protested against a scheme for deviating the Clanis into a new channel lest they should have to take their turn of being flooded by the new efferent.[3] Yet the waterlogging cannot have been extensive, for in laying out their main road to Arretium, the Via Cassia, the Romans did not find it necessary to by-pass the upper valley of the Clanis.

Among the cities of eastern Etruria the northernmost, Arretium, shared the industrial activities of the northern towns of the coast-land. Its clay-beds supplied a ceramic industry which attained a great if passing vogue in the days of Augustus, when its so-

[1] Diodorus, v. 13; Strabo, p. 223; O. Davies, *Roman Mines*, pp. 65–9. Small deposits of silver and tin were also worked in ancient times (Davies, loc. cit.; Daubrée, *Revue archéologique*, 1881, p. 235).

[2] On the drainage tunnels of Etruria and Latium see De La Blanchère in Daremberg–Saglio, *Dictionnaire des antiquités grecques et romaines*, i. 2, cols. 1591 ff. Export of Etruscan grain to Rome is mentioned in Livy, iv. 12. 9, xxviii. 45. 9. According to Varro (i. 44. 2) some Etruscan corn-lands yielded 15-fold (say, 20–30 bushels per acre, proportionately to the density of the sowing).

[3] Tacitus, *Annals* i. 79. In the seventeenth century Torricelli raised the water-shed and accelerated the flow-off by trapping the sediment of the floods, while the flood-water was discharged through sluices.

called 'Samian Ware' commanded the market for fine pottery in western Europe.[1] Of the more southerly cities, Cortona, Perusia, Clusium, and Volsinii sat proudly on high eminences overlooking choice strips of a well-watered plain. Volsinii stood at the northern edge of the fertile volcanic zone of western Italy; Perusia probably was a centre of the lumber industry which furnished Rome with constructional material (pp. 131–2).[2]

The southern section of Etruria is partly cut off from the rest of the country by the cross-ridge of the Ciminian range, whose dense forest had seldom been traversed until a Roman general, bent on a surprise raid into the country beyond, hacked his way through it.[3] The towns in this area accordingly tended to be drawn into closer connexion with Rome and Latium than with the rest of Etruria. Falerii retained a Latin element in its population, and Caere habitually cultivated good relations with Rome. But Veii was Rome's chief rival among the towns of Etruria. Perched on a broad platform of hard rock between two river gullies, it was long able to defy the attempts of the Romans to capture it by storm. Its eventual reduction gave the victors an additional piece of fertile land and complete control of the lower Tiber valley.

The breakdown of Etruria's early ascendancy in Italy and the decay of its civilization may be ascribed in the main to political causes. But the exhaustion of the copper-mines of Populonia was probably a contributory factor; and it may be surmised that the introduction of slave labour into the large estates of the Etruscan nobles may have resulted in a lower standard of cultivation and a neglect of the drainage canals on which the prosperity of the Tuscan lowlands depended.

§ 4. The Central Apennines

The central section of the Apennines contains the highest peak of peninsular Italy, the Gran Sasso d'Italia (c. 9,700 feet); but its loosely jointed ridges leave room for open valleys and level basins, and the friable texture of some of its rock formations favours a more rapid accumulation of humus and a richer provision of crop-land and pasture than is usual in Mediterranean

---

[1] On the export trade in Arretine ware see F. Örtel, *Cambr. Anc. Hist.* x, p. 394. (Arretium, however, was not the only place where 'Arretine' ware was made. H. Comfort in Frank, *Economic Survey*, v, p. 188.)

[2] Strabo, p. 222.

[3] Livy, ix. 36.

uplands.[1] But the cultivable area was reduced by the lack of natural outlets for the flood-water from some of its most fertile basins. In Varro's day the Rosei campi in the valley of the Velinus could be described as 'the breast on which Italy feeds';[2] but before the valley could become productive it had to be drained by an emissory channel half a mile long, which drew off the imprisoned waters of the Velinus (a work accomplished by Curius Dentatus *c.* 275 B.C.).[3] A similar but larger operation, by which the Lacus Fucinus was to be discharged into the river Liris through a three-mile tunnel, was not undertaken until the reign of the Emperor Claudius, and was partly frustrated by the subsequent choking of the conduit with limestone deposits.[4]

Lack of room for expansion, and consequent pressure of a growing population upon the means of subsistence, were no doubt the main reasons for the continual irruptions of the Apennine tribes, and especially of Rome's closest neighbours, the Sabines and the Aequi, into the Tiber valley, which fill the pages of early Roman history. The peoples of the central Apennines, however, were too scattered to form any lasting political union or military alliance. The small and loosely compacted federations of cantons which went by the names of Sabines, Aequi, Marsi, Paeligni, and so forth, could not stand up in the long run against the organized man-power of Rome and Latium.

By 300 B.C. a counter-offensive by the Romans had carried their arms across the Apennine watershed to the Adriatic foot-hills. The strategy by which the mountain peoples were finally pacified was based on Roman possession of the principal passes through the central Apennine chain. By a northward thrust they occupied the trans-Apennine route of the future Via Flaminia[5] and sundered the Umbrians in the north from the Sabines in the north-east. Reaching out eastward along the line of the later Via

---

[1] No other parts of Italy have received a richer tribute from Latin writers than the well-watered glens of central Italy. Cf. Ovid's reminiscence of his native Sulmo in the Paelignian country ('with bounteous flush of cooling waters': *Tristia* iv. 10. 3) and Pliny the Younger's description of that infant prodigy, the river Clitumnus (*Letters* viii. 8).

[2] i. 7. 10.

[3] Cicero, *Ad Atticum* iv. 15. 5. It is strange that Varro nowhere mentions the beautiful cascades of Terni by which the Velinus finally breaks out of the Sabine uplands into the valley of the Nar.

[4] Tacitus, *Annals* xii. 56–7.

[5] This route struck across the Apennine foot-hills and then threaded the base of the main ridge to the pass of Forum Sempronii, the best opening south of the Bologna passes. The colony of Spoletium which the Romans founded half-way was selected by the Lombards as their sub-capital of Italy.

Valeria, they took possession of the shortest cross-cut to the Adriatic and isolated the Sabines and Aequi from the Marsi and Paeligni. In the Italian War of 91–88 B.C., during which the Italian rebels operated on a wide front astride of the Via Valeria, the possession of this route was of decisive importance. In recognition of this the insurgent confederacy set up its capital at Corfinium, where two important side-valleys debouched on the main trans-Apennine route; but their failure to carry the Roman stations of Carseoli and Alba Fucens, the counterparts of Corfinium on the western slope of the Apennines, denied them the chance of a break-through to the western plains, and allowed the Romans in due time to resume their splitting strategy and by the recapture of Corfinium to disintegrate the rebel alliance.

§ 5. Latium

Occupying the central part of western Italy from the mouth of the Tiber to that of the Liris, Latium was described by Strabo as 'entirely fortunate and productive of all plants, except for a few marshy and unhealthy places along the coast and such parts as are mountainous and rocky'.[1] This picture was too flattering, for the mountainous and rocky section extends over a considerable part of central and southern Latium, and the seaboard is not only swampy but devoid of good harbours. As a result, perhaps, of a subsidence in the sixth or fifth century B.C., the coast hardly rises above sea-level, and although some attempts were made in ancient times to improve its drainage—the canal from Rome to Terracina may have been intended for this purpose as well as for transport[2]—the Pomptine marshes along it have retained their bad reputation until recently.[3]

But Latium also possessed tracts which merited Strabo's encomium. At its south-eastern end the valley of the Liris broadened into a fertile alluvial basin; at the north-western edge of the mountains and in the valleys of the lower Tiber and Anio, the volcanic dust poured forth in prehistoric times from the Alban Mount formed a rich topsoil. This friable upper layer, it is true, needed protection against winter wash-outs;[4] but a system of *cuniculi*—perhaps a legacy from the Etruscan occupa-

[1] Strabo, p. 231.

[2] Horace, *Satires* i. 5. 11 ff.; Strabo, p. 233.

[3] A systematic project of *bonificazione* has been in process of execution since 1920.

[4] T. Frank, *Economic History of Rome* (2nd ed.), pp. 4–11. The neglect of the drainage system in the early Middle Ages converted the Roman 'Campagna' (to use a modern name) into a desolate marshland.

tion—provided the necessary drainage. The tall-grown forests of Latium which evoked the admiration of Theophrastus[1] probably did not survive him for long; but the vineyards of its volcanic zone, which gained a high reputation under the early Roman emperors,[2] were a lasting token of its productiveness. Latium as a whole was therefore able to subsist a relatively large population.

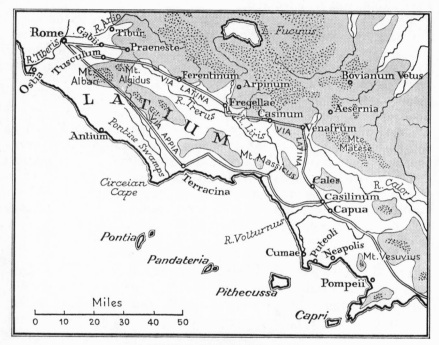

LATIUM AND CAMPANIA

Apart from Fregellae in the Liris valley and Rome at the other extremity, the principal towns of Latium were situated at the north-western edge of the upland zone on spurs of high ground overlooking the Roman plain. Such were Tibur (Tivoli), girt by a loop of the Anio; Praeneste, which stood commandingly on a ledge of 1,350 feet and was in turn dominated by a citadel rising to 2,500 feet; and Tusculum (Frascati), peeping out from its woodlands over the Tiber valley.

Two natural lines of communication extended from end to end of Latium. A lower route, along which the Romans eventually

---

[1] *Historia Plantarum* v. 8. 3.   [2] Pliny, xiv, §§ 48–52; Columella, iii. 2.

laid out their most famous trunk road, the Via Appia, ran straight across the coastal plain after a rise and fall over the foot-hills of the Alban Mount; the upper route ascended from the Tiber valley to the low col of Mons Algidus and followed the easy reverse slope into the basin of the Liris. The latter route had the advantage of rising well above inundation level, and it was along this line that the earliest of Roman military highways, the Via Latina, was constructed.

The facility of internal communications across Latium and the need for common defence, whether against the Etruscans across the Tiber or against the peoples of the Apennine border (the Aequi to the north and the Volsci to the east), pointed to an early association of the Latin communities. In the sixth century, if not earlier, a political league had been formed *ad caput Ferentinae*, at an unidentified point beneath the Alban mount;[1] but it was disrupted (probably *c.* 500 B.C.) by a thrust of the Volscians across the Liris valley to the coast, and never restored in its completeness. Contrary to the indications of geography, the political leadership of Latium was eventually assumed by the border town of Rome. But this city was marked out by Nature to achieve a dominion far wider than over Latium, and it was able to take Latium, as it were, in its stride.

§ 6. ROME

The site on which the city of Rome stood bore little resemblance to the usual location of an early Greek or Italian town. Instead of being built compactly on and around a single dominating eminence, it sprawled over a tumbled area of small bluffs and intersecting valleys.[2] The explanation of this abnormality is that Rome was an afterthought. The city was the product of an amalgamation of earlier village settlements on the upper ranges of the several hills.[3] Though these heights in no case exceeded 200 feet above sea-level, they rose for the most part in steep slopes above the surrounding valleys, and at some points presented sheer cliffs to them; and the valleys served for part of the year as ditches,

[1] On the early federating movements in Latium see A. N. Sherwin-White, *The Roman Citizenship*, pp. 11 ff. The league which had its headquarters at the temple of Jupiter on the Alban Mount was purely religious.

[2] The original 'City of the Four Regions' occupied 700 acres, and the 'Servian City' extended over nearly 1,100. Most of the Etruscan towns covered no more than 300–450 acres.

[3] On the genesis of the city of Rome see H. M. Last (*Camb. Anc. Hist.* vii, pp. 352–63) and H. H. Scullard (*History of the Roman World from 753 to 146 B.C.*, pp. 25–8).

for it required extensive draining and embanking operations before they were rendered immune from the Tiber floods.[1] But although the hills formed natural strongholds, they were of too narrow compass to offer refuge to any considerable population— the summit of the Palatine extended over twenty-five acres only, and that of the Capitoline over a mere twenty; and the defensive position of the city of Rome as a whole was by no means formidable.

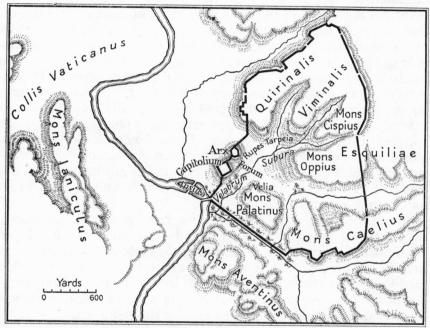

ROME, THE CITY OF THE FOUR REGIONS

But if Rome was not a natural fortress, it possessed the far greater advantage of being a natural centre of communications such as no other city of Italy could equal. Though its river, the Tiber, was not the largest of Italian streams—at Rome it did not exceed 100 yards in width—it carried a relatively large and equable volume of water and was the most easily navigable in its lower course. Its upper reaches served to convey to Rome a

---

[1] The Augustan writers were well aware that the valley-bottoms had once been marshland. Livy, i. 12 and Dionysius, ii. 42 (a *lacus Curtius* in the Forum); Propertius, v. 2. 7; Ovid, *Fasti* vi. 401. The level of the valleys has been raised since ancient times by accumulation of debris, mounting at some points to a height of forty feet.

large part of the timber and stone which the city required for construction-work,[1] and its last fifteen miles between Rome and Ostia could take sea-going vessels of light draught.[2] The Aventine mount, at the foot of which the up-river traffic discharged, therefore became an emporium for Latium in general in the days of the Roman kings.

But if Rome possessed the largest river-port of Italy, it never attracted to itself a maritime traffic comparable to that of the principal harbours on the Italian coast. The bulk of its imports from overseas had to be transferred to lighters at the river mouth and towed to the Aventine quays by means of oxen. The seaport of Ostia, moreover, suffered from the fact that it was a mere roadstead on an open coast and was rendered more and more inaccessible by a bar formed from the river silt; as a properly equipped harbour with protected basins it did not come into existence until the time of the Emperor Claudius (p. 27). In spite of its proximity to the sea, Rome could never become a world-centre of maritime trade like the chief river-ports of north-western Europe; its foreign trade was the result rather than the cause of its imperial expansion, and it was mainly limited to its own requirements.[3]

Rome, however, was more than a river-port. It was also a bridge-town, being situated at the lowest point of the Tiber where firm abutments for a bridge could be found, and an island in mid-channel at the most convenient locality for a bridge facilitated the spanning of the river.[4] By possession of this crossing-point Rome controlled the main line of communications along the western and more populous side of the peninsula.

Lastly, Rome had the advantage of a central situation within the Italian lands, being roughly equidistant (in a bee-line of *c.* 350 miles) from the corner points of Augusta Taurinorum, Aquileia, Brundisium, and Rhegium. It was therefore the natural starting-point of the fan-work of trunk roads across the peninsula, up the Tiber valley, through the Umbrian and Marsic gaps of the Apennine chain, down the river Liris, and along the Latin coast. As a river-port, bridge-town, and focusing-point of roads, Rome

---

[1] Strabo, pp. 222, 235.
[2] Dionysius, iii. 44. On the Tiber in general see Nissen, op. cit. i, pp. 315 ff.
[3] T. Frank, *Roman Imperialism*, ch. 14.
[4] S. B. Platner, *Topography of Ancient Rome*, p. 78. The site of the original Pons Sublicius is unknown, but by 291 B.C. at latest a two-armed bridge had been built where the island divides the river channel. Near the island there was a ford, but this could be used only at very low water.

equalled London, and within Italy it was less eccentric than London is in Britain.[1]

Thus Rome was marked out by Nature to be the capital of a unified Italy, just as Italy, by virtue of its large man-power and relatively central situation within the Mediterranean lands, was the natural seat of a Mediterranean empire. Rome's lordship over the ancient Mediterranean world was in accordance with the basic facts of Mediterranean geography.

§ 7. Campania

The name of 'Campania', anciently given to the hinterland of Naples, suggests that it was the plain *par excellence* of peninsular Italy. Yet it is not the most extensive of the peninsular lowlands, for it occupies no more than a narrow zone between the sea and a steeply rising façade of the Apennines, and it is cut in two by the mountain spur which ends in the promontory of Amalfi. But in the estimation of ancient writers it surpassed all other districts of Italy in its natural advantages, and indeed it is one of the most favoured spots of Europe.

At the present day the Neapolitan country is thought of first and foremost as a tourist centre. Its fame as a holiday resort was already established in ancient times. Its summer heat is tempered by a brisk sea breeze, and even the Mediterranean could scarcely offer a fairer seascape than the Bay of Naples as viewed from one of its enfolding heights, such as Posilippo in the north or Sorrento in the south. The Campanian coast accordingly used to celebrate a yearly 'high season', when well-to-do visitors from Rome resorted to it in order to escape the stuffy August weather of the capital; and all the year round it harboured a population of invalids and retired persons.[2] The inland, too, was reputed to be healthy; for this reason Capua enjoyed the doubtful advantage of being a centre for the training of gladiators.

But ancient writers reserved their most exuberant praise for the extraordinary natural riches of Campania.[3] This surpassing wealth it owed predominantly to Mt. Vesuvius. For many centuries previous to the great eruption of A.D. 79 Vesuvius had remained quiescent, and although it has been in frequent activity from that date, its later outbreaks have been on a far less devastat-

[1] The advantages of the site of Rome were aptly summed up by Cicero (*De republica* ii. 6. 11) and Livy (v. 54. 4). They went too far in describing the hills of Rome as 'particularly healthy', unless this be taken in relation to the lower city.
[2] Strabo, p. 246.
[3] Polybius, iii. 91. 2; Strabo, pp. 242–3; Pliny, xviii, § 111.

ing scale. But in prehistoric times it had carpeted Campania with an exceedingly thick layer of lava dust. The soil was therefore unusually well stocked with phosphorus and potash (two articles of plant-food contained in lava which are less easily replaced by ordinary means than nitrogen); and the spongy texture of the lava retained sufficient of the winter flood-water to keep the sub-soil moist throughout the summer drought, which extends over three months in this latitude of Italy.

Campania accordingly was the chief granary of peninsular Italy. In particular districts of it no less than three grain crops could be taken year after year, with perhaps a vegetable catch-crop to follow.[1] By the time of Cato the Elder it had also become a centre of olive culture,[2] and in the days of Augustus some of the choicest of ancient wines, including the strong and dry Falernian (the ancient sherry), were produced from the grapes of Mt. Massicus at the north-western edge of the plain.[3]

Industrial materials were also at hand which contributed to-wards making Campania one of the chief manufacturing centres of Italy. The clay-beds of Cales were utilized from the fifth or fourth century B.C. for the making of fine ceramic ware, and about the time of Augustus the pure white sand at the mouth of the Volturnus attracted the newly imported industry of glass-making to Capua.[4]

Lastly, Campania had the advantage of a good sea-front, which was denied to that other favoured land, Cisalpine Gaul. The northern side of the Bay of Naples was lined with a regular pro-gression of harbours, though these were not of equal value. Under the lee of Cape Misenum a submerged crater provided a sheltered basin which Augustus converted into the principal station of the Roman imperial fleet.[5] The port of Misenum, however, lay some-what far out from the Campanian centres of industry, and there-fore was not brought into use as a commercial emporium. A little farther inside the bay the crater of Lake Lucrinus provided an almost land-locked pool, where Agrippa could train Octavian's fleet in security from the weather and from Sextus Pompeius'

[1] Strabo, pp. 242–3; Pliny, xviii. 111.
[2] It is significant that Cato recommended Pompeii as the best place for purchasing oil-presses (*De re rustica*, ch. 135).
[3] Horace, *Odes* i. 27. 9–10, ii. 3. 8. Columella also mentioned the 'Massicum' and the 'Surrentinum' as among the 'noblest' vintages. Pompeii was also a centre of wine-production, though apparently it had no brands for export (Frank, *Economic Survey*, v, pp. 258–9).
[4] Pliny, xxxvi. 194.
[5] C. G. Starr, *The Roman Imperial Navy*, pp. 14–15.

raiders. But the 'Portus Iulius' which he constructed there was of narrow compass, and its bottle-neck entrance was liable to be completely sealed with silt. Augustus therefore abandoned it in favour of the more open but also more capacious station at Misenum.

In the farthest recess of the bay, the Greek colony of Naples occupied a site which was partly sheltered by the ridge of Posilippo and had easy communications with the inland centre of Capua. After 400 B.C. it displaced the older Greek settlement at Cumae, which lay near an open shore outside the bay; but it developed into a health and holiday resort rather than into a commercial town, and it did not become the principal city of the bay until the Byzantine age. Under Roman rule it was eclipsed as a mercantile station by its neighbour Puteoli, situated at the western edge of the Posilippo ridge. For reasons unknown to us the Romans preferred this more open site to the better sheltered station at Naples, and they improved it by means of extensive harbour works (completed by the time of Strabo), using for their breakwaters the local lava-earth (*pozzolana*), which was an ideal ingredient for hydraulic cement.[1] Thus Puteoli became the principal port of western Italy until Claudius built the new harbour at Ostia; and Puteoli held this advantage over the port of Rome, that Campania could provide it with industrial goods for export to balance its imports, whereas the traffic to Rome was mostly one-way.

The favourable situation of Campania for oversea commerce enhanced its natural advantages as a centre of industry. Thus Capua, which probably originated as an Etruscan bridge-town on the Volturnus, and may have attracted a select body of skilled craftsmen for the service of its Tuscan overlords, eventually became the principal manufacturing town of Italy. In addition to its glass-making industry, which was based on local materials (p. 134), it produced finished metal-ware with iron and copper imported from Etruria by the sea route. The iron, which came from Populonia in the form of partially smelted blooms,[2] was made up in Capuan forges into cutlery and ironmongers' goods, so that its secession to Hannibal in the Second Punic War provided him with an arsenal of the first magnitude. The bronze was cast into pots and pans which found a market at Carthage in the fourth and third centuries, and in the days of the early Roman Empire were shipped as far as Scotland and Scandinavia.[3]

---

[1] A point duly noted by Strabo (p. 245). [2] Diodorus, v. 13. 2.
[3] Frank, *Economic Survey*, v, pp. 197–9.

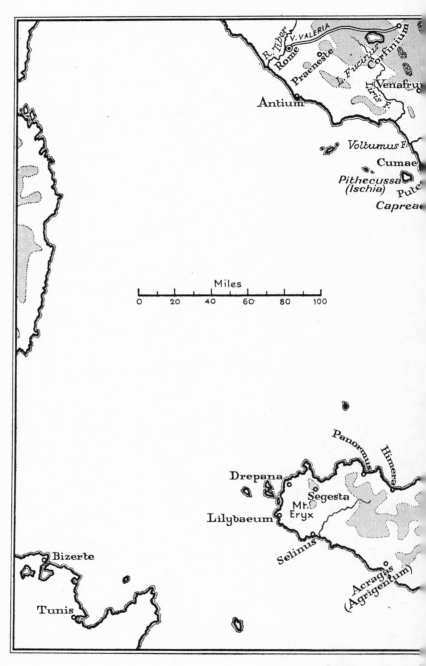

Miles

0   20   40   60   80   100

SOUTH ITALY

Sovianum vetus

A P U L I A

Luceria

(Mt. Matese)

Aufidus F.

Cannae

Beneventum   Canusium   (Bari)

Capua

Neapolis   Venusia

Pompeii

Brundisium

C A L A B R I A

Posidonia   L U C A N I A   Tarentum

Paestum   Metapontum

Pyxus   Sybaris (Thurii)

Laüs

B R U T T I U M   Croton

Mons Sila

Lipari Islands

Messene   Locri

Rhegium

(C. Spartivento)

Heraean   Naxos

Mountains

Aetna

Catana

Simaethus F.

Heraean Mts.

Gela   Leontini

Syracuse

Even the small town of Pompeii took advantage of its proximity to the sea in order to set up a small specialized trade. By way of its river, the Sarnus, it supplied itself with sprats and sardines, and re-exported them in the form of fish-sauce.[1]

The large man-power and varied resources of Campania fitted it to be the seat of a powerful state, such as might have rivalled Rome in a contest for predominance in Italy. But the Campanians failed even in the problem of warding off the marauders from the Apennine hinterland, who naturally coveted the rich spoils of the plain spread at their feet and had a convenient approach to it by the valley of the Volturnus. The Romans, called in to expel the highland raiders, naturally were slow to move out again, and it was in Campania that they fought their hardest battles, after Cannae, in the Second Punic War. The possession of Campania was indeed a stake of major importance to the Romans, for in addition to its native wealth and man-power it gave them for the first time a good sea-front and a convenient window on to the Mediterranean. With Campania firmly in their grasp, the Romans for the first time had a prospect of becoming a world state.

§ 8. THE SOUTHERN APENNINES (SAMNIUM AND LUCANIA)

The southern range of the Apennines is of lesser altitude than its central division: its highest point, Mons Tifernus (modern Matese), falls short of 7,000 feet. But it forms a more compact massif and offers fewer openings for routes from coast to coast. The two best approaches from the western lowlands were by the valley of the Volturnus and its tributary the Calor, which gave access respectively to the only two considerable towns of the Samnite country, Aesernia and Beneventum. The other chief places of Samnium, including the federal capital, Bovianum, could be reached only by upland tracks. Farther south, two practicable routes cut across Lucania from Pyxus to Metapontum and from Laüs to Sybaris, but there is no good evidence that either of these passages served as an 'isthmus route', so as to by-pass the Straits of Messina.[2]

The texture of the southern Apennines is also more uniform, consisting of the typical hard Mediterranean limestone, with few outcrops of softer formations. In ancient times Samnium and

[1] Frank, op. cit. v, pp. 252 ff.
[2] For a description of the Laüs–Sybaris pass see L. Ponnelle, *Mélanges d'archéologie et d'histoire*, 1907, pp. 263–9, where no archaeological evidence of an isthmus route is adduced. The pass rises to nearly 3,500 feet.

Lucania were still well wooded;[1] but with the exception of the sheltered upper valley of the Volturnus, where the olive-groves of Venafrum produced fine table-fruit,[2] they contained few pockets of cultivable land in their interior.

A special feature of the Apennines is that their steep front does not face in the same direction along their entire length. In their northern sector they fall abruptly to the Ligurian coast and descend more gently to the north Italian plain. In the central range they rise more gradually from the Tyrrenian Sea and drop more steeply to the Adriatic. In the southern division the gradient is once more reversed, for here the crest-line again approaches the western sea, and south of the beach from Salernum to Paestum, which marks the end of the Campanian lowland, the mountains scarcely leave room for any coastal plains. On the other hand, the slopes eastward to the Adriatic and southward to the Gulf of Otranto are less sharply tilted, and along the shore of the Gulf Lucania possessed several strips of good arable land. The more northerly of these cultivable belts, the plain of Metapontum, was in the early days of Greek colonization one of the principal cornfields of south Italy, a fact of which the ear of wheat on the Metapontine coins[3] is a grateful and graceful reminder.

On the southern border of Lucania the alluvial plain of Sybaris was another prolific wheat-land; it was ringed with sheep downs carrying good summer pasture and was traversed by a soft-water stream from the Bruttian country, the Crathis, which was well suited to wool-washing and dyeing operations. The fleeces of Sybaris were therefore exported as far as Miletus in Asia Minor (p. 164). A further contribution to the wealth of this favoured region may have been made by a silver-mine which is not mentioned in our ancient texts but was under exploitation in early modern times.[4]

The fabulous riches of Sybaris in the sixth century B.C. stood in sharp contrast with the comparative penury of its country-side in later days. This deterioration was no doubt due to the destruction of Sybaris by its Bruttian neighbour Croton (c. 510 B.C.), and a delay of some sixty-five years before it was replaced by the town of Thurii on a neighbouring site.[5] Long neglect of

---

[1] Livy, ix. 2. 7 (the Caudine Forks); Plutarch, *Pyrrhus* 25, § 2 (the field of Beneventum in 275 B.C.).   [2] Horace, *Odes* ii. 6. 16; Pliny, xv. 8.
[3] B. V. Head, *Historia Numorum* (2nd ed.), pp. 75–9.
[4] Nissen, op. cit. ii, p. 919.
[5] Thurii lay a little farther up the Crathis.

the water-channel in an almost level plain must have resulted in extensive marsh-formation, and the Thurians probably arrived too late to catch up with the damage and reclaim all the lost land.

§ 9. APULIA AND CALABRIA

The term 'Apulia' is now applied to the entire south-eastern stretch of the Italian peninsula from Cape Garganus to the tip of the heel. In ancient times it was restricted to the northern half of this region, while the heel went by the separate name of Calabria[1] (or Messapia). Geographically the two districts belong together.

With the exception of the detached block of Mt. Garganus, which presents a steep face to the Adriatic Sea, the eastern slope of the southern Apennines is nowhere abrupt, and some of the most extensive plains of peninsular Italy lie at their foot. A glance at a contour map might indeed suggest that Apulia and Calabria were eastern counterparts of Campania, but this impression would be deceptive. South-eastern Italy has the lowest rainfall of the peninsula, and the place of the Campanian lava is here taken by a dry top layer of limestone.[2] Consequently, in spite of its moderate elevation and low relief the inland does not lend itself to intensive tillage, and is suitable for little else besides sheep-grazing. Of the coastal plains, the northern section by way of contrast almost suffers from a surfeit of water, because of an abundance of springs which an under-bed of stiff clay here casts up to the surface. The rich rank grass of Apulia was the principal horse-pasture of ancient Italy. In the dry but sheltered coastal strip south of the river Aufidus a continuous olive-grove now stretches for 100 miles towards Brundisium.

Apart from the town of Canusium, the centre of the local textile industry,[3] the Apulian and Calabrian interior was sparsely settled; the larger part of the population was strung out among the towns of the coast. None of the sea-board towns achieved any marked pre-eminence over the rest, except the two outlying cities of Brundisium and Tarentum. The lack of a natural political centre among them may help to explain why the peoples of south-

---

[1] The name 'Calabria' has been transferred since Roman times from the heel to the toe of Italy (ancient Bruttium).

[2] For the dust-storm that blinded the Romans at the Battle of Cannae see Livy, xxii. 46. 9.

[3] On the woollen industries of Apulia and Calabria see Frank, *Economic Survey*, v, pp. 164–5.

eastern Italy never entered into any comprehensive political union, although theirs was a land of easy communications.

The history of this part of the peninsula is therefore almost summed up in that of its two chief towns, Tarentum and Brundisium. Tarentum enjoyed a unique combination of natural advantages among the Italian cities. It was built on a triangular tongue of land which interposed like an isthmus between an outer bay and an inner basin, eleven miles in circumference, with a narrow entrance which was spanned by a bridge and dominated by a citadel rock.[1] Its harbour was one of the safest and most capacious along the entire coast of Italy; in the absence of other good ports on the Gulf of Otranto, and on the Adriatic coast to the north of Brundisium, it was an indispensable station for ships plying between Greece and the Straits of Messina, and in the fourth and third centuries it became an important base for Adriatic trade.[2] But the harbour possessed more than a mercantile value. It was so well stocked with fish that Tarentum had a large fishing element in its population,[3] and it contained one of the richest purple-beds in Mediterranean waters. The hinterland produced a wool-clip which, in conjunction with the purple-fisheries of the harbour, made Tarentum the chief seat of the finer textile industry in Italy. Lastly, the local clay-beds gave the city a leading position in the manufacture of ceramic ware during the fourth and third centuries.[4]

With these natural endowments, Tarentum commanded sufficient wealth to engage in power politics on a large scale and to cross swords with Rome in a contest for supremacy in southern Italy. Its eventual decline may have been partly due to the increase of open-sea navigation in the Hellenistic age, which would diminish its value as a port of call; but it was mainly brought about by the Romans, who not only sacked the city during the Hannibalic War, but inflicted a more permanent injury upon it by diverting part of its traffic to Brundisium.[5]

[1] Polybius, x. 1; Strabo, p. 278.
[2] This may be inferred from the copious finds of Tarentine coins of this period in the Po valley (J. Déchelette, *Manuel d'archéologie préhistorique*, 2nd ed. iv, p. 1076).
[3] Aristotle, *Politics* 1291 b 23.
[4] P. Wuilleumier, *Tarente, des origines à la conquête romaine*, pp. 443–68. In the fourth century Tarentum produced tolerable imitations of Attic red-figure ware; in the Hellenistic age it helped to create the fashion in pottery with decorations in relief.
[5] The entrance to the inner harbour of Tarentum was in consequence allowed to silt up. A new cut into it has been made in modern times.

On the outer side of the 'heel' of Italy Brundisium possessed
a harbour equalling or even surpassing that of Tarentum, for it
was both commodious and completely sheltered.[1] The approach
to it led up a funnel-shaped bay and through a narrow channel
from the inner end of which two roomy basins bifurcated antler-
fashion. Given such an excellent situation and good crop-land
in addition to its grazings, it is strange that Brundisium never
received a permanent Greek settlement[2] and remained in a seem-
ing state of neglect until the coming of the Romans. Though the
general mercantile traffic of the Romans was directed, as was
natural, to the western ports of Ostia and Puteoli, Brundisium
under Roman rule became the principal packet-boat station for
cross-channel passages to Corcyra and western Greece. For this
traffic, which it has resumed in modern times, Brundisium was
particularly well fitted, for of all Italian ports it lay closest to
Greece.[3]

§ 10. BRUTTIUM

The peninsula of Bruttium (modern Calabria) is a surviving
remnant of an older land-mass ('Tyrrenis'), the greater part of
which now lies sunk under the Tyrrenian Sea. Its backbone,
Mt. Sila, is not a continuation of the Apennine chain; it forms,
as it were, a dam of older granitic formation within the ring of
folded limestone chains. It rises in sharp escarpments to a height
of nearly 6,500 feet, leaving scarcely any room for cultivable levels.
On its western coast, which is the most rugged of peninsular Italy,
Rhegium stood out as a pleasant garden city within a narrow
fringe of orchard country; but it possessed no natural harbour
and lay some ten miles away (to the south) from the Sicilian
Straits, the control of which usually lay in the hands of its *vis-à-
vis*, Messina (p. 147).[4]

The steep western face of Bruttium induces a copious fall of
'orographic' rain (rising to forty-three inches). It is therefore
still well wooded both with conifers and with deciduous trees,

---

[1] Strabo, p. 282.

[2] It has been suggested by J. L. Myres that the early Greek navigators, drifting
on a current that sets across the Adriatic, were carried on by it to the tip of the
Italian heel, i.e. towards Tarentum and away from Brundisium (*Proceedings of the
Classical Association*, 1911, p. 58).

[3] In winter the narrows of the Adriatic are frequently visited by gales, as Caesar
found out in his crossing of them in 49–48 B.C.

[4] The consul P. Popilius, who completed the Via Popilia from Capua to Rhegium
in 132 B.C. (Dessau, *Inscriptiones Latinae Selectae*, 23), had reason to be proud of a
difficult engineering achievement. Before the completion of the railway to Reggio,
modern traffic to Sicily mostly went by sea from Naples.

and in ancient times it was one of the most densely forested districts of Italy.[1] The lumbering industry was therefore the chief means of subsistence for the Bruttians, the principal centres of timber export being at Locri and Croton, which lay on the eastern and less precipitous side of Mt. Sila. But the high prosperity which Croton attained in the sixth and fifth centuries indicates some additional source of income. Some argentiferous slag-heaps in its neighbourhood are perhaps relics of an ancient silver-mine which gave to Croton a 'boom' period while it lasted.[2]

§ 11. SICILY

In terms of geology Sicily is not a prolongation of Bruttium but a resumption of Campania. The limestone of the Apennines here makes its reappearance, and the volcanic chain of western Italy, re-emerging from a submarine stage across the Lipari Sea, where the Lipari islands mark its course like a line of buoys, rises in Mt. Etna to its highest and largest peak (10,700 feet, with a perimeter of c. 80 miles). This monarch of European volcanoes has been active throughout the range of historical time, and in the prehistoric age it upheaved even greater masses than Vesuvius and flung them farther afield. The good work was also carried on by a cluster of lesser submarine volcanoes which delivered a rich mixture of lava and marine sediments. Thus the limestone core of Sicily has been streaked with heavy coatings of a highly fertilizing deposit. In the words of Strabo, 'the ash works havoc for a time but subsequently benefits the land, so that it produces fine grapes and rich crops'.[3]

Sicily therefore surpasses all other Mediterranean islands in the abundance and variety of its products.[4] True, it suffers from an apparent handicap in its summer drought, which extends over full four months: only 3 per cent. of its rainfall is delivered in summer. Yet for various reasons the drought is less detrimental than would appear on first consideration. In the north-eastern angle of the island Etna and the Heraean mountains rise high

---

[1] Strabo, p. 261. The 'timber from Italy' which Alcibiades enumerated among the prospective winnings of Athens from the Sicilian Expedition (Thucydides, vi. 90. 3) was no doubt the oak and beech and conifer wood from Mt. Sila. It may also be assumed that the close connexion which Dionysius of Syracuse established with the Bruttian town of Locri was partly in view of Locri's importance as a lumber port.
[2] Nissen, op. cit. ii, p. 940.
[3] p. 269.
[4] For details see V. Scramuzza in Frank, *Economic Survey*, iii, pp. 253–85.

enough and with a sufficiently steep scarp to command rainfall in all seasons. The flanks of the Heraean mountains were formerly well covered with oaks whose tall stature and huge acorns ('twice the size of any others') evoked the admiration of Diodorus.[1] These forest giants were no doubt the material foundation of the thalassocracies exercised by Dionysius and Sextus Pompeius. At the eastern end of Sicily the river Simaethus and its tributaries, fed by the snows of Mt. Etna, maintain a broad strip of perennial meadowland, which in ancient times made the island famous for its racehorses and milch-cows.[2]

But Sicily's chief compensation for its dry summers was an adequate supply of spring rain, which usually came at the right time for the growing wheat.[3] Thus climate and soil combined to produce an unusually heavy yield of cereals, with an average of not less than eighteen bushels per acre[4] and rising in certain districts, according to modern calculations, to twenty-eight bushels.[5] By the time of the Punic Wars, if not earlier, Sicily had become the principal grain-exporting country of the Mediterranean, and it probably remained so until the end of the pre-Christian era.[6]

Furthermore, the Sicilian lava-soil, like that of Campania, absorbs the winter rainfall like a sponge, so as to retain a store of water against the summer drought. The hilly interior of Sicily, therefore, instead of being given over to maquis, contains an abundance of good summer grazing; by the third century B.C. Sicily had become a large exporter of wool to Egypt.[7]

An allowance of sunshine which was generous even on Mediterranean standards—it was reputed that at Syracuse not a day passed without a spell of sunshine[8]—favoured the cultivation of vines and olives, which throve particularly in the undulating

---

[1] iv. 84. 1.

[2] Readers of Pindar will remember the prowess of the Sicilian racers at the Olympian and Pythian games, and students of Horace will recall Agrippa's Sicilian estate with its 'hundred herds of kine and steeds' (*Odes* ii. 16. 33).

[3] Theophrastus, *Historia Plantarum* viii. 6. 6.

[4] Scramuzza, op. cit., p. 260.

[5] J. Carcopino, *Vierteljahrschrift für soziale und Wirtschaftsgeschichte*, 1906, p. 142; A. Jardé, *Les Céréales dans l'antiquité grecque*, p. 58.

[6] The volume and importance of the trade in grain with Greece is somewhat problematic, though it is certain that by 480 B.C. Sicily held surpluses for export (Herodotus, vii. 158. 4). There is abundant evidence that, under the later Republic, Sicily was the 'provision-chamber and foster-mother of Rome' (Cato the Elder, quoted by Cicero, *In Verrem* ii, pt. 2, § 5).

[7] Rostovtzeff, *Social and Economic History of the Hellenistic World*, ii, p. 1257.

[8] Cicero, op. cit. ii, pt. 5, § 26.

country round Acragas. In Hellenistic times, it is true, Sicily had become an importer of wine, if we may judge by the many Rhodian wine-jars which have been discovered there. This decline in wine-production may have been due to the eventual loss of the Carthaginian market for this commodity, and to the intensification of grain-cultivation in response to growing demands from Rome. About 400 B.C. Acragas was a large exporter of wine to Carthage.[1] The storage accommodation of the principal producer at this period is described by Diodorus, on the authority of an eyewitness, in the following words: '300 vats were hewn out of the rock, each containing 860 gallons, and alongside them was a "swimming-pool" (κολυμβήθρα) with a lining of white-wash, out of which the wine was decanted into the vats.'[2] On the other hand, it is uncertain whether ancient Sicily produced an equivalent of the excellent Marsala vintages of the present day.[3]

Even the shrubs of Sicily made their contribution to the island's food-supply. No ancient honey was reputed superior to that which was collected from the thyme-blossoms of Hybla.[4]

A by-product of Sicily's volcanic activity was mined in the extensive sulphur beds of the low mountains behind Acragas. Since sulphur was the principal disinfecting and bleaching material known to the ancient world, it may be assumed that its extraction was actively pursued in Greek and Roman times, though the only references to these workings are contained in some stray Latin inscriptions.[5]

Another link between Sicily and Campania is formed by the great natural beauty of either district and the temperate climate of their breezy coastlands.[6] Under Roman rule Sicily followed Campania in becoming a tourist centre. Visitors in search of running waters and cool forest glades spent their holidays in the 'Sommerfrischen' of the Heraean Mountains.[7] But the principal attraction was Mt. Etna. The usual starting-point for the ascent was the small town of like name on its south-western border,

[1] Diodorus, xiii. 81. 4–5.
[2] Ibid. 83. 3.
[3] The lemon-groves of Catania and the orange orchards of the Conca d'Oro near Palermo are products of the Saracen invasion of the ninth century.
[4] Varro, iii. 16. 14. The Sicilian honey of the present day has an even finer flavour than the now better-known honey of Athens from Mt. Hymettus.
[5] Scramuzza, op. cit., p. 353.
[6] Naples and Palermo both have a mean January temperature of 50°; in July an afternoon sea-breeze blows refreshingly over them.
[7] Diodorus, iv. 84. 1.

which furnished the necessary night-accommodation and expert guides.[1]

But great as were the natural resources of Sicily, its prominent place in ancient history was due not so much to these as to its unique position in the centre of the Mediterranean and at its principal cross-roads.[2] Situated at the point where Europe and Africa reach out to one another, the island confines the intervening seas to two relatively narrow channels: the Straits of Messina are less than four miles wide opposite the town of that name, and from the north-eastern tip of Sicily the distance to the mainland is barely two miles; from Lilybaeum (Marsala) the Fair Promontory in Tunisia (C. Bon) is visible at a distance of seventy-five miles. Sicily therefore could serve both as a stepping-stone between Europe and Africa and as a gate by means of which the western and eastern basins of the Mediterranean could be shut off from one another. In ancient times it fulfilled either of these functions in turn.

Nay more, in view of its commanding position Sicily was fitted to be the seat of a central Mediterranean empire, and indeed in the days of the tyrant Dionysius, and again of the Norman kings of the eleventh and twelfth centuries, it appeared as if it might attain such a position. But a condition of such an ascendancy was that the island should be united within itself. From the geographic point of view such a union was not difficult to attain. Except in its north-eastern angle, the mountains of Sicily are neither compact nor uniformly high, and in between them several long corridors facilitate the passage from sea to sea. The crossing from Selinus to Segesta or from Acragas to Thermae involved no serious climb; and the Simaethus valley provided a broad avenue from the east coast to Enna (Castrogiovanni), from which two easy passes forked off to the north and south coasts.

So long as the focal point of Enna remained in the hands of the native Sicel population, there remained, geographically speaking, a chance of their reasserting themselves against the Greek and Carthaginian intruders.[3] But once Enna had been absorbed into

[1] Strabo, p. 273; Scramuzza, op. cit., p. 358.

[2] This point was well brought out by E. A. Freeman in his shorter *History of Sicily*.

[3] In the Slave War of 135–132 B.C. the insurgents set up their capital at Enna, which they recognized as 'the acropolis of the whole island' (Diodorus, xxxiv. 2. 24 b). When Ducetius set up a Sicel stronghold at Palice on the southern edge of the Simaethus plain (c. 450) he provided himself with a good raiding base but did little to disrupt communications between the Greek towns.

the Greek sphere of influence (after 400 B.C.), the Sicels were left without a good rallying-point, and the field was cleanly divided between Carthaginians and Greeks. The prolonged conflict between these two peoples was more than a scramble for the possession of Sicily itself: the main issue between them was rather which of them was to hold the gate between east and west. The Greeks were bent on keeping the gate open so that they might pass freely into the western basin of the Mediterranean, whereas the Carthaginians were intent on making it fast against Greek interlopers among their commercial preserves.

According to their own tradition the Greek settlers in Sicily made their first landfall at Naxos, under Mt. Etna. This belief was entirely in accord with geographic facts, for to a mariner following the south Italian coast the shining top of Etna reveals itself as soon as he has rounded C. Spartivento, and with this landmark in clear view there is no need for him to make his crossing at the Straits of Messina. From Naxos the Greeks spread out in either direction so as to occupy three-quarters of the coast and to acquire two of its best harbours. At the north-eastern tip of the island the semicircular port of Messina was sheltered from the gusts and currents of the Straits by a projecting spur of land; farther down the east coast the peninsula, on which stood the citadel of Syracuse (the so-called 'Island'), reached far out to meet an opposite headland, so as to leave only a narrow entrance into a sheltered and capacious bay.[1] Given its 'Great Harbour', where war-fleets of the largest size could be accommodated, and a central position within the horseshoe of the Greek colonies, Syracuse seemed to be marked out for leadership among them. On the land side it was comparatively isolated; this may be one reason why it always coveted the possession of the neighbouring town of Leontini, which gave access to the Simaethus valley and so to the easiest avenue towards the interior of the island.

At the western end of Sicily the Carthaginians held the three ports of Panormus, Drepana, and Motya-Lilybaeum. True to its name, Panormus possessed a roomy basin at the foot of the shapely Mt. Pellegrino, which gave complete protection from westerlies, together with a small recessed inner harbour. But it lay too far from Africa to serve as a main base for a Punic province in Sicily; therefore it did not come into its own until the Romans

---

[1] On the reverse side of the 'Island' a small funnel-shaped harbour gave full shelter from southerly and westerly winds. The main harbour is exposed to squalls from the land side.

developed it as the natural link between Sicily and Campania.[1]
Of the two ports at the western tip of the island, Drepana was
safe, but too narrow for large armadas. Motya, which stood on
an island in a sheltered bay and was artificially connected with
the mainland by a mole,[2] was excellently adapted to be a naval
station, but was less suitable as a base for land operations. In the
fourth century, when the Carthaginians were frequently drawn
into wars in the interior, Motya was replaced by Lilybaeum, which
lay farther south in the same bay in a more open position, but had
easier access into the hinterland.

The eventual and final conquest of Sicily by the Romans
deprived it of its function as a gate between the western and
eastern basins of the Mediterranean; or rather, the gate was now
thrown open to all. Henceforth the major axis of the island ran
from north to south; during the Punic Wars, and under the
Roman Peace that followed, it was the link between Italy and
Africa,[3] and it became for the first time an appendage of Italy.
This relation to Italy, which we nowadays take for granted, was
tardy in its inception. The reason for the comparative aloofness
of Sicily in earlier times may be found in the fact that Bruttium,
the nearest part of Italy, exerted little attractive power, and that
in virtue of its central position in the Mediterranean the island
was held for several centuries within the gravitational field of
Greeks and Carthaginians.

§ 12. Corsica and Sardinia

The other large islands of the western Mediterranean, Corsica
and Sardinia, have never played a part comparable with that of
Sicily. Corsica, the Cinderella of the Mediterranean family,
resembles Bruttium, in that it too is an emergent corner of the
sunken land of Tyrrenis; it is mainly composed of the same granite
and exhibits the same stark relief. Its highest peak, Mt. Cinto,
falls little short of 9,000 feet, and the whole land has a high
average elevation. Except for a narrow coastal strip on its eastern
face, Corsica remains largely uncultivated. The interior is now
mostly shared between forest and maquis; in ancient times it was

---

[1] Palermo resumed this relation after the Norman conquest in the twelfth
century and maintained it until the fall of the Neapolitan Bourbons in 1860.

[2] J. L. S. Whitaker, *Motya, a Phoenician Colony in Sicily*.

[3] For a power in possession of Sicily, Malta, in spite of its fine harbour, is superfluous as a shipping station. It therefore hardly figured in ancient history.

noted for its grand growth of trees.[1] But its lumber industry does not seem to have been developed like that of Bruttium, which lay much nearer to the principal ship-building centres.[2]

Sardinia is another survival of Tyrrenis, but it is not a mere replica of Corsica on a larger scale. In its southern half the Corsican granite makes way for softer schistous rock, on which a good loam for cereals has formed. In addition, Sardinia possesses a varied assortment of minerals, inclusive of silver, lead, copper, and zinc. Lying somewhat closer to Africa than to Italy, and having its only good commercial harbour, Caralis (Cagliari), on its southern coast,[3] it came first under Carthaginian occupation. After passing into Roman hands it momentarily became of vital importance, for in the Second Punic War, while Italy was being devastated by Hannibal and Sicily was lost to Rome, it became the city's chief granary; and when this function was taken over by Sicily it continued to be one of the 'frumentary subsidies' of the Roman Republic.[4]

Yet the Romans paid no such constant regard to Sardinia as they did to Sicily. One reason for their neglectfulness may be found in the bad reputation for insalubrity from which the island already suffered in ancient times. The fertile lands in the southern zone are low-lying and liable to turn into swamp in the absence of careful drainage, as they are partly cut off from the dry northerly winds by the central and northern mountain ranges, which strike across from west to east.[5] It is not certain whether the Sardinian fens were already infested with malaria in ancient times; but it is significant that the Romans made no attempt to colonize it, except with settlements of the Botany Bay type.[6]

Sardinia also shared with Corsica the disadvantage of lying off the main lines of traffic in the western Mediterranean. It may have been a station on an early Greek route from south Italy to Spain,[7] but from the point of view of the Carthaginians, who took sole possession of it c. 540 B.C., it lay in a commercial backwater.

[1] Theophrastus, *Historia Plantarum* v. 8. 2.
[2] The value which the Etruscans attached to Corsica in the sixth century (Herodotus, i. 166–7) suggests that its timber was imported by them for ship-construction or for smelting.
[3] The port of Olbia on the east coast provides good harbourage, but is cut off by mountains from the hinterland.
[4] Cicero, *De Imperio Cn. Pompeii*, § 34; Horace, *Odes* i. 31. 4.
[5] E. S. Bouchier, *Sardinia in Ancient Times*, ch. 4.
[6] Witness the 4,000 Jewish undesirables deported to Sardinia in A.D. 19. 'Si ob gravitatem caeli interissent, vile damnum' (Tacitus, *Annals* ii. 85. 5).
[7] Cary and Warmington, *The Ancient Explorers*, p. 22.

When Sardinia and Corsica passed into Roman hands, neither island became a regular stage on the route from Rome to Spain. Ancient sailors avoided the Straits of Bonifacio, which still have a bad reputation for their cross-currents and reefs: Roman ships bound for Spain usually put out from Luna or Portus Pisanus and struck a course well to the north of Corsica. Both islands therefore were isolated from a navigational point of view, whereas Sicily stood in the very centre of the Mediterranean fairway.

VI. THE ASIATIC NEAR EAST

§ 1. ASIA MINOR

WITH an area of *c.* 200,000 square miles, Asia Minor is the only considerable land-mass of Asia that has a Mediterranean front. It consists of a block of older formations that has been overfolded at its edges with two converging ridges of the characteristic Mediterranean limestone (p. 7). Its centre consists of a plateau, ascending eastward from 2,500 to 5,000 feet; its northern and southern rims, rising to 9,000 and 10,000 feet respectively, are made up of a series of overlapping ridges that admit of only a few narrow and tortuous passages between the coast and the interior. On its eastern frontier, where the southern coastal chain bends inwards and rises in Mt. Taurus to 13,000 feet, it is sharply separated from Syria and Mesopotamia. The easiest pass across the Taurus massif, the 'Cilician Gates' leading from Tyana to Tarsus, was regarded in ancient times as impregnable, and armies like those of Cyrus the Younger and Alexander, which contrived to carry this defile by surprise, marvelled at their good fortune.[1] In the north-east the border mountains run on into the still higher ranges of Armenia.

The only open face of Asia Minor is towards the west and north-west, where the plateau ends in a 'staircase' down to a piedmont country with river valleys shelving gently down to sea-level. The broad corridor of the central tableland is loosely streaked with isolated mountain chains which scarcely hinder communication along its major axis, and the river Halys, well known from a famous Delphic oracle as the boundary between Croesus' Lydia and Cyrus' Persia,[2] appears nowhere else in ancient history as an important political frontier. The passage along the corridor was facilitated by two trunk roads, both of them probably of Hittite origin. The northern or 'royal' highway ran from Sardes to Melitene on the middle Euphrates by way of Gordium and Ancyra; the southerly route, taking off from Ephesus, skirted the southern border range to Iconium and led up to the Cilician Gates.[3]

[1] Xenophon, *Anabasis* i. 2. 21; Quintus Curtius, iii. 4. 11. The tunnel driven under Mt. Taurus during the First World War ranks as a major achievement of modern engineering.

[2] Aristotle, *Rhetoric* 1407 a. The oracle is not mentioned by Herodotus.

[3] W. M. Ramsay, *Historical Geography of Asia Minor*, pp. 27 ff.; W. M. Calder,

ASIA MINOR

The historical function of Asia Minor accordingly has been to serve as the principal land-link between Asia and Europe. Being solidly joined to the Asiatic but not to the European continent, it might be compared to a jetty with its point of attachment on the Asiatic mainland; and this comparison might seem justified by the numerous invasions which Asia Minor has experienced at the hands of armies from inner Asia or Syria, and especially by its permanent conquest and colonization by the Turks. In earlier days, however, the invaders from the east for the most part were mere raiders who made quick progress along the central gangway but came in such small numbers that they could effect no lasting occupation. Parthians, Sassanids, and Saracens came and went; the only durable conquest from the mainland in ancient times was made by the Achaemenid kings of Persia, and this was not followed by any extensive colonization.[1] The land-approach to the jetty was broad, but it was obstructed by mountain masses and could not cope with much inward traffic. Ancient Greek writers indeed went so far as to assume that Asia Minor at its continental end tapered to an isthmus, and made a wild surmise that from a peak in its interior (Mt. Argaeus?) both the Black Sea and the Levantine Sea came into view.[2] This theory, however inaccurate, was essentially correct when considered in the light of Asia Minor's communications.

On the other hand, the sea end of the jetty was easily accessible and offered good berthing-spaces. None of the waters adjoining Asia Minor afford an easier passage than the Aegean Sea or the Dardanelles and Bosporus, and no portion of its coast provides better landing-grounds. In ancient times, therefore, most of the invasions of Asia Minor that had lasting results were launched from Europe. Phrygians in the twelfth century and Galatians in the third won a permanent foothold in its centre[3]; for over a thousand years (63 B.C.–A.D. 1170) the whole country was under Roman or Byzantine rule; Greek colonists were established in it from 1200 B.C. to A.D. 1922, and from the time of Alexander to the coming of the Turks Asia Minor was an integral part of Hellenedom.

Classical Review, 1925, pp. 7 ff. (where Herodotus' hazy notions about these roads are corrected).
   [1] Apart from an Assyrian settlement in Cappadocia in the third millennium (probably by peaceful penetration), no Semitic people has colonized Asia Minor. Cilicia was an Assyrian province in the early years of the first millennium B.C.
   [2] Herodotus, i. 72. 3; *Hellenica Oxyrhynchia* xvii. 4; Strabo, pp. 534, 538.
   [3] The question of Hittite origins is here left open.

After the downfall of the Hittite confederacy (c. 1200 B.C.) Asia Minor was never again united in ancient times except under the pressure of foreign conquerors. Its political partition was a natural result of its geographic incoherence, as shown in the seclusion of the midlands from the coastal borders to north and south, and of the comparatively small resources, and consequently thin population, of the central districts. The relative poverty of the centre was not due, as in others of the less productive Mediterranean regions, to sheer lack of level land, for its relief on the whole was flat or well rounded, but to an adverse climate.[1] While it shared the deficiency of summer rainfall which is common to most Mediterranean lands, it was also cut off by its mountain rims from the wet winds of winter, and only its western edge came well within their influence.

On the western borderland the annual rainfall, amounting to 16–20 inches, was sufficient for fair crops of cereals, though the statement which we read in Herodotus, that its harvests were exceptionally rich, was propagandist exaggeration.[2] Towards the opposite end of the plateau, in western Cappadocia, the tallest of Mediterranean volcanoes, Mt. Argaeus (13,000 feet high), fertilized the neighbourhood with lava dust and supplied it with snow-water in summer. In this region fruit-orchards of the Mediterranean type made their reappearance,[3] and the best horse-pasture of the Near East was found, on which a favourite strain of racers for the Roman circus was bred. Still farther east the region of Commagene, in the folds of Mt. Taurus, derived an adequate rainfall from westerly winds breaking in from the Gulf of Issus. But large tracts of the plateau were steppe-lands which produced little else but rough grazing for sheep and goats, and its midmost area was occupied by a large salt pool (Lake Tatta).

Some compensation for the infertility of central Asia Minor was provided by its varied store of mineral wealth. Cappadocia possessed silver-deposits which were already being worked in Hittite days[4] and still gave a good yield under the Roman emperors,[5] and a mine of cinnabar (sulphide of mercury), a rare

[1] On the climate of Asia Minor as a whole, see T. R. S. Broughton in Frank, *Economic Survey*, iv, pp. 602 ff.
[2] v. 49. 5. Herodotus did not give this as his own opinion, but put it into the mouth of an Asiatic Greek visitor to Sparta as bait for drawing the Spartan government into Asiatic adventures.
[3] Strabo, p. 535.
[4] Tell-el-Amarna letters, nos. 1 and 3. (Quoted in F. Petrie, *Syria and Egypt*.)
[5] The Cappadocian town of Caesarea was one of the chief imperial mints for the issue of silver money.

pigment which commanded a high price in the Greek and Roman markets.[1] At the western end of the plateau the marble of Docimium, a white stone streaked with purple, was extensively quarried for the use of Roman builders.[2]

But taken in its entirety, the central plateau was a land of slender resources, and it has never carried a large population.[3] Its inhabitants were sparsely distributed, and it was not until the Hellenistic and Roman periods that town life developed. Among the Greek cities (mostly foundations of the Seleucid dynasty) Antioch-in-Pisidia attained importance as a military base for the protection of the plateau against the robber tribes of the southern mountain border[4]; and Apamea, at the junction of the up-country roads from the Hermus and Maeander valleys, became the principal trading-depot of the interior. But at all times the larger towns have been strung out along the edge rather than across the heart of the tableland. Of the indigenous centres, the Hittite capital, Hattusas, and the present chief town, Ankara (ancient Ancyra), are to be found near the northern rim; Koniah (ancient Iconium), the original seat of Turkish rule, is close to the southern border. The middle part of the plateau has never produced an important co-ordinating centre.

The several coastlands of Asia Minor were not favoured by Nature in equal measure. Its southern seaboard entered little into ancient history. Along almost its entire length the mountains descend steeply to the sea; save in the region of Pamphylia, where the towns of Aspendus and Side once lay in a fertile plain, there is hardly any cultivable land along the coast. Lying open to the southerly winds of the winter season, the mountain slopes receive sufficient rainfall for a rich growth of tall forest. The coast of Lycia therefore became a dependency of the Ptolemaic kings of Egypt, who needed an oversea supply of ship-timber. The rugged interior on the other hand was left over to the native tribes, despite their predatory habits, until the period of Roman rule. This is not to be wondered at, for there was only one tolerable road from the seaboard across the mountain zone (from

[1] Strabo, p. 540. W. Leaf (*Journ. Hell. Stud.*, 1916, pp. 10 ff.) has pointed out that Strabo's '$\mu i \lambda \tau o s$' must be cinnabar and not red-lead (a cheap material that could not bear the cost of distant transport).

[2] Strabo, p. 577.

[3] Inclusive of its populous borders, Asia Minor now has less than 15 million inhabitants.

[4] The Seleucid colonies mostly stood on the rising ground of the foothills; the Attalid settlements, made in a less turbulent age, lay within the plain (Ramsay, op. cit., pp. 85 ff.).

Attalea to Apamea). The most trackless part of the coast, western or 'Rough' Cilicia, had no points of entrance except some narrow creeks which provided ideal hiding-places for corsairs working the trade-route between Rhodes and Syria. This stretch accordingly became the chief pirate base of the ancient Mediterranean.[1] Farther west, near Phaselis, a piece of the coast known as the 'Ladder' ($\kappa\lambda\hat{\imath}\mu\alpha\xi$), was described by Strabo as follows: 'It overlooks the Pamphylian Sea, leaving a narrow passage along the shore which is clear of water during calm spells, so as to be practicable for wayfarers, but when the sea washes over it by the action of the waves it is deep under water. The by-pass over the mountains is circuitous and steep, so in fine weather the journey is made by the coast road.'[2] The pacification of the mountain zone was eventually accomplished by the Romans; but it is significant that their most successful generals, Servilius Isauricus (78–5 B.C.) and Sulpicius Quirinus[3] (under Augustus), operated from the central plateau, where the pitch of the mountains was less abrupt.

The northern seaboard of Asia Minor falls into two sections: an eastern one (Pontus and Paphlagonia) facing the Black Sea, and a western one (Bithynia and Mysia) fronting on the Bosporus, the Sea of Marmora, and the Dardanelles.

The remoteness of the eastern section from Mediterranean influences is reflected in a different climate, which falls under the sway of a persistent northerly wind and is cool and moderately rainy all the year round. Strangely enough, the warmest part of the north coast is its extreme eastern zone, where Trebizond (ancient Trapezus) enjoys the weather of a Mediterranean Riviera. This paradox is due to the proximity of Mt. Caucasus, which screens it from the cold blasts of the Eurasian steppe. Though somewhat harsh in its skies, the rest of the Pontic and Paphlagonian seaboards belongs to the better-favoured regions of Asia Minor. Its mountains were as well clad with forest as those of the south coast; besides the usual varieties of shipwright's and carpenter's timber it produced more costly materials for furniture

---

[1] H. A. Ormerod, *Piracy in the Ancient World*, ch. 6. Observers were posted in crow's-nests on the cliffs to espy ships standing out to the open sea.

[2] p. 666. Strabo adds that Alexander's army struggled along the coast road with the water up to their waists. But according to Arrian (*Anabasis* i. 26. 1–2) a providential fall-wind from the north swept the sea away.

[3] For Servilius, see Ormerod, *Journ. Rom. Stud.*, 1922, pp. 35–56; for Sulpicius, R. Syme, *Klio*, 1934, pp. 131–5. Sulpicius was probably governor of the combined province of Galatia–Pamphylia.

and cabinet-making, such as boxwood and walnut.[1] Moreover the mountains, rising from the sea in terraces rather than in sheer cliffs, left room for a wider belt of cultivable coastland, and on their inner side they opened on to fertile valleys. Strabo's native district of Amasia, in the sheltered Iris valley, is extolled by him in these words: 'The plain is decked with dew and rich in meadow-grass, so that it can provide pasturage for kine and horses alike; of grain it is most partial to millet, which never fails here, for the abundance of water renders it proof to any drought.'[2] But Pontus was equally noted for its stone-fruit, which throve here in a land of summer showers.

In addition, the northern fringe of Asia Minor was rich in metal deposits. It contained workings of silver[3] and realgar[4] (disulphide of arsenic, valuable as a pigment), and in the land of the Chalybes (in the north-eastern corner of Pontus) it possessed hematite ore of rich iron content, which probably gave rise in Hittite days (c. 1400–1200 B.C.) to the earliest iron industry of Nearer Asia, and in Hellenistic days was reputed to produce the best steel.[5]

For internal communications the valley of the longest river of Asia Minor, the Halys, was of small use, being narrow and sunken; but the broad corridor of the Lycus served as a main artery for the Pontic area. This region therefore was a natural site for a well-compacted kingdom, such as the Mithridatic dynasty created in the Hellenistic age. On the other hand, the coast of Pontus and Paphlagonia was ill provided with shelter from the prevailing northerlies, for it contained only two good harbours, at Heraclea and Sinope. The latter was a typical 'anvil' port, and herein lay its chief importance. Sinope had poor natural communications with its hinterland, and as a gate of entry into Pontus it was inferior to its neighbour Amisus, at the lower end of the Iris valley. But because it had a secure

[1] Catullus' yacht, 'the fastest craft afloat', was built of Pontic timber which 'knew full well the box-clad heights of Mt. Cytorus' (Ode 42).

[2] p. 547.

[3] We may follow Strabo (p. 549) in locating Homer's 'Alybe, birthplace of silver' among the Chalybes of north-eastern Pontus (J. L. Myres, *Who were the Greeks?*, p. 313; M. Cary, *Mélanges Glotz*, i, pp. 135–6).

[4] Strabo, p. 562 (a horrifying description of the fume-laden mines).

[5] H. Peake points out that Pontus was likely to be the first important seat of iron-working, for its ores are easily accessible and *look* metallic (*Early Steps in Human Progress*, pp. 288 ff.). For a conspectus of Pontus' mineral resources, see S. Przeworski's map on p. 91 of *Internationale Zeitschrift für Ethnographie*, Supplementary vol. xxxvi. A good quality of coal is now worked near Eregli (Heraclea).

harbour it became the collecting-point for Pontus' maritime trade.[1] It therefore replaced Amasia as the capital of Pontus when its kings set themselves to convert their realm from a self-contained unit into an active and expanding member of the Hellenistic economy.

The western sector of the northern seaboard (Bithynia and Mysia) has a similar climate to that of Paphlagonia and Pontus. It does not share the mineral wealth of its eastern neighbours, but it possesses compensating advantages. In this region the mountains stand farther back from the coast, and several large belts of undulating and well-watered lowland extend between them and the sea. The open plain behind the Bosporus is excellent country for grain, and the Greek colonists who selected Calchedon in preference to Byzantium were 'blind' only in the sense that they had too good an eye for Calchedon's fine hinterland, so as not to observe the more varied advantages of Byzantium (p. 300); and the sheltered valley of Prusa is a delectable orchard country.

Bithynia and Mysia also have a better water-front than Paphlagonia and Pontus. The Sea of Marmora is as it were a natural creel for trapping the shoals of fish that migrate annually from the Mediterranean towards the Black Sea; the tunny, which was a standing coin-type of Cyzicus, was also one of its chief sources of wealth. Still more important was this sea as a meeting-point of trade routes. Its Asiatic shore, it is true, possessed only one good port, for Nicomedia was too deeply recessed in its long ditch-like gulf. But Cyzicus was excellently situated as a port of call on the shipping route between the Mediterranean and the Black Seas, and as an entrance gate into Asia Minor. Lying on a broad-headed offshore island, it had a commodious natural harbour in the intervening channel, and the bridges linking it with the mainland opened on to an easy avenue into the interior by way of the Macistus valley.[2] In addition to the wool of the Phrygian plateau, Cyzicus imported the electrum of Sardes (p. 161), which it long continued to use for its coinage.[3] The wide range which this currency commanded was a token of Cyzicus' advantageous position as a clearing-station for several lines of commercial traffic.[4] From Nicomedia another easy land route along the Sangarius valley led into the heart of Phrygia

---

[1] Strabo, p. 545 (also 'wonderful tunny-fisheries'); Leaf, op. cit., pp. 1 ff.

[2] See the enthusiastic description by Strabo (p. 575).

[3] B. V. Head, *Historia Numorum* (2nd ed.), pp. 522–5; P. Gardner, *History of Greek Coinage*, pp. 33–5.

[4] On Cyzicus' trade connexions see Rostovtzeff, *Hellenistic World*, i, p. 586.

and made connexion at Gordium with the Royal Road (p. 151). Lastly, Bithynia and Mysia lay on two main lines of communication between Asia and Europe, by way of the Bosporus and the Dardanelles. From 2000 B.C. at least these routes formed the principal link between the two continents in ancient times, and if they did not carry much merchandise before the Byzantine era, they were used again and again in either direction by migrating peoples and invading armies (p. 297).[1]

The north-western corner of Asia Minor thus held a key position at one of the Old World's principal cross-roads. One of the minor problems of ancient history is why its coast was not occupied more densely by Greek settlers, and how the kings of Bithynia contrived to maintain their independence in the Hellenistic age, when the importance of both the thoroughfares, transcontinental as well as transpontine, had become manifest to the Greeks.

But it was the western fringe of Asia Minor that contributed most to the country's history in Greek and Roman days. This region was credited by some Greek writers with having the best climate of all lands inhabited by their countrymen,[2] and indeed this claim was not ill founded. The eastern margin of the Aegean Sea shares the general weather conditions of the Greek homeland, but it is favoured by a milder winter; the summers are dry, but the heat is tempered by brisk sea breezes. In fertility of soil it far surpasses Greece proper. Besides several strips of good alluvial soil along the seaboard (as in Aeolis), it includes four broad river valleys—those of the Caïcus, the Hermus, the Caÿster, and the Maeander, whose waters are heavily charged with fertilizing silt; and in the hinterland of Sardes it contains a volcanic region (Lydia Combusta) with pockets of highly productive soil.[3]

The western rim of Asia Minor was particularly suited to the growing of figs, which require a warm as well as a wet winter; the Maeander valley and the plain of Caunus[4] in Caria were

---

[1] The original importance of Troy, as revealed by the remains of the Second City (c. 2000 B.C.), was as a station on the trans-continental route (V. G. Childe, *The Dawn of European History*, ch. 4). But in Homeric and historic times it had ceased to be an important gateway into Asia (Leaf, *Troy*, pp. 257 ff.). The chain of Mt. Ida cut its communications.

[2] Herodotus, i. 142. 1; Pausanias, vii. 5. 4.

[3] The volcanoes were extinct in the Greek and Roman era. But a severe earthquake in A.D. 17 served as a reminder that the Lydian earth still 'worked' (Tacitus, *Annals* ii. 47. 1).

[4] 'Caunus figs' were cried by hawkers at Rome (Cicero, *De Divinatione* ii, § 84).

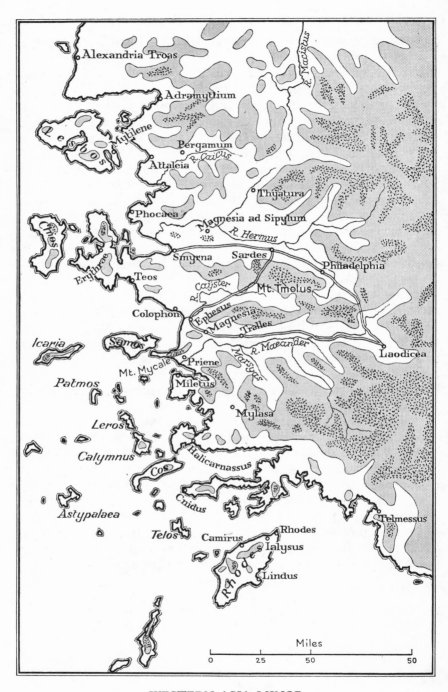

Miles

| 0 | 25 | 50 | 50 |

WESTERN ASIA MINOR

reputed to yield the choicest varieties of this fruit, the ancient equivalents of our present 'Smyrna figs'. The wines of Cnidus (at the south-western edge of the peninsula) commanded an oversea market and may have contributed to the extensive export trade of Rhodes (p. 102).

The towns of western Asia Minor also profited by their proximity to the wide sheep-downs of the Phrygian tableland to derive from them the material for their textile industries, in which they led all Greece. Before the Persian Wars Miletus had become the 'Manchester', or rather the 'Bradford', of the Greek world; in the Hellenistic and Roman periods Laodicea (on the Phrygian border) was noted for its soft 'raven-black' wool,[1] and Pergamum for its brocades and other fineries.[2] In ancient times the Angora goat had apparently not been introduced into Asia Minor, but the ordinary short-haired goats of Phrygia supplied the stuff for the felted cloths and blankets which were also a staple product of the Greek textile cities.[3] From Phrygia Pergamum also drew the sheeps' hides for the manufacture of parchment (*charta Pergamena*), which began to displace papyrus as the chief material for book-making under the later Roman emperors.[4]

The metallic resources of western Asia Minor were neither copious nor varied, but in the heyday of Lydian history the wealth of kings Alyattes and Croesus partly derived from the washings of electrum from Mount Tmolus. This rare substance, which was rated at ten times the value of silver, was in request as the principal material for the early coinage of Lydia and the adjacent Greek cities. A zinc-mine at Andeira in Aeolis was not much more than a curiosity.[5]

But the natural resources of western Asia Minor were of no higher importance than its communications. On land it commanded the easiest approaches to the central plateau, by way of the Hermus and the Maeander valleys, from which the two trunk roads of the tableland took off. The route that threads the valley of the Maeander and of its tributary the western Lycus was particularly convenient, for it made the most gradual ascent

---

[1] Strabo, p. 578.
[2] Rostovtzeff in W. H. Buckler and W. M. Calder, *Anatolian Studies presented to Sir William Mitchell Ramsay*, pp. 380 ff.
[3] Broughton, op. cit., pp. 619, 821.
[4] F. G. Kenyon, *Books and Readers in Ancient Greece and Rome*, pp. 87 ff.
[5] Strabo, p. 610; Leaf, *Commentary on Strabo, Book XIII*, 284–9. The reduction of the ore to metallic zinc was successfully accomplished at Andeira, as Leaf has made evident; but the process does not seem to have found imitators elsewhere.

to the plateau. Oversea communications were equally favourable, for the western coast was at sufficiently short range from the Levantine and the Black Seas to acquire a substantial share in the traffic of either, and, above all, it lay within reach of the Greek homeland.

The importance of these connexions finds expression in the fact that Ionia, which lay in the centre of the west coast and contained the starting-points of the two axial routes, was the real heart of the east Aegean lands. Farther north the district of Aeolis, being shut off from the interior by a belt of broken and forested mountain land (the western end of the northern coastal range), remained dependent on its agricultural wealth. The southern coastal strip of Doris was similarly hemmed in by the Carian abutment of the Levantine border chain; the excellent natural harbours of Cnidus and Halicarnassus, besides being cut out as ports of call on the Levantine route by Rhodes (p. 101), had little opportunity of hinterland traffic.[1]

Of the Ionian ports Phocaea achieved transient importance in the seventh and sixth centuries as a trading-station. At this period it may have served as the coastal terminus of the trunk route down the Hermus valley; but its chief scene of activity was, strangely enough, in the western Mediterranean, and its early fame was mainly due to the sheer enterprise and bold seamanship of its mariners.[2] As a collecting-point for the merchandise of Asia Minor it was subsequently eclipsed by Smyrna, ensconced at the head of a sheltered gulf, and more easily accessible from the interior.[3] In the Hellenistic and Roman periods Smyrna shared the commerce of the Hermus route with Ephesus. This latter city had a river-mouth harbour and was in consequence troubled with silting, and a mole which Attalus II of Pergamum built across the harbour mouth in order to narrow the river channel and to reinforce the scouring action of its waters had the opposite result of serving as a trap for the sediment.[4] But Ephesus had the advantage of a dual connexion with the interior by means of the two main river valleys. Its own river, the Caÿster, had indeed a

---

[1] Cnidus was screened from the open sea by an islet which was attached to the mainland by moles (Strabo, p. 656).

[2] Cary and Warmington, *The Ancient Explorers*, pp. 22–3. We may compare Genoa and Amalfi in medieval Italy, or Boston and Salem among the early trading towns of North America.

[3] Smyrna now suffers from the silt discharged by the Hermus farther down the gulf. Nothing, however, is said of this in Strabo (p. 646), who considered the site a fine one.   [4] Strabo, p. 641.

very short course, but an easy pass across Mt. Tmolus gave
it access to the Hermus valley, and a gap between two other
detached ridges, Mts. Messogis and Mycale, offered a· ready
passage into the Maeander basin. The landward orientation of
Ephesus is well illustrated by its history in Greek times. It took
no part in the brilliant naval expansion of early Ionia; it stood
out of the Ionian Revolt against Persian rule; and it was an intermittent and unpunctual member of the Delian League. But it
came into its own as the main base for Agesilaus's anabasis into
Asia.[1] As the terminal point of the southern trunk road Ephesus
secured the Seleucid kings' line of communications with the
Aegean area and therefore rose to be one of their sub-capitals.
Under the Romans, conversely, it became the principal port of
entry from Italy and 'the greatest mart of the Asian countries this
side of Taurus'.[2]

The other chief city of Ionia, Miletus, was not so well placed
as a collecting-point for the trans-continental trade. It was
separated from the Maeander valley by the Gulf of Latmus, and
its alternative route into the interior, over the cross-range of
Mt. Latmus, was never developed to the same extent as the roads
from Ephesus. The river Maeander, which continually chokes
itself with its own deposits and by-passes its own channel with
fresh loops, has, in addition, carried such masses of detritus into
the Latmian Gulf as to convert it into fenland, and Miletus is now
cut off from the Aegean. But in ancient times it still had, like
Smyrna, an unencumbered access to the open sea, and its inner
harbour was well protected by a protruding headland and the
offshore island of Lade.[3] Though it was also an important seat of
textile industry (perhaps deriving some of its wool by the sea route
from its daughter city Cyzicus), and probably also a large producer
of pottery in its earlier days,[4] its brilliant career before the Persian
Wars, when it was 'Ionia's jewel',[5] was mainly due to its position
as the focus of naval communications in the eastern Aegean.
This gave it pre-eminence in the early trade with the Black Sea[6]

[1] Xenophon, *Hellenica* iii.. 4. 16–19.
[2] Strabo, loc. cit.
[3] Lade is now a brown hummock jutting out of a rank green marsh.
[4] Eleanor R. Price, *Journ. Hell. Stud.*, 1924, pp. 190–202.
[5] Herodotus, v. 28. As the birthplace of Greek natural science, Miletus might
also be called an 'eye of Greece'.
[6] Of the ninety or more colonies credited to Miletus (Pliny, v, § 112), more
than forty-five have been verified (F. Bilabel, *Philologus*, Supplement xiv, pt. 1,
pp. 19 ff.). Most of them lay on the coast of the Black Sea and its approaches.

and with Egypt,[1] and brought it into close relations with Sybaris at the western margin of the Greek world.[2]

Appendix

CYPRUS

THE island of Cyprus may be affiliated to Asia Minor on the ground that this is the part of the Asiatic mainland to which it lies closest. But this attribution is not wholly borne out by its general geography and history. Its entire northern side is occupied by a mountain range which falls sharply to the sea, and the harbourless coast is exposed to violent fall-winds sweeping across from Mt. Taurus.

The south-western seaboard is similarly penned in by the massive ridge of Mt. Aoüs (modern Troödos), which rises to more than 6,000 feet. The only open parts of the coast, on which the principal towns of ancient times were situated, lie at the east and west ends, and the only extensive plain forms a broad corridor across the centre of Cyprus. Cut off to north and south-west from rain-bearing winds, this plain experiences a severe summer drought; an air-current from the south will sometimes bring clouds—but of locusts—from the African desert. Yet a good supply of snow-water from Mt. Aoüs compensates for lack of rainfall.

The chief product of the plain was its wine, which still holds first place among Levantine vintages, and its grain, which was being exported to Athens in the fourth century B.C., if not before. But in ancient times the peculiar wealth of Cyprus lay in its mountains, which, besides being densely forested,[3] contained some of the richest copper-mines of the Mediterranean area. It was these natural products rather than its central position in the Levantine Sea that gave Cyprus its former importance.

Partly, perhaps, because of its lack of natural harbours, and because of interception of its traffic by Rhodes (p. 102), Cyprus played a lesser part as a station on the route between Greece and Syria or Egypt than might have been expected. Though it was intensely colonized by Achaean settlers in the Late Minoan age, it apparently made no regular contacts with the Minoans from

[1] H. Prinz, 'Funde aus Naukratis' (*Klio*, Beiheft vii, pp. 14–39).
[2] Herodotus, vi. 21. 1. This trade connexion may have rested on the importation of a special count of wool from Sybaris.
[3] According to Eratosthenes (quoted by Strabo, p. 684) even the lowlands of Cyprus had once been overgrown with jungle.

Crete[1] and received no large numbers of Greek immigrants after 1000 B.C. At the end of the Persian Wars it came into temporary prominence as an Athenian base for descents on Phoenicia and Egypt—a function which it resumed during the Third Crusade— but it was eventually abandoned to Persia, presumably because it lay beyond the effective radius of action of the Athenian fleet. In the Hellenistic period it was a valuable prize for the Ptolemies because of its supplies of ship-timber, a commodity which Egypt lacked (p. 211). But it benefited less than Rhodes from the opening up of the Levantine Seas, and under the Romans also it remained, relatively speaking, in a commercial backwater.[2]

§ 2. SYRIA

The term 'Syria' is here taken to include Palestine, Transjorda- nia, and the eastern part of Cilicia (Cilicia Pedias). The range of Mt. Amanus which marks off eastern Cilicia from Syria does not constitute an effective barrier between them; it consists of a single narrow ridge and offers an easy passage by way of the 'Syrian Gate' (the Beilan Pass, 2,400 feet high). The real dividing- line between Syria and its western neighbours is the great mass of Mt. Taurus (p. 151), which the Greeks and Romans rightly regarded as the natural boundary for the Seleucid kingdom towards the west.[3]

Syria is situated at the very margin of the Mediterranean area, yet it conforms closely to the general Mediterranean type, and has a better claim to rank as a Mediterranean country than its more centrally situated neighbour Asia Minor.

The climate of Syria has apparently undergone some modifica- tion since the days of Greece and Rome, for the area of culti- vated land along its eastern border has undoubtedly shrunk since ancient times.[4] But it is not clear how far the disappearance and the desiccation of river courses has been due to sheer lack of rain, and to what extent it has been caused by neglect of water regula- tions consequent on political insecurity and by the choking of water-points under the dust stirred up by Bedouin raiders from the desert margin. In any case, Syria as a whole has been con- tinuously under a climate of Mediterranean type. Its winters

[1] S. Casson, *Ancient Cyprus*, ch. 2; G. F. Hill, *History of Cyprus*, i, ch. 3.
[2] Broughton (op. cit.) comments on the paucity of information about Roman Cyprus; Rostovtzeff (*Roman Empire*) never mentions it.
[3] In 189 B.C. the Romans imposed upon Antiochus III the following condition: 'excedito urbibus agris vicis castellis cis *Taurum montem*' (Livy, xxxviii. 38. 3).
[4] M. P. Nilsson, *Imperial Rome*, pp. 186–9; E. Huntington, *Palestine*, ch. 12.

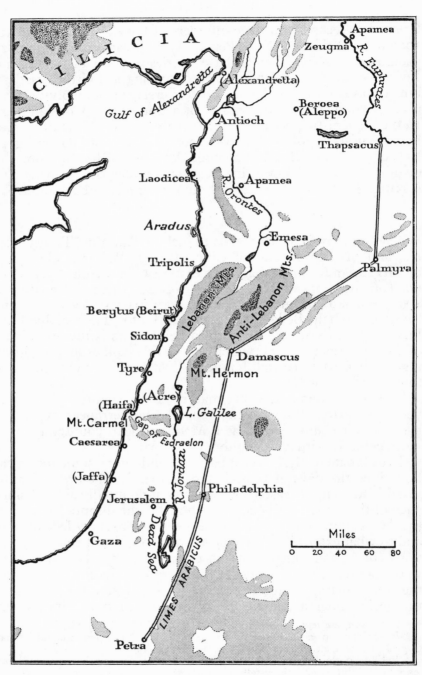

PALESTINE AND SYRIA

are wet and boisterous and sunny, with maxima of rainfall in
early autumn and early spring (the 'former' and 'latter' rains of
the Bible); its summers are almost rainless, and in Palestine the
drought may last from May to October.

A unique feature in the structure of Syria is the deep fissure,
caused by the greatest of all subsidences in the earth's crust,
along the line of the lower Jordan valley and the Dead Sea,
which lies 1,300 feet below sea-level.[1] But the chief tectonic
agency in the making of the country has been an upfolding of
a series of limestone ridges running parallel to the coast. The
texture of Syria is therefore similar to that of Greece and Italy;
its limestone formations store the rain-water in subterranean
caverns rather than in the topsoil, so that cultivation and settlement are largely dependent on the vicinity of springs. The
mountains are now largely stripped of their forest growth, but
the cedars and firs of Mt. Lebanon supplied the shipyards of the
Levant from at least 3000 B.C. to the end of ancient times.[2] The
lesser heights are covered with bush and scrub, and it was in this
sense that ancient Judaea was a 'land of milk and honey'—its
uplands were pasturing-ground for sheep and goats and bees.
Under the influence of the spring rains the lowlands yielded an
excellent wheat,[3] and the products of its orchards, figs, olives,
and especially wine, were exported as delicacies.[4]

The area of good land in Syria is relatively large: in this respect
the country is more comparable to Italy than to Greece. On its
north-western margin Cilicia Pedias occupies a wide belt of level
country which is well watered by the snows of Mt. Taurus;
in ancient times its flax supplied the material for an important
linen industry at Tarsus.[5] Another choice piece is the valley of
the river Orontes, which follows a leisurely course through water-
meadows reminiscent to Macedonian colonists of their native
glens by the Axius and the Haliacmon. At Apamea on the middle

[1] Other earth-convulsions on this faulting-line have produced the secondary
subsidence which engulfed Sodom and Gomorrah, the great earthquake of Antioch
in A.D. 115, and the volcanoes of the land of Midian (near the Gulf of Akaba).

[2] J. R. Breasted, *Ancient Records*, i, nos. 146–7.

[3] F. M. Heichelheim, in T. Frank, *Economic Survey of Rome*, v, pp. 127–8.
Syrian wheat was of better quality than Egyptian. But the theory that Syria was
the native place of wheat has been invalidated by Prof. Vavilov, who traces the
origins of wheat back to Abyssinia or Afghanistan.

[4] The cultivation of olives in Syria has declined since Roman times, but numerous
surviving oil-presses testify to its former importance.

[5] Dio Chrysostom, *Oratio 34*, §§ 21–3. Paul of Tarsus plied his craft as a tent-
maker at Corinth (Acts xviii. 3).

Orontes the Seleucid kings set up their 'Poona encampments', with stud farms for their corps of cavalry and elephants.[1] Farther down the river they planted the groves of Daphnae, the garden suburb of Antioch, thanks to which Antioch was reputed the most delectable of ancient capitals, the Vienna of the Hellenistic world. Another garden city of Syria, Damascus, is beholden for its plum orchards to the river Pharpar, which irrigates the environing plateau with the snows of Mt. Hermon before it loses itself in the desert. In Palestine the loosely jointed mountains of Samaria make room for numerous combes of arable land and good pasture. The gently shelving plain of Sharon on its seaboard is dependent for its harvests on careful water-conservation, but whenever its irrigation system has been in good working order it has been one of the chief seats of the Levantine orchard industry.[2]

Farther inland the valley of the lower Jordan makes amends for its stifling heat, which now and then is stoked up to a veritable oven atmosphere by fall-winds from the mountains on its western edge, with its tropical exuberance of vegetation. The date-palms and balsam-trees that flourished here[3] would not thrive anywhere else within easy distance of the Mediterranean coast, and their produce commanded such prices as an exotic rarity might fetch. Lastly, the plateau of Transjordania is lined with a continuous belt of fertile land, and it is sprayed with a steady jet of moisture due to the condensation of the vapour-bearing air that ascends the long and steep eastern scarp of the Jordan valley (by a rise from c. 1,000 feet below sea-level to 2,000 feet above). Its southern end, the land of Moab, and the volcanic soil of the Jebel-Hauran at its northern edge, receive a sufficient water-supply to produce large crops of wheat. The intermediate district of Gilead, which benefits further by its copious springs, is a parkland with rich grazing and patches of deciduous woodland; it has been compared with the more fertile regions of South England.[4] The remoter parts of Transjordania, where desert conditions begin to set in and irrigation for crops is essential, were made productive by the Romans, who not only guarded them against Bedouin raids, but made systematic provision for storing their intermittent rain-water.

[1] Strabo, p. 752 (an excellent description).
[2] The Sharon valley has now captured a world market with its export of 'Jaffa' oranges.				[3] Diodorus, xix. 98. 7.
[4] Good descriptions of Transjordania will be found in C. F. Kent, *Biblical Geography and History*, ch. 7, and E. Huntington, *Palestine*, chs. 10 and 11.

Deposits of copper and iron were formerly worked in Mt. Lebanon and at other stray points of Syria, but nowhere on a large scale. The cutlery of Damascus, which is first heard of under the Roman emperors, probably derived its material in the form of crucible steel from India.[1] On the shores of the Dead Sea a malodorous mineral welled up. In the words of Diodorus, 'all round the lake a smell of asphalt assails one with a noisome breath'.[2] This material was exported to Egypt as an ingredient in mummification, but not in any large quantities. The Mediterranean Sea was the source of the Phoenicians' industrial as well as of their commercial prosperity. The fine sand of the Sidonian beach was suitable for glass-making,[3] and the shallow waters near Tyre were rich in mussel-beds from which the most lustrous of purple dyes was extracted.

Syria was neither a mass-producer of cereals nor a seat of heavy industry in ancient times; but it raised choice brands of orchard produce and manufactured goods of high quality. Its export trade was not as voluminous as that of Egypt, but it was probably more lucrative.[4]

The ancient history of Syria was determined even more by its peculiar lines of communication than by its special natural resources. Its outer frontiers form a series of difficult barriers, albeit with considerable gaps in them. It is sundered from its Asiatic neighbours, Asia Minor and Mesopotamia, by the high chain of Mt. Taurus (p. 151) and by a wide belt of desert; and another desert zone cuts it off from Egypt.[5] Its sea-front is of very unequal value. The coast of Cilicia Pedias and the Gulf of Skanderoon provide good landing-places, but the hinterland is a cul-de-sac between Mts. Taurus and Amanus.[6] The northern

---

[1] E. H. Warmington, *The Commerce between the Roman Empire and India*, p. 258; Rostovtzeff, *Hellenistic World*, ii, p. 1218. The reason why Damascus became a seat of the cutlery industry was no doubt because of its position as a receiving centre of the overland trade from the East. The waters of the Pharpar were neither better nor worse than others for the tempering of steel.

[2] xix. 98. 6.

[3] Glass-making, however, did not have its origin in Phoenicia, as Pliny asserts in a well-known story (xxxvi, §§ 190–1), but in Egypt. The chief contribution of the Sidonians to the glass-making industry was the invention of the blow-pipe (T. Frank, *Economic History*, 2nd ed., pp. 225–7).

[4] It is significant that the cost of living in Syria was higher than in Egypt or Mesopotamia (Heichelheim, op. cit., p. 178).

[5] The successful crossing of this desert by large armies has only been possible as a result of careful organization, e.g. by Cambyses (Herodotus, iii. 9) and Antigonus (Diodorus, xx. 73. 3) in ancient times, and more recently by Allenby.

[6] The harbour of Skanderoon (Alexandretta) lies on a recently formed strip of alluvium (C. L. Woolley, *Journ. Hell. Stud.*, 1938, pp. 2–3).

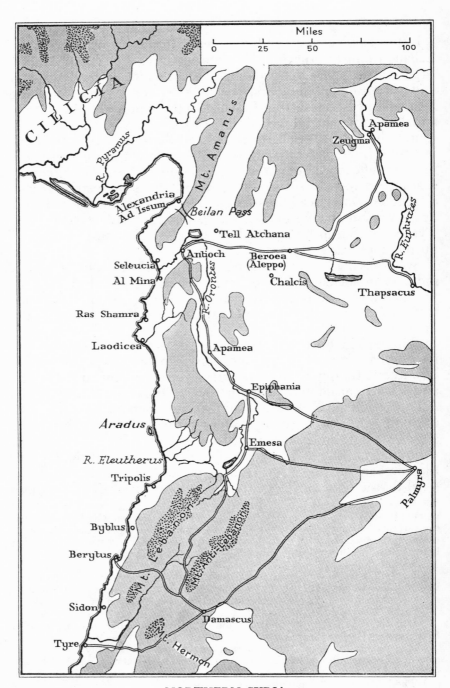

NORTHERN SYRIA

seaboard of Syria proper is rocky and harbourless; Seleucia, the
port of Antioch, lay on an open roadstead, five miles from the
mouth of the Orontes,[1] where sea-going vessels discharged their
cargoes into lighters for towage up the river. The southern
stretch of coast, on the other hand, is a continuous flat beach,
but it extends all the way to Mt. Carmel in an almost unbroken
straight line and offers scant protection against the westerly winds,
which here set up a strong indraught against a lee shore. Its
only good harbour in ancient times, Caesarea, was an artificial
basin, constructed at enormous expense by King Herod.[2]

Yet Syria, far from being a hermit country, has functioned
continually as a land of passage. It is the inevitable land-link
between Asia and Africa, and it also provides the shortest and
easiest connexion between the Mediterranean and inner Asia.
The ancient starting-points for journeys into the continent
(Zeugma-Apamea, equivalent to the Carchemish of the Old
Testament, and Thapsacus) were situated on the middle course
of the Euphrates, where the river approached most closely to the
Mediterranean seaboard and had an easy land-connexion with
the Orontes valley by way of the low plateau of Aleppo (ancient
Beroea). No other road on earth has a longer record of the
passage of armies and of peaceful traders than the route between
Upper Syria and Mesopotamia. From the time of Sargon of
Akkad (c. 2800 B.C.) Mesopotamian war-lords used it for their
breaks-through to the western sea; conversely, Egyptian Pharaohs
ever since the campaign of Thothmes III (c. 1475 B.C.) struck
back along it towards the Euphrates. In the fifteenth and four-
teenth centuries Minoan seafarers perhaps established trading-
posts at the near end of this thoroughfare at Ras Shamra and
Minet el Beida, some thirty miles south of the Orontes,[3] and at
Tell Atchana, fifteen miles north-east of Antioch.[4] A neighbouring settlement at Al Mina, on the high south bank of the Orontes
delta, similarly served Greek merchants between 750 and 300
B.C.[5] Greco-Macedonian kings from the time of Alexander set
out along the same highway for their anabases into the heart of

---

[1] Strabo, p. 151. In spite of its distance from the Orontes, the site is now
silted up.

[2] Jaffa is situated on an open roadstead.

[3] C. F. A. Schaeffer, C. Virollaud, and others in *Syria*, vols. x–xx (1929–39). But
see Sydney Smith, *Antiquaries Journal*, 1942, pp. 87–112.

[4] C. L. Woolley, *Journ. Hell. Stud.*, 1936, pp. 125–32.

[5] C. L. Woolley, ibid., 1938, pp. 1–30, 133–70 (especially pp. 3–4); M. Robertson,
ibid., 1940, pp. 2–21. It is noteworthy that commercial intercourse at Al Mina
was not interrupted in the period of the Persian Wars.

Asia, and Roman generals used it for their invasions of the Parthian empire. In the days of the Sino-Roman world peace (first and second centuries A.D.) the Aleppo road formed the last stage of the 'silk-route' from the Yellow Sea to the Mediterranean.[1] When the Seleucid monarchs established their capital at Antioch, they chose a site which gave them a window on to the Mediterranean and easy communications with the Asiatic continent.

Another link between Syria and Mesopotamia was furnished by a more southerly track which took off from Damascus or Emesa and proceeded by way of Palmyra to Dura-Europus. Albeit a desert route, it could be made practicable for caravans and even for armies (pp. 186–7).

On the sea-front of Syria the coast under Mt. Lebanon contains small strips of fertile land whose foreshore receives some protection against wind and wave from adjacent islands or lines of reefs. These were the sites on which the Phoenicians built their cities and the bases from which they opened up the entire Mediterranean for mercantile traffic. Sidon was screened by an island, and Tyre by a chain of reefs.[2] Thus Syria became the starting-point of travel to the Yellow Sea and to the Atlantic Ocean.

Like a true Mediterranean country, Syria is a complex of mountains and valleys. Its internal communications are therefore canalized along certain predestined routes. In its central latitudes the parallel ranges of Lebanon (10,500 feet) and Anti-Lebanon (8,500 feet) form a double barrier between Phoenicia and its hinterland. In Palestine the river Jordan, which in its upper course cascades from a plateau of 1,000 feet above sea-level into a valley 700 feet below, descends another 600 feet on its way to the Dead Sea; on either side the land rises in steep gradients to 2,000 feet or more above sea-level. Thus isolated at the bottom of a trough, the Jordan valley is of slight value as a line of communications from north to south, and its only regular cross-roads lie at either end of the basin, under Lake Galilee and by way of Jericho. Furthermore, the land of Judah between the Dead Sea and the Mediterranean border forms a mountain block of no

---

[1] Discoveries of Chinese silk in Syria: Heichelheim, p. 203. The region of the Roman empire visited by the Chinese envoy in A.D. 97 and described by him is probably to be identified with Syria. (Quotations in W. Schoff, *The Periplus of the Erythraean Sea*, pp. 275 ff.)

[2] Tyre stood on an offshore island which was connected with the mainland by a mole. Neither Beirut nor Haifa, which receive partial protection from crooks in the coast-line, were of any importance in ancient times.

great height, but bristling with steep scarps and seamed with
deep ravines, and clad with little vegetation save scrub and arid
pasture. But for the attractive power of its only considerable
city, Jerusalem, it must always have remained remote from the
main avenues of ancient traffic.

Yet all the internal barriers can be crossed or circumvented
at chosen points. The ridge of Mt. Lebanon is notched in the
neighbourhood of Tyre by a gully through which the river
Leontes breaks to the sea, and from the head of the Leontes
gorge a plateau road leads past the isolated mass of Mt. Hermon
to Damascus. It was by this route that the Phoenicians drew their
share of the perfume and spice trade of Arabia.

From the southern border fortress of Gaza an easy road leads
along the coastal plain of Palestine to Mt. Carmel; ascending over
a shoulder of this ridge, it bends inward through the Gap of
Esdraelon under the southern edge of Lebanon to the Jordan,
which it crosses near Lake Galilee, and runs on in two branches,
leading to Damascus and along the Orontes valley towards
Mesopotamia. This is the thoroughfare by which invading
armies from Egypt ever since the days of Thothmes III down to
A.D. 1918 have struck across Syria.[1]

The easiest of Syria's longitudinal lines of communications
extends from Damascus by way of the Transjordanian plateau
to Petra on the Arabian border (p. 186), and thence to the Gulf
of Akaba.[2] In ancient times this route was exposed to raids by
the desert nomads until Trajan advanced the Roman frontier
across the tableland to the desert edge. The trunk road which
he then constructed from Damascus to the Red Sea rendered
service not only as a military *limes*,[3] but as a trade route for
Arabian and Indian imports into the Mediterranean lands.

Given the position of Syria as a centre of communications
between three continents, its people should have played a commanding part in the ancient political world, had they been able to
form a united state. This, however, they never accomplished.

[1] In the Middle Ages the Gap of Esdraelon served as an avenue for trade
between Damascus and the port of Acre. The present railway connecting Damascus
with Haifa passes through it.

[2] This was the Israelites' main route of entry into the Promised Land. Its line
is now followed by the Mecca railway. A branch road which crossed the southern
continuation of the Jordan rift by a dam of high ground to the south of the Dead
Sea served to connect Ptolemaic Egypt with its Transjordanian outpost at Philadelphia (Amman).

[3] The Roman frontier fortifications, as delimited by an aerial survey, are described
by G. Macdonald in *Antiquity*, 1934, pp. 373–80.

Their failure was largely due to the natural barriers within their own territory, which favoured the erection of separate political units, like those which were formed in Greece under similar conditions. The Phoenician cities backed on to a mountain range; the Jordan valley made a rift between east and west; and Judah stood geographically as well as politically aloof from Israel. Thus a fragmented Syria became a land of passage and a battle-field for other powers, which coveted it for its natural resources, such as the ship-timber preserves on Mt. Lebanon, and even more for its commercial and strategic situation. Despite the industrial and mercantile ability and the general high civilization of its people, the history of ancient Syria was mostly one of political passivity.

One city of Syria, however, habitually went its own way and maintained its own individuality. Ensconced within the mountain fastness of Judah and safeguarded against attack by steep ravines on three sides, the isolated bastion of Jerusalem was by nature a 'city of refuge' rather than a centre of communications or a seat of empire. Significantly, it makes its first appearance in history as one of the last outposts of Egyptian rule in the declining years of the Eighteenth Dynasty (c. 1375 B.C.)[1] and again as one of the last Canaanite fortresses to be carried by the incoming Israelites. When its captor, King David, converted it into a breeding-ground of power politics, he thrust upon it a part for which Nature had not cast it;[2] indeed its subsequent political history was largely taken up with protracted but generally successful sieges. But when David made it the capital of a spiritual realm he prepared it for its true function in world history. Jerusalem in Palestine, like Delphi in Greece, was well situated to be a place of 'withdrawal', where contemplative minds could at their leisure think out a New Order.

§ 3. ARMENIA AND THE CAUCASUS LANDS

The distinctive feature of Armenia among the lands of the Near East is its great altitude. Its highest mountain, Ararat, rises to 17,000 feet, and its valleys range from 4,000 to 7,000 feet. Mere elevation isolates Armenia from its neighbours, and particularly so from the Mesopotamian lowlands. A series of mountain chains which strike across the country from west to east contributes further to make it impenetrable from the south. Another deterrent

---

[1] In the Tell-el-Amarna letters (F. Petrie, *Syria and Egypt*, letters 107 ff.).

[2] The natural capital of Palestine was at Samaria, a more central and accessible site.

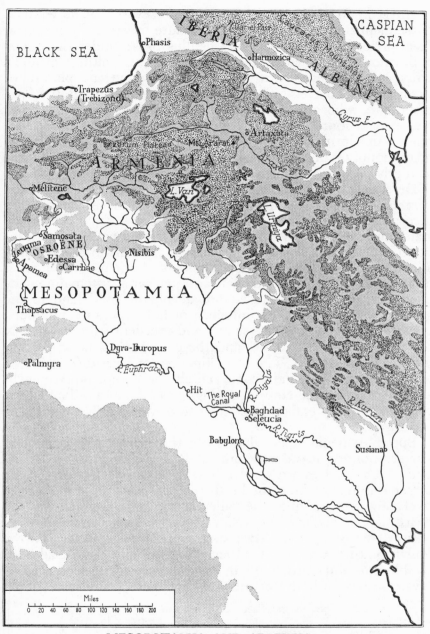

MESOPOTAMIA AND ARMENIA

to travel in Armenia lies in the extreme severity of its winters, consequent on its height and its exposure to winds from central Asia. The veteran soldiers of Lucullus broke under the rigour of the mountain climate in the early autumn; Domitius Corbulo's army suffered severely in its winter camp on the plateau of Erzerum (6,000 feet high);[1] and the achievement of the Ten Thousand, who crossed Armenia from end to end in the cold season, was more amazing than one would gather from Xenophon's unadorned story. The Armenian winter, moreover, is made doubly dangerous by its avalanches of snow, which were formerly reported to have swept away entire caravans.[2]

Defended by Nature against frequent encroachment on the part of stronger neighbours, Armenia was never thoroughly incorporated into the Persian empire or into any Hellenistic state; and the Romans twice drew back from a policy of annexation (initiated by Mark Antony and by Trajan) to one of loose alliance. Conversely, the population of Armenia was neither large enough nor sufficiently concentrated for a systematic policy of aggression. It was indeed not devoid of good land in the valleys, which, under the influence of hot and rainy summers, could produce good horse-pasture and excellent fruit.[3] But only the valleys were cultivable, and the country had no important industrial resources.[4] The early kingdom of Urartu (c. 750 B.C., centred round Lake Van) could merely make raids on Armenia,[5] and the 'ramshackle empire' of Tigranes I could no doubt have come to an early end without the intervention of a Lucullus or a Pompey.

But if Armenia stood aloof from the main current of Near Eastern politics, it was not completely sealed off from its neighbours. On its western border it was accessible by way of the upper Euphrates; from the head-waters of the Euphrates a relatively low pass led into the valley of the Araxes which was the heart of Armenia, and this valley also gave good communication with Media Atropatene (Azerbaijan) and Media proper. By the fourth century A.D., if not earlier, a regular 'silk route' had been established along this line;[6] in earlier centuries it served as an invasion alley for both Romans and Parthians. Domitius Corbulo

---

[1] Plutarch, *Lucullus*, ch. 32; Tacitus, *Annals* xiii. 35. 5–6.
[2] Strabo, p. 528.   [3] Strabo, loc. cit.
[4] A silver-mine in northern Armenia is mentioned by Marco Polo (*Travels*, ch. 4). It was apparently unknown to ancient reporters.
[5] A. H. Sayce, *Cambr. Anc. Hist.* iii, ch. 8.
[6] G. F. Hudson, *Europe and China*, pp. 108, 119.

and Trajan followed this route in their marches upon the Armenian capital at Artaxata, and Mark Antony traversed its entire length during his Parthian campaign. It was the accessibility of Artaxata by either limb of this thoroughfare which made Armenia a 'shuttlecock between Romans and Parthians',[1] provoking attack and counter-attack.

The mountains of Armenia are not subsidiary chains to the main ridge of the Caucasus; they are a continuation of the two coastal ranges of Asia Minor, whereas the Caucasus is a prolongation of the Balkan and Crimean mountains (p. 7). Between the Caucasus and the Armenian highlands, moreover, a broad belt of low ground extends from the Black Sea to the Caspian, the ancient land of the Iberians (towards the Black Sea) and Albanians (towards the Caspian). This region is well watered by the snows and 'orographic' rains from Mt. Caucasus. It is therefore a rich country of orchards and pasture, and its tall forests supply a great variety of timber.[2] The gold-washings in the streams of the Caucasian foot-hills, where the precious metal was collected in fleeces, were little more than a curiosity in Strabo's time,[3] reminiscent perhaps of a former 'boom' that drew the Argonauts as to an Eldorado.

The sub-Caucasian lands, however, were too remote from the Mediterranean to give rise to any regular export trade in food and forest produce; their excellent timber chiefly served the needs of the local pirates.[4] Their economic value to the Greeks and Romans, if any, was as a link in a trans-Caspian route for the importation of luxury ware from Bactria, India, and the Farther East. But the existence of such a route in ancient times is problematical. It is possible that formerly an arm of the Oxus (Amu-Darya) gave through communication by water from Bactria to the Caspian Sea (p. 199), and the portage from the Caspian to the Black Sea should have offered no serious difficulties, for the watershed between them does not rise above 3,000 feet. No doubt Seleucus I had such a route in mind when he commissioned his admiral Patrocles to explore the Caspian,[5] and it may have been with a similar end in view that Pompey and Antony's lieutenant, Carrinas, overran the cis-Caspian country.[6] In times of political unrest the Caspian route might have served a useful

[1] Tacitus, ii. 56. 1.   [2] Strabo, pp. 497–8.   [3] Ibid., p. 499.
[4] Strabo, pp. 495–6; Arrian, *Periplus Ponti Euxini*, ch. 15.
[5] Pliny, vi, § 58.
[6] The 'road fit for wagons' (Strabo, p. 498) may have been built by Carrinas.

purpose in enabling transcontinental traffic to by-pass Parthia, but in normal times it could offer no advantage over the well-established Parthian route farther south (p. 192). In the days of Strabo, at any rate, the Caspian Sea 'carried no traffic and did no work';[1] and the general ignorance of ancient writers in regard to the Caspian (which was commonly mistaken for an open sea with a through connexion to the Northern Ocean)[2] suggests that the hypothetical trade route never had any existence.[3] The same conclusion may be drawn from the chronic infestation of the sub-Caucasian coast of the Black Sea by pirates, whom the Roman Black Sea fleet apparently made no attempt to extirpate.

But if Iberia and Albania were of no economic significance to the Greeks and Romans, they possessed a distinct strategic importance through their control of the Caucasus passes. The coastal tracks along either end of the range are indeed not practicable for large invading forces, and the best inland road, the 'Caucasian Gates' (Dariel Pass), rises to a height of 8,000 feet. Yet by this gap Cimmerians and Scythians had broken into Asia Minor and Mesopotamia in the seventh century B.C., and in the early Christian era the risk of Sarmatian incursions by the same route was an object of constant concern to the Roman government. Therefore, from the time of Vespasian, if not earlier, a Roman garrison was stationed at Harmozica (near Tiflis).[4]

§ 4. MESOPOTAMIA

The land through which the rivers Euphrates and Tigris flow after emerging from the mountain zone of their upper courses is a plain of some 35,000 square miles, with borders of steeply scarped mountains to the west, north, and east, and a more gradual acclivity towards the north Arabian steppe. Cut off by Mt. Taurus from the temperate sea winds of the Mediterranean, Mesopotamia is exposed alternately to chilly winter blasts from the Armenian and Persian highlands, and to the furnace draught that blows up the Persian Gulf in summer. Consequently its climate is one of the extremes on the globe, ranging from 20° to

[1] Strabo, p. 509.

[2] H. F. Tozer, *History of Ancient Geography* (2nd ed.), pp. 136, 345.

[3] On the whole subject see W. W. Tarn, *The Greeks in Bactria and India*, Appendix 14.

[4] Strabo, p. 500; Dessau, *Inscriptiones Latinae Selectae* 8795. Nero planned an expedition to secure the Caucasian Gates. (Suetonius, *Nero* 19, § 2. The Gates are here mistakenly called 'Caspian'.—J. G. C. Anderson, *Cambr. Anc. Hist.* x, p. 777 and n.)

120° (with a recorded shade maximum of 137°). Except in the northern or Assyrian end of Mesopotamia, where the border mountains induce 'orographic' rain, drought prevails throughout summer; in the lower part of the plain the total annual rainfall does not exceed six to eight inches, and over the greater part of the country it is insufficient for the production of crops.

The prosperity of Mesopotamia therefore depends almost wholly on the systematic irrigation of the river strips that lie below flood-level, or are capable of being saturated by means of water hoists.[1] The downland that rises above the valleys (especially in western Mesopotamia) affords little else than rough herbage for sheep. But the régime of the rivers requires elaborate works of engineering to keep them under control. The floods of the Euphrates and Tigris, which proceed from the melting of the snows in the Armenian highlands, reach Mesopotamia in May; and the powerful adjunct inundation of the river Karun, which reinforces the lower Tigris with the overflow from the Persian border range, occurs at the same season. Consequently by midsummer the floods have subsided, and the land will be dried out before the maturing of the crops, unless the surplus water is conserved in storage basins for subsequent release into the irrigation canals.[2] Moreover, the rivers do not pass over such natural filter-beds as those of the Nile cataracts (p. 207, n. 5), and are thus in danger of choking themselves with their coarser detritus. Their channels therefore need periodical dredging, and new cuts must be made now and then, to prevent permanent waterlogging. The peril of leaving the rivers to their own devices may be illustrated from the history of Lower Mesopotamia, which was originally a dismal swamp and required generations of assiduous toil before it became a fertile and populous land; it had partly relapsed into marshland by the end of the Achaemenid era.[3]

But given human control and direction—and in Mesopotamia the hydraulic engineer had begun his beneficent work by 3,000 B.C.—the river valleys could produce harvests which set ancient writers marvelling, and romancing. Said Herodotus: 'Of all lands

[1] The hand-worked swing-beams used for this purpose were noted by Herodotus (i. 193. 1).

[2] Strabo, pp. 740–1 (where the double problem of storage basins and irrigation canals is clearly set forth); W. Willcocks, *The Irrigation of Mesopotamia* (2nd ed.). A natural storage basin, analogous to the Fayum in Egypt (p. 209), was provided in the depression of Habbaniah (west of Babylon).

[3] Strabo, p. 729; Arrian, *Anabasis* vii. 21 (Alexander plans the restoration of the Pallacopas canal below Babylon).

that we know, this is by far the best for its yield of the fruit of Demeter' (wheat, barley, and sesame);[1] and Strabo put about a story that the barley reproduced three-hundredfold.[2] In Babylonia, which received the finest and richest ingredients of the river sediment, a system of catch-cropping was already in operation in ancient times, by means of which two harvests were raised annually, and these were sometimes followed up with a mow of grass.[3] But the choicest produce of Mesopotamia came from its fruit gardens. In these, to be sure, two familiar Mediterranean species, the fig and the olive, were not planted at all;[4] but in no country of the world are better dates grown than in southern Mesopotamia. The peculiar conditions required by the date-palm, 'a hot head and wet feet', are provided to perfection in Lower Mesopotamia, and nowhere else was its cultivation better understood.

The chief industrial material of Mesopotamia was the wool of its downlands. In Assyria a short-staple spun silk was produced from native silkworms,[5] and papyrus was prepared from the reeds of the Babylonian fenland.[6] But only the northern rim of the country possessed any carpenter's timber, building stone, or minerals.[7] Mesopotamia was therefore a long way from being a self-contained country; but it could easily provide for its imports with its surplus crops. Consequently it was the first country of the Near East to engage in long-distance trade on a regular footing.

Mesopotamia was almost cut off from Armenia and Asia Minor by its frontier mountains. Passages across two dips in the Middle Euphrates gorge gave an opening into Asia Minor at Melitene and Samosata, from which points two relatively easy routes passed through openings in the Taurus chain. But the main line of communications with the west was by way of the Aleppo plateau and Syria (p. 171). An alternative route to Syria traversed

---

[1] Strabo, i. 193. 3. Rice and maize are now grown under the same system.
[2] Ibid., p. 742. The yield is now 36-fold (c. 40 bushels per acre).
[3] Pliny, xviii. 161.
[4] Herodotus (loc. cit.) asserted that the vine was not grown, and Strabo (p. 731) maintained that the Macedonians were the first to introduce this plant. But vines are represented on Assyrian reliefs.
[5] Pliny, xi, § 75. The traditional skill of the Assyrians in the textile industry was transferred in the Middle Ages to the production of cotton 'muslins' (i.e. fabrics from Mosul).
[6] Ibid., xiii, § 73; Heichelheim, op. cit., p. 134. Pliny states that the papyrus industry was of recent origin. This is broadly confirmed by the fact that cuneiform script died out in the days of Augustus.
[7] Remains of forests have been observed on the Arab border, and attempts at tree-planting are mentioned by Theophrastus (*Historia Plantarum* iv. 4. 1).

the North Arabian steppe from Hit or Dura-Europus (p. 185); but farther down river, where the steppe makes way to real desert, regular communications across Arabia were impossible.

On the eastern boundary the Persian border range formed a broad and compact wall; but in Susiana (near the Persian Gulf) it sloped down to a fertile piedmont ledge. The shortest crossings of the range were by routes approached through the valleys of two Tigris tributaries, the Diyala and the Karun. The Persian Gulf gave easy access to the Indian Ocean and perhaps brought Mesopotamia into contact with India as early as the third millennium. The best communications of Mesopotamia were accordingly with India and Syria, her richest and most cultured neighbours.

The main arteries of internal traffic were, of course, the Euphrates and Tigris. In their upper and middle courses the twin rivers were too rapid for navigation up stream. The descending journeys were made on rafts (modern 'keleks'), which were broken up on arrival at their destination, or on circular vessels with an osier framework and a covering of hides, like the modern 'guffas'. Herodotus describes how the materials of the guffas were disposed of: 'Each vessel carries a live donkey, the larger ones several. So when they have ended their course at Babylon and disposed of their cargo, they just sell the ribs of the vessel and all its straw stuffing by auction; but the hides they load up on the donkeys and so carry back to Armenia.'[1] Sea-going ships could ascend the Euphrates to Babylon, and the Tigris as far as Seleucia; but the lowest reaches of the Euphrates, of whose waters the irrigation canals took heavy toll, ran shallow in summer. In modern times Baghdad has become an important steamboat station;[2] yet no Greek or Roman writer described its former counterpart, Seleucia, as a busy port.

For travel by road the valley of the Euphrates was not such a convenient route as a glance at the map might suggest. On its middle course, from Melitene to Zeugma or Apamea,[3] the river flowed in a ravine; thenceforward it traversed a steppe country which extended, but for a fertile strip round Thapsacus, as far down-stream as Dura-Europus.[4] Overland travellers could avoid

---

[1] Herodotus, i. 194. 3. I am informed by Miss M. Drower that he may here have fallen into confusion. Nowadays only the keleks are used for long-distance journeys, and they alone are dismantled at the end of the trip.

[2] The Tigris was one of the first rivers in the world to carry a steamboat service.

[3] Zeugma and Apamea were twin settlements on opposite banks.

[4] Xenophon reports that Cyrus's forces suffered from lack of provisions on this

the intermediate tract of steppe by striking inland from Zeugma across a strip of cultivable land to Carrhae (already an important road-station under the Assyrians), and thence by way of Nisibis to the Tigris valley, which was flanked by a broader strip of fertile land.[1]

But the easiest as well as the shortest transit from river to river was on the line between Babylon and Seleucia, where the two streams converged within twenty-five miles of one another and the intervening country lay within the zone of irrigation.[2] In this area, which is both the centre of communications and the widest expanse of cultivable land, the largest city of Mesopotamia has usually been situated.[3] By 1750 B.C. Babylon had become the capital of the entire country, and it remained the most populous town to the time of Alexander, who intended to make it the centre of his empire. But under the Seleucid kings it was superseded by Seleucia, and since then either this city or Baghdad has been the principal seat of commerce and of power. This transference of the country's centre of gravity from the Euphrates to the Tigris may have been due in the first place to a political accident, in that the Seleucids, having set up their court at Antioch, required a subsidiary capital for the administration of their eastern provinces. And Seleucia as the starting-point of the 'Great Eastern Road' across Asia (p. 192), was well situated for this purpose. But it was also justified by the broad facts of Mesopotamian geography, for the Tigris valley provided the best longitudinal line of communications within the Land of the Two Rivers.

Mesopotamia hardly entered the political or commercial horizon of the Greeks until the time of Alexander, but in the following two centuries it was an indispensable portion of the Seleucid monarchy. So long as the Seleucids retained possession of their eastern provinces, it was the focus of communications within their dominions, and after the loss of their eastern terri-

---

stage of their journey (*Anabasis* i. 5. 5). Dura-Europus combined the advantages of a commanding situation on a bluff overlooking the Euphrates, of being the terminus of a caravan route (p. 185), and of lying at the margin of the fertile zone.

[1] An alternative route went farther north by way of Edessa. The Baghdad railway follows a somewhat more southerly track. On the 'fertile corridor' see K. Regling, *Klio*, 1901, pp. 443 ff.

[2] Water transit between Euphrates and Tigris was effected along this line by the 'Royal Canal' (modern Nahr Malik), which was fed by the Euphrates.

[3] Nineveh originated as a trading-station on the Tigris route to the north and west. Its situation was better suited to the capital of a wider Near-Eastern empire than to a Mesopotamian kingdom.

tories it continued to be one of their principal sources of revenue.[1] Its eventual conquest by the Parthians (*c.* 125 B.C.) reduced the Seleucid realm, both territorially and financially, to a second-class state.

The Roman emperors, on the other hand, were under no similar obligation to hold any territory beyond the Euphrates. By wresting Mesopotamia from the Parthians they might indeed hope at one stroke to replenish their own resources and to cripple the finances of their rivals, and it was perhaps for this reason that Trajan decided to annex and not merely to overrun it. But the consequent lengthening of the Roman lines of communication was such a serious offset that the new acquisitions were abandoned by Hadrian. Under Marcus Aurelius, it is true, the Romans set up a client-state in Osroëne (in the westernmost bulge of the Euphrates near Samosata),[2] as a bridge-head for future defensive attacks upon Parthia, and Byzantine emperors fought stoutly against Sassanid kings for the retention of the town of Edessa. But this forward move did not mark a resumption of Trajan's policy as a whole. In Europe the Roman emperors had valid reasons for advancing their frontiers into the heart of the continent, but a sound instinct warned them not to progress into Asia far beyond the smell of the Mediterranean brine.

§ 5. ARABIA

Extending over an area of 1¼ million square miles, Arabia is by far the largest territory of the Near East. To the Greeks and Romans it always remained a land of mystery, for very few ancient explorers ventured to probe its secrets; but as a medium of communications between the Greek and Roman world and the countries of the Indian Ocean it played a by no means negligible part.

[1] Judging by Herodotus' list of tributary payments to Achaemenid Persia (iii. 91–2), we may infer that in the second century B.C. the Seleucids drew half their revenue from Mesopotamia. This revenue probably included a considerable sum derived from tolls on trade between Seleucia and India. (On this commerce see Tarn, op. cit., p. 261 and Appendix 12. Tarn's conclusions are not invalidated by the paucity of Seleucid coin-finds in India, as suggested by Rostovtzeff, *Hellenistic World*, pp. 457 and 1429, n. 243). Unlike the Roman emperors, the Seleucid kings may have controlled their Indian trade so as to avoid the export of specie.

[2] The Roman frontier road, recently traced by M. A. Stein (*Geographical Journal*, xcii, 1938, pp. 62–6), followed the lower valley of the river Chaboras for fifty miles, and then struck north-eastward past Singara to meet the Tigris some eighty miles above Nineveh.

The structure of Arabia is that of an immense uptilted block, with a rim of mountains 5,000 to 9,000 feet high at its raised western and southern edges and a gentle dip towards Mesopotamia and the Persian Gulf. Its body consists of a granite and limestone mass which towers up into the coastal ranges and crops out in lesser ridges at scattered points of the interior. But this core has been overlaid with an extensive stratum of sandstone, and it is the disintegration of this cap under the influence of the Arabian climate that has converted the greater part of the country into a sand desert.

The climate of Arabia is not wholly uniform. The south-westerly and south-easterly fronts of the peninsula lie within the extreme range of the Indian Ocean monsoon and obtain sufficient rain in summer to permit of intensive cultivation under a careful system of water-conservation.[1] Its north-western face receives a small allowance of winter rain under the influence of Mediterranean winds blowing in across the low coast of Palestine. But the greater part of Arabia lies in a rain-shadow. Its high coastal ranges absorb the monsoon downfalls; the mountain chains of northern Syria cut off the greater part of the Mediterranean winter cyclones; and the Persian highlands intercept the damp weather from the Caspian Sea. In general, therefore, the climate is as extreme as that of Mesopotamia, with showers of snow in mid-winter and temperatures rising to 115° in summer; and the rainfall is even more scanty. The effect of the drought is intensified by the pulverization of the sandstone rocks under the influence of alternate fierce heat and frost.[2] The rare rainstorms of the interior may attain such violence as to cause sudden floods in the 'wadis' or valleys. To quote a recent traveller: 'Very soon the whole surface of the desert was covered with a sheet of water, and a shallow valley which we had motored up an hour or two before turned into a river like the Thames.'[3] But an Arabian Thames is soon dissipated into nothingness through the top layer of loose sand.

The choicest of the fertile fringes of Arabia, the land of the Sabaeans in the south-west and south, formerly carried the surname of 'The Blest', and its wealth was a subject of fable. While some observers noted that the sown lands yielded two harvests

---

[1] Remains of an immense dam which the ancient Sabaeans built across the Wadi Dena are still on view (J. G. C. Anderson, *Cambr. Anc. Hist.* x, p. 249).

[2] Observations at Palmyra and Petra suggest that desiccation has spread since ancient times (E. Huntington, *Palestine*, ch. 13).

[3] D. Vesey Fitzgerald, *The Listener*, 19 Dec. 1945, p. 616.

of grain annually,[1] attention was naturally centred on its groves of perfume-bearing shrubs, which were the main source of its native wealth.[2]

Central Arabia is interspersed with considerable patches of grazing-land wherever the limestone outcrops are high enough to induce a local 'orographic' rainfall, and its northern regions, coming partly under the influence of the Mediterranean climate, are steppe-land rather than desert.[3]

But the monsoon belt is the only part of Arabia which can furnish more than a precarious subsistence out of its own resources. The chief importance of Arabia Deserta in ancient times was as a land of transit for exotic luxuries that could bear the high cost of conveyance across the wilderness. The Arab caravan trade dealt not so much with the home products of the country, which were mostly exported by the sea route (p. 187),[4] as with the highly prized condiments of India and the Far East, especially cinnamon and pepper.[5] Two main 'spice routes' ran across Arabia. The southern one took off from Gerra (half-way along the coast of the Persian Gulf), and after crossing the central desert reached the distributing-station of Petra, from which the main limb was directed to Damascus and the Phoenician ports, while branch roads went to Gaza and the Gulf of Akaba.[6] The northerly track conveyed merchandise which had been carried by sea-going ships to Seleucia and thence by canal boat to Hit or Dura-Europus. From these two points the caravans proceeded to Palmyra, an oasis town with a good supply of spring-water within an arid belt of fifty miles. From Palmyra the Phoenician coast was reached by way of Damascus or Emesa.

The transit across the desert was effected in large convoys under expert camel-masters (συνοδιάρχαι) along definite routes containing water-points or caches of jugs in underground

---

[1] Strabo, p. 768.

[2] Herodotus, iii. 107–13 and Diodorus, iii. 46–7. (Not to be taken literally.) For a modern description see Schoff, op. cit., pp. 120–6. The coffee-shrub, which does not figure in Greek or Latin literature and is first mentioned by late-medieval travellers in Abyssinia, had perhaps not been acclimatized in Arabia in ancient times.

[3] No ancient author makes mention of Arab horses. The pasturage may have been reserved in Greek and Roman days for sheep and camels.

[4] Some incense may have reached the Gulf of Akaba by the route used by Aelius Gallus in reverse (p. 187).—Miss Freya Stark, *The Southern Gates of Arabia*, Appendix.

[5] See esp. Warmington, op. cit., pp. 186 ff., 228 ff.

[6] Mecca played no important part in Greek or Roman trade. It is a good water-point, but lacks a safe harbour.

chambers.[1] The same system prevails at the present day, and we may infer from modern practice that the ancient caravans could cover twenty or twenty-five miles in a day and carry three days' supply of water with them.[2] The northern and southern routes would appear to have been competitive, for Petra and Palmyra took it in turns to be prosperous. In the Achaemenid and Hellenistic eras Petra was the principal desert emporium, but by the second century of the Christian era Palmyra had taken the lead. In any case the northern route had the double advantage of a shorter land transit and of lying along a ledge of hard gravel which gave a better foothold than the sand or scree of central Arabia.[3]

The caravan trade of ancient Arabia was highly lucrative,[4] but it was too much concentrated along certain well-marked routes to relieve the general poverty of the country. Its neighbours therefore had always to reckon with an outward pressure on the part of its Bedouin population. The Arab tribes indeed, until recently, lay too scattered, and were politically too disunited, to attempt any mass-invasion of the borderlands;[5] but eternal vigilance was needed to cope with raiding-parties. These razzias would naturally provoke a desire to retaliate, and a further motive for an occasional anabasis into Arabia offered itself in the hope of wresting the profits of the caravan trade from the natives. But no ancient invader of Arabia solved the problem of supply or found the right answer to 'desert tactics'—the storage of immovable wealth in fortified places and wholesale retirement of men and flocks into the farther wilderness.

In 311 B.C. an officer of Antigonus I did indeed succeed in carrying Petra by a *coup de main*, but at the price of overstraining his troops, who were overcome by exhaustion on the return journey and massacred under an Arab counter-attack; and a second expedition under Demetrius Poliorcetes beat a timely retreat after a vain attempt to regain Petra by siege.[6] In 63 B.C. Pompey started out on the road to Petra, but doubled back before he had put his army to the full test. In 24 B.C. the Roman general

---

[1] Diodorus, xix. 94. 6–8; Rostovtzeff, *Caravan Cities*.

[2] Christina P. Grant, *The Syrian Desert*.

[3] This hard track also affords good going for motor-cars. It has been used by regular services of six-wheel coaches during the last twenty years.

[4] According to Pliny (vi, § 101) wares from India were sold in Rome at rates a hundredfold above their original price.

[5] The recent union of Arabia under Ibn Saud has been achieved by means of a tank corps.

[6] Diodorus, xix. 94–8.

Aelius Gallus made a remarkable march of some 900 miles from the Gulf of Akaba to the verge of the Sabaean land, followed by an equally notable retreat; but his water-supply gave out a few days too soon, and Arabia Felix remained unsubdued.[1] In A.D. 272 the Emperor Aurelian twice captured Palmyra after forced marches through its surrounding waterless zone; but when he destroyed the town he also made an end of its caravan traffic. At best these expeditions could not have diverted the transit trade into Greek or Roman hands, for only the native travellers had enough knowledge of the water-points, and sufficient experience in organizing camel-trains, to exploit it successfully. With characteristic prudence accordingly the Ptolemies contented themselves with diplomatic overtures to the Arab chiefs.[2] The Emperor Trajan solved the problem of frontier defence for Syria by means of the *limes Arabicus* (p. 173).

Arabia also entered into Greek and Roman history as the country that bordered on the Red Sea and the Persian Gulf, two water-ways which gave the easiest lines of communication between the Mediterranean lands and the Indian Ocean. Both these seas, it is true, presented peculiar difficulties, and Greek writers dilated on the perils of navigation in the Red Sea.[3] Though these authors omitted to mention its stifling heat (which raises its surface water to a temperature of 80–85°), its sudden squalls, and its cross-currents, they duly noted its numerous shoals and reefs and the pirate haunts on the Arabian coast.[4] The plans of Alexander for the opening up of a trade route from Egypt to India along the Arab seaboard were therefore soon lost out of sight, and for two further centuries navigation of the Red Sea remained mostly in the hands of the Sabaeans, who had long been accustomed to export the frankincense of their homeland by the sea route, and also to forward merchandise conveyed to Aden from India. Greek and Roman writers were consequently deluded into the belief that Indian seasonings, such as cinnamon, pepper, and cane-sugar, were products of Arabia.[5] Towards the end of the second century B.C. Greek seamen began to assume a

---

[1] Strabo, pp. 780–2; Anderson, op. cit. x, pp. 249–51.
[2] Tarn, *Journal of Egyptian Archaeology*, 1929, pp. 9 ff.
[3] Agatharchides, ch. 83 (in C. Müller, *Geographici Graeci Minores*, i, p. 171), followed by Diodorus, iii. 40; *Periplus of the Erythraean Sea*, ch. 20.
[4] Reefs can be detected by observing the greenish-yellow patches of water surrounding them. But these do not show up distinctly under all weather conditions, unless viewed through dark goggles (*The Red Sea Pilot* (8th ed.), pp. 10–12).
[5] Herodotus, iii. 107–13; Diodorus, iii. 46. 3, xix. 94. 10; Warmington, op. cit., pp. 186–7.

direct part in the Indian trade (p. 204), but not until the time of Augustus was a regular sea route established between Egypt and India.[1] The long delay in securing this line of traffic may have been due to opposition on the part of the Sabaeans, who appear to have withheld the use of the ports of Hodeida and Aden—the only two good harbours on the Arab side of the Red Sea[2]—from foreign interlopers, until a Roman expeditionary force conquered and probably retained possession of Aden.[3]

The Persian Gulf, though not devoid of reefs and shoals, is a less dangerous piece of water than the Red Sea, and it was successfully explored by Alexander's admiral Nearchus.[4] But while it is probable that the Seleucid kings controlled its eastern coast (p. 193), there is no evidence of active interference on their part with the commerce of Gerra.[5] It may be assumed that Arab seamen imported the goods from India which were forwarded from Gerra by the caravan route.

[1] Strabo, p. 118.
[2] Aden is a typical 'isthmus' harbour.
[3] *Periplus of the Erythraean Sea*, ch. 26: οὐ πρὸ πολλοῦ τῶν ἡμετέρων χρόνων Καῖσαρ αὐτὴν κατεστρέψατο. It is generally agreed that 'Καῖσαρ' here must mean 'Augustus'. The middle form κατεστρέψατο ('conquered for his own sake') suggests a permanent occupation.
[4] Arrian, *Indica*, chs. 18–42 (*Geographici Graeci Minores*, i, pp. 329 ff.).
[5] Antiochus III apparently levied a tribute or danegeld on Gerra, but he did not occupy it (Polybius, xiii. 9. 4–5).

VII. THE ASIATIC MIDDLE EAST

§ 1. PERSIA

THE territory of Persia reproduces on a larger scale several of the characteristic features of Asia Minor. It is a plateau of similar altitude (3,000–5,000 feet), though of far greater extent (c. 650,000 square miles); it is similarly encompassed by mountain rims, which rise in the northern range of Elburz to 18,600 feet (Mt. Demavend), and expand at the western edge (in the Zagrus chain) to a width of 300 miles. In addition, it is streaked by a central chain, some 800 miles in length, with peaks rising well above 10,000 feet. Persia differs most notably from Asia Minor in that its seaboard not only is much shorter, but is almost cut off from the open waters of the Indian Ocean by the land-mass of Arabia.

In accordance with its more continental position, Persia has a more extreme climate than Asia Minor, and it suffers more severely from drought. It is cut off from the rain-bearing winds of the Black Sea by the Armenian highlands, and from those of the Caspian by the Elburz range; and it is screened from the Indian Ocean monsoon by the mountains of south Arabia and of its own coastal border. The average rainfall therefore ranges between a mere five and ten inches, and in eastern Persia immense tracts of former lakeland have become desiccated into salt desert.[1] In the coastlands, which lie in the lee of the summer northerlies, the heat is as intense as in Arabia and Mesopotamia;[2] on the plateau the winter cold could render campaigning impossible even to seasoned troops. In 316 B.C. Antigonus I had to forgo the chance of a surprise attack on his adversary Eumenes, because his veterans had been obliged to light camp fires in order to survive a severe night frost;[3] and the Parthian kings would not venture to expose their troops to a winter campaign.[4]

[1] From the time of Marco Polo (*Travels*, ch. 19) the deserts of Persia have made a deep impression on travellers by their utter desolation. Ruins of towns in the desert area attest desiccation since ancient times (E. Huntington, *The Pulse of Asia*, ch. 16). But the causes of desiccation may have been partly political (Sven Hedin, *Overland to India*, ii, chs. 49–50; T. Peisker, *Cambridge Medieval History*, i, pp. 325 ff.).

[2] Strabo, p. 731. Marco Polo (ch. 16) relates that during the heat of the day the people of Ormuz immersed themselves up to the neck in cisterns!

[3] Plutarch, *Eumenes*, ch. 15.

[4] Plutarch, *Antonius*, ch. 40.

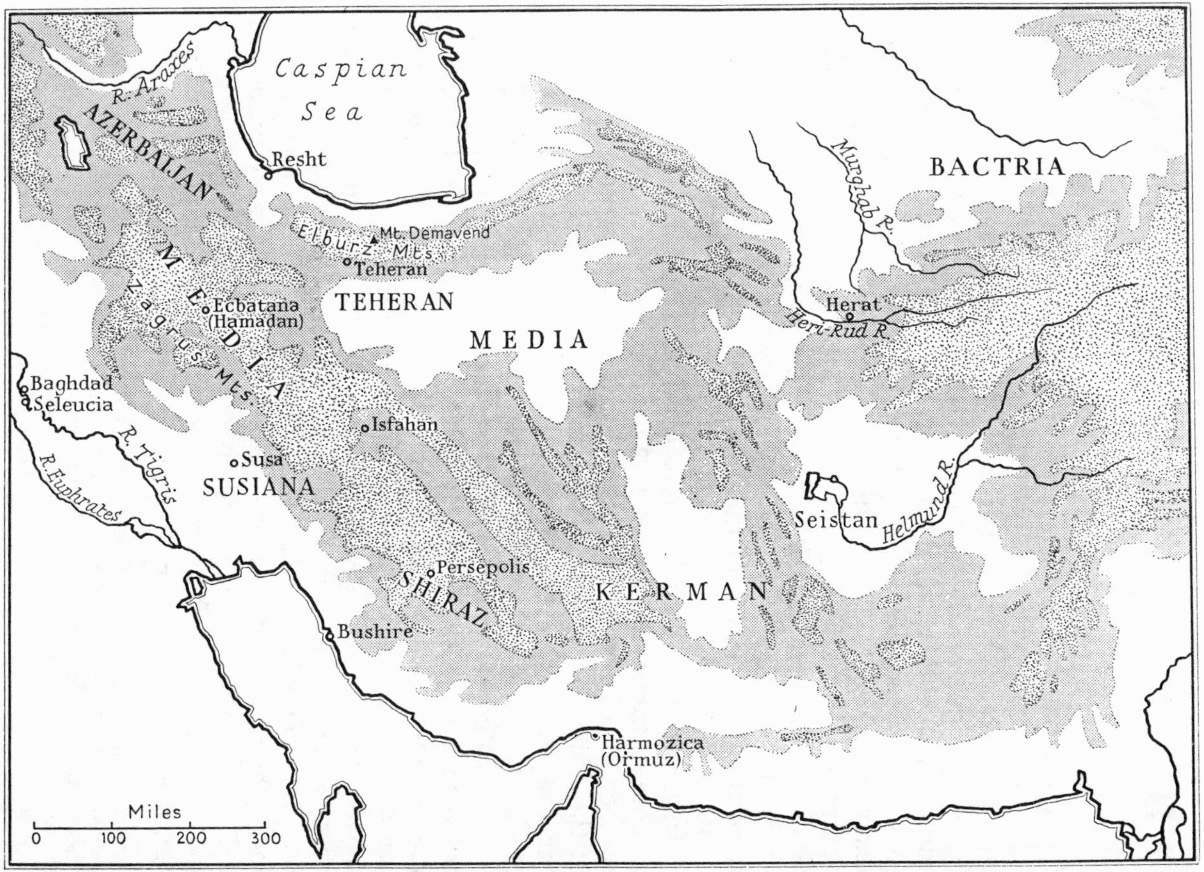

Caspian Sea

BACTRIA

Murghab R.

Herat
Heri-Rud R.

Seistan Helmand R.

KERMAN

MEDIA

TEHERAN

Mt. Demavend
Elburz Mts.
Teheran

Isfahan

Harmozica
(Ormuz)

SHIRAZ

Persepolis

Bushire

Resht

R. Araxes

AZERBAIJAN

M E D I A

Zagros Mts.
Ecbatana
(Hamadan)

Susa

SUSIANA

R. Tigris

Baghdad
Seleucia

R. Euphrates

Miles
0   100   200   300

As compared with Asia Minor, Persia derives one advantage
from the greater height of its mountains, in that it receives a
larger supply of snow-water from them. Its interior therefore
contains a number of highly fertile valleys—those of Shiraz in
the south, of Kerman (ancient Carmania) in the south-east,[1] of
Isfahan in the centre, and above all the plain of Teheran under
Mt. Elburz (ancient Media Major). Of its borderlands, Azerbaijan in the north-west (ancient Media Atropatene) and the
strip to the north of Mt. Elburz (ancient Parthia in the narrow
sense) benefit by the rainy northerlies from the Caspian Sea; the
western piedmont, especially in Susiana, is irrigated by Mt.
Zagrus. On the eastern margin the sunken basin of Seistan
(ancient Drangiana), to which the river Helmund and its tributaries convey the off-flow from the highlands of Afghanistan,
might be compared with Egypt, but for the lack of systematic
water-regulation. It was in such favoured tracts that the Persian
grandees laid out their parks with game preserves and orchards
of apples and peaches (*mala Persica*), or raised crops of alfalfa
(*herba Medica*) as fodder for their big-boned chargers; and that
the subsequent Greek settlers planted their vineyards.[2] Persia
has recently become one of the world's chief sources of mineral
oil, and it is known to contain large deposits of metal ores. In
ancient times Carmania was worked for a variety of metals,[3] and
the tin of Seistan[4] may have been the alloy on which the early
Sumerians drew for their bronze-casting (*c.* 3000 B.C.). But the
so-called 'Parthian' iron may have been, like the 'Damascus steel'
(p. 169), an importation from India or from China;[5] and the
well in Susiana, from which petroleum and bitumen were collected in Herodotus' day in a quite unhurried fashion,[6] was little
more than a curiosity. Similarly Persia's hard-wearing carpets
were mentioned as an oddity rather than a staple commodity for
export.[7]

Even when full allowance is made for its checkered zones of
delectable land, it remains true that Persia in ancient times was
not a highly productive country and could not have carried a large
population; at present it is reckoned to contain not more than

---

[1] Strabo, p. 726 ('Carmania grows everything and provided grand fruit-trees,
except olives'). Cf. p. 725 (a similar eulogy of Seistan).
[2] Strabo, p. 525; Tarn, *Hellenistic Military and Naval Development*, pp. 78–83.
[3] Strabo, p. 726.   [4] Ibid., p. 724.
[5] Pliny (xxxiv, § 145) mentions Parthian and Chinese iron as being of similar
workmanship.
[6] Herodotus, vi. 119. 2–3.   Pliny, viii, § 191.

ten million inhabitants. Yet again and again its people have made substantial contributions to world history, whether in the Persian art,[1] literature, and science of various ages, in the religion of Zarathustra, or in the statecraft of the Achaemenian dynasty. So far as the Persian achievement has been due to natural causes, it may be ascribed in part to the exhilarating quality of its dry and salty air, together with the sharp-set character of its landscape,[2] and partly to its situation between the Mediterranean and the eastern centres of civilization.

Communications across Persia are confined to a few routes which thread their way, so far as possible, between the mountain ranges and the desert belts. The most convenient and important of these thoroughfares is the 'Great East Road' which, taking off from ancient Seleucia or modern Baghdad and descending from Mt. Zagrus to the hill station of Hamadan (ancient Ecbatana), strikes across the Median plateau, traverses Mt. Elburz by the Dervend Pass (the strangely named 'Caspian Gates' of ancient authors), and eventually branches to Merv and Herat.[3] The central road from Isfahan to Seistan, which in later days formed part of an alternative trans-continental route, may not have been in regular use before the Middle Ages, as it is not mentioned in Greek or Roman authors. In Hellenistic times, if not before, a southerly road extended from Susa to Persepolis and Carmania;[4] it is not known whether it was prolonged to Seistan or threw off a branch to Ormuz. Either of the two last-named routes had to interweave through several difficult bands of mountain country. The principal south-and-north line of communications, from Bushire or Bunder Abbas to Teheran and Resht (on the Caspian Sea), can now be traversed in comfort on the recently built motor-road and railway;[5] but these are veritable *tours de force* of engineering across a continuous switch-back of mountain and valley.

Because of the difficulties of internal communication, and of the sheer magnitude of the country, the unification of Persia in

[1] On ancient Persian art see F. Sarre, *Die Kunst der alten Perser.*

[2] The stimulating character of the Persian air has been emphasized by modern travellers, e.g. D. G. Hogarth and Sir Percy Sykes. The latter has compared the Persian landscape with that of Spain, because of its strong contrast of colour and its hard outline (*History of Persia*, 3rd ed., i, p. 7).

[3] The stages of this route are marked off in a surviving road-book from the time of Augustus, the *Parthian Stations* of Isidorus of Charax (ed. W. H. Schoff).

[4] Strabo, p. 744.

[5] The road was built in the thirties by Shah Riza, the railway in 1942 by the Western Allies.

ancient times lagged far behind that of Mesopotamia. When unification came, the rallying-point was naturally in Media, as being the largest tract of fertile land and the focal point of communications. Ecbatana, on the 'Great East Road', was the first capital of the consolidated state, and after the downfall of the native Median dynasty it continued to serve as a summer station for the Achaemenid and Arsacid lines. But the disjunctive tendency of Persian geography reasserted itself under the Arsacid kings, whose government was decentralized to a dangerous degree.[1]

Of Persia's external lines of communications, the sea route never attained importance in ancient times. The broad band of mountains that encases the country on its southern side all but cuts it off from the waterside. It is true that, no doubt as a result of Nearchus' voyage of exploration along the coast, one of the Seleucid kings constructed a port at or near the island of Ormuz, commanding the entrance of the Persian Gulf.[2] But the so-called 'Macedonian harbour' at this point was mainly intended as a station on the long-distance sea route between India and Mesopotamia, and we may doubt whether it established any extensive trading connexions with the Persian mainland. In any case, its ancient trade was mainly in Greek or Arab hands.

The mountain border of Persia, however, has never isolated the country from its neighbours to east and west. On its comparatively open eastern side it had easy access to Bactria and the east Iranian lands, which formed an integral part of the Achaemenid and Arsacid dominions. The 'Great East Road' brought Persia into commercial contact with India and China and allowed its rulers, whether native dynasts (Darius I and Nadir Shah) or foreign overlords (Alexander, Antiochus III, and the Saracens), to pour invading hosts into India. Conversely, this route needed close guarding at its entrance-points into Persia, by way of the Murghal and Heri-Rud valleys, against successive raids of nomads from the grasslands of central Asia.

But Persia's most important outlets were towards the west. The northernmost of the westward exits, leading by way of the

---

[1] On the structure of the Parthian empire see Tarn, *Cambr. Anc. Hist.* ix, ch. 14. The greater centralization of Persia under the Achaemenids and Sassanids may have been due to the 'challenge' of formidable neighbours in the west, the Assyrians and the Romans. The danger to the Arsacids from the Seleucids was less formidable.

[2] Pliny, vi, § 110 ('portus Macedonum'); Tarn, *Greeks in Bactria*, App. 12. Nearchus found the isle of Ormuz deserted (Arrian, *Indica*, ch. 37, and note by C. Müller in *Geographici Graeci Minores*, i, pp. 358–9).

Araxes valley into Armenia, was indeed of lesser consequence in ancient times, except in that it gave the Parthians easy access to Armenia and enabled them to contest its possession with the Romans. But the western end of the 'Great East Road' and the route from Persepolis to Susa[1] were the principal links of Persia with the outer world. It was by these lines of communication that the Median and Achaemenid rulers acquired their knowledge of Assyrian war-craft and state-craft, and that the Achaemenids broke in upon the Mediterranean world. And although Persian civilization was native and always remained distinct from that of its neighbours, the foreign cultural influences that exercised the most effect upon them were derived from western Asia and from Greece.[2]

§ 2. THE EAST IRANIAN LANDS

The broad belt of territory between Persia and India which has been summed up here under the name of 'East Iranian Lands' is in reality a composite region falling naturally into three separate units, a gigantic mountain spine in the centre and two shelving plateaux to north and south. These three 'ridings' will require separate treatment.

(a) The southern division (ancient Gedrosia, modern Beluchistan) is a scalloped tableland with a rib-work of mountains which follow a general trend from west to east. It lies within a double rain-shadow, being cut off from the summer monsoon by the mountains of southern Arabia, and from the rain-bearing west and north-west winds of winter by the Persian highlands; and it derives no snow-water from its internal system of ranges, which hardly exceed 5,000 feet, nor from the central spine, whose off-flow is drained away to Seistan (p. 191). It is therefore an almost unrelieved desert of bare rock or hard-baked clay, and its only historical importance is as a land of passage between Persia and India.

The corridors between the mountain flutings are mostly level and provide a floor of firm gravel;[3] in the Middle Ages two of these passages were put to regular use by traders plying between Ormuz or central Persia and India. The northerly route connected Seistan with the Punjab by way of Kelat and the Bolan

---

[1] Susa, the chief seat of government under the Achaemenid kings, subsequently became one of the principal and most durable Greek settlements in the eastern lands (Tarn, *The Greeks in Bactria and India*, pp. 27-30).

[2] For western influences on Persian art see Sarre, op. cit., Introd., p. vi.

[3] The Earl of Ronaldshay, *An Eastern Miscellany*, ch. 6. (A description of a journey from Quetta to Seistan.)

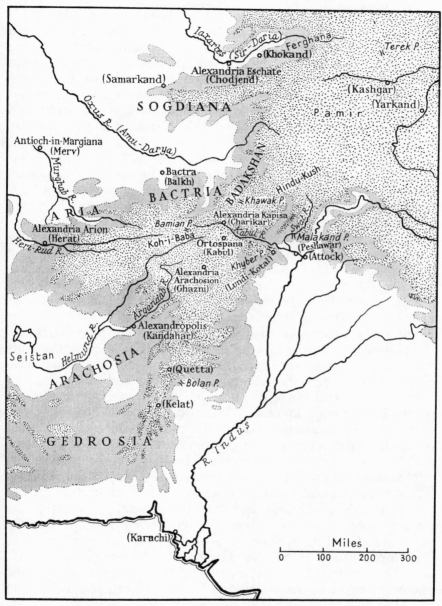

EAST IRAN AND NORTH-WEST INDIA

pass; the southerly one, taking off from Kerman, slanted towards the sea and ended at Karachi. Remains of forests, of dikes, and of terraces along these tracks are evidence that formerly they were bordered by patches of cultivable land.[1] The second route would have been the natural one for Alexander to take on his return from India. But his main concern at this stage of his march was to establish a naval line of communications between India and Persia, and with this end in view he determined to pick his way along the coast so as to keep in touch with his ships on their voyage of exploration. The coastal track was not wholly impracticable for a small and lightly equipped force, for the country through which it passed was mostly level and provided a little brackish water from wells. But an isolated spur of high land (the Malan block) compelled Alexander to turn inland, and before he could regain the shore he had to follow the course of an arid valley with water-points as much as seventy miles apart.[2] It gave him but temporary relief and added to his embarrassments when one of his night-camps was washed out by one of those rare cloud-bursts which dissipate themselves over the Beluchi desert as they do over that of Arabia (p. 184).[3] It is not known whether Alexander's successors made any attempt to explore either of the two inland thoroughfares. In any case, no Greek settlements were planted along them, and any traffic which they may have carried must have been gathered in native or Indian hands.

(b) The central block of the east Iranian zone comprises the territories anciently known as Aria and Arachosia (roughly equal to modern Afghanistan). The greater part of it consists of a broad belt of mountains rising in its centre (Koh-i-Baba) to 17,000 feet, and in its north-eastern extension (Hindu-Kush) to 18,000 feet. Afghanistan suffers from the same general sterility as Beluchistan. The climate, besides running to extremes of temperature (30° to 110°),[4] is only a little less arid, and the general elevation of the country raises much of it above the level of cultivation. But the sheer altitude of its peaks ensures a supply of snow sufficient to feed three strong rivers, the Heri-Rud, Helmund, and Kabul, and the irrigation lands dependent on these streams are prolific enough to subsist three considerable cities, Herat, Kandahar, and

[1] T. Holdich, *The Gates of India*, ch. 8.
[2] Holdich, op. cit., pp. 144 ff.; Sykes, op. cit., pp. 276 ff.
[3] Strabo, p. 722.
[4] On the march from Kabul to Kandahar in August 1880 the British troops suffered from the severe chilliness of the nights (F. S. Roberts, *Forty-one Years in India*, 2nd ed., p. 480).

Kabul. The Hindu-Kush contains silver-mines from which no doubt the Greco-Bactrian dynasts derived the bullion for their copious and splendid mintage. Partly for these reasons, but chiefly because of its importance as a focus of communications, Afghanistan was well colonized by Alexander and his successors.

In the Greek road system of Afghanistan the starting-point was Alexandria Arion (Herat), which was within easy reach of Persia by way of the Heri-Rud valley. From Herat two roads led to Alexandria-Kapisa (Charikar), which lay in the corridor between the Koh-i-Baba and Hindu-Kush, and was the focus of communications between Arachosia, Bactria, and India.[1] One of these routes skirted the Koh-i-Baba range on its northern side and descended upon Kapisa after crossing an arm of the Koh-i-Baba by way of the Bamian pass (13,500 feet). The more southerly route, after making a wide detour towards Seistan (where it may have linked up with a road from southern Persia), ascended the Helmund and Argandab valleys to Alexandropolis (Kandahar); from this point it crossed an eastern extension of the Koh-i-Baba by a relatively easy pass (10,000 feet) leading by way of Alexandria Arachosion (Ghazni) and Ortospana (Kabul) to Kapisa. Perhaps because of its double connexion with Persia, Alexander made use of the second route. In 330 he followed it in his outward march across Afghanistan, and in 325 he sent back the main part of his army on the return from India by the same track.

From Alexandria-Kapisa the direct route to India went through the Khyber pass. This route has always been the main avenue to India for peaceful travellers, for it rises nowhere to more than 7,000 feet, and at the Lundi-Kotal gate it is down to 3,400 feet. But the pass narrows to a mere cleft in the mountains which, to say nothing of its stifling heat, can easily be blocked against an invading force and is much exposed to marauders on its flanks. On his expedition to India Alexander, who had the good fortune to win over the raja Taxiles, guardian of the Khyber pass, directed his main column to march through it. But the king in person led a flank-guarding corps by a more northerly route up the broad Kunar valley and across the Bajaur range to the river Swat. His original plan, no doubt, was to descend the Swat valley and to rejoin his Grand Army near Peshawar by way of the Mala-kand pass, which despite its height of 15,000 feet has been a

---

[1] It was known to Strabo (p. 723) as ἡ ἐκ Βάκτρων τρίοδος. For the identification of ancient with modern place-names see W. W. Tarn, *The Greeks in Bactria and India*, Appendix 9.

favourite avenue of invaders into India. But from the Swat valley he was lured eastward into a loop of the Indus by the challenge of the hitherto impregnable mountain-fortress of Aornos (Pir-Sar), rising 5,000 feet above the river valley. After the reduction of Aornos the king cut his way directly across an untrodden mountain jungle to a lower point on the Indus (near Attock), where he regained touch with his main force.[1]

The Khyber pass continued to be the chief entrance-gate into India under the Seleucid and Greco-Bactrian kings. But on the homeward journey Alexander sent his main army back by one of the more southerly passes leading to Quetta and Kandahar— probably by the Bolan pass (6,000 feet), the easiest in northwestern India.[2] The Quetta–Kandahar route, with its continuation down the Helmund valley to Seistan, remained a secondary line of communications with India under the Greco-Bactrian kings.[3]

Kapisa was also the starting-point of the routes leading northwestward into Bactria. The lower but more circuitous road crossed the eastern shoulder of the Hindu-Kush by the Khawak pass (11,500 feet); the higher but more direct one went by way of the Bamian pass (p. 197), which nowadays is the main line of communications between Afghanistan and Turkestan.[4]

(c) Between the northern fringe of the Afghan mountains and the desert lowlands extending to the Caspian and Aral Seas lies a piedmont country, ancient Bactria and Sogdiana (Afghan and Russian Turkestan), which receives little rainfall but is plentifully watered by the snows from the Pamirs melting into the drainage basin of the Oxus (Amu-Darya) and its tributaries. Its irrigation system has shrunk since ancient days,[5] but in the Achaemenid and Hellenistic eras it was highly developed, so that the country could be described as 'the gem of all the Arian [i.e. east Iranian] land'.[6] Like the irrigation lands of Persia, it reared

---

[1] M. A. Stein, *On Alexander's Track to the Indus*, esp. chs. vi, xvii–xxii.

[2] The alternative to the Bolan pass, the equally high Mulla pass, is more tortuous. There is no evidence of its use in ancient times (T. H. Holdich, *India*, p. 49).

[3] Tarn, op. cit., pp. 93–4.

[4] A. Foucher et Mme Bazin-Foucher, *La Vieille Route de l'Inde de Bactres à Taxila*, pp. 1–58 (Mémoires de la Délégation Française en Afghanistan, vol. i, 1942).

[5] According to Holdich (*Gates of India*, p. 75) the level of Bactria is now higher than in ancient times, and this has restricted the area of irrigable land. Under Soviet administration, however, the zone of intensive cultivation has been greatly increased, so that Turkestan has become an important cotton-growing region.

[6] Strabo, p. 516 (τῆς συμπάσης Ἀριανῆς πρόσχημα); Tarn, op. cit., pp. 102–13.

a powerful breed of war-horses on alfalfa grass, and it was the 'farthest east' of Greek viticulture. It was ill provided with metals, but the province of Badakshan near its eastern border was the source of lapis lazuli, a stone greatly prized among the ancient monarchies of the Near East.

The Greek capital of this choice country was established at Bactra (Balkh), on the border-line between the Afghan highlands and the plateau. Situated at the meeting-point of the roads from Afghanistan and India, it was Alexander's sally-port into the Oxus plain, and the base from which the Greco-Bactrian rulers of the second century B.C. once more extended Greek dominion into India. Whether it also served as a starting-point for a trade route down the Oxus valley to the Caspian is uncertain. True, a direct connexion between the Oxus and the Caspian, by way of the Uzboi channel, has recently been re-established,[1] and a similar passage may have existed in ancient times. But the Oxus at best is a bad cargo-carrier because of its rapids and bars, and for three months of the year it is ice-bound. We may probably write off the Oxus trade route in the same way as its companion piece, the trade route between the Caspian and the Black Sea (pp. 177–8).[2]

But Bactra was also the converging-point of several routes from China, which cross the Pamirs by three passes of no great difficulty at a height of about 12,000 feet. The southernmost road proceeds from Yarkand, at the south-western edge of the Tarim basin, to the valley of the Murghab, and so to the Oxus. The central one takes off from Kashgar, at the western extremity of the basin, and reaches the Oxus by way of the Alai valley.[3] The third leaves Kashgar by way of the Terek pass (now furnished with a motor-road), and goes across Ferghana to Samarkand. No regular silk trade, to be sure, was established along these routes before the Parthian era, but the Greek kings of Bactria received occasional samples of Chinese merchandise (nickel and perhaps crucible steel in addition to silk) over one or other of these roads.[4]

Yet the situation of Bactra, however enviable in a geographic sense, was politically precarious, in that it was within easy reach of the central Asiatic steppe country and offered a tempting prey to its marauding populations. This danger had been clearly realized by the Achaemenid kings, who had drawn a line of

[1] N. Mikhaylov, *Soviet Geography* (2nd ed.), pp. 129–31.
[2] Tarn, op. cit., pp. 112–13 and Appendix 15.
[3] Sven Hedin, *The Silk Road*, ch. 18; A. Herrmann, *Das Land der Seide und Tibet im Lichte der Antike*, i, pp. 101–6.
[4] Tarn, pp. 110–12.

advanced forts along the river Iaxartes (Sir-Daria). Alexander imitated their precautions by founding Alexandria Eschate (Chodjend, near the great bend of the Iaxartes); Seleucus I built an outpost, Antioch-in-Scythia, beyond this point; and Antiochus I established an inner ring of military settlements round Antioch-in-Margiana (Merv), which also had a direct connexion with Persia by means of a branch from the Great East road. Yet it was from this quarter that the Greco-Bactrian dominion was finally invaded and overthrown (c. 150 B.C.) by one of the 'Sacae' tribes of the central Asiatic grasslands. Thus the great hiving-ground of world-disturbers, the home of Huns and Tatars and Turks (but also the origin of the Pax Tatarica and Pax Ottomanica) made its first prominent entrance into history.

§ 3. INDIA

From the north-west frontier the natural route for invaders of India lies along the ledge which skirts the Himalayan foot-hills in the direction of Delhi and the Ganges basin. At a height of 1,000 feet, this platform stands well above the flood-level of the Punjab streams, and in the dry season it offers easy crossing-places. Alexander accordingly struck out eastward from the Indus, and apparently no natural difficulty stood in the way of his final goal, the 'eastern Ocean' (Bay of Bengal). But for some unexplained reason he did not set out until the eve of the wet season (c. May–June 325 B.C.). He contrived to force the position of the river Hydaspes (Jhelum) against opposition, but he sustained losses in putting across the Acesines (Chenab), whose flood-bed had widened out to 15 stades (1¾ miles).[1] Meantime the monsoon had broken, and seventy days of wild weather bore down the discipline of his army,[2] so that the king had to surrender to their resolve to advance no farther. The Indian rain it was that inflicted on Alexander his one and only defeat.

Rejoining the Indus, Alexander followed the river to its estuary and set out thence on his return journey (p. 196). In restricting his Indian dominion to the basin of the Indus and its tributaries, he gave his empire a good natural frontier, for this basin is

[1] Arrian, *Anabasis* v. 20. 8–9 (on the authority of Ptolemy). The channels of some of the Punjab rivers have shifted considerably since ancient times.

[2] Diodorus, xvii. 94. 3. According to this writer the deluge 'so happened' (κατὰ τύχην χειμῶνες ἄγριοι κατερράγησαν)! A native of Sicily who had travelled little might have assumed that summer is everywhere a dry season. But Alexander, whose intelligence service was excellent, can hardly have ignored the risks he was taking.

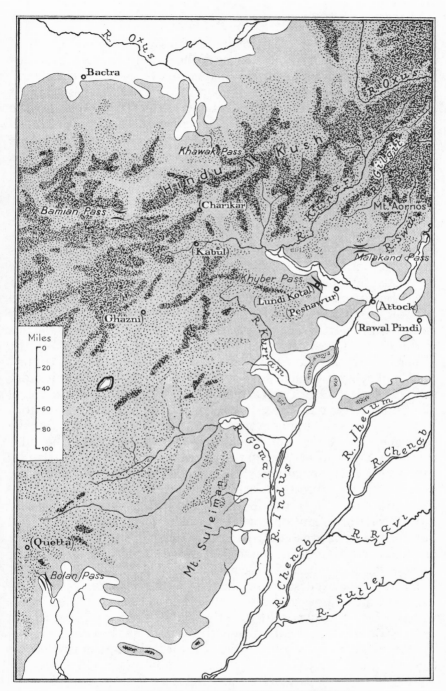

THE INDIAN NORTH-WEST FRONTIER

flanked for the greater part of its length by the 150-mile belt of the Thar desert. On the other hand, the empire which the Greco-Bactrian kings set up in the second century (c. 185–150 B.C.) stood in sheer defiance of political geography. These dynasts, albeit completely cut off from the main body of the Greek world by the intervening barrier of a hostile Seleucid monarchy, outdistanced Alexander in both directions. Thrusting eastward along the piedmont route, they penetrated into the Ganges valley and took possession of it as far as Palibothra (Patna); in their southward advance they overpassed the Indus estuary and following the coast as far as the mouth of the Nerbudda they reached out by way of its valley as far as Ozene (Ujjain).[1] It is a further geographical paradox that the second Greek dominion, with its far-flung frontiers dangling in the air, should have eked out its existence until c. 30 B.C.; that its final extinction should not have been accomplished from the east or south-east by a native Indian ruler, but by Sacae from the central Asiatic steppe, who pushed on after their conquest of Bactria; and that the Sacae did not enter India by the north-western passes, but thrust down from Bactria to the Indian Ocean (by an unknown route) and squeezed out the Greeks by working their way in reverse direction up the Indus.[2]

A final geographical absurdity in this true but improbable story is that the last Greek dynast in India, Hermaeus, was a vassal of China.[3] He may have made contact with Chinese territory by way of the Khyber route and the Panjshir pass (at the eastern end of the Hindu-Kush), and a final stage along the 'silk-route' to Yarkand or Kashgar (p. 199). It was no doubt also by this route that specimens of Greco-Roman art subsequently found their way into the Tarim basin (at Miran and Lop-Nor).[4] The direct road from north-west India by way of the Gilgit and Hunza territories and one of the Karakoram passes may be ruled out in spite of its greater directness, because of the extreme height and arctic weather of the passes (18,000 feet), which put them out of bounds for political intercourse.

Despite the excursions of the Greco-Bactrian rulers into the basins of the Ganges and the Nerbudda, the history of the Greeks in India is virtually confined to the Indus territories, and within this region their chief sphere of activity, as might be expected, was in the vicinity of the north-west frontier. The majority of the (mostly ephemeral) Greek colonies in India was planted near the

[1] Tarn, op. cit., ch. 4.　　　[2] Ibid., ch. 8.　　　[3] Ibid., pp. 339–50.
[4] M. A. Stein, Serindia; L. Halphen, Cambr. Anc. Hist. xii, p. 98.

northern end of the Indus valley,[1] and the Greek kings' chief
seat of government, Taxila (Bhir), lay between the Indus and
Jhelum, within easy reach of the north-western passes.

The Indus basin which was the only real home of the Greeks
in India is a land of high mountains in the far north, and of desert
at the southern end (Sind), which is situated just too far west to
get the benefit of the monsoon. Contrary to the reports of Greek
prospectors,[2] this region had no important mineral deposits, and
the 'ant-gold' which according to Herodotus was furtively fetched
in the Kabul district, what time its fierce and gigantic guardian
insects could be caught napping, had been exhausted before the
Hellenistic age, if indeed it was not a mere product of fancy.[3]
Moreover, the heat of Sind and of the sub-Himalayan valleys is
almost beyond the endurance of Europeans.[4]

But the monsoon rains which by-pass Sind are partly deflected
by the central Himalayas towards the upper Indus valley, and the
floods which this river and its tributaries roll down in July and
August inundate a wide area, thus enabling rich crops to be
raised even in the rainless belt of Sind.[5] The time of the floods,
moreover, is most convenient for purposes of cultivation, for the
inundated land remains moist until the end of the hot season.[6]
The typical 'monsoon' crops of cotton, cane-sugar, and rice[7] were
therefore grown in the Indus valley, where the Greeks first made
acquaintance with them. In addition to the monsoon deluge,
the Punjab also receives sufficient winter rain for the raising of
wheat and barley as a preliminary spring crop. This capacity of

[1] Of the seventeen Greek colonies in India, three were near the Indus estuary,
and seven close to the north-west frontier (V. Tscherikower, *Philologus*, Supplement
xix, pt. 1).

[2] Strabo, p. 700 (Γόργος ὁ μεταλλευτής).

[3] iii. 102. The real provenance of this gold has been located by G. F. Hudson
(*Europe and China*, ch. 1) in the Altai mountains, and by H. G. Rawlinson (*Inter-
course between India and the Western World*, pp. 71–4) in Dardistan (north of
Kashmir).

[4] 126–7° at Jacobabad in Sind; similar temperatures at Peshawar and Kohat.
The range of temperature in Punjab is 55–95° (as in northern Egypt). Another
deterrent to European settlers in India, its profusion of dangerous animals and
especially of reptiles, was duly reported by Greek writers. Nearchus (quoted by
Strabo, p. 706), particularly noticed the '16-foot vipers' (pythons) and the small
snakes (kraits), which are 'difficult to guard against' because of their inconspicuous-
ness and their habit of lurking in houses.

[5] A good description of the floods is in Strabo, pp. 691–3. Their full benefit was
not realized until the recent construction of irrigation works in Sind.

[6] The Nile observes the same convenient time-table for Egypt (p. 209).

[7] Cotton: Herodotus, iii. 106. 3; Strabo, p. 693. Sugar: Theophrastus, *Historia
Plantarum* iv. 4. 10; Strabo, p. 694 ('the canes make sugar without bees'). Rice:
Strabo, p. 692 (a good description of its cultivation).

Indian soil to produce two annual harvests attracted the special attention of the Greeks.[1] The products of the Indus valley did not indeed give rise to such an extensive trade with Mediterranean lands as those of central and southern India; but rice, sugar, and cotton all figured in the list of imports in Roman times.[2] At that period too consignments of Chinese silk which had reached Bactra by the trans-continental route were forwarded from that point to Barygaza (Broach) on the Indian coast and ended their westward journey by the sea route.[3]

Direct oversea traffic between India and Mediterranean lands was not established until the end of the pre-Christian era. It came in the first instance as the result of a discovery made by two Greek venturers, Eudoxus and Hippalus,[4] who ascertained the 'law of the monsoons' in the Indian Ocean: sail outward from Egypt between June and August, when the summer monsoon blows regularly from the south-west, and return from India between October and March, when the counter-monsoon of winter is set from the south-east; avoid the intermediate period, during which gales are frequent. This law not only fixed the season for navigation in the Indian Ocean, but gave Greek seamen confidence to attempt open-sea voyages across it, with the assurance that they would find a landfall in India and make the African coast on their return trip. By A.D. 50 or 60 they had established direct routes not only to the ports of the Indus basin but to the whole of the west coast of India;[5] and the more southerly tracks to this coast offered a double advantage. The north-western seaboard of India is lacking in good harbours. Its low alluvial land is fringed with shoals; the tides run strong in the Gulfs of Cutch and Cambay; and in the latter the bore caused by the meeting of the tide with the flood-waters of the Nerbudda was a serious menace to ancient shipping.[6] Neither could a permanent port be constructed at the Indus estuary, for the river continually cuts new channels across its delta. On the other hand, the table-land of south-west India had an easy approach from an open

---

[1] Megasthenes and Eratosthenes, quoted by Strabo (p. 693).
[2] E. H. Warmington, *The Commerce between the Roman Empire and India*, pp. 208–11.   [3] *The Periplus of the Erythraean Sea*, § 64.
[4] Warmington, op. cit., pp. 44–8; J. H. Thiel, *Eudoxus van Cyzicus*; W. Otto and H. Bengtson, *Abhandlungen der bayerischen Akademie der Wissenschaften*, philosophisch-historische Klasse, 1938, pp. 194 ff. Eudoxus made his trips to India c. 115 B.C. Hippalus was perhaps his shipmate (as Thiel suggests), but may belong to the first century B.C.
[5] Warmington, loc. cit.; M. P. Charlesworth, *Classical Quarterly*, 1928, pp. 92 ff.
[6] *Periplus*, §§ 39 ff., verified point for point by the *Indian Ocean Pilot*.

sea, and at Muziris (Cranganore) and Nelcynda (Kottayam) it possessed good river-ports. Moreover, it was the southern emporia to which the products most in demand in the Western world, spices and jewels, were brought for export.[1] In the centre of the west coast Calliena (Bombay)[2] was of little account in ancient times; there may have been political reasons for this, but its staple export, cotton, was not in great request among the Greeks and Romans.

It may seem strange that commerce between India and the ancient Mediterranean world should have been most active at a period when the Greeks had lost the whole of their Indian dominion. But, once discovered, the sea route between India and Egypt provided the easiest line of communications between East and West, and after the Roman occupation of Aden (p. 188) it offered the additional advantage of freedom from interruption on political grounds.

By A.D. 60 a few Greek pioneers had doubled Cape Comorin and had felt their way up the east coast of India to the Ganges estuary,[3] where they tapped another silk-route, leading from Tibet across the Himalayas by way of the Chumbi valley (c. 14,500 feet high) to Darjeeling and the Ganges basin.[4] In the early second century some bolder spirits applied the 'law of the monsoons' to the Bay of Bengal and thus discovered a short cut from Ceylon to the Malay peninsula.[5] A voyage due east would carry them to the Isthmus of Kra, where the peninsula slims down to some twenty-five miles. We may infer that those occasional Greek travellers who made their way to the Gulf of Siam and pushed on to Cambodja or China applied the 'law of isthmuses' in this case and went overland across Malaya instead of sailing through the Malacca Straits, for these are never mentioned by Greek or Roman authors, and the belief persisted that the eastern shore of the Indian Ocean trended southward to meet Terra Australis. If this was so, they presumably took passage on a Chinese vessel for their last stage.[6]

[1] Warmington, op. cit., pt. ii, chs. 2 and 3.   [2] *Periplus*, § 52.
[3] Ancient seamen were very hazy about the size of Ceylon, which they usually exaggerated. This suggests that they did not circumnavigate the island, like modern shipping, but sailed through the reef-infested Straits of Comorin. With shallow-draught vessels the risk may not have been excessive.
[4] *Periplus*, § 64, and note by Schoff, p. 272.
[5] E. H. Warmington, in Cary and Warmington, *The Ancient Explorers*, pp. 82–3.
[6] No ancient or medieval writer mentions tea, which was first brought from China to Europe in the sixteenth century. The tea-plant was not acclimatized in Assam, India, and Ceylon until the nineteenth century.

VIII. NORTH AFRICA

§ 1. THE RED SEA BORDER

THE only parts of East Africa beyond Egypt with which the Greeks or Romans had any regular dealings were Abyssinia and Somaliland.[1] These two countries form the northern extremity of the East African plateau. Somaliland is a featureless country with a fairly uniform altitude of 3,000 feet, whereas Abyssinia is a land of towering peaks (rising to 15,000 feet) and deeply sunk valleys. Both districts have this in common, that they present a steep face to the Red Sea and the Gulf of Aden, the Abyssinian coastal range attaining a height of 8,000 feet. The climates of their hinterlands differ greatly, for while both countries lie on the track of the Indian Ocean monsoon, the clouds do not break readily over the level and equably heated plateau of Somaliland, but they empty themselves in 'orographic' rain over the Abyssinian mountains. Yet this difference is not apparent on the Red Sea border, for the Abyssinian coast lies in the rain-shadow of the adjacent mountains, and is therefore as dry and desert as that of Somaliland. The desolation of the seaboard is enhanced by its lack of good harbours along a straight and reef-infested shore. Between Suez and Cape Guardafui the only good natural port is at Massowah (ancient Adule), in a bay between two headlands.

The hinterland, however, had a peculiar attraction for the Ptolemaic kings of Egypt, for it was one of the chief haunts of the African elephant.[2] In the Hellenistic period this beast was in request as an instrument of war and became the object of organized hunts, which were conducted from the station of Ptolemais Theron (Suakin). In the second century B.C. the use of elephants for military purposes came to an end, but their tusks continued to be in request for the ivory trade, which gave the East African ports a lingering importance in the Roman era. A subsidiary import from Somaliland was frankincense, which grew on the coastal range behind Berberah, in a limited region of more generous rain.

[1] Occasional Greek venturers ran down the east African coast to Rhapta (Zanzibar) for cargoes of ivory (*Periplus of the Erythraean Sea*, ch. 16).

[2] The statement of Polybius (v. 84. 6), followed by a train of other ancient writers, that the African elephant is smaller than the Indian, is defended in an (as yet unpublished) article by Sir William Gowers, the manuscript of which I have been able to consult, by courtesy of the author.

§ 2. EGYPT

As defined by its present political frontiers, Egypt is a square-shaped territory of *c.* 600 miles in either direction; but throughout historical times its habitable area has been confined to the Nile valley, and in the days of Greek and Roman history it extended southward no farther than the First Cataract.[1] Above the Delta the cultivable land nowhere has a width of more than fifteen miles, for on either side the river valley is hemmed in by a steeply scarped limestone ridge, and the transition from the sown land to the desert is utterly abrupt. The entire productive area does not exceed 25,000 square miles.

The reason why Egypt outside the Nile valley is a desert is because in regard to the world's weather systems it is a no-man's-land. It lies too far north to come within range of the summer monsoon from the Indian Ocean, yet only the Delta lies within reach of the Mediterranean winter cyclones. The prevailing wind is a breeze from the north which, blowing across the Mediterranean waters, mitigates the summer heat and is relatively warm in winter. Thus Egypt is not exposed to the extremes of temperature which characterize Arabia, Mesopotamia, and Persia: at Cairo the mean annual range lies between 55° and 95°. But because the Egyptian air progresses at a uniform speed rather than circulates at varying velocities, it induces hardly any rainfall south of Cairo.[2] Alexandria receives a yearly average of eight inches, but in Upper Egypt any measurable downpour is news.[3]

In spite of its desert climate, the Nile valley has, ever since Pharaonic days, been the most intensively tilled and the most densely peopled of Mediterranean lands. As a cultivable area it is quite literally the 'gift of the Nile',[4] for it owes its abundant and inexhaustible fertility to the process by which it has been and is still built up out of the river's sediment, and its assured supply of water to the Nile floods.[5]

[1] Beyond Assuan the Romans occupied a strip of some fifty miles (the 'Dodeca-schoenus') as a neutral zone between Egypt and Ethiopia, analogous to the modern Gibraltar.

[2] In winter and spring a trough of low pressure over the Levantine Sea may induce a strong south-westerly wind (the 'khamsin'), which is hot and sand-laden like a Scirocco. But these 'desert storms' never last long.

[3] Herodotus went a little too far when he remarked that a shower on Egyptian Thebes in 525 B.C. was the first ever (iii. 10. 3).

[4] Hecataeus, quoted by Herodotus (ii. 5. 1—without acknowledgement), and by Arrian (*Anabasis* v. 6. 5).

[5] This sediment is a fine and tractable mud; the coarser detritus is intercepted by the natural dams of granite within the river-bed in the Cataract zone.

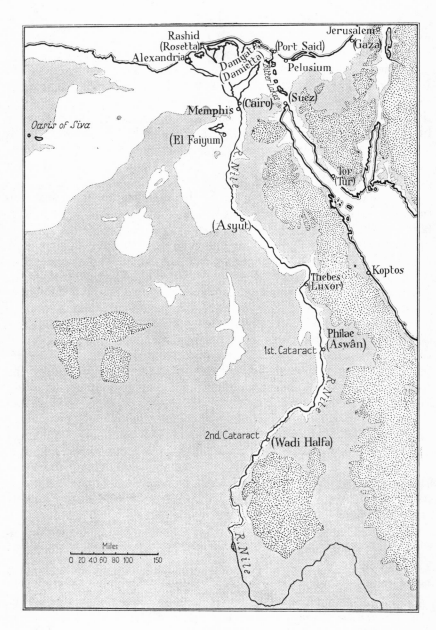

EGYPT

Taking its rise in the equatorial belt of Africa, where the Great Lakes serve as a storage basin for the copious and regular rains of that region, the Nile has a remarkably steady flow throughout the winter and spring, despite its intermediate course through a thousand miles of Sudanese steppe and Nubian desert.[1] Between July and September it receives successive spates from its chief tributaries, the Blue Nile and the Atbara, which are then swollen by the breaking of the monsoon on the Abyssinian highlands.[2] The season of inundation thus coincides with the period of greatest heat, and the drenched land therefore does not dry out until the crops are sown and well set. Moreover, the full utilization of the flood water is expedited by the elevation of the river's bed (through the accumulation of sediment) above the rest of the valley. By means of a simple system of sluices in the longitudinal dykes that enclose the river channel, the inundation water can be drawn off and passed by gravitation through a series of compartments into which the crop land has been banked off, so as to soak the land systematically, and the surplus can be returned into the main stream when the floods have subsided.[3]

On the margin of the inundation area additional strips of land could be brought under cultivation by means of water-hoists. For this purpose swing-beams had been employed since Pharaonic times; under the Ptolemies water-wheels were also brought into use.[4] The 'uninundated' (ἄβροχος) land had a higher value, because it could be irrigated and cropped more than once in a season.[5]

Another increment to Egypt's productive area was obtained by reclaiming the Fayum basin (the 'Lake Moeris' of the ancients), situated some fifty miles south-west of Cairo, at a level considerably below that of the Nile. In prehistoric times a slight upheaval of the intermediate land cut off the Fayum from the river and brought about its partial desiccation; but under the first or second Ptolemy a canal was cut through the bar and furnished

[1] The rainfall of the Lakes district is heaviest from January to April. This extra measure maintains but does not raise the Nile level.

[2] On ancient speculations about the Nile flood see Herodotus, ii. 20–5; Tozer, op. cit., pp. 62–3. Aristotle divined that it was due to tropical rains, and Agatharchides (a second-century writer conversant with the Red Sea) pointed out that the rains came from Abyssinia.

[3] A. C. Johnson, in Frank, *Economic Survey*, ii, pp. 7–19.

[4] Rostovtzeff, *Hellenistic History*, i, p. 363. It is not unlikely that the Archimedean screw was also used in Ptolemaic times.

[5] On the régime of the γῆ ἄβροχος see W. L. Westermann, *Classical Philology*, 1919, pp. 158 ff.; 1920, pp. 120 ff.

with a sluice, by means of which the volume of water admitted from the Nile could be controlled.[1] It was on this reclamation area that most of the Greek settlements in Egypt were made.[2]

But Egypt, albeit a gift, was not a free gift of the Nile. Its prosperity has at all times depended on incessant regulation of the river's waters. Left to itself the Nile, like the Euphrates and Tigris, will encumber its bed with detritus and convert the seasonal flood into a permanent one. In the pre-dynastic age of Egypt, before a regular and comprehensive system of water-control had been established by a centralized government, the Nile valley was a straggle of extensive fenlands; and it required centuries of dike-construction, so as to embank the stream in a permanent channel, and to contain its flood-water in the catchment basins, before the valley became continuously cultivable.[3] Even so, the problem of keeping the Nile water in hand at all places and seasons was not definitely solved until the British occupation of Egypt. In ancient times insufficient provision was made for reserve stores of water against an occasional 'low Nile', so that there were seasons in which Egypt had to import foodstuffs,[4] and the risk of a crop failure was not finally averted until the building of the Assuan dam. Neither were adequate measures taken to ensure the run-off of the flood-waters from a 'high Nile' in the Delta, of which large tracts remained liable to relapse into morass until the recent installation of sluices near Cairo.[5] But in any normal year, once the Nile had been put into harness, it could be made to provide the requisite volume of water at the right time and place. Under such conditions the Egyptian cultivator was presented year after year with an all but ready-made seed-bed, for the soil was re-fertilized with finely ground detritus at the same time as it was water-flushed, and it required no further preparation than to be opened up with a hoe or a light plough.[6] He had no need to leave half his land fallow in order

[1] Miss G. Caton Thompson and Miss E. W. Gardner, *The Desert Fayum.* (This work has superseded all others on the pre-Ptolemaic history of the Fayum.) Strabo erred in stating that the Ptolemaic sluice also served to let the irrigation-water run back into the Nile after the flood had subsided (p. 811). The Fayum was permanently below the level of the Nile bed.

[2] The Greek Fayum towns have been our chief source of papyri.

[3] On the 'challenge' of the untamed Nile, see A. J. Toynbee, *A Study of History,* i, pp. 302–15.   [4] Pliny, *Panegyricus* 30, §§ 2–5 (under Trajan).

[5] Hence in times of unrest 'kings of the marshland' like Athens' ally Amyrtaeus (Thucydides, i. 112. 3) could assume the part of Hereward the Wake in a Deltaic 'Isle of Ely'.

[6] But Herodotus went too far in saying that the peasantry merely had to cast their seed and turn on their hogs to trample it in (ii. 14. 2).

to conserve its ground-water, or to find time for repeated tillage.
The 'undrenched' areas which were irrigated by hoists could be
made to yield two harvests in a season.[1]

The main crop of Egypt was wheat. By the fifth century B.C.,
if not before, a surplus was available for export to Greece, and
under the early Ptolemies the Nile valley became one of the
principal granaries of the Aegean area. Whether it contributed
a regular supply to Rome in the republican era is uncertain, but
under the emperors it provided sufficient to subsist the capital
for three or four months of the year.[2] A considerable acreage was
under forage crops which supplemented the natural pasture of the
fenlands, so that Egypt was also abundantly provided with live-
stock.

On the other hand cotton, which is now one of the country's
main cash crops, was probably not acclimatized before the Roman
era, and then only on a small scale (p. 22). Moreover, while the
Nile valley is almost ideal as an arable country, it is not well
suited to the typical garden industry of the Mediterranean lands.
Although the Greeks of the Ptolemaic era raised the production
of wine to a considerable volume, only a few brands, such as the
'Mareotic' vintage of the Alexandrian region,[3] could have been
fit for the royal table. In the Fayum the Greeks obtained a large
yield of olives, but the oil had a rank smell, and in the days of
Strabo olive-cultivation was restricted to this area and to the
outskirts of Alexandria.[4] In Upper Egypt the summer was hot
enough for dates,[5] but these were never a staple product, as in
Mesopotamia. Still less did the Greeks succeed in acclimatizing
trees suitable for ship-building, such as the larger conifers, for
the sedimentary soil of the Nile valley is too powdery to give a
firm hold to tree-roots.[6] Consequently the Ptolemies, like the
Pharaohs before them, had to derive their timber from Phoenicia
or Cyprus or Lycia. But in the papyrus plant of the fenlands
Egypt formerly possessed a highly lucrative asset. The pith of
the Deltaic variety of this reed produced the smoothest writing-
material of the ancient world; hence Alexandria became its

[1] An experiment in following up a main crop of barley with a catch crop of
'three-month' wheat, at the instance of Ptolemy II, is mentioned in C. C. Edgar,
The Zenon Papyri (Cairo), no. 59155. On Ptolemaic land-work in general, see M.
Schnebel, *Die Landwirtschaft im Ptolemäischen Ägypten.*
[2] Josephus, *Bellum Judaicum* ii, § 386; Frank, *Economic Survey*, v, p. 219.
[3] Strabo, p. 799; Horace, *Odes* i. 37. 14: '[Cleopatrae] mentem lymphatam
Mareotico.'   [4] p. 809.   [5] Ibid., p. 818.
[6] The 'wood-cutting' (ξυλοκοπία) which is often mentioned in Ptolemaic papyri
refers to the clearing of brushwood from reclamation-land.

principal book market, and by a judicious thinning down of the reed-beds the stationers of that city were able to command monopoly prices.[1]

The surrounding deserts contributed to Egypt the mineral resources which the Nile valley lacked. Gold, copper, and iron were extracted from the mountains of the Red Sea border.[2] The chief deficiency was in silver, which had to be imported from Asia Minor, or perhaps from Spain by way of Carthage.[3] From the desert the architects and sculptors of Egypt drew an abundant and varied supply of stone. The limestone ridges bordering on the Nile valley produced the material for their monumental buildings; the Red Sea border and Nubia supplied the hard stones (granite, porphyry, &c.) for statuary and decoration.[4] From desiccated lake-basins of the desert zone saltpetre and soda were obtained (both of these for mummifying, soda also for soap- and glass-making), and alum (for dye-fixing).

With the exception of timber, Egypt had at call every prime necessity of civilized life, and despite the density of its popula- tion (p. 216) it became one of the chief exporting countries of the Mediterranean area. Consequently under the Ptolemies it accumulated large stocks of money from its trading balances, and under the Caesars it became one of the most prolific milch cows of the Roman empire.

As a barrier to intercourse the deserts which encompass the Nile valley are even more formidable than a glance at the map might indicate. The eastern desert ascends to a ridge of barren mountains 6,000 feet high, which shuts off access to the Red Sea almost completely. The Red Sea coast of Egypt was therefore scarcely inhabited, but for a few settlements of cave-dwellers whose primitive ways of life aroused the curiosity of Greek travellers.[5] The western or Libyan desert contains several large oases within the present Egyptian territory, but taken as a whole it is a featureless plateau with insufficient relief to induce local

[1] Strabo, pp. 799–800.

[2] Ibid., p. 821. Diodorus (iii. 12–13) gives a gruesome account of the ruthless methods by which the criminals and prisoners of war who provided the labour for the mines were literally worked to death. In the age of the Tell-el-Amarna letters (c. 1375 B.C.) the gold of Egypt was a potent diplomatic asset.

[3] This scarcity may help to explain the poor quality of the coinage issued by the Ptolemies after 200 B.C. and by the Roman emperors for local circulation.

[4] A. Lucas, Ancient Egyptian Materials and Industries (2nd ed.), chs. xii and xiii.

[5] Diodorus, iii. 32–3, following Agatharchides (Geographici Graeci Minores, i, pp. 153–6).

rainfall, and its water-points sometimes lie as far as 180 miles apart. No trans-Saharan route takes off from Egypt, and the only desert station that frequently attracted visitors from the Nile was the oasis of Siva (*c.* 300 miles west of Cairo), where lay the oracular seat of Amon.

Travel to and from Egypt by water is also beset with difficulties. Navigation up Nile is interrupted near Assuan by a staircase of cataracts, and beyond these lies the Nubian section of the desert which extends at points right up to the river banks. These barriers, it is true, have never wholly cut off Egypt from the Sudan. Intercourse with ancient Ethiopia dated back to the early Pharaonic dynasties; but in Greek and Roman days it amounted to little more than outpost skirmishes and an occasional punitive expedition under Ptolemaic generals or Roman prefects. Above Khartum the Nile is encumbered with floating masses of 'sudd' (vegetable debris) which baffled the explorers of the river until 1860, and its navigators until the present century. The Nile valley therefore was not an easy road to inner Africa, and Egypt has always been a land of the Mediterranean border rather than of the African continent.

The Mediterranean sea-front of Egypt, taken as a whole, is no more inviting than that of Palestine. For the greater part of the year it is swept by a brisk north wind, and that stretch of it which lies between the arms of the Nile is an alluvial marsh-land behind a fringe of shoals. In 306 B.C. Demetrius the Besieger, after annihilating the Ptolemaic fleet at the battle of Cypriote Salamis, was unable to follow up his advantage with an invasion of Egypt, because the strength of the onshore wind made a beach landing impossible.[1]

Nevertheless Egypt was predestined by its isthmus position to be a meeting-point of peoples by land and sea. Not only do the Mediterranean and Red Seas here approach within 100 miles of one another, but communication between them is easily established. Some forty miles below Cairo a desiccated river-bed stretches between the easternmost arm of the Nile and the Bitter Lakes (south of Ismailia), from the southern end of which another corridor extends to Suez.[2] To dig an equivalent of the Suez Canal along this line was a work for spades and shovels unaided by picks,

---

[1] Diodorus, xx. 74; Plutarch *Demetrius*, ch. 19, § 3.
[2] Herodotus, ii. 158; How and Wells, commentary ad loc.; G. Poesener, *Chronique d'Égypte*, 1938, pp. 251–73. Presumably the canal became choked by desert sand-storms.

and it was completed in the first instance by Pharaoh Necho
(*c.* 600 B.C.), if not before. No adequate provision indeed would
seem to have been made for upkeep, so that major works of
renovation became necessary under Darius I, Ptolemy II, and
Trajan. But the fact that these repairs were undertaken again
and again suggests that for light craft at any rate, if not for ocean-
going ships, this waterway had a permanent value. The canal
route, moreover, could be supplemented by an overland track
connecting Thebes with Koptos (on the Red Sea, near Kosseir)
through a gap in the coastal range. This line of traffic was
organized for caravans by Ptolemy II, who equipped the necessary
rest-stations; but characteristically it was left to Augustus to
provide a water-supply by digging wells and building reservoirs,
so that the freight-camels could be relieved of their extra load of
drinking-water.[1] Henceforth Koptos became the regular port of
departure for East Indiamen.

For the absence of good harbourage on the Delta coast compensation was found until the time of Alexander in river ports,
the most important of which was Naucratis on the westernmost
branch of the Nile.[2] This station, however, was not commodious
enough for the far-sighted ambitions of Alexander, who selected
a new site for a harbour on a shelf of firm ground beyond the
western extremity of the Delta. The foreshore at this point was
not liable to shoaling, for the eastward current which usually
sets along the Egyptian coast would carry the Nile sediment in
the opposite direction; and it was sheltered from the prevailing
northerlies by the adjacent island of Pharos. A mole which
Alexander built to connect Pharos with the mainland made
Alexandria into a double harbour of a familiar Greek type, so as
to afford protection against winds from any direction. The
lighthouse which Sostratus, the architect of Ptolemy I, set up
on Pharos may have been primarily intended to guide vessels
leaving port on the off-shore breeze which usually springs up
on this coast after dark.[3] A short canal provided through travel
(for smaller craft at least) between Alexandria and the Nile, and
solved the city's problem of drinking-water.

[1] *Corpus Inscriptionum Latinarum*, iii. 6627 B, ll. 10 ff.—a record of *lacci* and
hydreumata installed by Roman troops. The reason why the canal route was not
used for East Indian traffic was presumably that it would not take ships of 'India-
man' displacement. According to the *Red Sea Pilot* conditions of navigation at the
northern end of the Red Sea are no worse than elsewhere.

[2] The port of Daphnae on the eastern (Pelusiac) arm fell into disuse *c.* 600 B.C.

[3] W. Leaf, *Proceedings of the Classical Association*, 1921, pp. 31–2.

Communications between Egypt and the outer world by the coastal routes from either end of the Delta are impeded by protrusions of the desert to the Mediterranean's edge. Even after the Romans had constructed a road from Alexandria to Cyrene, intercourse between Egypt and Cyrenaica continued probably by sea rather than overland. On the other hand, the road from Pelusium into Palestine had a relatively short stage in the desert and was indispensable as a link between two of the world's most ancient seats of civilization. Though merchandise in bulk was sent by the sea route to or from Phoenicia since at least 3000 B.C.,[1] light traffic plied at all times by the Pelusium route, and invading armies again and again forced it on the way from Asia to Africa, or vice versa.

Road travel along the Nile valley is facilitated by the dikes that line the river on either bank.[2] In flood time the dike roads provided the only connexion between the riverside settlements, which mostly stood on isolated and artificially constructed knolls. But at all seasons the main artery of traffic was the Nile itself. Boats proceeding up stream could at need be towed from the dike-ways, but the north wind blowing constantly up the valley was strong enough to permit the use of sails. To obtain steerage-way for vessels drifting down river heavy stones were taken in tow (as the equivalents of our anchor-drags).[3]

The fording of the Nile is not wholly impossible in the low-water season, but it is rendered precarious by the lack of firm gravel deposits in its bed. The Macedonian regent Perdiccas discovered this to his cost when he sought to force a crossing against Ptolemy I, for the channel sagged under the weight of his elephants and engulfed part of his army.[4] But outside flood-time the Nile is well suited to ferry services, for it is generally free from squalls and eddies.[5] The numerous river-arms and extensive marshes in the Delta, however, compelled traffic to follow rather than to cut across the water-courses; hence the road from Alexandria to Pelusium went round by way of Memphis (fifteen miles south of Cairo).

[1] The Egyptian war-lord Thothmes III habitually used the sea route to convey his invading armies to Syria (c. 1475 B.C.). It is not unlikely that the Ptolemies maintained their hold on Phoenicia by means of their fleet.

[2] Since Ptolemaic times these roads carried a regular postal service (B. P. Grenfell and A. S. Hunt, The Hibeh Papyri, no. 110).

[3] Herodotus, ii. 96. 4.

[4] Diodorus, xvii. 35. 2.

[5] A fortuitous squall prevented Antigonus I from forcing a passage in 306 B.C. (Diodorus, xx. 76. 4).

The high fertility of the Nile valley, and the absolute aridity of its borderlands, has brought about such a concentration of its inhabitants that it has always been the most densely populated of Mediterranean lands (apart from the large modern conurbations). It numbered 7,000,000 inhabitants *c.* 50 B.C., and *c.* A.D. 70 it contained 7,500,000 exclusive of Alexandria (which would account for at least another half-million).[1] But within its area the settlements were strung out evenly. The uniform productivity of the valley, the abundance of water at all seasons, the lack of natural strongholds and the absence of need for them, all contributed to the equable distribution of the people over a large number of villages[2] and the slow growth of town life. It was not until the second century A.D. that any widespread tendency to 'synoikismoi' became apparent,[3] and before the reign of Septimius Severus only the Greek colonies possessed municipal constitutions.

The consequent absence of municipal patriotism in Egypt reinforced two primary geographical causes that facilitated the political union of the country under an autocratic government: the imperative need of systematic and centralized control of the Nile waters, and the facility with which the king's writ could be made to run along the Nile valley. It is true that the great length of the valley (even if reckoned no farther up stream than Assuan) favoured a tendency to polarize control in two rival capitals in Upper Egypt and the Delta respectively. Hence in the Pharaonic era the seat of government shifted to and fro between Thebes and one or other of the Delta towns (Memphis, Bubastis, Tanis, or Sais). Yet as early as 3300 B.C. Upper and Lower Egypt had been welded into a single realm; and as the country was progressively drawn into the sphere of Near Eastern and eventually of general Mediterranean politics, its administrative centre of gravity moved definitely towards the Mediterranean seaboard.[4]

The genial but somewhat monotonous climate, the easy conditions of life in Egypt, and its partial isolation, made for conservatism and pacifism among its people. Though Pharaonic Egypt had an interlude of imperialism in the Eighteenth Dynasty (1580 B.C. ff.), this came in answer to a special challenge, the first great invasion from Asia (by the 'Hyksos' people). Among the

---

[1] Diodorus, i. 31. 8; Josephus, *Bellum Judaicum* ii, § 385.
[2] According to Diodorus (i. 31. 7) more than 30,000 villages had been enumerated under Ptolemy I!
[3] Rostovtzeff, *Roman Empire*, pp. 271–3.
[4] The marginal position of Alexandria was expressed in its full name, 'Alexandria *ad* Aegyptum'.

Hellenistic dynasts the Ptolemies, while intent on holding certain outlying possessions of special economic value (such as Phoenicia and Cyprus), made it their chief object to cultivate their Egyptian 'home farm'. And Egyptian culture, after an early period of eager apprenticeship and self-improvement, became self-contained and merely traditional.

Yet the natural wealth of the country could not fail to draw foreign adventurers to it. The approach from Syria became a regular invasion route, and the frontier line at Pelusium, though protected by a desert belt in front of it (p. 215), was sometimes ill guarded. From the time of the last Assyrian kings (c. 675 B.C.) Egypt was almost continuously under foreign domination. In view of the density of the native population none of the successive conquerors was able to colonize the country on any considerable scale. Apart from Alexandria the only compact centre of Hellenism lay in the reclamation lands of the Fayum; and the Romans never made a settlement of any sort in it. Thus Egypt, under its alien masters, became an exploitation colony. Because of its self-replenishing riches and the self-satisfied passivity of its indigenous folk, it was able to sustain this role from century to century.

§ 3. Cyrenaica and Tripolitania

(a) *Cyrenaica.* The same conditions of climate which have converted all Egypt outside the Nile valley into a desert have also determined the characters of its western neighbours, Cyrenaica and Tripolitania, which are waste lands with coastal oases.

Directly south of the Greek mainland the general flatness of the shore of north-eastern Africa is relieved by a line of hills rising to a height of 1,800 feet, and behind this coastal range an interior ridge reaches up to 3,300 feet (Jebel Akudar, near Barce). The terrace between these two chains is shielded by the inner range from desert sandstorms,[1] and it receives winter rains, varying from twelve to twenty inches, which are precipitated by the cooling of the northern and western winds as they ascend the mountain flanks.[2] The rain, it is true, is absorbed very rapidly by a highly porous limestone rock, so that over the greater part of Cyrenaica cultivation is made possible only by the systematic

---

[1] The inner range, however, is no barrier to occasional invasions of locusts from the desert.

[2] Here, according to Herodotus (iv. 158. 3), the 'sky had holes in it'. The sea winds and rains maintain the mean temperature of Cyrenaica within a range of 50–90°.

collection of the water in reservoirs; but in some districts a band of impervious clay in the rock gives rise to powerful springs.

At one favoured spot, some ten miles from the coast, an upland glen receives a copious supply of water which gushes in cascades from springs in the enfolding mountain-sides. Here Greek immigrants, after some unavailing gropings for good land, established the flourishing colony of Cyrene.[1] The domain of Cyrene included tracts of woodland and of horse-pasture: readers of Pindar will remember the trophies which the city-kings of Cyrene gathered in the chariot races at Delphi.[2] Between Cyrene and the sea lay a zone of orchard land, and behind it a tract of arable country which yielded surpluses of grain for export.[3] Lastly, the steppe on the reverse side of the inner range produced a medicinal plant, silphium, whose juice was reputed a specific for ailments ranging from a chill to a snake-bite.[4] This magic herb disappeared before long from the hinterland—we may presume that it was carelessly picked without attempts at re-planting; but while it lasted it made the fortune of Cyrene, and it was fitly adopted as a standing type on the coinage of the city.

Beyond the Cyrenaic hill-country the Libyan plateau extends over 1,000 miles to the Sudan. Save for a chain of small oases running from east to west, this wide belt of land is utter desert, and Cyrenaica in ancient times was never the terminal region of a caravan route.[5] To east and west the coastal zone was equally uncultivable over a stretch of 500 miles. On its Egyptian border Cyrenaica lay barely within the grasp of a well-equipped expeditionary force; but it never fell into the hands of the Pharaohs, and its later attachment to the Persian and Ptolemaic empires was loose and discontinuous.

The Cyrenaic coast is firm and unencumbered with fluvial deposits. But it lies exposed to all the weathers, and only at a few points could ships draw upon it for a scanty supply of brackish water.[6] Of its three principal stations Ptolemais (Barce) was 'storm-tost' (ἐπίσαλος); Berenice (Benghazi) offered better shelter but had a shallow approach and stood at the far western edge of

---

[1] For an account of the Greek colonization, see Herodotus, iv. 150–9.

[2] *Pythian Odes* 4 and 5.

[3] *Supplementum Epigraphicum Graecum*, ix. 1. 2.

[4] Pliny, xxii. 101–6.

[5] The trans-Saharan trip made by some young dare-devils of the Libyan border-tribe of the Nasamones (Herodotus, ii. 32) was a mere escapade and had no permanent results.

[6] The water-points are carefully noted in the *Stadiasmus Maris Magni* (C. Müller, *Geographici Graeci Minores*, i, pp. 429 ff.).

the cultivable zone; away towards Egypt Antipyrgus (Tobruk) was securely recessed up a narrow creek but opened on to mere desert.[1]

Thus even on its sea-front Cyrenaica was in large measure isolated. Despite its proximity to Greece it was never drawn into the main current of Greek politics or commerce,[2] and its political history was almost summed up in its local faction-fights. When the Romans received the land as a gift from its last Ptolemaic ruler, they hesitated for some twenty years (96–74 B.C.) before occupying it.[3] But they subsequently made amends for their tardiness by the energy with which they organized water-conservation and irrigation so as to extend the area of cultivation to its limits.[4]

(b) *Tripolitania.* A 500-mile strip of desert separates Cyrenaica from the coastal oasis of Tripolitania. Here a range of heights rising to 2,800 feet (the Takat ridge) induces 'orographic' rain in sufficient quantities to supply a broad plain with water for the intensive cultivation of date-palms and olives. This stretch of the north African seaboard was also the best point of departure for the trans-Saharan caravan trade, for the two large oases of Jerma and Murzuk to the south of Tripolitania provided advanced bases for the final desert stage on the routes to Lake Chad and the Niger.[5] A caravan route was probably explored, if not established, by the Carthaginians,[6] and with the introduction of the camel into north Africa under Ptolemaic or Roman rule the traffic no doubt became more regular.[7] But just as the Greeks relinquished the caravan commerce of the Near East to the Arabians (p. 187), so the Romans left the trans-Saharan traffic in the hands of the oasis tribe of the Garamantes.[8] In any case, the trade of the African desert in ancient times was not to be compared with that

[1] Ibid., §§ 38, 55, 57.

[2] It is now generally agreed that the early Greek pottery formerly called 'Cyrenaic' was made in Laconia.

[3] The occupation of Cyrenaica may have formed part of the Roman plan for a general drive against the pirates who then infested the Mediterranean.

[4] H. I. Bell, *Cambr. Anc. Hist.* xi, p. 672.

[5] This route was taken in reverse by Gen. Leclercq in 1943, during the Battle of Tripolitania.

[6] Athenaeus, ii. 22, p. 44e. (A Carthaginian had repeatedly crossed the Sahara on a diet of dry barley without water! In spite of its absurd detail, this story may be regarded as evidence for a Punic trade route.)

[7] King Juba I of Numidia possessed a few camels in 46 B.C. (*Bellum Africum* 68. 4); by the fourth century A.D. they had become plentiful in Tripolitania (Ammianus Marcellinus, 28. 6. 5).

[8] For an isolated Roman expedition across the Sahara under one Iulius Maternus, see Cary and Warmington, *Explorers*, pp. 182–3.

of Arabia for volume or value, though it probably helped to satisfy
the Mediterranean demand for ivory.

The coast between Cyrenaica and Tripolitania is of the same
type as that of southern Palestine. Built up by a slow elevation
of the land, it is flat and straight, and it offers no good harbourage,
except under the lee of a cape and a chain of small islands in the
bay of Tripoli. In ancient times it was peculiarly dreaded by
sailors, because a tide rising to five feet, and banked up by frequent north winds, used to cast up ships on to a fringe of shoals.[1]
Hence this piece of water was named the 'drag-net' ($\Sigma\acute{v}\rho\tau\iota\varsigma$).

Tripolitania thus resembled Cyrenaica in being half-isolated
from the world around. Under Roman rule its chief towns,
Leptis (Lebda) and Oea (Tripoli), achieved prosperity, because
the Roman market was near enough and large enough to absorb
its surplus stocks of oil. But the district as a whole played a far
smaller part in ancient history than its central position in the
Mediterranean would suggest.

§ 4. NORTH-WEST AFRICA

The eastern half of north Africa, though more Mediterranean
than African, differs markedly in structure and climate from the
Mediterranean norm; but in passing over to its western portion,
comprising Tunisia, Algeria, and Morocco (the ancient Roman
provinces of 'Africa', Numidia, and Mauretania), we return to
the true Mediterranean world. This protruding ledge of the continent projects so far northward that its coast runs close to the
central axis of the Mediterranean Sea. Structurally it belongs to
the Mediterranean region of folded mountains. Its highlands rise
in successive steps to the massive block of Mt. Aures (7,000 feet)
in the east and to the long-drawn-out range of Mt. Atlas (rising
to 15,000 feet) in the centre and west. The terraced plateau, which
extends between the seaboard and Mt. Atlas, attains an average
width of 300 miles (narrowing to 150 miles near Bescara (Biskra),
where the Sahara reaches out farthest to the north) and stands
at a general altitude of 2,500–3,000 feet. The rock-formations
consist for the most part of the typical Mediterranean limestone,
carved in high relief with citadel hills like those of Greece and
Italy. Among these natural fortresses we may instance 'Zaghouan'
and 'Long Stop' hills in Tunisia, which did duty as strong points
in the Battle of Africa, and the ancient Numidian capital of Cirta

[1] Strabo, p. 836. H. Weld-Blundell, *Annual of the British School at Athens*,
ii, pp. 115 ff.

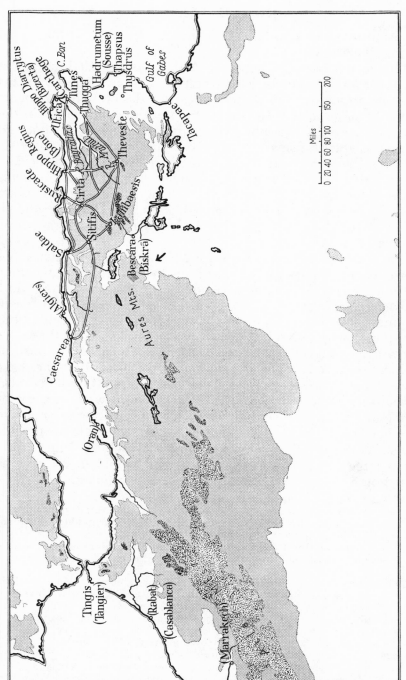

NORTH-WEST AFRICA

Miles
0 20 40 60 80 100   150   200

Tingis
(Tangier)

(Rabat)

(Casablance)

(Marrakech)

(Oran)

Caesarea
(Algiers)

Saldae

Rusicade

Hippo Regins
(Bône)

Sitifis

Cirta

Milevum

Milbaesis

Bescarae
(Biskra)

Aures Mts.

Theveste

Thugga

Tunes

Carthage

C.Bar.

Hippo Diarrhytus
(Bizerta)

Utica

Hadrumetum
(Sousse)

Thapsus

Thysdrus

Gulf of Gabes

Tacapae

Tacapae

(Constantine), situated like many an Italian city on a high bluff between two rivers.

The greater part of north-west Africa was included in ancient times within the zone of Mediterranean climate, and it remains so at the present day, for in these latitudes desiccation has not set in on any large scale.[1] In winter the prevailing weather is of the cyclonic type, with variable winds and sharp gusts of rain, and occasional spells of severe cold.[2] Its summers are monotonously fine; but in Morocco the heat is tempered by a current of cold water in the Atlantic,[3] and on the plateau the mean July temperature does not, as a rule, rise above 80°. The weather conditions are therefore congenial to immigrants from south Europe,[4] and in ancient times the robust health of the native population impressed Roman observers.

But north-west Africa, like most Mediterranean countries, has a problem of water-supply. The rains in winter are heavy along the north coast, where by a curious inversion they grow more copious from west to east,[5] and in the central highlands; but in summer they give out completely, except for some torrential but very rare downpours.[6] Over most of north-west Africa the year's rainfall does not exceed sixteen inches; in southern Tunisia it dwindles to seven inches; here and there the local salt-mines have served since ancient times as quarries for building-materials.[7] Save in the higher ranges of Mt. Atlas, the rain-water is not supplemented to any appreciable extent by the melting of snows in summer. It is debatable whether the Sahara has made any notable gains in historical times by means of its encroaching sandstorms;[8] but a large portion of north-west Africa would in no case be cultivable without a strict régime of water-conservation.

[1] S. Gsell, *Histoire ancienne de l'Afrique du Nord*, i, pp. 40–99.

[2] On several occasions French troops have perished in snowdrifts on the uplands.

[3] The effect is like that of the cold submarine springs which induce San Francisco's cool summer breeze.

[4] The amount of this immigration in ancient times is problematical. On its importance in the last hundred years see Elizabeth Monroe, *The Mediterranean in Politics*.

[5] Thirty-two inches per annum at Algiers, forty-eight inches at Bône (mostly in winter). Operations in the Battle of Africa (1942–3) were much delayed by winter rains.

[6] According to Orosius (v. 15. 15) a severe rainstorm supervened to help the Romans in a desperate encounter with Jugurtha.

[7] Herodotus, iv. 185. 2, and note in How and Wells's Commentary.

[8] Encroachment by the desert in historical times is accepted by E. F. Gautier, *Le Sahara*, p. 71, and A. G. P. Martin, *Les Oasis Sahariennes*, pp. 339 ff.; it is denied by H. Schirmer, *Le Sahara*, ch. 7, and A. Berthelot, *L'Afrique Saharienne et Soudanèse*, pp. 88 ff.

North-West Africa contains a large pocket of alluvial soil in Tunisia, with an unusually rich potash content, and much good land on the lower edge of the plateau (the 'Tell', in modern parlance). Where the supply of water is generous, its vegetation is rich and even rank. Extensive forests survive not only in the solitary mountain zones of Atlas and Aures, but near the rain-washed coast of northern Tunisia, which is still densely clad both with conifers and with hardwood trees, despite continuous felling by Romans and Arabs.[1] Mt. Atlas supplied Roman connoisseurs in furniture with ebony and the highly prized wood of the thuya tree (Latin *citrus*; a rare conifer). The north-eastern tip of Tunisia was laid out with olive-plantations whose oil, if somewhat crude, was at any rate plentiful. Central Tunisia, the Algerian coastlands, and the Tell are well adapted to the growth of cereals, which benefit from a generous fall of rain in spring-time and are ready for cutting before the summer sun can parch them.[2] The cultivation of grain, which was first developed by the Carthaginians in Tunisia and by King Massinissa on the Tell, was intensified by the Romans to the almost complete exclusion of other products in the areas suitable for corn-production.[3] Under the later Republic north-west Africa supplemented Sicily as a source of Rome's corn imports; under the emperors it became the capital's chief granary.[4]

Though the Algerian Tell is well suited to viticulture, and now has a large export trade in wine, in ancient times this form of husbandry was sacrificed to corn-production. On the other hand, the valley of the Bagradas (modern Medjerda) was planted with fruit-gardens by the Carthaginians and remained a rich orchard country under the Romans. Successive invaders of Tunisia from the time of Agathocles to that of Belisarius feasted themselves right royally in this land of paradise.[5] In other parts of central Tunisia, where water was less plentiful, the land was given over to olives. Southern Tunisia remained half-desert until the Romans planted it with olive-groves.

[1] The statement of Sallust (*Bellum Iugurthinum* 17, § 5), that north-west Africa is ill suited to tree-growing, holds good only of the high plateau.

[2] But the statement of Pliny (xvii, § 41), that near Byzacium (in central Tunisia) the grain reproduced itself 150-fold, cannot be accepted. This is more than has been achieved in any modern force-bed.

[3] R. M. Haywood, in Frank's *Economic Survey*, iv, pp. 16–22, 39–49.

[4] According to Josephus (*Bell. Jud.* vi, § 383) the import from Africa was double the import from Egypt.

[5] Diodorus, xx. 8. 3; Procopius, *Bellum Vandalicum* i. 17. 9–10. Dates were not yet a staple product of Tunisia, as at the present day.

On the higher plateau the rainfall is also insufficient for tillage, and the water of the shallow lakes ('shotts'), which form a chain across it, is too brackish for irrigation. Steppe conditions, therefore, have always prevailed here, and the only notable product of the region in ancient times was a wiry breed of horses which provided excellent mounts for the light cavalry of Massinissa and Jugurtha and for the auxiliary forces of the Roman imperial army.

North-West Africa is well provided with minerals, whose extraction plays a considerable part in the modern economy of the country. Of its varied metallic resources the high-grade iron ores from Morocco and the region of Constantine are the most important; in addition, beds of coal and lignite and extensive deposits of potash contribute to its industrial output. In ancient times, however, the only mineral that was extensively worked was the yellow marble of Simitthus in Numidia, which attained a vogue at Rome from the time of the later Republic.

The purple-beds in the Gulf of Gabes were probably among the first objects to attract Phoenician settlers to African shores, and they provided the material for the principal industry of pre-Roman Carthage; but it is doubtful whether they were still being fished in the Roman era. Apart from an abundance of cheap pottery, some of which, curiously enough, found export markets all round the western Mediterranean, there is no evidence of any large industrial activity in north-west Africa under Roman rule.

The isolation of north-west Africa from its hinterland has now been overcome by regular services of trans-Saharan motor coaches to the African west coast. The western half of the desert has a more broken relief than its eastern plateau, and in the range of Mt. Ahaggar it rises to 10,000 feet. Though it does not receive rainfall from the Atlantic cyclones (which hold a more northerly track), it benefits from local 'orographic' downpours and is therefore more closely dotted with oases than the Egyptian and Cyrenaic hinterland.[1] In Strabo's day some of the desert tribes traded with the city of Cirta by way of the Biskra gap, using horses to carry their packs.[2] But the Gaetulians who tenanted the western oases in ancient days were raiders rather than traders, and it was not until the Arab conquest that camel transport to and from Timbuctoo was organized on any considerable scale.

[1] Gautier, op. cit., pp. 11 ff.
[2] Strabo, p. 828. The horses also carried water-skins slung under their bellies. For light travel in the Sahara horses and donkeys have been found no less suitable than camels.

The Atlantic seaboard of Morocco possesses some good road-steads and shelving beaches, but part of the coast is rendered difficult of access by breakers, and it is lacking in commodious natural harbours. It has recently leapt into importance as a trans-Atlantic terminal, but in ancient times its eccentric position in relation to the Mediterranean area deprived it of commercial importance. The greater part of the long Riff coast of northern Morocco and Algeria is steep-to, and the ports in its small erosion bays, while giving shelter from westerly winds, lie open to the north. Tingis (Tangier) presumably served the Carthaginians as a stage on their trade-route to west Africa (p. 229); it subsequently became the principal Roman gate into Morocco (p. 227). This and some lesser stations on the Riff coast which the Carthaginians founded and the Romans re-established (from the time of Augustus) seem at any rate to have performed a useful coastguard duty, for little is heard in ancient authors of the 'Barbary corsairs' who subsequently infested the western Mediterranean for over 1,000 years and required successive expeditions by U.S., French, and British war-fleets to suppress them.[1] But there is no evidence of any considerable trade between the ancient Riff ports and Italy or Spain.

The northern coast of Tunisia possesses in Bizerta (ancient Hippo Diarrytus) a land-locked basin at the end of a long sea-arm which provides perfect harbourage. But as a gateway to the interior Bizerta is almost useless, for its hinterland is extremely broken and densely wooded; until it became a French naval station it never attained more than local importance. The east Tunisian seaboard is mostly flat and marshy. At Hadrumetum (modern Sousse) and Thapsus two rocky knolls protruding into the sea provide fair shelter, but these ports are not roomy enough for any extensive trade.

On the other hand, the north-eastern apex of Tunisia formerly contained two harbours which were at once safe and commodious, and well situated both for local and for long-distance commerce, Utica and Carthage. These two towns lay in the recesses of a wide bay enclosed between the Fair Promontory and the boldly out-stretched arm of the Hermaean Promontory (C. Bon). Their foreshore, it is true, was liable to become silted with deposits

---

[1] The pirate head-quarters were at Algiers and Tripoli, but one of their principal spheres of operations was near the Gibraltar bottle-neck. The absence of a strong base for police patrols at Gibraltar (corresponding to the ancient stations on the Riff coast) facilitated their depredations. Jefferson's 1804–5 expedition was the first U.S. entanglement in the Old World.

from the river Bagradas, indeed the long neglect which these
ports have suffered from the time of the Arab conquest has led
to their becoming completely choked; but in ancient days the
sedimentation had not yet endangered the harbour entrances.[1]
Moreover the Bagradas valley offered an easy approach into the
best territory of Tunisia, so that Utica and Carthage became the
chief receiving points for the exports of north-western Africa.
Above all, the twin cities occupied commanding positions on the

TUNISIA AND ALGERIA

'waist' of the Mediterranean Sea, at the centre of its basin, where
its passage-way narrows to some seventy-five miles. The preponderance which Carthage achieved over Utica, however, is not to
be explained by any special advantages in its situation as compared with its neighbour's; the reason should rather be sought in
a personal factor, the high enterprise and organizing capacity of
its governing nobility.

The internal communications of north-west Africa are largely
determined by the general trend of its mountains from east to west.
This trend is followed both by the main chain of Atlas and by the
many small subsidiary ridges of the plateau.[2] The gaps which

[1] The site of Carthage was originally an island, whose eventual attachment to
the mainland enhanced the value of the port. The outlines of the ancient harbour
are now largely obliterated (Gsell, op. cit. ii, pp. 58–78). Utica and Carthage have
been superseded by Tunis, which is connected with the sea by a modern canal.

[2] On the communications of the plateau see A. N. Sherwin-White, *Journal of
Roman Studies*, 1944, pp. 1–10, and especially fig. 3 on p. 3.

these ridges leave between the uplands and the coast are mostly tortuous, and the rivers that wind through these mazes are ravine torrents of the Greek type and useless for navigation. Ancient Numidia indeed possessed two nodal points upon which the roads from the seaboard converged, at Sitifis, and more especially at Cirta, the predestined seat of government in the days of Numidian independence; but the long Mediterranean coast of Mauretania was cut off from the interior, except only at Caesarea (Cherchell) and Tingis, the two provincial capitals under Roman rule.

From the Atlantic coast of Morocco a broad staircase leads by easy stages to the plateau, but further progress is impeded by a tangle of small mountain systems which leave but one passage (the 'Taza corridor') as a bottleneck for traffic from west to east. Morocco is therefore almost cut off by land from Algeria; in ancient times its main line of communications ran through Spain, just as nowadays its principal link with France is the sea route from Casablanca to Bordeaux. In Algeria the lower plateau is cut up by short cross-ridges and belts of forest, so that the most practicable roads from west to east lie along the coast and on the open steppe of the inner table-land. In Tunisia, on the other hand, the valleys of the Bagradas and the Muthul provide easy ascents to the plateau in the direction of Cirta and the Aures massif.

The mere extent of north-west Africa, which stretches over 1,000 miles from east to west, and the difficulty of its internal communications, have always been an impediment to its union into a single state. Until its absorption into the Roman empire Mauretania always formed a separate kingdom, and although Massinissa accomplished the remarkable feat of holding all Numidia together in a common allegiance, his realm was liable to become a prey to rival pretenders. Still less could the Punic settlers in north-west Africa hope to consolidate it into a single dominion, in view of their slender man-power and their natural tendency to rely mainly on naval communications. Although the Carthaginians eventually appropriated the entire Tunisian plain and made a good beginning of bringing it under intensive cultivation, their advance into the interior came as an afterthought,[1] and it never gave them a secure footing on the plateau. The main

[1] As late as c. 400 B.C. the Carthaginians had to import their wine and oil from Sicily; they had as yet no plantations in Africa (Diodorus, 13. 81. 4–5).

importance of Tunisia for them was that it gave them control of the Sicilian Straits and a good base for the closing of the western Mediterranean against commercial interlopers.

The Roman penetration of north-west Africa also remained incomplete.[1] Mauretania never became an area for Roman settlement on any large scale. The concern of the Roman occupying forces hardly went beyond the safeguarding of the Spanish coast against raiders, the recruitment of auxiliary forces into the Roman army, and prospecting along the Atlas border for rare species of timber and wild beasts for the circus.[2] In Algeria the forest belts were left untouched, and the border steppe was patrolled rather than colonized. Broadly speaking, only the north-eastern sector of north-west Africa, comprising Tunisia and the adjacent part of the Algerian Tell, were intensively occupied.

Yet in north-west Africa the Romans, while recognizing certain limits to their power of taming a wild country-side, gave a conspicuous example of their ability to utilize those natural features of a land which could be harnessed for its development. In advancing their garrisons on to the plateau, in the first instance to Theveste, and subsequently to Lambaesis (near the foot of Mt. Aures), they stationed them in an open country where they could move quickly and discharge efficiently their main task, which was to safeguard the cultivable zones against depredations by the nomads of the steppe at the outer edge of the plateau, and by raiders from the Saharan oases. In planning their road system they used Tunisia as a base for divergent trunk roads along the northern seaboard (as far as the rugged Riff coast), along the Algerian Tell (to Cirta and Sitifis), and towards the strategic centres adjoining Mt. Aures. Their north-and-south roads, cutting across the grain of the land, were subsidiary lines of approach to the military frontier,[3] or service routes for the conveyance of grain from the Tell to the ports.

In the area of deficient rainfall, where steppe country could be rendered cultivable, but only by systematic water-conservation, the Romans excelled themselves as hydraulic engineers. In the uplands they built barrages to trap the winter torrents at the exits of the cross-valleys, and along the foot-hills they constructed canals

[1] Sherwin-White, op. cit.; M. Holroyd, *Journ. Rom. Stud.*, 1928, pp. 1–20.
[2] J. Carcopino, *Le Maroc antique*, pp. 15–45.
[3] A French general who gave himself credit for opening up a difficult mountain pass in the Atlas range went on to discover an inscription recording that the Romans had previously driven a road through the defile. (M. Nilsson, *Imperial Rome*, pp. 218–19).

to conduct the water to the irrigation-fields and the town reservoirs. In the plains they eked out the canal-borne supplies with vaulted cisterns fed from the local springs.[1]

In southern Tunisia, where the soil was fertile, but the rainfall fell short of ten inches, the Romans introduced a successful system of 'dry' cultivation in olive-yards, by spacing out the trees widely, by cutting all the smaller roots in order to induce strong growth in the tap-roots, and by constantly turning over the top-soil to check capillary evaporation. It was by direct imitation of the Roman methods that recent French planters for a second time redeemed the territory of Sfax and Gabes from sterility.

In view of its slight industrial development, north-west Africa in ancient times was never a land of large cities. The only major aggregates of population in the Roman era, Carthage, Utica, Cirta, and Thugga (in western Tunisia), were the receiving-points for oversea exports; the remaining centres were mostly market towns. But in the central Tunisian plain, and near the springs of the piedmont, the towns lay unusually close together, and in the aggregate they carried a numerous and prosperous population.[2] No other part of the Roman empire shows up better that its prosperity was due, not merely to the Roman soldier, but to the Roman planter, road-builder, and civil engineer; and success in their pursuits entails a close study of the land and its resources.

§ 5. WEST AFRICA

About 500 B.C. a Carthaginian navigator named Hanno made a voyage of exploration along the west coast of Africa; passing the river Senegal, he pushed on to Sierra Leone or, as some scholars maintain, as far as the Equator.[3] Whichever was his journey's end, he penetrated farther south than any European traveller before c. A.D. 1450, and his cruise was not without practical results, for he established a trading-post at a place called Cerne, possibly

[1] See especially J. Toutain, Les Cités romaines de la Tunisie, i, ch. 4, pp. 56–75. Masons' marks on the cisterns near Carthage prove that these were of Roman, not of Punic construction (Corp. Inscr. Lat. viii. 12420). For a time-table regulating the admission of water to the irrigation-plots at Lamasba (in Algeria), see Dessau, Inscr. Lat. Sel. 5793. Ibid. 5795: a report on an amateurishly conducted boring through a hill-side, in which 'apparuit fossuras a rigorem [sic] errasse'.

[2] This prosperity is attested by the high rates of footing-money paid by the entrants into the local magistracies and senates, and by the absurdly big amphi-theatre of the moderate-sized town of Thysdrus, which could hold 60,000 on-lookers.

[3] Müller, Geogr. Graeci Minores, i, p. 1; Cary and Warmington, Explorers, pp. 47–52; R. Hennig, Terrae Incognitae, pp. 70–8.

to be identified with Herne Island in the bay of the Rio de Ouro (on the Tropic of Cancer). It was probably at this depot that the Carthaginians obtained gold by 'silent haggling' with the natives.[1]

With the fall of Carthage, however, this traffic came to an end, in spite of an attempt by the historian Polybius (acting on a commission from Scipio Aemilianus) to open up the west African coast to Greek and Roman shipping,[2] and all knowledge of the African coast south of Morocco was lost. The abandonment of this lucrative field of commerce was probably due in lesser measure to any special difficulties of navigation in west African waters[3] than to the completely desert character of the coast for some 700 miles beyond Morocco, and to the complete absence of harbourage along this shore. In the late Middle Ages the Saharan coast baffled explorers for over 100 years; once they had won through to Cape Verde their further progress was rapid.

[1] Herodotus, iv. 196; Carcopino, op. cit., pp. 73–163.
[2] Pliny, v. 9.
[3] Beyond C. Verde lies a zone of doldrums variegated by occasional tornadoes, and north-easterly trade winds may delay the return journey. But taken by themselves these difficulties were not insurmountable even in ancient times.

IX. WESTERN EUROPE

§ 1. THE SPANISH PENINSULA

SPAIN and Portugal compose a territory more than twice as large as Italy. With an area of 230,000 square miles, they equal in size the other two largest peninsulas of the Mediterranean, the Balkan peninsula and Asia Minor. The resemblance of the Spanish peninsula with Asia Minor goes farther. Like its eastern counterpart, it is a plateau with high rims at the northern and southern edges (the Pyrenees and the Sierra Nevada, either of which rises to c. 11,200 feet), and its central tableland is likewise fringed with coastal plains of a contrasting texture.

The core of the peninsula, the Castilian plateau or *Meseta*, is a solid block of older rock comprising all the inland sierras and extending from the Portuguese frontier to the vicinity of the Mediterranean Sea.[1] Its average elevation exceeds 2,500 feet, so that the peninsula as a whole stands higher above sea-level than any other large land-mass of Europe except Scandinavia. Despite its proximity to the Atlantic, the climate of the meseta is distinctly continental, with marked contrasts of temperature and a deficiency of rainfall.[2] At its western rim it is cut off from the rain-bearing ocean winds by a belt of high ground which rises in the Sierra de Estrella (dividing the Douro and Tagus valleys) to 6,500 feet. The summers of Castile are fully as hot and dry as those of Italy and Greece;[3] its winters are equally sunny but even more boisterous—according to Cato the Elder a Spanish gust of wind 'gave you a mouthful'[4]—the cold more severe, and the rain less generous. The total annual precipitation, e.g. Madrid's yearly ration of fifteen inches, is barely sufficient for agriculture.

The absolute shortage of rain on the plateau is not relieved over any large area by snow-water in the summer season, for the inner sierras nowhere attain the level of permanent snow.[5] The

---

[1] A good description in A. Schulten, *Numantia*, i, esp. pp. 149–78.

[2] Yet Justin (xliv. 1. 4) praised the temperateness of the Spanish climate! Presumably his information came (at several removes) from a Greek writer such as Ephorus, whose knowledge of Spain was restricted to its southern and eastern lowlands, if indeed it was not a conventional romance about *terra incognita*.

[3] For a story about the choking dust-storms of the plateau, see Plutarch, *Sertorius*, ch. 17.

[4] 'Buccam implet' (Cato *ap.* Gellius, ii. 22. 29).

[5] The Sierra de Gredos (west of Madrid) rises to 8,750 feet.

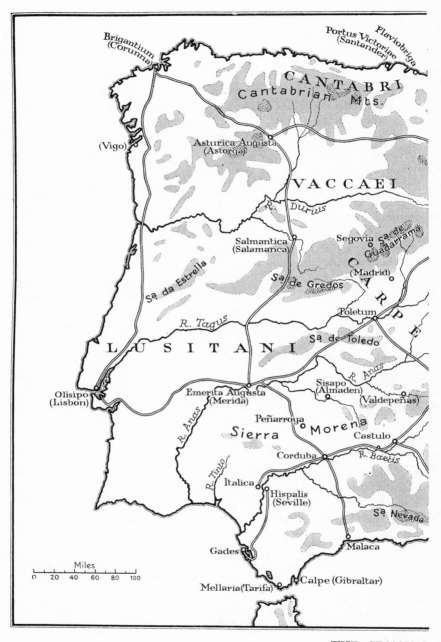

THE SPANISH

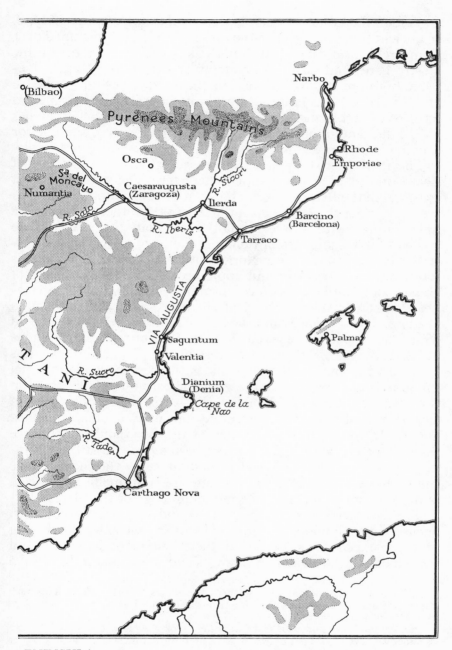

PENINSULA

vegetation therefore is mostly of a stunted drought-resisting type. In ancient times, it is true, large preserves of forest remained over from prehistoric days on the south slopes of the Pyrenees (now mostly bare) and on the mountains of the interior,[1] and olive-plantations are still to be found in sheltered nooks under the lee of the Sierra de Guadarrama; but throughout the historical period most of the tableland has been treeless. The cultivated patches yield but scanty crops of cereals, and large areas are suitable for rough grazing only.

The fringes of the plateau are more extensive than those of Asia Minor, and of more varied character. The north and west coasts from the Pyrenees to Lisbon and the hill country of Galicia are fully under the influence of the Atlantic weather and combine mild winters with ample rainfall throughout the year: Bilbao receives forty-six inches of rain, and Santiago no less than sixty-six.[2] Galicia is as green as Normandy or Devon, with deciduous forest and cow pastures and apple orchards.[3] The lowlands of eastern and southern Spain conform in general to the Mediterranean climate. At either end of the east coast, under the rain shadow of the Pyrenees and the Sierra Morena, belts of semi-arid land extend which have given rise to the illusion that 'Africa begins at the Pyrenees'. The esparto grass of the Spanish steppes was in demand among ancient sea-folk as the best available material for ropes,[4] thus taking the place which Baltic hemp occupied in the economy of the Middle Ages. But these 'bad lands' stand in sharp contrast with the adjacent regions of Catalonia, Valencia, and Andalusia. The lower valley of the Ebro and the concave plain of Valencia are the collecting basins of the east coast rainfall, while Andalusia is irrigated in summer by the snows of the Sierra Nevada; and all these districts are continually refertilized with river-borne silt from the mountain edge of the plateau.

The productiveness of the eastern and southern lowlands in ancient times should not be judged by their yield since the coming of the Saracens, who perfected their system of irrigation and introduced the cultivation of oranges and sugar-cane.[5] But in the

[1] Strabo, pp. 137, 162; Schulten, op. cit. i, pp. 161–2, 165–8.

[2] Strabo (p. 137) guessed that northern Spain was 'utterly cold'. This rash inference from latitude is on a par with his assertion that Ireland was a sorry place to live in for its icy climate (p. 72).

[3] Strabo (p. 155) informs us that butter here took the place of olive oil: a sure sign that we have passed out of Mediterranean into Atlantic lands. Portugal as yet was not an important wine-growing district.

[4] Pliny, xix, §§ 26–30.

[5] Spanish sugar-cane was one of the chief sources of sugar for Europe until the

days of the Roman emperors their cereal crops were heavy, and in addition to grain they exported great quantities of wine and oil.[1] The volume of the export trade may be gauged by its surviving monument, the Monte Testaccio, an artificial hillock on the southern outskirts of Rome, with a perimeter of half a mile, which is mainly composed of fragments of Spanish jars.[2] The Andalusian wine of ancient times, it is true, was not rated as highly as its modern counterpart, the Tarragona vintages being considered superior;[3] but the oil was regarded as second only to the best of Italy.[4] In the Ebro valley the cultivation of flax, an exacting plant which requires a rich and well-watered soil, was already a staple industry; it was worked up on the looms of Emporiae, the ancient industrial equivalent of Barcelona.[5]

The agricultural wealth of the southern and eastern lowlands was matched by the abundance of the adjacent seas in fish and other marine products (crustaceans and oysters). No mention is made in ancient writers of the Portuguese sardine-fisheries, but the variety and imposing size of the marine animals on either side of the Straits of Gibraltar stirred their imagination.[6] Not only did these waters receive visits from whales and cachalots, but they were well stocked with fish and crustaceans of unheard-of dimensions. Even these monsters were surpassed in food-value by the shoals of tunnies which came in lean and emaciated from the Ocean, but gorged on the acorns of a marine plant that grew profusely inside the Straits, and filled out to an 'incredible obesity':[7] Spain therefore was a large exporter of fish as well as of other foods, and fish-pickling was the staple industry of several coast towns ranging from Gades to Malaca and Carthago Nova.

But the most distinctive feature of Spain's natural resources consisted in the quantity and high grade of its minerals.[8] The

development of beet cultivation in the eighteenth century. The productiveness of the *huertas* of eastern Spain may be measured by their purchase price, which is thirty to forty times that of unirrigated land.

[1] Strabo, pp. 144–5. Some of the land now yields two or three crops, or ten to twelve mows of alfalfa grass.

[2] Frank, *Economic Survey*, v, p. 220; *American Journal of Philology*, 1936, pp. 87–90. According to a recent estimate Spain has 300 million olive-trees, as against Italy's 100 millions (E. Ludwig, *The Mediterranean*, p. 49).

[3] Pliny, xiv, § 71.   [4] Strabo ,p. 144; Pliny, xv, § 8.

[5] Strabo, p. 160; Pliny, xix, § 10.

[6] Strabo, p. 145; Pliny, ix, § 12; Festus Rufus Avienus, *Ora Maritima*, ll. 128–9.

[7] [Aristotle], *De Miris Auscultationibus*, § 136; Strabo, p. 145.

[8] Descriptions of Spanish mines from the pens of Polybius and Posidonius have been partly transmitted to us by Diodorus (v. 37–8) and Strabo (pp. 146–8). For a modern survey see J. J. van Nostrand in Frank, *Economic Survey*, iii, pp. 150–66.

coalfields of the north-west escaped the attention of ancient prospectors, but the general riches of the country in metals was known to them from prehistoric times, and it was the quest for these that first drew Spain into the economy and politics of the Mediterranean world. The principal deposits were in the Sierra Morena, in the Pyrenees and their western continuations, but the ore was widely distributed over the peninsula. The Sierra Morena contained large deposits of silver, whose product was transported down the Guadalquivir to Tartessus (situated perhaps on the site of Seville),[1] until the Carthaginians diverted it to New Carthage. At Sisapo (modern Almaden) in the same range was to be found one of the world's richest cinnabar-mines.[2] In the Pyrenees the iron that fed the Catalan forges of medieval days was not yet exploited in large quantities, but the local silver-mines supplied the Roman conquerors in the second century B.C. with large hauls of *argentum Oscense* (from Huesca). Under Augustus the high-quality iron ore of Bilbao was probably brought into production;[3] the gold-mines of the Cantabrian mountains and the tin-deposits of the north-western region were certainly opened up about that period.[4] Another high-grade ore was extracted in the Sierra de Moncayo (the Ebro–Douro watershed), from which (unless we should allow for the local patriotism of our informant, Martial) the best of all steel was prepared.[5] Of the remaining minefields the most notable was the vast deposit of copper ore at the mouth of the Rio Tinto in Andalusia, which is still under active exploitation, although the Romans are estimated to have fetched away from it 21 million tons of ore, yielding 1·2 million tons of copper.[6]

In spite of its mineral wealth, Spain was not the seat of any large industry in ancient times. Spanish armourers acquired a high reputation for their perfectly annealed steel; on the other hand, despite the production of copper and tin within easy dis-

---

[1] Herodotus, iv. 152–3. For the site of Tartessus, see A. Berthelot's commentary on Avienus, pp. 81–2.

[2] Cinnabar (mercury sulphide) was highly prized as a pigment because of its rich vermilion colour. Greek and Latin writers have wrought much confusion by using the same term (μίλτος, minium) for cinnabar and common red-lead.

[3] Pliny, xxxiv, § 149. Large Roman slag-heaps are reported by Davies (*Roman Mines*, p. 99).

[4] W. C. Borlase, *Tin Mining in Spain*, pp. 15 ff.

[5] iv. 55, ll. 11–15.

[6] Davies, op. cit., p. 114 n. 6; R. Thouvenot, *Essai sur la Province Romaine de Bétique*, p. 255. The Metallum Vipascense at Aljustrel in south Portugal, concerning the administration of which invaluable details are preserved in a long inscription (Dessau, *Inscr. Lat. Sel.* 6891), does not appear to have had any great economic importance.

tance of one another, no important bronze industry came into being within the peninsula. Though Spanish wool (especially the black variety) had a good name, there was no manufacture of woollens for export;[1] and the better sorts of pottery had to be imported from Gaul. Apart from its chief ports, the country had no large towns, and it may be assumed that its population was considerably less than that of Gaul or Italy.[2]

The barrier which separates Spain from France has isolated it more effectually than the Alps have sundered Italy from Europe. At first sight the Pyrenees would appear a less formidable obstacle. Their central passes do not rise above 5,000–6,000 feet;[3] the Roncesvaux pass at their western end is 3,500 feet high, but the Col du Perthus at the Mediterranean edge falls short of 1,000 feet. Their width varies from 20 to 60 miles, that of the Alps from 30 to 180. On the other hand, the Pyrenees have no easy river approach on either flank, for the Ebro and Garonne flow roughly parallel with them, and their side valleys are few and narrow. Again, while the gradients on the southern face of the Pyrenees are relatively gentle, in contrast with the sharp southward tilt of the Alps, the Spanish piedmont, unlike that of Italy, is dry and barren, being cut off from the rain-bearing westerlies by the Cantabrian and Aragonese mountains. The Pyrenees therefore provide one reason why Spain has never been an integral part of Europe to the same extent as Italy.

The southern rim of the peninsula, the Sierra Nevada, has also had a segregating influence upon it, for it not only surpasses all the other sierras in height, but it offers only two practicable passes (leading to Malaga and Almeria). Contacts between Spain and north Africa have therefore been almost confined to the eight-mile gap at the Straits of Gibraltar; and this link between the continents, whose importance in the Middle Ages was far-reaching, in ancient times merely served as a gangway for small relays of Roman soldiers and administrators into Mauretania, and for bands of Moorish raiders into Spain.

The Spanish and Portuguese coast-lines contain several excellent ports on their western face. The deeply re-entrant *rias* in which Vigo and Corunna (Artabrorum Portus or Brigantium) are situated, afford safe shelter, and as they contain no river estuary

[1] The fine merino strain was a product of the sixteenth century.
[2] The present population of Spain and Portugal is *c.* 25 millions.
[3] H. Belloc, *The Pyrenees*. Stiff climbing is required near some of the summits, but no more so than in the Alps.

they are not liable to become silted. Corunna was the starting-point of the open-sea route to Cornwall, discovered by the Carthaginians and exploited for a short time by the Romans; but after the conquest of Gaul it had little further interest for the latter.[1] Near the estuary of the Tagus, where the river meets the largest and deepest of the *rias*, Lisbon (Olisipo) occupies one of the best harbour sites of Europe.[2] Under Roman rule Lisbon collected the exports of the entire western coast for shipment to Rome in craft of ocean-going size; but only the immense economic pull of the imperial city could bring it within the field of ancient Mediterranean connexions, and its fortunes were not fully established until the Atlantic coast ceased to be the world's end.

The produce of Andalusia and the Sierra Morena was partly conveyed from the river-port of Hispalis (Seville), which sea-going vessels could reach on the flood tide, though Mediterranean seamen found the strength of the ebb and flow 'not a little hazardous'.[3] But the early Phoenician colonists naturally set up their principal station at Gades (Cadiz), which was built on an off-shore island (now attached to the mainland by a mole), and was therefore relatively immune, like modern Gibraltar, from mainland attacks; under the Roman Republic and the Caesars it maintained its old-established supremacy. On the other hand, the Rock of Gibraltar in Roman times merely served as a landmark. Strabo describes it in words such as may have occurred to many a modern traveller: 'the mountain of Calpe is not large in circumference, but it stands up straight and tall, so that it looms up from a distance like a detached island.'[4] Although the Carthaginians jealously guarded the gates of the Atlantic, they would seem to have used Gades, or possibly Malaca inside the Straits, as their control station.

The south coast inside the Straits crinkles into a series of small erosion ports like those of the opposite African shore. The chief of these, Malaca, was an important station for fish-pickling and exported oil from the fertile plain which here occupies a gap in the Sierra Nevada. At the south-eastern corner of Spain New Carthage occupied the head of a secure and capacious bay, but was partly cut off from the hinterland by a lagoon. But the richness of

---

[1] Strabo, pp. 175–6.

[2] Its position was duly appreciated by Strabo (pp. 151–2). The full official title of the city ('municipium civium Romanorum Olisipo Felicitas Iulia') suggests that it received Roman franchise from Caesar as a reward for services rendered as an advanced base for his Atlantic pirate-drive in 61 B.C. (Dio Cassius, xxvii. 53. 4).

[3] Strabo, pp. 142–3.   [4] Ibid., p. 139.

the silver-mines in its neighbourhood secured for it a leading position among the Spanish ports.[1]

On the east coast the only good natural harbour is the capacious semicircular bay of Rosas at the foot of the Pyrenees; but the little Greek colony of Rhode which lay ensconced in it had scarcely any economic hinterland, and its neighbour Emporiae, on a more open site, was almost equally shut off from the interior. Barcino (Barcelona), Tarraco, and Valentia, the natural reception-points for the produce of the fertile plains of eastern Spain, were situated on open roadsteads.[2] Another feature of the eastern seaboard is that it trends in a different direction from the west coast of Italy, so that the distance between the two peninsulas is far greater than between Italy and the Balkans. Thus by sea as well as by land Spain lies comparatively isolated from the rest of Europe, and until Rome provided the attraction of an inexhaustible market for Spanish produce the eastern seaboard remained undeveloped.

The Castilian plateau not only stands high above the coastal borderlands, but is sharply cut off from them by steep scarps. Of the intermediate river valleys those of the Tagus and Guadiana (ancient Anas) are the most commodious, and an easy pass between Merida and Lisbon links the two rivers in their lower reaches. The Douro has an open road across the plateau, but on the way to the coast it plunges through deep ravines. The Ebro, likewise, has an open middle course, and together with its tributary the Jalon (ancient Salo), provides the best avenue from the eastern seaboard to the plateau; but its lower reaches, like those of the Douro, are hemmed in by a narrow gorge. The Guadalquivir (ancient Baetis) provides easy communications by road or boat as far as Cordova, but in its upper course it does not cut through to the plateau, and the steep southern rim of the Sierra Morena which it skirts offers no easy ascent. The plateau itself is intersected by a number of loosely jointed ridges which rise to no great height and can be crossed by passes below the 5,000-foot line. But their approaches are mostly through arid and desolate country.

Despite its compact shape, the Spanish peninsula has hardly ever experienced political unity except under Roman rule.[3] The

[1] Ibid., p. 158. The strong gust that temporarily scooped the water out of the lagoon, so as to afford a passage for Scipio Africanus's storming party, was probably a 'full wind' from the neighbouring heights (H. H. Scullard, *Scipio Africanus*, pp. 76–9).

[2] Until the seventeenth century Barcelona was, like pre-Claudian Ostia, an open port with a sandbank.

[3] It was united in modern times from A.D. 1581 to 1640.

sharp contrasts between tableland and lowland have always impeded co-operation between their several inhabitants, and in ancient times the Celtiberians of the plateau had little in common with the people of the plains.[1] Moreover the Celtiberians, whose central situation and military aptitude seemed to mark them out for leadership, just as the Castilians have been the political leaders of modern Spain, never succeeded in uniting themselves into a single realm or confederacy. In addition to the difficulties of intercourse mentioned above, another factor which impeded political union was the lack of any natural centre of communications in the middle of the plateau: the setting up of Madrid as a political capital and the suppression of local liberties which laid the foundations of modern Spain were a political *tour de force*.[2] In the absence of a masterful hand acting in disregard of Nature's dispositions, Celtiberia in ancient times remained split up into a number of small cantons, each with its independent hill fortress, and no connecting link between them, except some incompact tribal confederacies.[3] The integration of Spain in ancient times was therefore left to its foreign invaders.

In the early days of their colonial expansion the Greeks probably made their approach to Spain, not by way of Massilia, but by a directer route from Sicily or south Italy which led past Sardinia and the Balearic Islands to Cape Nao, and thence followed the south-eastern and southern coasts to Tartessus.[4] But the occupation of Gades by the Carthaginians (*c*. 600 B.C.) shut the Greeks off from the Atlantic, so that Pindar could subsequently affirm, 'what lies beyond the Straits is forbidden ground to wise men and unwise alike'.[5] After their conquest of Sardinia (*c*. 540 B.C.) the Carthaginians were able to intercept all foreign vessels bound for the Straits by the open-sea route,[6] thus restricting Greek traffic to a trickle from Massilia along the eastern coast.

The first result of the Carthaginian occupation of the Straits was that Spain for a while anticipated its future role as the gate

[1] In the Middle Ages the economic contrast between the settled and highly civilized Moslem populations of the lowlands and the ruder pastoral Christian folk of the highlands was an even greater obstacle to union than their religious differences.

[2] H. A. L. Fisher, *History of Europe* (2nd ed.), pp. 627–8: 'All ways in France led to Paris, no ways in Spain led to Madrid.'

[3] Schulten, *Numantia*, i, pp. 228 ff.

[4] Schulten, *Tartessos*, ch. 4. The Greek landfall in Spain was probably the Puenta de Ifach, a Gibraltar-like rock to the south of C. Nao (R. Carpenter, *The Greeks in Spain*, p. 20 and pls. i and ii).

[5] *Olympia* iii. 76–8; *Nemea* iii. 35–6.   [6] Strabo, p. 802.

of the Atlantic. Corunna became the starting-point of an open-sea route to Cornwall, and the possibility of reaching the Indies by a westward journey from Spain was discussed by Greek geographers.[1] But after the destruction of Carthage and the institution by the Romans of a good road system to the Atlantic through Gaul (pp. 256–7), Spain ceased to be a base for Ocean adventures and once more turned its face to the Mediterranean.

The Anabasis of the Carthaginians into the interior of Spain which was undertaken by Hamilcar and his successors (237 B.C. ff.) might on first impression appear as ineffectual as Caesar's invasions of Britain. But, to adapt Tacitus' *mot* about Caesar to Hamilcar and Hannibal, they 'laid Spain open for the Romans'. In particular, Hannibal's first Spanish campaign, in which he carried Punic arms across the grain of the land as far as the territory of the Vaccaei (on the middle Douro) and returned through the land of the Carpetani (New Castile), appears as a fruitful voyage of exploration.[2] On the way out he presumably used the Peñarroya pass across the Sierra Morena and proceeded by a corridor of comparatively level ground to Salamanca; on the return journey he probably took the Segovia pass through the Sierra de Guadarrama and regained Andalusia by the Valdepeñas pass. If this was his route, he discovered the two best north-and-south roads across the heart of the peninsula.

By the end of the Second Punic War the Romans had acquired possession of the eastern and southern lowlands from the Pyrenees to Gades, with a coast-line of nearly 1,000 miles. Since this territory was in respect of mere length too unwieldy to control from a single centre, it was divided into two provinces, whose seats of government were at Carthago Nova and Corduba. The choice of these towns as capitals shows that the Romans were primarily interested in the tract containing the best land and the richest mines. But from a strategic point of view the two provinces were in a precarious position, for they were dominated by the central plateau and exposed to constant if not concentrated attacks by the Celtiberians.[3] The Romans were therefore drawn on to the plateau and across it, and thus were committed to a protracted warfare in which they were pitted against long distances, large tracts of semi-desert land, and an enemy who knew how to take

[1] Cary and Warmington, *The Ancient Explorers*, p. 193.
[2] Livy, xxi. 5.
[3] The failure of the Moors to gain a broad foothold on the plateau in the Middle Ages made their eventual expulsion from Spain a mere matter of time, despite their superiority of civilization over the Castilians.

full advantage of the surviving forest coverts and the desiccated river-valleys (resembling the 'nullahs' of Anglo-Indian warfare) for springing ambushes. On the other hand they had learnt from the Carthaginians the best avenues for the penetration of the plateau from the south, and in 195 B.C. Cato, as governor of Hither Spain, found the master-key that opened the doors of Aragon and Castile from the east, the valley of the Salo. In the campaign of 179 B.C., which definitely gave the Romans a secure foothold on the plateau, the two governors (Sp. Postumius and Tiberius Gracchus the Elder) combined to squeeze the Carthaginians in a pincer operation from the south and the east.[1] Once established along the lines of the Ebro and the Douro, the Romans could pen up the Spanish armies in the watershed between the two valleys. The reduction of the last native stronghold, Numantia, cost them heavily in lives and reputation. Unlike other cantonal capitals of Spain, Numantia was not perched on a high eyrie, but it was almost water-girt, and the approach to it was rendered difficult by dense forest.[2] The importance of the native hill-fortresses as centres of resistance was early recognized by the Romans, for it was in Spain that they first applied in a systematic manner their policy of *deductio in plana* in regard to conquered peoples.[3]

Conformably to the natural lines of communication in Spain, the Romans built their main roads on a peripheral rather than a radial pattern.[4] Their basic route threaded the east coast to Carthago Nova, throwing off a branch which ascended the valley of the Sucro (south of Valentia), and cut across an eastern bastion of the Sierra Morena into Andalusia, and so on to Gades. From this main circular road 'service' routes were thrown off to the ports and mining centres.

Of the principal Roman road stations in Spain, Caesaraugusta (Zaragoza) lay in the Ebro basin near the turning-off point up the Salo valley; Corduba was situated at the head of navigation up the Baetis and near the entrance of the Peñarroya pass across the Sierra Morena; Merida was at the principal cross-roads of the peninsula, where the western section of the circular road intersected the solitary diagonal road across the plateau, from

[1] Soullard, *The Roman World from 753 to 146 B.C.*, pp. 315–16.
[2] Schulten, op. cit. ii, pp. 40–79.
[3] So Aemilius Paullus in 190 B.C. (Dessau, *Inscr. Lat. Sel.* 15); Caesar in 61 B.C. (Dio Cassius, xxxvii. 52. 3); Augustus in 24–19 B.C. (ibid. liv. 11. 6).
[4] For details see M. P. Charlesworth, *Trade Routes and Commerce of the Roman Empire*, pp. 151–6.

Caesaraugusta to Olisipo. No road centre of any importance was established in the heart of the plateau.

§ 2. GAUL

The territory of Gaul, which included France, Belgium, the western part of the German Rhineland, and 'Helvetia', i.e. the valleys of the Aar and the upper Rhône, was ethnically divisible into the ridings of Aquitania, Belgica, and Lugdunensis,[1] but geographically it formed a single unit. With an area of c. 250,000 square miles, it was of the same order of magnitude as the Spanish peninsula, but here the resemblance between the two countries might be said to end.

In structure Gaul bears a closer resemblance to England than to its Mediterranean neighbours. Being the product, not of a vast earth-convulsion, but of lesser shifts and stresses, it lacks the bold relief of the Mediterranean lands, and the higher ground between its valleys, like that of England, consists for the most part of rolling country with gentle declivities rather than of steeply scarped ridges and tablelands.

The uniformity of Gaul is least apparent in its climate, which exhibits a clearly marked local variation. In its south-eastern section, comprising roughly the Roman province of Gallia Narbonensis or the old French provinces of Provence and Languedoc, we meet again all the main characteristics of Mediterranean weather—abundant sunshine, winter rain and gales between bright intervals, and summer drought. The most trying climatic feature of this region is the mistral, the north wind of winter and spring, which blows down vehemently from the Alps like a Mediterranean fall-wind. Its action in the plain of La Crau (behind Marseille) is thus described by Strabo: 'This bleak plain is swept by a violent and ice-cold blast. In fact it is said that under the force of its gusts people are pounded off their carriages and have their tools snatched out of their hands and their clothes stripped off their backs.'[2] But all the rest of Gaul falls into the Atlantic weather-zone. It is comprised all the year round within the belt of ocean westerlies, and it lies entirely open to the sea winds, which are nowhere fended off by a coastal barrier, as in the case of Spain. Its climate therefore is equable, with adequate rainfall distributed over the seasons.

[1] Caesar, *Bellum Gallicum* i. 1. 1.
[2] p. 182. The wind-breaks of poplar or conifer trees which are now a feature of Provence are not mentioned by Strabo.

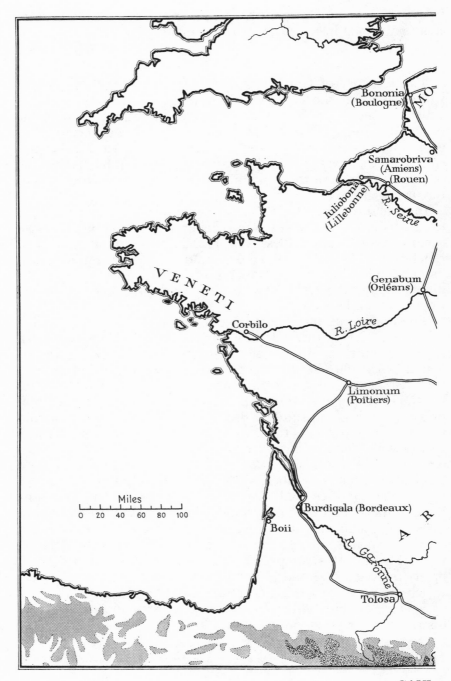

GAUL

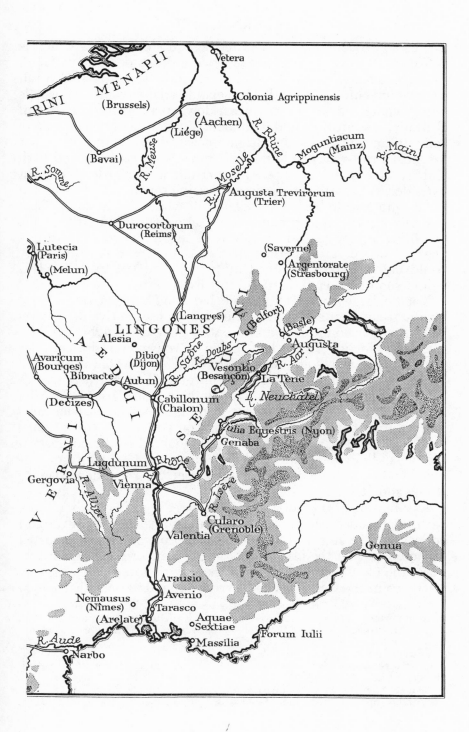

The sharp contrast between fertile and sterile tracts which is a feature of Mediterranean countries is less apparent in Gaul. Some 'bad lands', of course, are to be found. The Massif Central, a surviving core of an eroded tableland, is largely an area of fells with thin grazing. Another worn-down plateau, the district of Brittany, is scantily coated with moorland and mattings of spongy soil. In ancient times the Belgian coast, whose dunes were not yet held firm with plantations of star-grass, was furrowed with shifting creeks and swamps. Farther inland the Ardennes forest extended even farther than now, covering much of north-eastern Gaul; and a wide belt of woodland, of which the Fontainebleau Forest is a surviving remnant, spread across the basin of the Seine. In the relatively humid climate of Gaul, moreover, the forests were of denser growth than in the Mediterranean lands; they could not be rapidly thinned by firing,[1] and left to themselves would soon recover the ground lost by clearing.

Yet no large region of Europe has a higher general level of fertility than Gaul. Its uplands are hardly less cultivable than its valleys, and even in the Massif Central there exist highly productive areas, for its eastern half, being of volcanic origin, contains pockets of richer soil. Moreover, Gaul as a whole achieves a balanced economy in its agrarian output. The north possesses several large tracts of natural cornland (the Paris basin, Picardy, Brabant, and Hainault); the west, with its somewhat heavier rainfall, has rich pasture in the lowlands on either side of Brittany; and the Mediterranean border is well adapted to the cultivation of vine and olive. By way of supplement, the Gallic forests provided enough pig-food to maintain a large export trade in ham to Rome and Italy.[2]

As a mining area Gaul in ancient times did not hold equal rank with the Spanish peninsula.[3] It was not so well off for silver and copper, and its stocks of Breton tin had probably been exhausted by 500 B.C.[4] On the other hand, at the time of the Roman conquest the Gallic temples were irresistibly rich in gold from river washings in the Cévennes and Pyrenees,[5] and various districts of

[1] According to G. Clark (*Antiquity*, 1939, pp. 57–71) neolithic man cleared large tracts of northern and western Europe by firing. If so, he was more successful than the airmen of the Allies in the Battle of Germany, who made little impression with their incendiaries on the woods of the Rhineland.

[2] Strabo, pp. 192, 197.

[3] For a comprehensive survey see A. Grenier in Frank, *Economic Survey*, iii, pp. 455–64.

[4] M. Cary, *Journ. Hell. Stud.*, 1924, p. 167.

[5] Strabo, pp. 146, 187, 190. Gold was also streamed in Helvetia (ibid., p.

Gaul were well stocked with iron ore. The great Lorraine iron-field, it is true, remained almost untouched,[1] but the neighbouring deposits in the Liége–Namur basin and in the Jura were under active exploitation: no doubt the Jura mines were the source of the metal from which the excellent broadswords of La Tène (near Neuchâtel) were produced in the pre-Roman period.[2] High-quality ore was also extracted at either edge of the Massif Central, near Périgord on the western side, and near Bourges on the eastern flank:[3] it was the latter minefield which made Avaricum (Bourges) into the chief arsenal town of Gaul.[4] Lastly, under the Roman emperors the district of Gressenich (near Aachen) produced suffi-cient zinc ore to become the centre of a brass-founding industry.[5]

Another important industrial material was provided by exten-sive beds of potter's clay. The principal deposits were situated on the southern and eastern edges of the Massif Central.

With its ample natural resources and flourishing industries (p. 258), Gaul under the Roman emperors probably equalled and possibly surpassed Italy in the number of its inhabitants.[6]

But the place which Gaul occupied in ancient history was not wholly due to its high productiveness; it also depended on its position as a land of passage, for it shared with the Balkan penin-sula the main lines of communication between the Mediterranean area and the European continent. Like the Balkan peninsula and Syria, it was indeed fenced off by formidable barriers on certain of its sections, but it also provided gaps between the barriers at convenient points.

Whatever Louis XIV may have said, the Pyrenees have always existed and have always precluded frequent communications between Gaul and Spain (p. 237). Unlike the Pyrenees, the western Alps have a relatively easy approach by way of the Rhône valley and those of its tributaries, and most of the passes from the Riviera as far as Mt. Simplon are sufficiently low to provide a

193). But the fabulous haul which Servilius Caepio made at Tolosa (estimated at 100,000 lb.—Orosius, v. 15) was no doubt derived in the main from the Cévennes or Pyrenees.

[1] Davies, *Roman Mines*, pp. 167–8. This field remained undeveloped until recent times. Its phosphatic ore could not be satisfactorily reduced until the inven-tion of the modern basic process.

[2] F. Cumont, *Comment la Belge fut romanisée*, p. 38; Davies, op. cit., p. 165. On the La Tène swords, see Grenier, op. cit., pp. 402 ff.

[3] Strabo, p. 191.   [4] Caesar, *Bellum Gallicum* vii. 22. 2.

[5] H. Willers, *Neue Untersuchungen über die römische Bronzeindustrie*.

[6] Grenier (op. cit., p. 455) estimates a population of 15–20 millions at the time of the Roman conquest, eventually rising to more than 20 millions.

snow-free path from May to September.[1] The difficulties of Hannibal's passage, who was encumbered with elephants and did not make his march until the first snows of the Alpine winter had strewn a treacherous blanket over patches of ice or névé,[2] were not typical. But before the Romans drove their metalled roads across the main passes (pp. 254–6) the journey was reckoned to take at least six days.[3]

On the north-eastern frontier the Vosges (scarcely exceeding 4,000 feet) and the Ardennes interposed a different but scarcely less effective obstacle in their cover of dense forest.[4] And farther north the Maas and Waal, with their complex system of shifting channels, provided a multiple water-barrier, as the Romans discovered in their pursuit of Civilis,[5] and the Allies in the Battles of Arnhem and Walcheren. The coast from the Maas estuary to Calais had not yet assumed definite shape and offered no firm landing places.[6] The Loire and Garonne estuaries possessed excellent harbours at Corbilo (the equivalent of Nantes or St. Nazaire) and at Burdigala (Bordeaux), but faced a limitless ocean.

On the other hand, Gaul stands wide open to incomers by the Mediterranean Sea. The Alpine barrier, it is true, detracts from the value of the small erosion ports along the Riviera and the capacious harbour, shielded by a projecting headland, at Toulon. But from Marseille to the Pyrenees the coast flattens out. Its lagoon port at Narbonne is indeed suitable for small vessels only, but Marseille has all the requisites of an international port. Its deeply recessed 'Vieux Port' is screened on its open western side by an angle-bastion in the coast, and it stands in right relation to

[1] There is no warrant for Dr. Arnold's statement (*The Second Punic War*, p. 25), that in Roman times the Alpine passes were snowbound all the year round.

[2] This point was duly made by Livy (xxi. 36. 5–6). If credence can be given to Polybius' statement (iii. 54. 2), that Hannibal's men from the summit saw Italy stretched out at their feet, the Col du Clapier will be singled out as the most likely route, in spite of its height (8,000 feet), for it alone of the western passes commands an extensive view (as on the photograph in Spenser Wilkinson, *Hannibal's March*, facing p. 8). A noted alpinist, R. L. G. Irving, says of this view, 'of all summit views this is the one that has impressed me most' (*The Alps*, p. 39). On the Clapier route see J. Knoflach, *Klio*, 1932, pp. 403–21.

[3] Polybius, quoted by Strabo, p. 209.

[4] The German break-through on this sector in 1914 and again in 1940 was due, paradoxically, to its very difficulties, for these were a temptation to the defenders to set an insufficient guard.

[5] Tacitus, *Histories*, v. 19 ff.

[6] On the former bifurcations of the Rhine and the conformations of the Dutch and Belgian coasts, see R. Hennig, *Bonner Jahrbücher*, pp. 166–222. Bruges did not attain importance as a port until the Middle Ages, and Antwerp not before the fifteenth century.

the Rhône estuary, being within easy reach but beyond the deposit area of the river silt.[1]

On the north-eastern frontier the Rhine has a swift flow from Lake Constance to Basle, but between Basle and the Dutch frontier it offers many convenient bridge-points; in particular, the reaches between Strasbourg and Mainz, and again between Bonn and the Dutch frontier, are convenient for crossing, for their approach on either bank is through open country. On the Channel front the French coast possesses, in addition to the two great basins of Cherbourg and Le Havre, a number of tidal inlets (Boulogne, Ambleteuse, Calais), which though small are adequate to the needs of coastal and cross-Channel shipping; and the crossing to Britain can be made from any of them without losing sight of land.

The internal barriers of Gaul are nowhere continuous, except in the region of the Jura, which fits tightly between the Rhône and the Rhine and as an offset to its moderate altitude (a little over 5,000 feet) has relatively high and tortuous passes. The Massif Central is an isolated block and can be by-passed on every side. Between the Jura and the Vosges the 'Burgundian Gate', or better, the 'Trouée de Belfort', provides an easy passage to the Rhine valley which has through the ages formed one of the chief links between the Rhine and the interior of France. Two subsidiary approaches to the Rhine are available by the Gap of Saverne between the Vosges and the hill country of the Palatinate, and by the valley of the Moselle. But most convenient of all is the piedmont road under the northern edge of the Ardennes through Liége and Aachen, which forms a natural causeway between the forest belt and the 'Mesopotamia' of the Maas and lower Rhine. This route has always provided the main avenue between the Rhineland and northern France or the Channel.

But the outstanding feature of the inner communications of Gaul lies in the excellence of its river system, which is the most commodious in all Europe. Unlike the Mediterranean streams, those of Gaul for the most part carry an equable volume of water at all seasons, and they have this advantage over the rivers of Germany and Russia, that they are almost wholly free from ice in winter. Moreover, the watershed between the flow-off to Mediterranean and Atlantic is neither high nor steep, so as to admit of a connecting system of portages.[2] It was thus possible in ancient

---

[1] In this respect Marseille resembles Alexandria.
[2] Strabo, pp. 177, 189; L. Bonnard, *La Navigation intérieure de la Gaule à l'époque gallo-romaine.*

times to travel from sea to sea by several water routes. From Narbo boats could ascend the Aude, and after being hauled over a col scarcely exceeding 600 feet in height they were carried on to Burdigala by the Garonne.[1] But the principal avenue from the Mediterranean into Gaul is by way of the Rhône valley.

In ancient times the entrance to the Rhône was impeded by silting and shifting of the Delta channels;[2] an attempt by Marius to avoid a bar in front of the eastern arm by means of a new cut (from Fos to the Delta head) gave but temporary relief.[3] Above the Delta the current was so rapid that only light barges could be hauled up stream; consequently the heavier consignments were sent by road, and cargoes conveyed on the river had to be transhipped at Lugdunum (Lyon) on to the heavier vessels which continued the voyage up the more placid waters of the Saône.[4] On the other hand, the Rhône offered the advantage of a constant volume of water, for during the summer drought it was fed by snow and, later on, by ice-water from the Alps, and Lake Leman acted on its flow like a great regulating basin. Moreover, merchandise carried up Rhône had a choice of routes for further transit across Gaul. It could be transferred to the Loire system by portages from various points along the Rhône itself and the Saône; the most important transit station was Chalon-sur-Saône, from which an easy road led to Decizes on the Loire.[5] Near its head-waters the Loire was too impetuous for heavy boats, but from the Chalon portage it offered an easy course, except for an occasional sand-bank. Still better was navigation up the Saône, a river that flows 'with incredible gentleness';[6] and from its upper reaches the journey could be carried on directly by the Doubs towards Belfort, or with an intermediate portage to the Moselle, Meuse, or Seine. The last-named river was reached by a gap-route from Langres, or from Dijon by way of its tributary, the Yonne. Of the rivers discharging into the Atlantic, the Seine had the steadiest current and was the most easy to navigate.

[1] Strabo, p. 189. This was the line of Louis XIV's Canal du Midi. This route has been impaired by excessive deforestation in Gascony, which has rendered the flow of the Garonne more inconstant.

[2] On the early braidings and floodings of the Rhône Delta see R. D. Oldham, *Quarterly Journal of the Geological Society*, xc (1934), pp. 445–61.

[3] Plutarch, *Marius* xv. 2–3. The Massiliotes set up towers to mark the entrance to the fairways (Strabo, pp. 183–4).

[4] Strabo, p. 189. The traffic on the Rhône has now been definitely abandoned to the railway.

[5] L. C. West, *Roman Gaul. The Objects of Trade*, ch. 2.

[6] Caesar, *Bellum Gallicum* i. 12. 1.

In ancient times the Rhine might also be claimed as a river of
Gaul, for it was closely linked up with the roads and waterways
of that country.[1] In its upper course as far as Basle this artery of
Europe has too steep a gradient for navigation; from Basle to
Strasbourg its channel is often obstructed with gravel deposits.
From Strasbourg to Bingen it has firm banks and a steady current,
but near Bingen its waters were formerly dammed up in a narrow
gorge and formed dangerous eddies;[2] below Wesel it requires continuous embanking to prevent inundations. But it is almost ice-
free and, like the Rhône, it receives the melted snow and ice of
the Alps, dispensed in level instalments from a great lake, so as to
maintain an even volume of water. Lastly, its estuary lies within
easy reach of one of Europe's greatest traffic centres, the Straits
of Dover.

In addition to its waterways, Gaul possesses a good natural
system of roads, which can either follow the river valleys or be-
stride the intermediate uplands without wide detours or sharp
gradients. Land travel accordingly was well developed before the
coming of the Romans with their metalled roads. Convoys of
pack-animals laden with ingots of Cornish tin plied between the
Atlantic and the Mediterranean seaboards in the short space of
thirty days,[3] and wheeled traffic was so much in use that the Gauls
could give the Romans lessons in the construction of coaches and
wagons. The prodigious marching performances of Caesar in
Gaul are not to be credited wholly to the *Caesariana celeritas*;
their explanation lies also in the fact that Nature had put a network of good tracks at his disposal.

Given these ready-made means of internal communication, the
political union of Gaul should not have been difficult of achievement, and indeed at the time of the Roman conquest its people
had made far greater strides towards a nation-state than the
Spaniards. One obstacle, however, to a comprehensive empire or
federation lay in the even balance of strength between the two
leading states, the Arverni (of Auvergne) and the Aedui (on the
Rhône–Loire watershed). The Arverni had the advantage of a
central position and of ample mineral resources. It was therefore
no mere accident that they twice led the resistance against the

---

[1] On the Rhine in general see A. Demangeon and L. Febvre, *Le Rhin*.

[2] News of these whirlpools had reached Cicero by 55 B.C. (*In Pisonem* § 81:
'Rheni fossam gurgitibus illis redundantem').

[3] Diodorus, v. 22. 4 (probably derived from Posidonius, and therefore descriptive of conditions *c.* 100–80 B.C.). The cavalcade probably went from Corbilo to
Massilia (Strabo, p. 147), a distance of over 400 miles.

Roman invaders, in 125–120 B.C. and in the days of Vercingetorix. But it was equally natural that the Aedui, who lay astride of the main line of communications between Mediterranean and Atlantic Gaul and stood to profit by close trading relations with the Mediterranean seaboard, should have taken the opposite side and made common cause with the Romans.

The Greek colonists on the Mediterranean face of Gaul apparently made no attempt to occupy the site of Narbo, despite its facilities for trade with the interior; and the settlement of Theline which they made at the head of the Rhône delta, on the future site of Arelate,[1] was short-lived: it may have lain too far inland for their undisputed possession. On the other hand their city of Massilia, besides possessing a good harbour,[2] reached up the brow of a steep bluff to a citadel which commanded the plain of La Crau on its other flank. The Massiliotes made the best of their stone-strewn hinterland by grazing sheep on its wild clover,[3] and from their safer point of vantage they eventually took over and developed the river trade of Theline. By 500 B.C. they had begun the penetration of Gaul by way of the Rhône valley,[4] and by 300 B.C. their commerce was extending along the various river routes of Gaul to the vicinity of the Rhine and the Atlantic.[5] The transfer of their inland trade to Arelate after the time of Caesar was due to political rather than to geographical reasons.

In constituting their first Gallic province, Gallia Narbonensis, the Romans drew its boundaries fairly close to the limits of Mediterranean France,[6] so that in due course it became 'more Italy than a province'.[7] But apart from the crest of the Cévennes, which provided an obvious line of defence, they left it without any strategic frontiers towards the north and west; indeed no such frontiers can be drawn anywhere across Gaul. The colony which they founded at Narbo may have been intended as the terminal

[1] Avienus, l. 690.
[2] The old Greek harbour was of narrower dimensions than the present Vieux Port (M. Clerc, *Massalia*, i, ch. 1).
[3] Strabo, p. 182.
[4] Avienus, ll. 637 ff., and commentary by Berthelot.
[5] This extension does not appear to have been rapid before 300 B.C., for this is the date at which Massilian coins began to spread across Gaul (Cary, *Journ. Hell. Stud.*, 1924, pp. 172–8). The very few genuine Greek vases of the fifth century B.C. which have been found in Switzerland and southern Germany may have been imported by way of the Danube rather than of the Rhône (P. Jacobsthal, *Germania*, 1934, pp. 14 ff.).
[6] Its northernmost town, Vienna, lay outside the Mediterranean zone.
[7] Pliny, iii. 31.

point of a new tin-route to supplement the traffic between Corbilo and Massilia (p. 252, n. 5) which the native merchants kept in their own hands;[1] but its purpose may equally well have been agrarian, for Italian settlers in its hinterland would find the conditions of soil and climate congenial to the traditional technique of Italian land-work.

The definitive conquest of Gaul by Caesar, whether premeditated or the result of a chapter of accidents, generally followed the best lines of a strategic advance for a conqueror from Italy. By choice or by chance, Caesar at the outset by-passed the Massif Central, which even at a later stage proved too tough a nut to crush by direct assault. Having advanced in his first campaign along the Rhône–Rhine corridor, he quartered his troops among the Sequani (in the Doubs valley), thus making fast the invasion-gate by the Trouée de Belfort. In turning westward to the Atlantic (56 B.C.) before he had secured the Liége–Namur avenue he took a risk, and in the following year he had to return to repair this omission. But his drive to the Atlantic and right down the west coast was a profitable move and may have been inspired primarily by strategic considerations,[2] for its effect was to ring off the centre of France in much the same manner as the German occupation of 1940. In the complicated pattern of marching and counter-marching which made up the campaign of 52 B.C. a distinctive feature was the recurrent racing of the antagonists for the control of the river passages. The rapidity with which Caesar crossed and re-crossed the Loire and the Allier, and Labienus seized the passages of the Seine at Melun and Paris, extricated the Roman forces from some dangerous situations and gave back the initiative into their hands. The brimming rivers of Gaul carried enough water in the campaigning season to have pinned down a less elusive couple of commanders than Caesar and his lieutenant.

The division of Gaul for administrative purposes, as devised by Augustus and Agrippa, generally followed the lines of the pre-existing ethnic boundaries. But it also conformed to the geographic structure of the country. Of Augustus' new provinces, Aquitania comprised the basin of the Garonne, Lugdunensis those of the Loire and Seine, and Belgica those of the Meuse and Rhine. The importance of the Gallic river system was fully realized by the Romans; already well developed before the Roman

---

[1] Strabo, p. 190.
[2] Caesar's invasion of Aquitania (Gascony) was a piece of pure aggression, as is pointed out by C. Hignett, *Cambr. Anc. Hist.* ix. 556.

conquest, it was henceforth put to the fullest use. An ambitious project by one of Claudius' governors for a canal to connect the Saône with the Moselle remained in the planning stage; the costs of its construction would probably have been prohibitive.[1] Similarly the widening of the Rhine narrows was a task beyond the technique of Roman engineers; but the elder Drusus built a dike at the fork of the Old Rhine and the Waal so as to divert floods from the low-lying lands on the west bank.[2] The extent to which the Romans exploited the Gallic waterways is attested by the survival of seventy-five inscriptions relating to the boatmen's guilds; even such a tear-away mountain stream as the Druentia (Durance) was pressed into service.[3]

The conquest of Gaul imposed upon the Romans the construction of paved roads across the western Alps.[4] In the absence of any clear reference to some of these passes in ancient authors, or of any ancient pavement or milestones, it may be assumed that the Romans did not build a highway across the Col de Larche (6,500 feet) or through the Mt. Cenis pass (parts of which are exposed to violent squalls).[5] Though they promptly followed up the annexation of Gallia Narbonensis with a road from the Rhône to the Pyrenees, they did not complete the corresponding section between the river and the Maritime Alps until the time of Augustus, apparently making shift in the meantime with an older Massilian track.[6] The passage of the Rhône was made by ferries at Tarasco and (in later days) at Arelate:[7] until the construction of the Pont d'Avignon in A.D. 1177–85 the lowest bridge over the river presumably stood at Lyon.

The first paved road across the Alps was probably by the low and comparatively sheltered Mt. Genèvre (6,100 feet), which may be attributed to Pompey.[8] After Caesar's conquest of central and

[1] Tacitus, *Annals*, xiii. 53. 3–4. The modern Canal de l'Est between the Saône and the Meuse is encumbered with some 150 locks and tunnels.

[2] Tacitus, *Histories*, v. 19. 3. It was not until the Middle Ages that the Waal replaced the Old Rhine as the main waterway. See the maps on pp. 382, 386, and 415 in A. W. Byvanck, *Nederland in den romeinschen tijd*, ii.

[3] Bonnard, op. cit.

[4] In general, see W. W. Hyde, 'Roman Alpine Routes', in *Memoirs of the American Philosophical Association* (Philadelphia), ii (1935).

[5] Both these passes have been in constant use since the Middle Ages.

[6] Strabo, p. 178. On the course of the Augustan road see W. H. Bullock Hall, *The Romans on the Riviera*, ch. 17; H. J. de Witt, *Transactions of the American Philosophical Association*, 1941, pp. 59–69. Near Monaco the Via Augusta surmounted *en corniche* a spur of the Maritime Alps.

[7] Strabo, loc. cit.; C. Jullian, *Histoire de la Gaule*, v. 119.

[8] This is the usual inference from a report made by Pompey to the Senate:

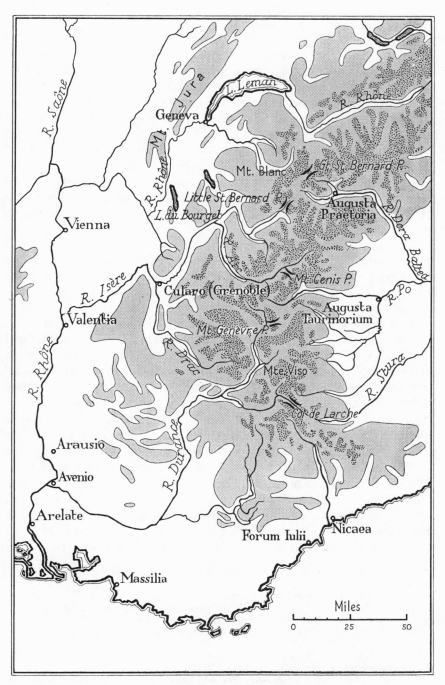

THE WESTERN ALPS

northern Gaul the Little and Great St. Bernard Passes (7,200 and 8,100 feet) had to accommodate more traffic and were metalled by Augustus and Claudius respectively.[1] While the roads across the Mt. Genèvre and Little St. Bernard converged on the Rhône at Vienna (modern Vienne), the Great St. Bernard route became the main line of communications with the Aar valley by way of Lousonna (modern Lausanne). The Simplon road was paved more perfunctorily, so as to meet the needs of local traffic, and not until c. A.D. 200.[2] Though this pass (rising to 6,600 feet) does not rank among the more difficult ones, its approach through the deep Gondo ravine on the Italian side has an alarming appearance, and on the Swiss side it debouches on a section of the Rhône valley which is liable to inundation.[3]

It is an eloquent commentary on the good workmanship and careful siting of the Roman roads in the Alps, that in A.D. 69 the Vitellian general Caecina led his army over the Great St. Bernard, apparently without any mishap, in the early spring, when the danger from avalanches is at its greatest.[4]

The internal network of Roman roads in Gaul was not peripheral, like that of Spain, but radiated from a number of local centres. While Vienna (modern Vienne) was the connecting-point of two Alpine roads (see above) and of the way from Arelate, the first important point of bifurcation was twenty miles farther north, at Lugdunum. This city lay far enough north to give a relatively easy passage to the 'Great West Road' which it sent forth to the Garonne and Loire estuaries, avoiding the higher levels of the Massif Central; and it was the natural starting-point for the valley roads up the Saône and the Doubs, and across the watershed to the Yonne, the Seine, and the Moselle.[5] An important secondary road-centre at Durocortorum (Reims) received several converging roads from Lyon and the Saône valley which made for the open country of Champagne between the Forests of the Ardennes and of the Paris district.[6] From the same town one

---

'per Alpes iter aliud atque Hannibal nobis opportunius patefeci' (Sallust, *Histories*, fr. 98, § 4, Maurenbrecher).

[1] The Little St. Bernard was repaved in 1871, and the Great St. Bernard in 1905. To offset its great height, the latter pass has easy approaches.

[2] F. Stähelin, *Die Schweiz in römischer Zeit* (2nd ed.), pp. 329 ff.

[3] The Rhône floods still cause much trouble in the canton of Valais.

[4] Tacitus, *Histories*, i. 70. 4: 'hibernis adhuc Alpibus'.

[5] Hence the international importance of Lyon Fair, which became one of the chief commercial exchanges in the later Middle Ages.

[6] Before Lyon gained ascendancy, the chief Fair Town of western Europe was Provins, a little to the west of the Roman 'Great North Road'.

main road branched off to the Moselle valley, and another across the dry and unencumbered plain of Picardy to Gessoriacum (Boulogne); and a continuation of the 'Great North Road' from Lugdunum went on to Bagacum (Bavai, near Maubeuge). From this last branching-point, one arm rejoined the direct road from Reims at Boulogne; another skirted the northern edge of the Ardennes and took the Liége corridor to Colonia Agrippinensis (Cologne), where it met the trunk road that skirted the left bank of the Rhine, all the way from the vicinity of Basle to Lugdunum (Leyden), at the estuary of the Old Rhine.[1]

Though Gaul was essentially self-contained in its agriculture, it could provide exports under the stimulus of a foreign demand, and under Roman rule it produced an overplus of grain and wine. The wheatfields of Belgica became the normal source of supply for the large Roman forces on the Rhine frontier.[2] But the principal innovation in Gallic land-work was the intensified cultivation of the vine. In ancient times, it is true, some of the chief vintage areas of modern times, the Côte d'Or, Champagne, and the Rhineland, had not yet acquired a high reputation, and the vineyards of the Moselle are mentioned only in Ausonius, an author of the fourth century.[3] The tardy development of these districts may have been due to the fact that they are best suited for the production of the choicer brands in moderate quantities,[4] and that the Roman market for the better beverages was adequately stocked from the vineyards of Italy itself. On the other hand, Provence and Languedoc (which latter is the most prolific producer of wine in modern France) and the Bordeaux district grew for export. The former two areas were probably the source from which Roman wine-merchants intoxicated Gaul (in pre-Roman days) and Germany;[5] the latter furnished Roman Britain with its 'claret' (p. 270).

For the export of oil from Gaul the evidence is scanty and

---

[1] The Roman road system bore a remarkable resemblance to that of eighteenth-century France (P. Vidal de la Blache, in Lavisse, *Histoire de France*, i, maps on pp. 378–9).

[2] Cumont, *Comment la Belge fut romanisée*, pp. 32–3.

[3] *Mosella*, xxi, ll. 155–62.

[4] The soil of the wine-producing area of Champagne is naturally unfertile, and the yield per acre is comparatively low.

[5] Exports of wine to Gaul: Diodorus, v. 26. 3; Caesar, *Bellum Gallicum* ii. 15. 4; to Germany, Caesar, iv. 2. 6; Tacitus, *Germania* 23, § 1. It may be surmised that the chief source of export was Narbonese Gaul, where the art of doctoring and drugging wine for unsophisticated palates was practised (Pliny, xiv, § 68).

fugitive; at best it was not comparable with that from Spain. But the plentiful remains of ancient oil-presses in Provence are evidence that the Roman planters here introduced the olive along with the vine.[1]

In the first and second centuries of the Christian era the industrial resources of Gaul were developed to such an extent that the country might almost have been described as 'the workshop of the Roman empire'. A more intensive working of the mines furnished abundance of materials both for munitions of war and for decorative metal-work. The exports from Gaul included iron and copper vessels with tin plating, household ware of brass, and enamelled brooches.[2] But the principal contribution of the soil of Gaul to the country's prosperity now came from its clay-beds, which provided the material for the most extensive manufactures of ceramic ware in the ancient world.[3] The Gallic *terra sigillata* (a highly glazed red ware, suggestive of sealing-wax, with embossed ornaments) captured the markets of all western Europe and found its way as far as Egypt. The principal centres of manufacture were La Graufesenque in the valley of the Tarn (*floruit* A.D. 40–75) and Lezoux in the valley of the Allier (*floruit* A.D. 75–160).

The industrial materials of northern Gaul, which had been less actively exploited in pre-Roman days, were henceforth put to fuller use. The manufacture of glass table-ware by blowing, which was introduced from Italy and attained a considerable vogue in the second and third centuries, had its chief seats near Cologne and in Normandy or the Pas de Calais.[4] The textile industry of Flanders also made its start under the Roman emperors. It did not as yet weave high-quality cloth with wool from Britain, but it used the heavy fleeces of its own rich but rank pastures to produce thick 'frieze' cloaks which found a ready market in Italy and in the eastern Mediterranean.[5]

The fuller utilization of Gaul's natural road and river facilities under Roman rule, together with the accumulation of surplus goods for export, inevitably gave a sharp stimulus to trade. But the most notable expansion of commerce was a result of the Roman invasion of Britain. The reconnaissances of Caesar in this strange land produced a speedy effect, so that under Augustus

[1] Grenier, op. cit., p. 585.
[2] Rostovtzeff, *Roman Empire*, p. 531 n. 17 (finds of Gallic brooches in Russia).
[3] Grenier, op. cit., pp. 540–62.
[4] Ibid., pp. 628–9.
[5] Cumont, op. cit., pp. 35–6.

four regular sea-routes between Gaul and Britain were under
regular operation. The routes are thus enumerated by Strabo:
'There are four crossings in habitual use between the continent
and the island; they take off from the mouths of the rivers, the
Rhine, Seine, Loire, and Garonne. Those who put out to sea
from the Rhine district do not take off exactly from its estuary,
but from the land of the Morini' (Pas de Calais).[1] Of these passages,
it is true, the one from the Loire, which had carried a regular
traffic in pre-Roman days, in connexion with the Cornish stannaries, lost much of its former importance with the temporary
suspension of tin-mining (p. 268). But a packet-boat and military
transport service inevitably developed on the 'short sea routes';
the route from the Garonne was established for the export of
wine, and that from the Rhine for the conveyance of other bulky
ware, such as pottery.

The growth of urban life in Gaul under Roman rule was particularly rapid in the Narbonese province, where dearth of water
in summer naturally makes for close settlement, and the general
resemblance of the country to Italy favoured the establishment
of numerous Roman colonies.[2] The greater number of the Roman
settlements was strung along the Rhône valley from Arelate,
which replaced Massilia as the main port of entry into Gaul, to
the river-fork towns of Avenio (Avignon) and Valentia (Valence),
and the road-centre of Vienna (p. 256). At the exit of Lake Leman
Genaba achieved local importance as a bridge town and a summer
resort for the well-to-do folk of Vienna,[3] but it was not and could
not be a major centre of traffic. It does not lie near any Alpine
pass; it is partly cut off from France by the Jura, and it cannot
serve as a head of river navigation, for below it the Rhône is con-
stricted into a series of rapids and tunnels.

In the rest of Gaul, where climatic conditions do not preclude
scattered settlement, the population in pre-Roman days was widely
diffused, and its walled *oppida* on hill-tops were for temporary
refuge rather than for permanent habitation, except in the case
of a few industrial centres, such as Alesia (a bronze-founding and
silver-plating town),[4] Avaricum (Bourges), and Bibracte (near
Autun). Here Roman colonization was more sparse, and mainly
confined to traffic centres such as Lugdunum, Augusta Raura-

---

[1] p. 199.
[2] It is pointed out by Vidal de la Blache (op. cit., p. 350) that the Provençaux are
still conspicuous among the French for their love of the stir and bustle of town life.
[3] Stähelin, op. cit., pp. 129–32.
[4] Pliny, xxxiv, § 162; Grenier, op. cit., p. 528.

corum (near Basle), Augusta Trevirorum (Trier), and Colonia Agrippinensis.

Of the native towns Lutecia (Paris) was of local importance as a station on a river route, but not as a road centre. It had a connexion with Genabum (Orléans) on the Loire, but was not a base of communications with northern France and Belgium, for which purpose it was ill suited until the surrounding forest had been cleared. The roads to the north went by the more open lands of Champagne (p. 256), and their starting-point was Reims. On the west coast the old town of Corbilo declined with the suspension of the Cornish tin trade, and Iuliobona (Lillebonne), which lay some twenty miles up the Seine, was but a feeble anticipation of the greater river-port at Rouen and the great ocean out-port at Le Havre. But Burdigala (Bordeaux), situated on the lowest piece of firm ground in the Garonne estuary, grew with the wine trade to Britain. For the Channel crossing Boulogne was preferred to Calais, which was backed by undrained marshland. Of the towns on the Rhine Strasbourg did not achieve importance as a port until the Middle Ages, and Moguntiacum (Mainz) was mainly a station for military patrols and commissariat. For commercial traffic down river and to the sea Cologne was the head of navigation. No harbour towns of any importance arose on the Dutch or Flemish coasts, which had as yet not assumed definite shape (p. 248).

§ 3. BRITAIN

The natural line of approach from the western or central Mediterranean area to Britain would seem to be the land route across France. From the Franco-Italian frontier to London the beeline distance is under 600 miles, i.e. less than from London to John o' Groats or from the Franco-Italian frontier to Brindisi. On the other hand, the shortest open-sea route between Britain and Gibraltar measures 1,000 nautical miles, and the coastal voyage is twice as long. Nevertheless an oversea connexion between Britain and the Mediterranean had been established for many centuries before Caesar opened up the land route from Italy. Maritime trade with Britain was initiated by the people of Tartessus perhaps as early as 2000 B.C.; by 500 B.C., if not sooner, the Carthaginians had taken over this traffic,[1] and at some later date they began to work an open-sea route from Spain to Cornwall (p. 238). The reason for the earlier development of this maritime

[1] On early Atlantic trade see Cary and Warmington, *The Ancient Explorers,* pp. 29-33 and notes.

ROMAN BRITAIN

traffic was no doubt that the tin of Cornwall had a monopoly value in Mediterranean lands, where this metal was rare, and that such a bulky commodity was more suitable for transportation by sea than by land. About 300 B.C. a Greek explorer, Pytheas of Massilia, not only followed the Carthaginians to Cornwall but outdistanced them by circumnavigating Britain;[1] but no other Greek seafarer ventured out on his track into the Atlantic, and it was left to a Roman governor of Spain, P. Crassus, to throw open to all comers the open-sea route.[2] Even so, the acquaintance of the Mediterranean peoples with Britain hardly extended beyond the Cornish stannaries.

By the second century, if not earlier, Cornish tin was being forwarded from the port of Corbilo on the Loire estuary to Massilia for distribution in Mediterranean lands (p. 251); but the provenience of the tin was kept secret by the Gaulish middlemen.[3] Consequently it was left to Caesar to put Britain on the Roman map.[4]

Caesar's invasions of Britain (55 and 54 B.C.), being directed to an unknown country, had perforce to begin with beach landings. For this purpose the shelving coast between Dover and the North Foreland was the most suitable, for the southern seaboard of Kent is dominated by high cliffs, and until the building of the modern sea-wall the Romney flats of east Sussex were liable to inundation. But it is strange that in both of his British campaigns Caesar, having successfully made his landing, neglected to seize his 'Cherbourg', the port of Rutupiae (Richborough) under the lee of Thanet Island.[5] Like the Allies in 1944, he may have banked on a respite from easterly gales, which indeed are rare in these waters during the summer.

The chief natural obstacles to Caesar's progress in the campaign of 54 B.C. were the Thames and the wooded country on either side of the river, in which he was continually ambushed by his adversaries. His line of advance through Kent was probably

---

[1] The details of Pytheas' voyage remain uncertain. (For a recent reconstruction see G. E. Broche, *Pythéas le Massaliote*.) But it is now generally acknowledged that his cruise round Britain was actually accomplished.

[2] Strabo, p. 176. His 'Publius Crassus' was probably the consul of 97 B.C., who proceeded to the governorship of Further Spain and was engaged in a campaign in the west of the peninsula.

[3] Strabo, p. 190.

[4] Tacitus, *Agricola* 13, § 2: 'Britanniam potest videri *ostendisse* posteris.'

[5] R. G. Collingwood in Collingwood and Myres, *Roman Britain and the English Settlements* (2nd ed.), pp. 45–6. No ancient author makes allusion to the Goodwin Sands, which have given the east Kent coast a bad reputation since the Middle Ages.

along the southern slope of the North Downs, which is still well
strewn with coppices, but avoids the marsh-land of the Medway
estuary. To ford the Thames, he must have marched at least as
far west as London, but he need not have gone farther up stream,
for until the building of the Embankment the river could occasionally be crossed on foot at low tide in the Chelsea reach. North
of the Thames he entered another wooded area of which Epping
Forest is an attenuated remnant. Here the Celtic strongholds
were not hill-top forts (like Maiden Castle in the open Dorset
country), but fastnesses protected by jungle and marshes.[1]

Caesar's invasion had at least the merit of dispelling some
prevalent errors about Britain, that being northerly it was very
cold,[2] and that it abounded in gold and silver.[3] It also brought
into regular use the four main crossings from the continent (p.
259). The shortest route, from Boulogne to Dover, usually took
seven or eight hours, because of those cross-tides which nowadays
retard or baffle the swimmers of the Channel.[4]

The additional knowledge of Britain which a century of regular
intercourse had brought to the Roman world made it possible for
the definitive invasion of Britain under Claudius (A.D. 43) to be
planned with better regard to geography.[5] By his immediate
seizure of Richborough Claudius' general Plautius provided the
Roman forces with a safe base and ensured the success of the first
campaign, which covered much the same ground as Caesar's
expedition in 54 B.C. Plautius' subsequent operations were in the
nature of a pincer movement from the lower Thames valley, in
which one arm cut northward across the corridor of open country
between the Arden forest of the central midlands and the Fens
(then extending as far as the line of the Great North Road) towards
Leicester and Lincoln, while the other arm thrust westward towards Bath and the Mendips. The western column presumably
followed the long line of the chalk escarpment between the Thames

---

[1] This holds good of the pre-Roman stronghold at Wheathampstead in the
upper Lea valley—probably the one which Caesar stormed—and of the one built
shortly after Caesar's time near St. Albans (Collingwood and Myres, pp. 46, 54–5;
R. E. M. and T. Wheeler, *Verulamium* (Reports of the Research Committee of the
Society of Antiquaries, no. XI). Strabo said too sweepingly of British fortresses:
πόλεις αὐτῶν εἰσιν οἱ δρυμοί (p. 200).

[2] So Diodorus, v. 21. 6 (probably from Posidonius or Ephorus).

[3] Cicero, *Ad Atticum* iv. 17. 6; *Ad Familiares* vii. 7. 1.

[4] Strabo, pp. 193–4. In the seventeenth century seven hours was still considered
a fair time for a crossing. It is estimated that coastal erosion has increased the
width of Dover Straits by one mile since the Roman era.

[5] For the Roman advance through Britain, see Collingwood and Myres throughout.

valley and the Channel, avoiding the densely wooded belts of the Sussex Weald and the New Forest; the division which the future emperor Vespasian led to capture the Isle of Wight[1] no doubt proceeded by the Winchester Gap between the two zones of woodland.

The line along which the pincers eventually closed was probably that of the 'jurassic escarpment', a belt of high ground running diagonally across the midlands from south-west to north-east, close to which one of the first Roman governors built the Fosse Way as a provisional *limes* or frontier road. The escarpment turns its steep face outward towards the valleys of the Severn, Avon, and Trent.

The second governor of Britain, Ostorius, proceeded to 'hold down with strong-points all the territory this side of Severn and Trent',[2] i.e. the central and west midlands. As this area was interspersed with large patches of forest, its reduction demanded methods of infiltration rather than a swift cut-through. But once astride of his new river line, Ostorius naturally went on through the Cheshire Gap between the higher lands of Derbyshire and Wales, so as to occupy Chester and complete a second diagonal crossing of England, from south-east to north-west. By A.D. 60, therefore, Roman Britain had assumed the shape of a quadrilateral with the outer angle-points at Lincoln, Chester, and Gloucester.[3]

But the Romans came to the same conclusion in Britain as they had previously reached in Spain, that to obtain complete security for the lowlands they must penetrate into the adjacent mountain country and either absorb it or establish a protective glacis across it: a policy which the Normans and Plantagenets adopted in their turn. Therefore the occupation of Wales, initiated by Ostorius and Suetonius (*c.* A.D. 60), was completed by Frontinus (74–7) and Agricola (77–84). Here the method of infiltration by river valleys was plainly indicated, and surviving Roman forts in the valleys of the Usk (Caerleon and Brecon) and of the Severn (Caersws and Caer Forden) attest that this strategy was adopted.[4] Another Roman fort at Carnarvon indicates that Agricola's march across north Wales may have been made by the inland route

---

[1] Suetonius, *Vespasian*, 4, § 1.   [2] Tacitus, *Annals*, xii. 31. 2.

[3] An early Roman occupation of Gloucester, long surmised, has recently been proved by archaeological finds (C. Green, *Journ. Rom. Stud.*, 1942, pp. 39 ff.; 1943, pp. 15 ff.).

[4] The medieval equivalent of Caerleon would be Chepstow or Caerphilly, that of Caersws would be Montgomery.

through Capel Curig (of which Carnarvon is the terminus), rather than by the coast road with its difficult section at Penmaenmawr. By using the inland route Agricola would have cut through the heart of the Gwynedd country, which is the chief natural stronghold of Wales and was the centre of resistance in Plantagenet days. But the substantial character of the fort at Carnarvon suggests that it did additional duty as a base for an accompanying fleet.[1]

Agricola's predecessor Cerialis (A.D. 71–4) had already prepared for the longer thrust across north Britain by occupying the plain between Humber and Tyne and transferring the northern Roman base from Lincoln to York. This city lay off the Roman Great North Road, which kept well inland by way of Doncaster and Castleford in order to avoid the fens and the Forest of Elmet in the Humber area[2]; its choice as a military headquarters no doubt rested on its river communications with the Humber, which gave it a position analogous to that of London in the south.

The advance of Agricola to the Scottish border was a pincer action by parallel advances on either side of the Pennines, and the occupation and fortification of the transverse routes across these mountains.[3] The main line of march, as in Plantagenet and Tudor times, was by the eastern route, which was not only easier in itself but gave better communications with the coast and so facilitated co-operation with the fleet. Instead of following the almost harbourless coast between this river and the Firth of Forth, Agricola used the later invasion route of English kings by way of the upper Tyne, so as to rejoin his fleet near Edinburgh.[4] In his progress beyond the Forth he again took advantage of the easier going and better facilities for contact with his fleet on the east side of the Grampians, his object being to turn this massif rather than to adventure himself up the Pass of Killiecrankie.[5]

---

[1] I. A. Richmond, *Journ. Rom. Stud.*, 1944, p. 38. The whole of this article is an excellent example of geography applied to elucidate campaigns.

[2] The Great North Road of the Middle Ages went through Pontefract (west of Castleford).

[3] Agricolan forts have been located along the chief river cross-routes, on the Tyne–Solway line, in Wensleydale and Wharfedale; also in the Hebden Gap, and on the Pennine ridge in the line between the base forts of York and Chester.

[4] Agricola's route is clearly marked by the large camp at Newstead in the middle Tweed valley which was his advanced base.

[5] J. G. C. Anderson, *Cornelii Taciti De Vita Agricolae* (2nd ed.), Introduction, p. lxviii, and Richmond, op. cit., p. 42. Richmond would locate Agricola's final battle in the open country north of Aberdeen.

In calling a halt to Agricola's advance Domitian relieved his generals of the Herculean task of subduing the wild west and north of Scotland. But he set them the difficult problem of making a choice between the two 'isthmus' positions at the Clyde–Forth and the Solway–Tyne gaps as a definite frontier line. Either of these would give the Romans a relatively short front to hold and a belt of high ground with a steep scarp on the south side of the gap[1]; but to decide between them was no easy matter. The Scottish line, it is true, had the obvious advantage of measuring only thirty-seven miles as against the seventy-three miles of the English one; but it involved the lengthening of the supply line by a hundred miles through a difficult and semi-desert country, and in the absence of permanent bases in north Britain for the Roman fleet it lay dangerously exposed to enfilading attacks by naval raiders.[2] Therefore after long hesitations the Romans finally endorsed Hadrian's decision to fall back on the English line (c. A.D. 185).

In the later days of the Roman occupation the need to repel marauders from overseas became paramount over that of land defence. In particular, the raids of the Saxons upon the eastern and southern coasts called for a redistribution of forces. The Romans met the fresh menace by constructing a chain of forts from the Isle of Wight to the Wash (c. A.D. 300), which was extended c. A.D. 375 along the Yorkshire coast as far as the Cleveland district. These forts were no doubt intended to serve as bases for small naval squadrons, enabling these to get quickly off the mark against elusive Saxon raiders.[3] The original dimension of the 'Saxon Shore' suggests that the invaders at first felt their way along the continental coast (where their visitations are also on record), and after putting across the Straits of Dover worked their way along either coast. Its later extension implies that the Saxons eventually explored an open-sea route, with a landfall at Flamborough Head. The inclusion of London and York in the scheme of fortifications, and the special care which was taken to strengthen the riverside sectors of their new ring-walls, indicates that the Saxons, like the Danes to follow, used the inland waterways as means of penetration into England.

[1] The strategic value of the Clyde–Forth line is duly emphasized by G. Macdonald (*The Roman Wall in Scotland*).

[2] A chain of forts along the Cumberland coast which served as a flank guard to Hadrian's Wall shows that the Romans realized the danger of such forays.

[3] The head-quarters of the Classis Britannica were at Boulogne. The deep-water inlets of Chatham and Portsmouth were not developed as naval harbours until the coming of the heavy 'ship of the line'.

In Gaul the Romans made few attempts at colonization beyond its Mediterranean face (p. 259). *A fortiori* they did not make numerous settlements in Britain. Spoilt by long hours of Mediterranean sunshine, they would not readily acclimatize themselves to our duller skies and wetter summers.[1] Moreover they were ill qualified to play the part of improving landlords in Britain, as they had been in south France, southern and eastern Spain, and in Tunisia. To say nothing of the difficulty of growing vines[2] and the impossibility of cultivating olives, they could not have raised good crops of grain by their Italian methods in the climatic conditions of Britain; still less would they have been disposed to clear dense forests of tough oak and beech. It is significant that, of the four colonies founded by the Romans in Britain (Colchester, Lincoln, York, and Gloucester), all except the last-named were situated in relatively dry and open country and on light soil. The cultivation of the stiff clay lands which are common in the south and the midlands was left by the Romans in the hands of an earlier group of invaders from northern Gaul, who had brought with them their deep-cutting and sod-overturning ploughs, without which the sticky clay soil could not have been adequately drained and aerated.[3] The most important land-operation of all, the clearing of the superfluous forest, was left over to the Anglo-Saxons.[4] The sole direct contribution of the Romans to the food-supply of Britain, so far as is known, was the introduction of the edible cherry, previously brought to Italy from Asia Minor.[5] But the indirect services rendered by the Romans to British agriculture should not be lost out of sight—political security, better roads, and wider markets. It is probably no mere accident that under Roman rule the eastern counties could produce a surplus of grain for shipment to the Rhineland,[6] and that by the time of

---

[1] The fogs of Britain were duly noted by Strabo (p. 200) and Tacitus (*Agricola*, 12, § 3). According to the German tribe of the Heruli, Britain was the gate of the nether world (Procopius, *Bellum Gothicum*, iv. 20, §§ 4–5).

[2] Attempts to produce a home-made wine which were made in the lower Severn valley during the Middle Ages were abandoned after the introduction of hop-growing from Flanders in the fifteenth century.

[3] Collingwood and Myres, p. 211.

[4] See the map on p. 5 of J. Ward, *The Roman Era in Britain*. Here it is shown that, apart from the mountain districts, the least cultivated parts of Roman Britain were the forested areas.

[5] Pliny, xv, § 102. The exact date of the importation, A.D. 47, is here given.

[6] It is pointed out by Collingwood and Myres that these shipments may not have been on a commercial basis. But in the fourth century at least they were regular. The exports to the Continent were resumed from time to time in the later Middle Ages.

Diocletian, if not before, the export of British wool to the Continent had begun.[1]

The Romans were not slow to discover the oyster-beds of the Thames estuary and to send their products to Rome, or to the officers' messes in the British frontier camps; and they toyed with the idea that where oysters were succulent, pearls must be plentiful.[2] But apparently they did not observe that the British seas, whose shallow beds are unusually rich in plankton, might become one of the world's greatest fishing areas.[3] Presumably the difficulty of transporting the catch to the Mediterranean centres of population shut their eyes to this unfailing source of wealth.

It is a paradox of the Roman occupation of Britain that the mining of tin in Cornwall, which had been the first means of bringing Britain into regular contact with the Mediterranean world, was suspended during the first two centuries of the Christian era, and that there is little evidence of the presence of Romans in south-western England beyond the Exe valley before A.D. 250. This dereliction of Cornwall may be connected with the discovery of tin-mines in north-western Spain which could be worked by surface streaming, whereas even in Pytheas' days the Cornish mines required underground operation; when the Spanish mines lost their initial advantage, mining in Cornwall could be resumed, and the Romans took possession.[4] In the meantime, by way of revenge, the younger lead-mines of England and Wales had displaced those of Spain as the principal source of material for the water-pipes of Rome and Italy.[5]

Of the metals exported from Britain in the days of Augustus, gold (from south Wales), and silver (embedded in the lead ores)[6] cannot have been produced in any large quantity, but iron was plentiful and mostly of a high grade. Besides the two principal ironfields of medieval and early modern times, the Sussex Weald and the Forest of Dean, where extensive slag-heaps of Roman

[1] See Diocletian's tariff, ch. xix, l. 36: 'byrrus Britannicus' (a hooded cloak). Frank, *Economic Survey*, v, p. 374 (text and translation by Miss E. R. Graser). If we may judge by the importance of Corinium (Cirencester) in the third century, the export of wool from the Cotswolds began in Roman times.

[2] Tacitus, *Agricola*, 12, § 6.

[3] Open-sea fishing round Britain did not begin until the sixteenth century.

[4] On tin-mining in Pytheas' days see Diodorus, v. 22. 2 (from Timaeus or Posidonius). On Roman Cornwall in general, see F. J. Haverfield and Miss M. V. Taylor, *Victoria County History, Cornwall*, i, pt. 5, pp. 15–24. According to Diodorus (v. 22. 2), whose description is probably drawn from Pytheas, the Cornish miners extracted the tin-stone by cutting galleries.

[5] M. Besnier, *Revue archéologique*, 1921, pp. 36 ff., 98 ff.

[6] Strabo, p. 199.

date have been found, the workings of the Roman period included those of the Jurassic escarpment from Oxfordshire to Lincolnshire (now again one of our chief sources) and the hematite deposits of the Furness district. The Cleveland minefield in the north of Yorkshire (one of the most prolific of the nineteenth century) was merely scratched in Roman times: presumably the ore was not of sufficient grade to be worth reduction by ancient methods. But smelting by coal (which did not definitely displace charcoal in this country until the eighteenth century) was not unknown,[1] and coal extraction for domestic purposes was carried on in most of the mining areas (Staffordshire being the only notable exception). Indeed Roman Britain was, with the possible exception of China, the principal coal-mining region of the ancient world. This was but natural, as no other European country has high-quality coal lying so close to the surface.

The British sand-beds that are suitable for glass-making were worked on a small scale only, and although ceramic industries flourished here and there (notably at Castor near Peterborough and in the New Forest), the clay-deposits of Staffordshire and Cornwall which have been the foundation of our modern Potteries were not laid under contribution.

Though ancient Britain lagged well behind Gaul as a manufacturing country, it gave promise of its future activity, especially in the heavy industries. Just as the full exploitation of Britain's industrial resources was stimulated by the internal peace and the widening world-market of the Hanoverian era, so their first extensive utilization was the result of similar opportunities under the Roman empire.

With the suspension of work in the Cornish tin-mines, the oversea trade between Britain and the Mediterranean lands was discontinued.[2] On the other hand, the traffic with Belgium and the Baltic, which became the main branch of English maritime commerce in the Middle Ages, had not yet been opened, and the only North Sea route of any importance was that which led to the Rhine estuary. In other words, almost the entire current of foreign trade flowed to and from Gaul. Consequently the sea ports of Roman Britain were confined to the strip of coast between Colchester and Southampton. Of these harbours Richborough and Dover were too cramped for the heavier traffic and therefore

[1] T. May, *Warrington's Roman Remains*, pp. 23 ff.
[2] This cessation of traffic is reflected in the extreme haziness of Roman geographers about the relative positions of Britain and Spain.

served mainly as military and 'packet' ports. Southampton had all the requisites of a commercial port, except that its natural feeders in Gaul were the relatively unimportant harbours of the Seine estuary. In Roman times its place was taken by Clausentum (Bitterne, two miles up the river Itchen), whose principal traffic was presumably in Bordeaux wine.[1] The greater part of the oversea commerce no doubt came up the Thames estuary, which lay opposite the important trade route of the Rhine. Here the first good berthing-place was in the London Pool reach, where either bank offered firm ground for quays; but it was also the last convenient spot for sea-going vessels, for farther up-stream there was no assurance of a sufficient depth of water at ebb tide. Once Britain had been securely hitched to the Continent, London was marked out to become its principal port. In Roman as in medieval times, it was not 'petted' by the state authorities, but grew up independently of them[2]; yet with an area roughly equal to that of the present City (c. 330 acres), it became one of the largest towns of western Europe.

A country whose innermost penetralia lie not more than seventy miles from the sea, and whose rivers are maintained at a constant level by an equable rainfall, should have good inland water-communications, and indeed in the interval between the activities of the Roman and the modern road engineers the rivers of England were its main arteries of travel. In selecting York as their chief military base in north Britain, and Corbridge (ten miles up the Tyne from Newcastle) as the supply depot for Hadrian's Wall, the Romans showed that they were not blind to the advantages of English river-communications. Yet several of the river ports that flourished in medieval and early modern times, e.g. Nottingham and Bristol, do not appear on the map of Roman Britain; Gloucester and Cambridge[3] were bridge or ferry stations rather than ports, and Leicester was merely a road-halt. The reason for this apparent neglect of natural opportunities lay no doubt in the fact that the Humber and Wash and the Severn estuary did not lie close to any ancient trade-route. But it is not so easy to explain

[1] Southampton imported Bordeaux wine in the Middle Ages; but it first came into its own in the fifteenth and sixteenth centuries, when maritime intercourse with the Mediterranean was resumed.

[2] After the inception of regular trade with the Continent, but before the Roman occupation, an urban settlement in Southwark began to replace the scattered hamlets which had previously been dotted over the London area.

[3] Cambridge lay on a road connecting Colchester with the Roman Great North Road (at Huntingdon) and the Fosse Way (at Leicester). Situated at the border of the Fens, it offered the lowest convenient place for crossing the Cam.

why the Thames above London played no part in Roman Britain, why the place of Reading was taken by the up-country town of Silchester, and why no trace of a Roman settlement at Oxford has been found.[1]

In a frontier province like Britain the network of Roman roads was bound to subserve a predominantly military purpose. The construction of secondary commercial roads was therefore on a lesser scale than, e.g., in north-west Africa or southern Spain. In Britain, as in Gaul, the natural features of the country offered no serious obstacle to the Roman road-maker, save in regions of forest or fen. The road system was therefore planned, like that of Gaul, on the radial pattern, as being the most economical in total mileage. But in Britain a single focal centre sufficed. For incomers from Gaul the first important road-objective was a convenient point for crossing the lower Thames, and the same physical features which predestined London to become Britain's chief port also indicated it as the principal bridge-town; the same stretches of firm bank that provided it with quay-space also furnished it with solid abutments for a bridge.[2] The general preference of the Roman engineers for dry and open land is illustrated by the siting of their roads in Britain, for these were usually laid out at some distance above the river valleys. The London–Chester road (the medieval 'Watling Street') skirted in an easterly trend round the modern Black Country in order to avoid the Arden Forest. It was presumably because of the barrier of Sherwood Forest that the Romans did not direct one of their highways to the Trent passage at Nottingham, whose site was almost ideal for a Roman road-station or colony.

The veil of mystery which Caesar and his successors tore from Britain was never removed from Ireland in ancient times. In prehistoric days, to be sure, Ireland had an active commerce with the Continent and even with Spain. But the gold of Wicklow which was the main article of this early traffic had been exhausted long before the Roman era, and its reputed tin-mines merely

[1] Miss M. V. Taylor, in *Victoria County History, Oxfordshire*, i, pp. 301–3. The Roman stations in the county, Dorchester and Bicester, lay on a service road of the Roman army from Southampton Water to the midlands. H. E. Salter has suggested that until the Thames was regulated by locks (not before A.D. 1635), it ran too fast in some reaches for commercial traffic, though Danish raiders might negotiate it (*Medieval Oxford*, p. 17). But ancient boatmen who could ply on the Rhône and Loire should have been able to battle up the Thames.

[2] The Roman bridge stood some 100 yards above the medieval and modern London bridge.

served as lairs for Irish snakes. Consequently Strabo imagined Ireland as situated to the north of Britain, and whereas he knew that the British winters were mild, he assumed that Ireland was miserably chilly.[1] Similarly Pomponius Mela, writing about the time of Claudius' invasion of Britain, could merely report that Ireland had rich pasturage—so rich that the grazing-time of the cattle had to be stinted for fear that they should 'leap apart'.[2]

Agricola gave a passing thought to the conquest of Ireland and may even have sent out a reconnaissance party across St. George's Channel. From his dispositions for the conquest of Wales, and from the actual beginnings of the invasions under Plantagenet rule, it may be assumed that his bases for his prospective expedition were at Chester and Carnarvon. It was probably also from these points that the later thin trickle of trade to the eastern and north-eastern coasts of Ireland was directed. The theory that in Roman times there was lively traffic between southern Ireland and Gaul lacks archaeological confirmation,[3] and it is improbable on geographical grounds, for it would entail an open-sea run of at least 250 miles (as against 50–60 miles from Wales to the east coast). In sum, the history of Ireland in Roman times confirms the dictum that whereas Britain is a detached piece of Europe, what lies beyond it is an island of the Atlantic Ocean.

[1] pp. 72, 201.
[2] iii. 53: 'nisi pabulo prohibeantur, diutius pasta dissiliant'.
[3] F. J. Haverfield, *English Historical Review*, 1913, pp. 1 ff.

X. CENTRAL EUROPE

§ 1. GERMANY

SO far as concerns the history of Rome, ancient Germany
might be roughly defined as the territory between the Rhine,
the upper and middle Danube, and the Vistula. This country is,
like Gaul and Britain, a land of good natural communications.
Its northern half forms part of the vast plain that stretches almost
unbrokenly from the North to the Yellow Sea, and the hill country of the southern portion is discontinuous and seamed with
easy passage-ways. Of the German rivers, the Vistula and Oder,
besides being ice-bound in midwinter, have the disadvantage of
ending their course in the Baltic backwater, but the Elbe and
Weser share with the Rhine (p. 251) a fairly constant flow of water
and an outlet on a sea which is potentially one of the principal
lines of European communications. The climate is of the Atlantic
type, with a moderate range of temperature and equable rainfall.[1]
Germany contains many patches of dry and open land, where
crops could be grown with simple equipment; its mineral resources
are large and varied,[2] and in its deposits of amber on the coasts of
Samland and Jutland it formerly possessed an almost unique
asset.

On the other hand, to say nothing of Roman fastidiousness in
the matter of warm sun and blue skies, ancient Germany, even
more than Britain, presented an unkempt appearance.[3] Its cultivable lands were surrounded with large areas of dense forest and
swamp. In the German midlands the present Thuringian, Fran-
conian, and Sudetic forests formerly coalesced into a 'Hercynian
wood', whose vast expanse had captivated the imagination of
Greek geographers[4] before it awed the soldiers and traders of
Rome. In northern Germany extensive tracts of almost dead-
level country have too slow a run-off of their spill-water, and a
hard pan of tightly rammed clay (a remnant of former Ice Ages)

---

[1] The boundary between the Atlantic and the continental weather systems lies
at the Vistula. The climate of Germany is rated among the best in the world by
E. Huntington (*Civilisation and Climate*, ch. x).

[2] The renaissance of mining in the fifteenth and sixteenth centuries began in
Germany.

[3] Tacitus, *Germania*, 5, § 1: 'silvis horrida aut paludibus foeda'.

[4] Caesar, *Bellum Gallicum* vi. 25: a sixty days' journey across it! (Probably from
Posidonius.)

T

under a thin top layer of sandstone retards subsoil drainage. Until the advent of modern science and machinery Germany contained large reserves of fenland and peat-bogs.

The minerals of Germany mostly lie at a deep level; in ancient times their very presence for the most part remained unsuspected. Of the seas adjoining Germany the Baltic is safe, but it was too deeply recessed from the main roads of ancient commerce. The North Sea is less boisterous than the Channel and Bay of Biscay, but it is not immune from summer gales, and at all seasons it is liable to be hemmed in with thick cloud or blurred with mist. Its Frisian and Jutish coasts are ill defined and partly submerged at high tide; and such conditions of low visibility and vanishing landmarks were peculiarly baffling to seamen trained in Mediterranean waters.[1] Consequently it remained a 'German Ocean'; and it is doubtful whether the Baltic ever carried a Greek or Roman keel.

Contrary to their early delusions about Britain (p. 263), the Romans never imagined Germany as an Eldorado, and their interest in it was almost exclusively one of frontier defence. From the economic point of view the Rhine appeared the limit of profitable expansion, and with its strong and equable flow of water it formed a good barrier against invasion; but once the Romans had drawn the remainder of their European boundary along the Danube, a re-entrant angle was formed between the two rivers which considerably added to the mileage requiring to be guarded.

In the days of Augustus accordingly the Roman armies reconnoitred in Germany for a shorter if more distant boundary, and at the outset of their quest they happened upon the best alternative line. Though the emperor could probably not have drawn a remotely correct map of Germany—not even the geographer Ptolemy could do this 150 years later—his choice of the Elbe as an alternative river barrier, and of the Czechoslovak plateau to close the gap between it and the Danube, was happily inspired, for his new German boundary, together with its prolongation along the Danube, made a clean diagonal cut across the European continent. In their advance across western Germany to establish their new front Augustus' generals made good use of the natural avenues of penetration. From their southern base at Moguntia-

---

[1] Witness the disaster to Germanicus' transport fleet in A.D. 16 (Tacitus, *Annals*, ii. 23–4). The subsidence of the coast of north-west Germany, which was probably part cause of the Saxon migrations (Collingwood and Myres, op. cit., p. 342), may also account for the Cimbric invasions of the late second century B.C.

cum (Mainz) they followed the valleys of the Main and the Saale, and from their northern camp at Vetera (near the German-Dutch frontier) they marched up the valley of the Lippe. Their commissariat fleets, based on Boulogne, made a circuit of the North Sea to the estuary of the Ems, Weser, or Elbe, and rowed up these rivers to the appointed meeting-place with the armies. But the last grand operation, a converging advance upon Bohemia by one force ascending the Main valley and another striking northward from the middle Danube (p. 286), had to be called off for reasons extraneous to the plan of campaign (a rebellion in the Danube lands); and a chance defeat of another Roman army which lost its way in the forests of Westphalia led to the complete abandonment of Augustus' scheme.

Augustus' plans were revived and carried into effect in an attenuated form by Vespasian and Domitian, who pinched out the salient between the middle Rhine and the upper Danube by occupying the Black Forest area and incorporated a zone of territory on the right bank of the Rhine from a point below Bonn, so as to take in the high ground of Mt. Taunus. The new frontier, which was marked out so as to follow the hill-crests beyond the valleys of the Rhine, Main, and Neckar, not only shortened the Roman line of defence, but by including the wooded areas of Mt. Taunus and the Black Forest it deprived German raiders of convenient mustering-grounds, and incidentally it annexed some of Germany's best agricultural land in Hesse and the Wetterau. One result of these frontier adjustments was that Argentorate (Strasbourg) became the starting-point of a military road across the Black Forest by way of the Kinzig valley. Thus Roman Strasbourg, though not yet a river port, acquired importance as a sally-port into Germany.

The Romans were too much preoccupied with the safeguarding of their German frontier to foster commerce with the natives; indeed they would not admit German traders into Roman territory save at selected points.[1] But they could not prevent Italian or Gaulish merchants from adventuring themselves in German lands. Finds of Roman or Gallic objects are most frequent in the Ruhr district, in Thuringia, and in north-western Germany.[2] Their distribution suggests that the traders partly used the old invasion routes by way of the Main and the Lippe, and partly worked their way up-river from the North Sea, in imitation of

[1] Tacitus, *Germania*, 41, § 1.
[2] Mrs. O. Brogan, *Journ. Rom. Stud.*, 1936, pp. 195–222 and map.

Augustus' transport fleets.[1] Numerous finds of Roman coins on German territory indicate that Roman exports (wine and metal ware) did not suffice to pay for the imports. Since the medieval trade in timber, hemp, and fur from the Baltic regions had not yet come into existence, and the amber traffic since the reign of Nero was directed to the middle Danube (p. 286),[2] it remains a problem how the balance of imports over exports turned against the Roman empire and had to be settled in specie, unless the Roman slave-traders brought home large hauls of captives from the German inter-tribal wars.

§ 2. THE ALPINE LANDS

The Alpine massif, extending from the Bernese Oberland to the Wiener Wald, is by far the largest mountain block in Roman Europe; from west to east it measures some 450 miles, and its width from north to south nowhere falls short of 100 miles. It does not, however, form a compact table-land like the Spanish meseta, but is furrowed by numerous river valleys, and the passes across the watershed between the Mediterranean river systems, and those between the Rhine and Danube, do not exceed those of the western Alps in height.[3] The more westerly passes, which take off from Lakes Lugano and Como and lead to the Rhine valley, vary from a summit height of 6,000 feet (Maloggia) to one of 7,600 feet (Septimer). Of the easterly ones, the Reschen-Scheideck and the Brenner, which connect the valley of the Adige with that of the Inn, rise no higher than 4,900 and 4,500 feet respectively; and the Pontebba pass, which lies in the saddle between the Julian and the Carnic Alps and gives access from Venetia to the valley of the Drave, is a mere 2,600 feet in altitude. But the breadth of the high mountain zone surpasses that of the western Alps,[4] and the passage to Germany by way of the Brenner or Reschen-Scheideck involves a further climb over the Bavarian Alps which separate the Inn from the upper Danube with a pass height of 3,200 feet.

[1] A regular North Sea traffic is assumed by A. Francke (Pauly-Wissowa, s.v. 'Nordsee') and A. W. Byvanck, *Nederland in den romeinschen tijd*, pp. 547–8.

[2] The prehistoric transport of Jutish amber across Germany to Italy appears to have died out not long after 1000 B.C. (J. M. de Navarro, *Geographical Journal*, 1925, pp. 484 ff.).

[3] The Stelvio pass, which takes the highest paved road in Europe (9,000 feet), connects the upper valleys of the Adige and the Adda, both of which drain into the Adriatic.

[4] G. E. V. Chilver, *Cisalpine Gaul*, pp. 3–4.

The chief economic resource of the Alpine lands consisted of the high-grade iron ores of Styria, which gave rise to the 'Hallstatt' civilization of the eastern Celts (*c.* 1000 B.C.), and are still in full production at the present day. It was no doubt with metal from this source that the iron-workers of ancient Comum made their prime steel,[1] as their neighbours of Brescia and Milan did in the Middle Ages. On the other hand, the Styrian gold mines,

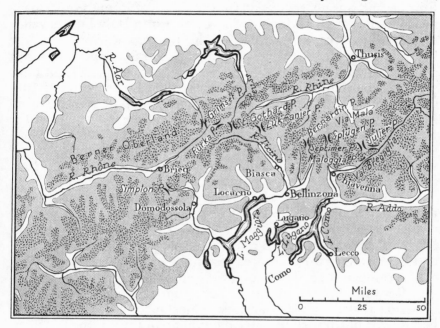

THE CENTRAL ALPINE PASSES

which caused a 'Klondyke rush' in the second century B.C., did not last long.[2] The larch-forests that clothed the Swiss Alps were occasionally exploited by Roman emperors in search of specially firm construction timber;[3] but costs of transport would prevent any regular trade in Alpine lumber.[4]

But the chief historical importance of the Alpine massif in ancient times was that it served in the first instance as a bulwark

[1] Pliny, xxxiv, § 144.
[2] Polybius, xxxiv. 10. 10–14. Strabo makes no mention of Styrian gold.
[3] Pliny, xvi, § 190. Extensive plantings of Swiss larch were made in Scotland *c.* A.D. 1800, as being suitable by its extreme toughness for the construction of war-ships.
[4] It required ships of special build before the modern trade in Burmese teak could be established.

for Italy, and subsequently as a means of direct communication between Italy and Germany. In prehistoric times the Brenner or Reschen-Scheideck pass was already being used for the conveyance of Jutish amber to the Adriatic[1] and of Italic bronze ware to northern Europe, and the Etruscans subsequently exported their metal goods by the same route.[2] This trans-Alpine traffic, it is true, was interrupted by the Celtic migrations across central Europe, and was not revived in the early days of Rome's supremacy in Italy. But the irruption of the Cimbri into Italy by the valley of the Adige (102–101 B.C.) gave the Romans warning that the barrier of the central Alps was not impenetrable, and the unrest among Alpine tribes which was the aftermath of the Cimbric invasions eventually taught them that the only sure method of safeguarding north Italy was to incorporate the Alpine massif within their empire. Finally, Augustus' plans for the extension of the Roman frontier from the Rhine to the Elbe entailed a corresponding advance of the boundaries from Italy to the Danube, failing which the Alpine block would form a huge salient between Italy and the newly acquired territory in Germany.

Invaders of later ages, Habsburgs and Burgundians, have found the Alpine lands a veritable hornets' nest. It is therefore all the more remarkable that Augustus' stepsons, Tiberius and Drusus, broke the back of native resistance in a single expedition (16 B.C.), and discovered two of the easiest lines of penetration in what was a campaign of exploration as well as of conquest. Marching eastward up the Rhine valley from the vicinity of Basle, Tiberius joined hands near Lake Constance with Drusus, who had moved northward up the Adige valley and across the Reschen-Scheideck pass. By means of this pincer operation the western and eastern halves of the Alpine massif were severed, and the western half was cut off from all hope of reinforcement from Germany. 'Mopping up' operations no doubt followed, but Tiberius was able to advance across south Germany to the Danube without serious fighting, and the eastern portion of the massif was apparently acquired by a prompt capitulation.

These conquests, besides bringing security to Italy, provided the Roman empire with the best substitute for the frontier line of the Elbe. The Danube, which formed the northern boundary of the two new provinces of Raetia and Noricum,[3] is the longest

---

[1] De Navarro, op. cit.

[2] F. Stähelin, *Die Schweiz in römischer Zeit* (2nd ed.), pp. 10–12.

[3] The frontiers of Raetia and Noricum cannot be determined exactly. According

river of Europe outside Russia, and the most voluminous of all. Though it is not fed directly from Alpine snowfields and glaciers, like the Rhône and the Rhine, it derives a copious supply of Alpine water from its numerous tributaries, among which the Inn carries a volume equal to that of the main stream. Moreover, beyond the Inn confluence the Danube flows through a region of wooded ravines and breaks into a series of almost impassable rapids. It was therefore the most effective of the empire's river barriers. A trans-Danubian zone from a point west of Regensburg to Lorch, the terminal point of the trans-Rhenane strip (p. 275), was formed by Domitian; but this, like the borderland east of the Rhine, was merely an outwork of the main line of defence.

But the Danube frontier needed new roads to connect it with Italy. Naturally the valley of the Adige served as the principal exit from Italy towards the upper Danube. Of the two passes which started out along this line, the Reschen-Scheideck, which follows the Adige past Merano to its source and joins the Inn near its head-waters, was the first to be paved (under Claudius). The Brenner, which diverges eastward at Bolzano along the Eisack valley, was apparently not metalled from end to end until the time of Septimius Severus, despite its shorter mileage and lesser altitude. The reason for the priority given to the more westerly pass was no doubt because it was comparatively open, whereas the Eisack runs through a difficult gorge.[1] From Innsbruck, on which the two Adige passes converged, a western arm crossed the Karawanken ridge by the Garmisch pass and followed the Lech to Augusta Vindelicorum (Augsburg), and an eastern limb accompanied the Inn through the Kufstein gap and cut across country to Castra Regina (Regensburg).[2] As the main approach to Noricum, the Pontebba road was probably the first to be paved; it may have formed part of Tiberius' road-building scheme.

to Kiepert (*Formae Orbis Antiqui*, map xxii) Raetia extended westward to the eastern tip of Lake Leman; according to Haug (Pauly-Wissowa, s.v.) its frontier with Gaul (and subsequently with Germania Superior) was formed by the upper Rhine and the Furka pass. Its frontier with Noricum probably followed the river Lech and the Brenner pass from Innsbruck.

[1] On the eastern Alpine passes, see especially W. Cartellieri in *Philologus*, Supplementband xviii (1926), Heft 1. In the Middle Ages the Eisack gorge was circumvented by a mountain detour. In 1944 it was a favourite target of American Fortresses.

[2] The two Roman roads through Bavaria by-passed Munich. This town is essentially modern, and a creation of the railway.

Of the group of passes which branched off from Lake Como and converged on the upper Rhine, at least three became regular Roman routes and were paved at least in part: the Septimer, the Splügen, and the Maloggia-Julier.[1] In spite of their greater height, the Julier (7,500 feet) and Septimer (7,600 feet) appear to have been in more frequent use than the Splügen (6,900 feet). The reason for this preference may have been that they were relatively immune from avalanches, and that they contained no specially difficult stages like the Rhine gorge ('Via Mala') on the Splügen, which in Roman times had to be circumvented by an additional steep detour.[2] The date of the Roman roads through the Swiss passes is uncertain; some of them probably formed part of Septimius Severus' scheme for strengthening the defences of the upper Danube.

In Roman times the St. Gothard route, which in the Middle Ages shared with the Brenner the greater part of the Alpine traffic, was apparently not used at all. This may have been due to the difficulties of two sections on its northern side, the wind-swept and snow-laden gorge of the Reuss near Andermatt, and the cliff road along the eastern lappet of Lake Lucerne, neither of which was made thoroughly safe for traffic until the nineteenth century. But the chief reason for the Romans' neglect of the St. Gothard pass may have been due to the fact that the chief purpose of this route, which is to link north Italy with Basle and the middle Rhine,[3] was equally served by the various pre-existing lines of communication across France and western Switzerland.

The Roman conquest of the Alpine lands led to a modest development of city life at the main road-stations, such as Augusta Vindelicorum (Augsburg), Castra Regina (Regensburg), and Pons Aeni (Innsbruck), and at industrial centres such as Iuvavum (Salzburg).[4] But both the Roman provinces, and especially Raetia, remained essentially lands of passage.

[1] On the Swiss passes, see especially Stähelin, op. cit., pp. 329–38; W. W. Hyde, *Memoirs of the American Philosophical Society* (Philadelphia), ii (1935); C. L. Freeston, *The Alpine Passes*.

[2] The Septimer was also favoured in the Middle Ages. The dangers of spring avalanches and of winter ice and snow, and the need of drag-ropes (held by men or attached to oxen) to hold back wheeled traffic on these roads, are vividly described by Ammianus Marcellinus (xv. 10. 4–5).

[3] In recent times the most important traffic along the St. Gothard route has been the movement of Ruhr coal to the industrial centres of north Italy.

[4] A. Dopsch, *Wirtschaftliche und soziale Grundlagen der europäischen Kultur-entwickelung*, i, p. 121.

§ 3. The Middle Danube Lands

The term 'Middle Danube Lands' is here taken to denote the territory lying on either side of the great bend of the Danube between Vienna and Beograd.

The country on the right bank of this bend, forming the Roman province of Pannonia, is mostly a region of plains or low hills, intersected by two large tributary rivers, the Drave and the Save, which in their lower courses offer no serious obstacle to cross-traffic, but for some belts of adjacent marshland. This region, moreover, is readily accessible from Italy by the 'Pear Tree' pass, connecting the Venetian plain with the valley of the Save. With a summit height of 2,900 feet, this pass is the second lowest across the Alps, and it is the shortest of all, for the distance from piedmont to piedmont is a mere thirty miles. The Pear Tree pass, indeed, was so little of an obstacle that in Roman days it could take heavy wheeled traffic,[1] and before the Romans put it accurately on the map the belief persisted among Greek writers that a branch of the Danube, divaricating from the main stream somewhere near Beograd, cut across it to the Adriatic.[2] On the other hand, a large area of this region is even now heavily forested, and it contains no important mineral resources.

Pannonia resembled Raetia in being pre-eminently a land of passage. It lay on the track of the eastern and in historical times the more important amber route, which ran from Samland up the Vistula to Torun, thence across country to Lower Silesia, and through the 'Moravian Gate' (between the Sudetic and the Carpathian ranges) to the neighbourhood of Vienna.[3] It also contained the principal line of communications between Italy and the Balkan Peninsula, which crossed the Pear Tree pass and then followed the Save valley to Beograd. This same valley also offered a back-door entrance into Illyria (Bosnia and Dalmatia) by way of its southern tributaries; to compensate for their greater length, the river routes into Illyria avoided the steep ascents on the direct roads from the Dalmatian coast.

The comparative ease of the approach to Italy by the Save valley made this a likely route for invaders. It was probably by this gate that the prehistoric migrants into Italy, the 'Terramara'

---

[1] Strabo, pp. 207, 214.

[2] Cary and Warmington, *The Ancient Explorers*, p. 228, n. 31. Even Roman writers like Mela and Pliny repeated this fable.

[3] V. Sadowski, *Handelstraßen der Griechen und Römer durch das Flußgebiet der Oder und Weichsel.*

THE MIDDLE DANUBE LANDS

and the 'Villanova' folk,[1] issued from their Danubian homes. In the days of the Roman Republic no danger actually threatened from this quarter; but ignorance of Balkan geography before the days of Augustus deluded the Romans into underestimating the distance across the peninsula and exaggerating the risks of an overland attack, whether by roving Bastarnae in the employ of Philip V of Macedon[2] or by an ambitious monarch like Burebistas of Dacia (p. 288). Even so, in spite of their apprehensions, they took no preventive action before the days of Augustus, who solved the problem of the Save corridor by annexing it.

Augustus' first expeditions into the middle Danube region (35–34 B.C.) merely served to explore the Save route and to complete Roman control of Dalmatia by penetration from the landward side. But his annexation of Balkan territories in 29–28 B.C. (p. 303) virtually compelled him to take permanent possession of the Save valley as the main line of approach to his Balkan acquisitions; and his subsequent decision to draw a river-frontier for the Roman empire across Europe, whether along the Elbe or along the Rhine and upper Danube, entailed a corresponding advance to the middle Danube as the intermediate boundary line.[3] The occupation of the large salient in the Danube bend by Tiberius (12–9 B.C.) forms one of the lost chapters of Roman history; and not much can be said about its recovery by the same general after the Pannonian Revolt of A.D. 6–9. But it is clear that in the Second Pannonian War Tiberius staked everything on the retention of the Save line, and that the success of the Romans in holding their two main stations on this route, at Sissia (Sisak) and Sirmium (Mitrovica), was the chief factor in their ultimate victory. So long as the Save route remained in Roman hands, the insurgents could be kept separate from an associated rising in Dalmatia, and a passage remained open for reinforcements, whether from Italy or from the Balkan peninsula and Asia Minor.

The road-making which followed the constitution of the province of Pannonia was mainly on a peripheral plan, as indicated by strategic requirements. Of the three main Roman roads the basic route, as we have seen, went by the Save valley; and an outer route followed the Danube frontier from Vindobona (Vienna) to

[1] H. H. Scullard, *History of the Roman World from 753 to 146 B.C.*, p. 7.
[2] F. W. Walbank, *Philip V of Macedon*, p. 254.
[3] It was probably on the preliminary expedition of 35 B.C. that the Romans definitely settled the problem whether the Ister of the Balkans was simply a continuation of the Danuvius of Germany (Sallust, *Histories*, fr. iii. 79 (Maurenbrecher)).

THE EAST ALPINE PASSES

Carnuntum (Petronell, near Bratislava), but kept at some distance from the river in the reach below Aquincum (Budapest) to Singidunum (Beograd), so as to stand above flood-level (see below). These two highways were supplemented by the rivers themselves, for the Roman navy comprised a Danube and a Save flotilla.[1] The other major line of communications skirted the eastern edge of the Alps and forked in the vicinity of the Danube, so as to serve both Vindobona and Carnuntum. The more direct but more mountainous routes from Italy by way of Graz or Leoben and the Semmering Pass (3,200 feet) were used at most for local purposes.

The stretch of the Danube on which Vindobona and Carnuntum were situated was bordered on its left bank by an open plain ('the Marchfeld'), which provided an easy avenue to the Moravian Gap. Either of these towns, therefore, was a natural crossing-point of the middle Danube on a trans-European route from north to south. Of these two stations Vindobona was the natural terminus for navigation up the Danube, for above it the river breaks into rapids (p. 279), and the crossing at this point is facilitated by an island in mid-stream. If the Roman emperors had ever carried out Augustus' plan of annexing the Bohemian-Moravian plateau, Vindobona might well have displaced Carnuntum as the capital of Pannonia. But since they dispensed with an outlying province on this sector of the Danube, they did not need to establish a regular crossing-point, and since Carnuntum lay in a more open and less forested region, they gave it the preference over Vindobona.[2] Beyond the Danube bend the site of Aquincum was the last to offer firm ground for a riverside foundation until Singidunum was reached. Farther down stream the flood-waters of the Danube, unable to clear the 'bottle-neck' of the Iron Gate, spilt over the adjacent flat country, which to this day remains comparatively desolate.[3] Aquincum was therefore the natural entrance from the region of the middle Danube into the Carpathian lands; but since the Romans made their main approach to these lands from the south or south-west (p. 283), they did not need to make the fullest use of their more northerly base.[4]

[1] C. G. Starr, *The Roman Imperial Navy*, pp. 138–41.

[2] In the days of Hungarian and Turkish invasions the towns on the plain below Vienna lay too exposed, and this city, which backed on to high ground, became the natural bulwark against attacks from the east.

[3] The only modern town of any importance on this reach of the Danube is Petrovaradin, not far distant from Beograd.

[4] Budapest first acquired importance as a sally-port for Hungarians and Turks into Austria.

The Roman occupation of Pannonia led to a resumption of traffic in Samland amber, after a long interruption. In Nero's time a Roman venturer who found his way from Carnuntum through the Moravian Gate to the amber country brought back such a rich haul that it was used to stud the safety-nets at the beast-hunts.[1] Large finds of Roman coins in the eastern Baltic (mostly from the time of Trajan)[2] suggest that this Roman trader set a durable fashion. But it is not certain whether most of these coins travelled by the Carnuntum route, or whether they were carried across the Russian plain by Gothic merchants or marauders (p. 276). In any case the importance of Pannonia to the Romans, like that of Raetia, was more strategic than economic.

Beyond the middle Danube the Bohemian and Moravian sections of Czechoslovakia constitute one of the most favoured regions of central Europe. Their soil is well adapted to tillage and garden industry and is rich in various minerals. It is now believed that before the opening of regular trade with the Atlantic lands the Mediterranean people drew the greater part of their supplies of tin from Bohemia.[3] Czechoslovakia presents a sharp edge, backed by extensive forests, against the Saxon and Silesian lowlands, and is therefore easily defensible on its northern and north-eastern sides; but it provides two easy passages, by way of the upper Elbe and of the Moravian Gate, between the middle Danube and the German plain.

Though the Roman emperors apparently never discovered the economic value of this trans-Danubian tract, they had some appreciation of its strategic importance. According to Augustus' project for an Elbe–Danube frontier all the land west of a line from Dresden to Brno and Bratislava would require to be included within the Roman empire. In A.D. 6, therefore, Tiberius set out from Carnuntum, probably by the route now used by the Vienna–Brno–Prague railway, to meet another Roman force advancing up the Main towards the postern gate of Cheb (Eger) in the mountains of north-western Bohemia. But the outbreak of the Pannonian Revolt (p. 275) compelled the invaders to draw back the arms of their pincer, and for nearly two centuries the plan to annex Bohemia and Moravia was lost from sight.

[1] Pliny, xxxvii, § 45.
[2] On finds of Roman coins in Germany and the islands off Sweden see S. Bolin, *Berichte der Römisch-Germanischen Kommission*, 1929, pp. 86–145.
[3] V. G. Childe, *The Dawn of European Civilisation*, pp. 33, 57. The earliest 'dollars' (thalers) were minted in the fifteenth and sixteenth centuries from the silver of Joachimsthal.

Towards the end of his reign Marcus Aurelius, having beaten off a heavy attack by the Marcomanni and Quadi, two German tribes then in possession of Bohemia and Moravia, resolved to forestall future invasions by occupying their country. Had this policy been carried out, his new province would have formed a projecting bastion rather than part of a general defensive line, with an exposed though easily tenable frontier on its western flank along the densely forested district of the Böhmer Wald. In this case Bohemia and Moravia might have assumed in ancient times the part which they have played since the Middle Ages, of a non-German bulwark over against the lapping tide of Germanic immigration. But after the death of Marcus Aurelius his successor Commodus definitely abandoned the project of a trans-Danubian annexe. On a purely strategic reckoning this may have been good policy, in view of the great value of the middle Danube as a protective barrier;[1] but on economic grounds the new province of 'Marcomannia' might have been a notable asset to the Roman empire.

The trans-Danubian country below the great bend of the river is a region of sharp contrasts. The valley of the Danube itself, and that of its tributary the Theiss, form part of a flat and mostly treeless champaign which might be regarded as the forerunner of the boundless Eurasian steppe. Like Roumania and south-west Russia, it is one of Europe's natural wheatfields; its powdery loess soil gives insufficient hold to the roots of trees, but is rich in plant-food. Yet in the absence of a large neighbouring market for cereal products, such as has been provided in modern days by the rapid growth of Budapest and Vienna, the plain of eastern Hungary remained in ancient times an uncultivated steppe. The Romans, who shunned treeless land as they avoided dense forest, felt no attraction to it, and they had no strategic reason for occupying it, for the Sarmatian nomads who tenanted it were not numerous enough to be a serious menace to Pannonia. This country therefore remained a blank on the Roman map.

On the other hand, between the Hungarian plain and the east European lowlands the folded range of the Carpathians interposes a zone of mountains and rich oak forests, and of good land for mixed farming in its river valleys. In its south-eastern angle the Carpathian zone broadens out into a table-land, the ancient territory of Dacia (modern Transylvania), in which the greater part

---

[1] The barrier was strengthened with a chain of turrets (*burgi*) along the right bank (Dessau, *Inscr. Lat. Sel.* 395).

of Carpathian history has been made. Here the mountains hold a varied store of mineral wealth, including iron, copper, and silver, and in ancient days they contained some of the largest gold-deposits of Europe (near Verespatak in the western Carpathians). With its diversified resources Dacia was economically a self-contained country, and with its numerous hill-fortresses it offered better opportunities for defence than the featureless plains around it: between the eras of the Roman and of the Ottoman Peace it served as an island of refuge within the invading tides.

But Dacia's appearance of security is somewhat delusive. It stands open on its west side, and several of the numerous and relatively low passes in the Carpathians are broad and open.[1] Consequently the plateau was swept over in succession by Scythians from the east (from 700 B.C.) and by Celts from the west (from 400 B.C.).[2] It may have been in response to this challenge that the normally peaceful and sedentary Dacians allowed themselves to be organized into a military monarchy and to pass over to the offensive under two ambitious kings, Burebistas and Decebalus, who drew their country into the sphere of Roman interests.

As a field of economic exploitation Dacia had been visited since the second century B.C. by the same Italian travellers who also ranged across Pannonia with their skins of wine and their panniers of hardware.[3] But it did not enter into the purview of Roman politics until Burebistas aggravated unrest in the Balkans (c. 60 B.C.),[4] and his timely death averted a clash for some 150 years, when Decebalus crossed the lower Danube and broke into the Roman province of Moesia (A.D. 85). In their counter-invasions of Dacia (A.D. 86–106), Domitian and Trajan delivered their main attacks on either side of the Iron Gates, in the neighbourhood of which their main bases lay (p. 283). This choice of route obliged them to force the relatively difficult passes on the steep southern and south-western edges of the Carpathians. Even so, the natural difficulties of the country were hardly greater than those which Augustus' stepsons had surmounted in their campaigns in central Europe (pp. 275, 278). But they had to deal with a compact defence which had the advantage of operating on inner lines.

[1] In particular, the 'Tartar' pass in the north-east has been a broadway for successive invaders from the steppes.

[2] V. Parvan, *Dacia*, chs. 4 and 5.　　　　　　　　　　[3] Ibid., pp. 152–6.

[4] It is not unlikely that about the time of Burebistas' death Caesar was meditating a preventive attack upon him from his base at Aquileia in Cisalpine Gaul (J. Carcopino, in Glotz, *Histoire Ancienne*, pt. iii, vol. ii, pp. 693–9).

The Roman commanders therefore did not attempt a major pincer movement, but thrust their main forces into one pass at a time. Apparently they directed their first attacks through the Iron Gate pass in the south-west, so as to gain access to the valley of the Mures, a main artery of traffic inside Dacia.[1] But in the decisive campaigns of A.D. 102 and 106 Trajan effected his entry from the south, by way of the Red Tower pass, which brought him out on to the Mures valley at a point farther up stream.[2]

Victory over the Dacians confronted Trajan with a new frontier problem. Strategically the incorporation of their country into the Roman empire was of doubtful value, for unless the Roman garrison were to line the entire horseshoe of the Carpathian ridge, their northern face and their western flank would be left, so to speak, in the air. On second thoughts the emperor nevertheless decided to retain Dacia in his grasp. This resolve was probably taken on economic grounds, for Trajan lost no time in drafting new settlers into the mining districts.[3] Market towns also grew up in the fertile valleys, and the population became sufficiently romanized to preserve a Latin form of speech. But the stray line of forts which was built to guard the open frontiers on the northern and western sides of the new province[4] was a poor substitute for the broad and continuous barrier of the Danube. Moreover, after A.D. 250 frequent sweeps of Gothic raiders across the Roumanian plain threatened to undercut the Roman position in Dacia from the south-east and south. The Emperor Aurelian therefore withdrew his garrisons and reverted to an all-Danube frontier. His successors held the line of the Danube, or soon repaired breaches in it, until the sixth century.

Apart from the Latin dialect still spoken in Transylvania, the Roman occupation of Dacia has left visible memorials in Trajan's bridge at Turnu Severin (below the Iron Gate rapids), the lowest over the Danube until the completion of the Costanza bridge in 1895, and the Via Traiana, a road driven through the Iron Gate river-gorge so as to provide lateral communications along the Danube front, and partly carried on corbels over the river surface.[5]

[1] Not to be confused with the Iron Gate narrows of the Danube, which lie considerably farther south. The approach to the pass of like name is made from Timisoara (Temesvár).

[2] On the Roman invasions of Dacia see G. A. T. Davies, *Journ. Rom. Stud.*, 1917, pp. 74 ff., and E. T. Salmon, *Transactions of the Philological Association*, 1936, pp. 83 ff.

[3] O. Davies, *Roman Mines*, ch. 8.

[4] The Roman frontier cannot be traced exactly.

[5] A. P. Gest, *Roman Engineering*, pp. 131, 162.

XI. EASTERN EUROPE

§ 1. THE BALKAN LANDS

THE term 'Balkan Lands' is here taken to denote the Balkan peninsula with the exception of Greece. This exclusion is justified on geographic as much as on historic grounds, for whereas Greece is a typically Mediterranean country, the region that lies between it and the Danube basin is transitional in character. Like Asia Minor, the Balkan Lands lie in a Mediterranean latitude and present two fronts to the Mediterranean Sea; but they also resemble Asia Minor in backing on to a large land-mass, and their historical function has similarly been that of a connecting link between two continents.

The intermediate character of the Balkan Lands stands out clearly in their climate, or rather climates. The Dalmatian coastlands experience Mediterranean weather of an uncompromising type. The winters alternate between bright sunshine and torrential rain. At some points (e.g. near Kotor), where a high and abrupt coast suddenly hoists the warm westerly winds into a cooler stratum of air and wrings the moisture out of them, the rainfall rises to 180 inches in the year and thus competes for the European record with Snowdonia (up to 197 inches). Spells of cold weather will also break in, during which the 'bora' swoops with dangerous suddenness down the valley funnels and over the Adriatic Sea.[1] On the other hand, Dalmatia enjoys long hours of sunshine the year round, with a lucid atmosphere and a vivid blue sky; but it pays the usual price for these boons with a prolonged summer drought.

On the Aegean front of the Balkan Lands Thrace and Macedonia lead up to a somewhat more open hinterland than that of Dalmatia, and are therefore more exposed to northerly or northeasterly winds. Blowing off the Russian steppes, these winds produce a colder and drier winter, which to the Greeks appeared inhumanly severe. Plato recalled that at Potidaea the Athenian investing force sat muffled and cowering in the trenches, while Socrates in one of his fits of meditation stood four-square and unprotected in a biting gale.[2] Conversely, the relatively high

---

[1] At Trieste in winter-time ropes are sometimes strung along the streets to save pedestrians from 'going with the wind'.
[2] *Symposium* 220a, b.

latitude of Macedonia and Thrace protects them from the full effects of a summer drought, for above the parallel of 40° the prevailing northerlies are not so completely desiccated as in their further progress over the central and southern Mediterranean. On the other hand, the eastern face and the interior of the Balkan Lands have a purely continental climate, with protracted as well as intensely cold winters and summers kept fresh with frequent convectional rain.[1]

The basic feature in the structure of the Balkan Lands is a continuous mountain range trending from north-west to south-east, like the Apennines in Italy; but the Balkan 'spine', instead of crossing from front to back of the peninsula, lies close to the back, i.e. the west, all the way: at one point the watershed is only five miles from the Adriatic coast. From its high western edge the land slopes down to wide expanses of plain facing the Black Sea, but these eastern lowlands are intersected by two transverse ribs which diverge from a central knot in the neighbourhood of Sofia. Of these two ridges Mt. Rhodope, trending south-east-ward, is an isolated remnant of an old granite massif; the Balkan Range (Mt. Haemus), striking due east, forms part of the Tertiary Age upfold which framed the Mediterranean zone (p. 7).

The spine of the Balkan peninsula is also a dividing line between its zones of vegetation. In its north-western section, the plateau of the Dinaric Alps, it exhibits the characteristics of the Mediterranean uplands in an almost exaggerated degree. Though this highland does not culminate in any high peaks, its general level is raised above the line of cultivation, and its constituent limestone is honeycombed with fissures that absorb the heavy rainfall and prevent the formation of a humid subsoil. The Dinaric tableland therefore is a region of bare rock or scrub with rare patches of vegetation in its valleys. At the foot of the Dalmatian mountains the Adriatic seaboard is seamed with small strips of alluvial land which is well suited to the Mediterranean orchard plants; in particular, the olive-groves of Istria produced an export surplus under the Roman emperors.[2] At the southern or Albanian end of this coast the zone of level land broadens out into a fertile tract of high potential value, but neglect of its water-courses has resulted in the formation of swamps and the spread of malaria.

Another region of typically Mediterranean plant life extends

---

[1] Herodotus remarked on the equableness of the rainfall in the Danube basin (iv. 50. 2).
[2] Rostovtzeff, *Roman Empire*, p. 218.

along the more sheltered stretches of the Aegean coast, and notably on the southern seaboards of the Chalcidic peninsula and of western Thrace, which was an important wine-growing district from the days of the Trojan War.[1]

Apart from these maritime borderlands, Balkan vegetation conforms to that of the European continent, but with much regional variety. The general standard of fertility is higher than in most Mediterranean lands, for the surface rock is mostly conducive to loam-formation, and the summer rainfall is adequate. The uplands of the Balkan interior (notably in Bosnia and Serbia) are well clad with deciduous forest. For the growth of cereals the champaign country of eastern Thrace and above all the wide loess lands of the Roumanian plain are specially well adapted. Serbia and Bulgaria are rich in plum and cherry orchards, and the modern rose gardens of Roumelia had their ancient counterpart in the 'gardens of Midas' on the Macedonian piedmont, 'where roses grow wild, each singly holding 60 petals, and more fragrant than any other'.[2]

The mineral resources of the Balkan Lands, though mainly concentrated in two areas, are varied in kind. The plains on either side of Mt. Pangaeus in western Thrace (Scaptesyle on the western flank, Philippi to the east) were formerly rich in beds of placer gold which made history while they lasted (during the fifth and fourth centuries B.C.).[3] From Mt. Pangaeus a zone of silver-deposits stretched across northern Macedonia. Bosnia and Serbia still possess considerable fields of silver, copper, and iron. In the Middle Ages the Italian republics imported silver and copper from these regions; the Romans supplied their Danubian armies from the Dalmatian iron-mines.[4]

For those approaching the Balkan peninsula from the continental side the Save is not a serious barrier, and its tributaries provide a gradual ascent to the plateau of Bosnia and Serbia (p. 281); but the plateau itself impedes further progress by reason of its dense forests. To the east of Beograd the Carpathians and the Danube cut off the peninsula more sharply from the continent. The lower Danube, which has a remarkably constant flow of water below the Iron Gates[5] (for these serve as a natural lock),

[1] S. Casson, *Macedonia, Thrace, and Illyria*, pp. 53–5.
[2] Herodotus, viii. 138. 2.
[3] Casson, op. cit., pp. 59–79; P. Perdrizet, *Klio*, 1910, pp. 1 ff.
[4] Davies, *Roman Mines*, pp. 182 ff.
[5] This fact evidently impressed Herodotus, who mentioned it twice over (iv. 48. 1 and 50. 2).

cannot be forded at any point, and until recently it has defied the bridge-maker (p. 289). As a line of defence against invaders from the north this reach of the river has the further advantage that its southern bank is high and dominates the crossing-points. But at its estuary, where the force of the current abates, it is frozen over in midwinter,[1] and the passage is facilitated by a chain of eyots. Here, accordingly, was one of the principal points of transit to and from the peninsula.

The Istrian and Dalmatian coasts are protected by a screen of small islands, and they contain secure and silt-proof as well as capacious harbours at Pola and Kotor. But the channels between the isles are suitable for small vessels only; Pola has a barren hinterland, and Kotor abuts on to a mountain wall.[2] The other ports of this seaboard (Trieste, Fiume, Split, Dubrovnik) gave but indifferent shelter until the modern engineer provided them with adequate breakwaters, and the valleys which lead inland from them are narrow and tortuous. The coast of Albania opens on to a cultivable plain and contains two harbours, of which Durres (Epidamnus or Dyrrachium) is well protected to the north, while Vlone (Apollonia) affords good shelter south-westward. The immediate hinterland of these ports, however, is marshy (p. 291), and not until the Roman road-builders cut through the ring of mountains that encircle the plain (p. 304) could Apollonia and Dyrrachium become terminal ports for long-distance traffic. In ancient times these two stations, and Ragusa (Dubrovnik) in the Middle Ages, were the only important gates of entry from the Adriatic into the Balkan Lands. Until the advent of the Roman Peace, and again before the Venetians patrolled the adjacent seas, the Dalmatian and Albanian coasts had an unenviable reputation as one of the Mediterranean's chief pirate haunts.[3]

The land frontier which marks off the Balkan Lands from Greece is difficult at every point (p. 44), and the northern end of the Aegean which forms the rest of their southern front is the least inviting part of that sea. The off-shore winds come in fierce gusts like the mistral and the bora, and the southerly gales of

---

[1] The river is icebound for about forty days. The ice facilitated Trajan's crossing in one of his Dacian expeditions (Pliny the Younger, *Panegyricus* 12, § 3). On the other hand, in A.D. 68–9 a premature thaw trapped some Sarmatian raiders on the south bank and exposed them to destruction in a Roman counter-attack (Tacitus, *Histories* i. 79).

[2] Until the construction of the motor road connecting it with Kotor, the former Montenegrin capital, Cettinje, was virtually cut off from the sea.

[3] H. A. Ormerod, *Piracy in the Ancient World*, pp. 166 ff. In the First World War the Dalmatian channels made an excellent base for U-boats.

winter (which here lasts well into spring) break on to a poorly sheltered coast.[1]

The Gulf of Salonika has been progressively reduced in size by silt from the river Vardar (ancient Axius). Between the time of Herodotus, when the town of Pella lay close to the coast, and that of Strabo, when it was situated fourteen miles inland,[2] its western pocket was filled up, and dredging is now required to keep open a fairway to Salonika. The head of the Gulf is marshy,[3] and it probably required extensive drainage operations before the obscure town of Therma could be replaced by Cassander's city of Thessalonica (c. 300 B.C.). But given a firm water-front, Thessalonica was assured of a large flow of traffic as a focal point of Balkan communications (p. 305).[4]

The east coast of Thrace is a lee shore which offers scant shelter from its frequent north-easterly winds. The 'jaw of Salmydessus, step-mother of ships' (some fifty miles from the Bosporus), had a particularly bad reputation because of its shoals and attendant wreckers.[5] But sea-going vessels of considerable tonnage can proceed up the Danube as far as its first bend (to Galati).

The Balkan peninsula's maritime communications are mainly concentrated in the 200 miles of waterway between the Aegean and the Black Seas, comprising the Dardanelles (ancient Hellespont), Sea of Marmara (Propontis), and Bosporus. Of the two 'bottlenecks' which terminate this passage, the Dardanelles are forty miles in length and slightly over a mile in width; the Bosporus is fifteen miles long and less than half a mile across at its narrowest point. The salt-water rivers that flow through these straits have too rapid a current—rising in the Dardanelles to five and in the Bosporus to six miles an hour—and are swept too frequently by north-easterly gales, to bear the yoke of a permanent bridge, but they have carried a ferry service from times immemorial. In ancient days the excellent harbour of Cyzicus on

[1] It was off this coast that Odysseus first became the sport of wind and wave (Homer, *Odyssey* ix. 67 ff.), and that the Persians lost their first invading armada (Herodotus, vi. 44. 2–3). In A.D. 1915 the Thracian coast was considered too insecure for a beach landing (Casson, op. cit., p. 36).

[2] Herodotus, vii. 123. 3; Strabo, p. 330, fr. 20.

[3] Hence the heavy casualties from malaria sustained by the British Salonika Force in 1917–18.

[4] The Gulf of Salonika was probably a gate of entry in prehistoric times for Aegean imports into the Balkan and Danube Lands (V. G. Childe, *The Danube in Prehistory*, pp. 91–3).

[5] Aeschylus, *Prometheus Vinctus*, ll. 726–7; Xenophon, *Anabasis* vii. 5. 12. For the ports of the east coast in general see G. A. Short, *Liverpool Annals of Archaeology and Anthropology*, 1937, pp. 141–55.

the Propontis (p. 158) also engaged in a brisk traffic with the Bosporus and the Black Sea.[1] Of all points of contact between the Balkan Lands and the outer world this has been by far the most important in the course of ages. From at least 2000 B.C. to the coming of the Ottoman Turks it has been the scene of a shuttle-service of migrations and invasions; and it was one of the main avenues by which the prehistoric culture of the Near East passed into Europe and fostered the civilization of that continent until the Greeks and Romans carried their culture to it by other routes.[2]

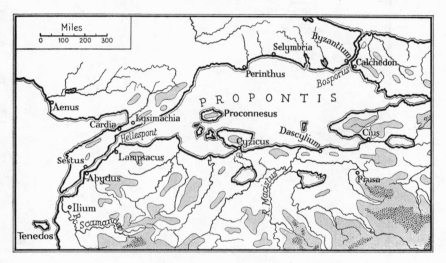

THE APPROACH TO THE BLACK SEA

Communications within the Balkan peninsula are most difficult in its western half. Though none of the mountains in this area attains a great height (Liubotrn in northern Albania falls short of 9,000 feet), they extend over a wide region, and their structure is highly complex. In Bosnia they form a grid-work of chains deeply grooved with winding gorges; in Serbia the valleys are more open, but the cover of forest remains to this day a bar to easy travel. In ancient times only the coastal fringe came within the purview of the Greek world, and it was left to the Roman armies to open up the western highlands (p. 303).

In the south-eastern quarter of the peninsula the chain of

[1] Rostovtzeff, *Hellenistic World*, i, p. 117.
[2] Childe, op. cit., *passim*. It is not unlikely that the art of iron metallurgy was brought to the European continent from Asia Minor by this route (*c.* 1200 B.C.). *Inter alia*, the Turks introduced into Europe the horse-chestnut and the tulip.

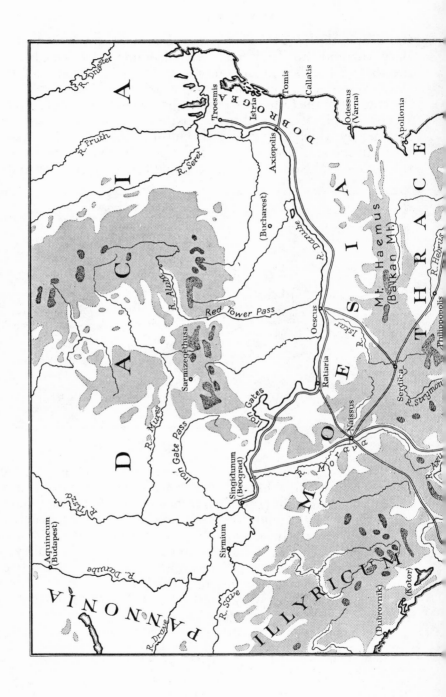

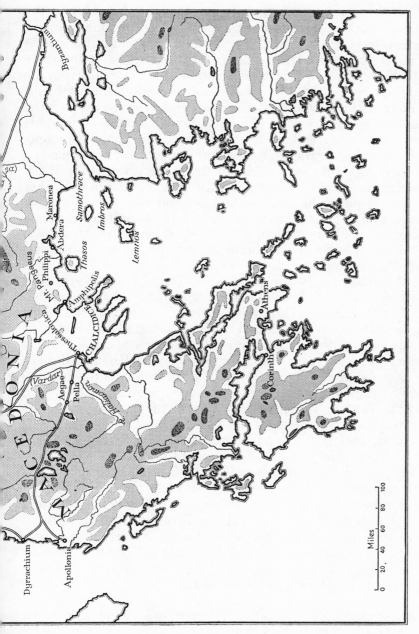

THE BALKAN PENINSULA

Rhodope thrusts itself like a bolt between the Aegean and the Black Sea sections. Its top ridge, which rises at one point to 9,000 feet, has not weathered down into a 'peak and pass' serration, and it presents a steep face to the south-west. It therefore was an effective bar to Greek penetration of the interior from the Macedonian coast, and it has at all times prevented the establishment of an 'isthmus route' to the Black Sea, so as to by-pass the Dardanelles and Bosporus. The Balkan range is a less formidable barrier. Its summit (at 8,000 feet) is not far below that of Rhodope, and its central pass, the Shipka, rises to 4,500 feet; but this is a fairly open col, and the declivity of the range towards the Black Sea facilitates alternative passages near the coast. On the other hand, the region where the Rhodope and the Balkan ranges converge and meet the western massif is encumbered with a tangle of small chains which, though of no great height, detract from the value of Sofia, the midmost town of the peninsula, as a centre of communications.

But if cross-country travel in the Balkan Lands is generally difficult, several well-defined corridors afford a passage through them. In the north the Danube is navigable up to the Iron Gates throughout the open season, and the Wallachian plain on its right bank has good natural communications along its Transylvanian piedmont. From a point near Beograd the main Balkan tributary of the Danube, the Morava, skirts the western massif towards the centre of the peninsula, and its line is continued to the Aegean Sea by the Vardar. Either of these rivers, it is true, has to cut its way through an 'Iron Gate' of its own, but most of their course is unimpeded, and the watershed between them is flat and low (c. 1,500 feet). The route from Beograd to Salonika is therefore the main artery for traffic between the Danube basin and the Mediterranean Sea. From Nish (Naissus) in the upper Morava valley another route forks off to Sofia (ancient Serdica) across a 3,000-foot pass and descends to the basin of the Maritza (Hebrus) and the open plain of south-eastern Thrace, which affords easy travelling as far as Istanbul. This diagonal road across the peninsula has always been the main line of communications between the European mainland and the Near East.

In the second millennium B.C. the eastern Adriatic coast was a stage on a trade-route which brought Baltic amber and, possibly, Bohemian tin to Greece.[1] This traffic, however, was discon-

---

[1] Childe, *Dawn of European Civilisation*, p. 33.

tinued after the Mycenaean Age,[1] and the Greeks of historic times
made but sporadic attempts to colonize the seaboard north of
Epidamnus, or to open up the Dalmatian interior.[2] It is not
unlikely that the Corinthians imported Bosnian silver and drew
upon the iris blossoms of the Dalmatian hill-sides for their manufacture of perfumery; and in the fourth century Greek wine-
merchants were threading their way up the valley of the Narenta
from the neighbourhood of Dubrovnik.[3] But these shy ventures
did not lead on to widespread settlement or systematic penetration of the hinterland.

On the other hand, the southern seaboard of the Balkan peninsula became one of the chief areas of Greek colonization. The
most numerous Greek settlements clustered round the coast of
the Chalcidic peninsula, most thickly on the south-westerly faces
of its three protruding prongs. Sheltered from the northerly
winds of the mainland by the coastal ridges on to which they
backed, these colonies enjoyed a Riviera climate and produced
an export surplus of wine.[4] But their chief asset lay in the
forests with which the adjacent mountain-sides were clothed in
ancient times. The timber area also included the foot-hills of
Mt. Pangaeus; it was probably the ship-building material of this
region, even more than the mines farther inland (p. 292), that
drew the Athenians on to found the colony of Amphipolis.[5] But
in spite of its earlier name, 'The Nine Roads', Amphipolis was
not an important centre of communications. Its value as a bridge
town was lessened by the shallowness of the Strymon, which was
fordable near its mouth, and its commercial usefulness by the
impenetrable ravine up stream, through which the Strymon
worms its way.[6] The more sparsely strung Greek settlements on
the southern coast of Thrace between Mt. Pangaeus and the
Thracian Chersonese (the Gallipoli peninsula) were primarily
agrarian colonies which exploited strips of good arable and
orchard land. Abdera and Maronea, which were usually on good
terms with the Odrysian Thracians of the hinterland, developed

[1] The theory that the offerings brought to Delphi from the 'Land of the Hyperboreans' in the time of Herodotus consisted of amber (iv. 33) will not bear close
examination.
[2] On this subject in general see R. L. Beaumont, *Journ. Hell. Stud.*, 1936,
pp. 159–204.
[3] Theopompus, quoted by Strabo (p. 317).
[4] [Demosthenes,] xxxv, § 10.
[5] Herodotus, v. 23. 2; Thucydides, iv. 108. 1. The north Aegean timber was
more straight-grained than that of Greece proper (Casson, op. cit., p. 53, n. 5).
[6] Casson, pp. 19–20 and fig. 12.

a lucrative commerce with them (presumably in their home-produced wine). But neither of them was well placed for maritime trade, for their harbourage was of the poorest.[1]

In the Gallipoli peninsula the best soil lies on the gentler declivity of its northern face, but the Greek settlements were naturally most frequent on its southern side, fronting on the Dardanelles. The European coast here had this advantage over its *vis-à-vis*, that it was sheltered from the prevailing northerlies and did not receive the full impact of the Dardanelles current. The principal Greek station was at Sestus, whose harbour gave protection from the current and from easterly winds. Abydus on the opposite coast offered no special advantage apart from its proximity to Sestus; like its neighbour Lampsacus farther up stream, it had a pocket of good alluvial land behind it, but it was lacking in natural harbourage.

The European bank of the Bosporus contained only one Greek settlement, because one site here combined every advantage of position. Byzantium, situated on a broad tongue of land on the western side of the Golden Horn, offered the initial attractions of a peninsular position which could easily be walled off from the mainland,[2] and of a self-delivered food-supply in the shoals of fish which were headed off the Bosporus as its emerging current was deflected into eddies, one of which skirted Seraglio Point at the tip of the Golden Horn. While the sea stocked the larders of Byzantium, the rich agricultural land in Thrace and on the opposite Asiatic shore (p. 158) filled its granaries. But Nature's chief gift to Byzantium was the Golden Horn. This deeply recessed backwater lay out of reach of the deflected Bosporus current, and, being riverless, it was not liable to silting. Here, accordingly, was the ideal halting-point for ships plying up and down the Bosporus, and the inevitable terminus of the inter-continental ferry.[3]

The relative importance of Byzantium as the gate of the Black Sea and the crossing-point between Europe and Asia varied from age to age. In the prehistoric era of land migrations, culminating c. 1200 B.C. in the Phrygian and Mysian invasions of Asia Minor, it was a ferry station and nothing more. But when the Greeks

[1] Casson, pp. 33–5.

[2] The walls of Constantinople were more elaborate than those of Rome, but they had a narrower front.

[3] The trend of the current which delivered the fish at the Byzantines' door was noted by Strabo (p. 320) and Tacitus (*Annals* xii. 63. 2). For a more general appreciation of the site see Polybius, iv. 43–4.

opened up and colonized the Black Sea, it took on the part of an
ancient Suez or Panama and drew its wealth from tolls on Black
Sea shipping. So lucrative indeed were these imposts that the
Byzantines had no need to engage in extensive maritime adventure on a large scale.[1] In the Hellenistic period, when the territories of King Lysimachus were spread astride the Black Sea
passage, and nomadic Galatians followed in the wake of Phrygians
and Mysians, Byzantium resumed the function of a link between
the continents, but not for long. Until the Hellenistic age the
Asiatic hinterland of the city remained undeveloped, and it was
not until the days of the Roman occupation that Thrace was
thoroughly opened up, so as to provide the basis for a peaceable
and permanent intercourse between the continents. In the days
of the Greek ascendancy, therefore, the prosperity of Byzantium
depended mainly on its trans-pontine traffic.

The Greek settlements in eastern Thrace bore a general
resemblance to those of the Aegean seaboard, for most of them
occupied sites that were better suited for land work than for
oversea trade. The strips of coast on which they stood were ill
protected against the prevalent north-easters, but contained good
arable soil, and gave relatively easy access to the interior. But the
sites selected by the Greek colonists for their domiciles suggest that
they did not feel sure of their welcome from the natives; Apollonia was built on an off-shore island,[2] and several others were
perched on hills that presented their steep face to the interior.[3]
If we may judge by position, these settlements had a modest
self-contained existence.

But sixty miles from the mouth of the Danube a deep bay
with a protective curtain of islands provided safer harbourage.
On one of these islands Greek settlers of the seventh century
founded the colony of Istria, which at first derived its living from
the fisheries of the Danube delta, but subsequently opened a
brisk trade up the river.[4] From an advanced depot (of unknown
name) near modern Braila—a counterpart in situation to Naucratis in the Nile delta—they pushed up the main stream of the
Danube as far as the Iron Gates, and up its lower tributaries,
with cargoes of Greek wine. The Istrian up-river trade was
short-circuited c. 300 B.C. by King Lysimachus, who established

[1] But there was a limit to the exactions which the Byzantines might impose
without provoking reprisals (Polybius, iv. 38).
[2] Strabo, p. 319.
[3] Short, op. cit.
[4] On Istria and Greek penetration of the Danube basin see Parvan, *Dacia*, ch. 3.

an overland route across the Dobrogea steppe, from Tomis
(Costanza) to the point where the railway from Costanza to
Bucharest now crosses the river, and here founded the colony of
Axiopolis. This settlement, it is true, disappeared in the ensuing
age of disorders, but under Roman rule the trade-route was
revived. Meantime silt from the Danube was choking the channels
of the Istrian inlet.[1] Tomis, therefore, supplanted it as the
emporium for the lower Danube, though its harbour (previous
to modern improvements) gave protection on the north side only.

For the Greeks the Balkan Lands could never be more than an
area of colonial exploitation; but their cousins the Macedonians
were not unfavourably placed for a political ascendancy in the
peninsula. The Macedonian homeland consisted of the lower
valleys of the Axius and the Haliacmon, together with the foot-
hills of their encircling mountains; but between 600 and 340 B.C.
a Greater Macedonia was formed which included the lowland
belt between the lower Axius and Strymon and the Chalcidic
peninsula. In its extended dimensions Macedonia formed a wide
plain or piedmont within a highland horseshoe. Thus situated,
it was exposed on several sides to raids by restless mountain tribes,
and it was liable to major incursions by migrating peoples breaking in from the Danube basin by the Morava route (p. 298).
The danger from this quarter was emphasized by the havoc which
the Galatians wrought in 279–277 B.C., when they found the
northern gate of Macedonia, the narrows of the Axius, denuded
of its defenders, and by the hard tussles which the Antigonid
kings had to sustain against the Dardanian invaders from the north-
western highlands. It was in recognition of the part which Macedonia had long played as a bulwark of Aegean civilization against
the wild folk of the European continent that its Roman conqueror
Flamininus granted it lenient conditions.[2]

On the other hand, the Macedonian plain, being largely built
up by alluvial deposits, was highly fertile;[3] its foot-hills were
strewn with silver-mines (p. 292), and the gold of Mt. Pangaeus
lay within easy reach of a resolute ruler like Philip II. The
country could therefore carry a large man-power, such as even
Athens among the Greek city-states could not rival, and once
the same strong king had centralized its government it could
embark on a policy of expansion. The new orientation of Mace-

[1] Polybius, iv. 41. 1–2.   [2] Ibid. xviii. 37. 9.
[3] Macedonia and western Thrace are now the principal European producers of
tobacco, a plant requiring a rich soil.

donian policy was marked by the transference of the seat of power from Aegae, which lay *perdu* on the western mountain border, to Pella, which at that time was still within easy reach of the coast (p. 294). Moreover, the central position of Macedonia, which exposed it to converging onslaughts in times of weakness, gave it the opportunity of quick counter-thrusts from inner lines. Thus from the time of Philip II to the coming of the Romans we find its kings laying about them in all directions—eastward across Mt. Rhodope into the Hebrus valley, where Philip II established Philippopolis (Plovdiv) as a bridgehead, northward across the Balkan range to the Danube (Alexander in 335 B.C.), and westward to the Albanian coast (Cassander in 314 B.C.). The lure of Greece and Asia, it is true, diverted Macedonian energies into other objects and reduced attempts at expansion in the Balkan Lands to spasmodic and uncoordinated thrusts. A more systematic policy of 'fanning out', such as the Romans carried out under similar geographic conditions in Italy, might have enabled the rulers of Macedon to establish a *pax Balcanica*.

The problems of frontier protection that confronted the rulers of Macedon, whether native or foreign, were no doubt one reason why the Romans hesitated for half a century (196–148 B.C.) before they annexed the country. Their first rough-and-ready expedient for the defence of their new province was to meet raid with counter-raid. Striking back at invaders by way of the Morava route, the Roman governors were repeatedly drawn on as far as the Danube (so M. Drusus in 112 and C. Curio in 75 B.C.), and thus no doubt they made the discovery that this river was the best protective line for the Balkan Lands east of Beograd.

We may surmise that Caesar would have advanced the Roman frontier to the Danube after his projected counter-attack upon the Dacians in 44 B.C.;[1] but it devolved upon Augustus to make this forward move. As a preliminary to this operation, while he was still Octavian the triumvir, he had occupied the highlands of Bosnia and Serbia, using the tributaries of the Save as his main avenues of penetration (35–34 B.C.). By this judicious strategy he reduced the difficult mountain country as rapidly as his stepsons Tiberius and Drusus carried the Alpine Lands (p. 278). But little is known of Octavian's wars in the Balkan peninsula, and even less of the remarkable campaigns in which M. Crassus (29–28 B.C.) and Cn. Lentulus (18 B.C.) crossed Mt. Haemus and secured the line of the lower Danube. Of the new provinces into which the

[1] Suetonius, *Divus Iulius* 44, § 3.

conquests of Augustus and his generals were divided Illyricum and Moesia[1] occupied the key positions, for Illyria marched with the valley of the Save and Moesia was conterminous with the Danube from Beograd to the Dobrogea.[2] With the usual Roman aversion from steppe country, the early emperors drew their frontier across the neck of the Dobrogea near the latitude of Tomis, but for greater security Trajan advanced it to the mouth of the Danube.[3] It was also left to the same emperor to extend the Roman empire beyond the lower Danube into the plain of Wallachia. His predecessors had resisted the temptation of acquiring one of the best wheatfields of Europe, the reason for their abstinence probably being that the supplies required by the Roman garrisons along the river could easily be raised on its southern bank, in Thrace and Moesia, and distant markets for the Wallachian grain would not have been any more available than for that of Hungary. But Trajan's decision to annex Transylvania carried with it the obligation to occupy permanently its approaches from the lower Danube. The trans-Danubian plain was therefore shared out between Moesia and the new province of Dacia. Under this arrangement Dacia received the central portion, including the valley of the Aluta, which gave the most convenient line of ascent to the Transylvanian plateau (by way of the Red Tower pass). But the occupation of Wallachia and the Dobrogea had a purely military purpose and was not followed up to any large extent by civilian settlement.

The first Roman road to be constructed in the Balkan Lands, the Via Egnatia, extended originally from the Adriatic ports of Apollonia and Dyrrachium (from which it took off by separate arms) to Thessalonica, but was subsequently prolonged to Byzantium.[4] Traversing the tumbled mountain system of Inner Albania and Upper Macedonia, with considerable stretches at a level exceeding 6,000 feet, it was a remarkable feat of engineering. It was indispensable as a link on the shortest route from Italy to Macedonia, and eventually it became the main road to Rome's Asiatic provinces.

[1] The date of which Moesia was constituted a province is uncertain. According to R. Syme (*Cambr. Anc. Hist.* x, pp. 367–8) it fell under Augustus; according to J. Keil (ibid. xi, p. 570) it was not anterior to Claudius.

[2] The valley of the Save was included in Pannonia, that of the Morava in Moesia.

[3] On the Dobrogea frontiers see R. P. Longden, *Cambr. Anc. Hist.* xi, pp. 170, 234. Under Trajan an advanced Roman base was established at Troesmis (modern Iglitza), some thirty miles south of the last Danube bend.

[4] A detailed description in Strabo, pp. 322–3 (following Polybius).

But Augustus' conquest of the Balkan Peninsula as a whole entailed the construction of a new road system so as to connect it directly with northern Italy and the Save valley, which henceforth was its chief gate of entry. The starting-point of this system was Singidunum, from which a trunk road descended the Danube valley. From this trunk a main branch diverged up the Morava valley to Naissus (Nish). At this point the branch forked into two limbs, of which one went by the Vardar valley to Thessalonica, while the other gained the Maritza valley by way of Serdica and followed it to Byzantium. The road to Byzantium threw off two junction roads to the lower Danube valley; one of these, taking off from Serdica, descended the Iskar valley to Oescus, the starting-point of the road to Dacia by the Aluta valley; another went across country from Adrianople to the Black Sea coast near Varna and continued along the seaboard to Tomis. Lastly, as an alternative approach to Dacia, Trajan built a diagonal road from Lissus on the Dalmatian coast which struck boldly across the Bosnian and Serbian highlands to Nish and ended on the Danube at Ratiaria (near Vidin).

Apart from the road stations mentioned above, the number of new towns founded under Roman rule was small. Of the older Balkan cities, Thessalonica acquired added importance as a T-junction of two main roads. Byzantium's role as a gate to the Black Sea was diminished, but it played a greater part than ever as a link between the continents.

The Balkan peninsula was unique among the countries of eastern Europe, in that it did not belong wholly to the Latin or to the Greek sphere of culture but was divided between them. Apart from the military stations along the Danube, all of which were naturally Latin-speaking, the zone of demarcation ran roughly along the Morava valley. In ancient times the Balkan peninsula formed an intermediate zone between Europe and Asia, between continental and Mediterranean Europe, and between the Latin and Greek civilizations.

§ 2. SCYTHIA

To the Greeks and Romans 'Scythia' meant that portion of the east European plain which extends from the Carpathians to the river Don, and from the Black Sea to the edge of the forest zone of central Russia (above the latitude of Kiev and Kharkov). This country is potentially one of the richest of Europe, for it is a veritable storehouse of raw materials. Part of its wealth, indeed,

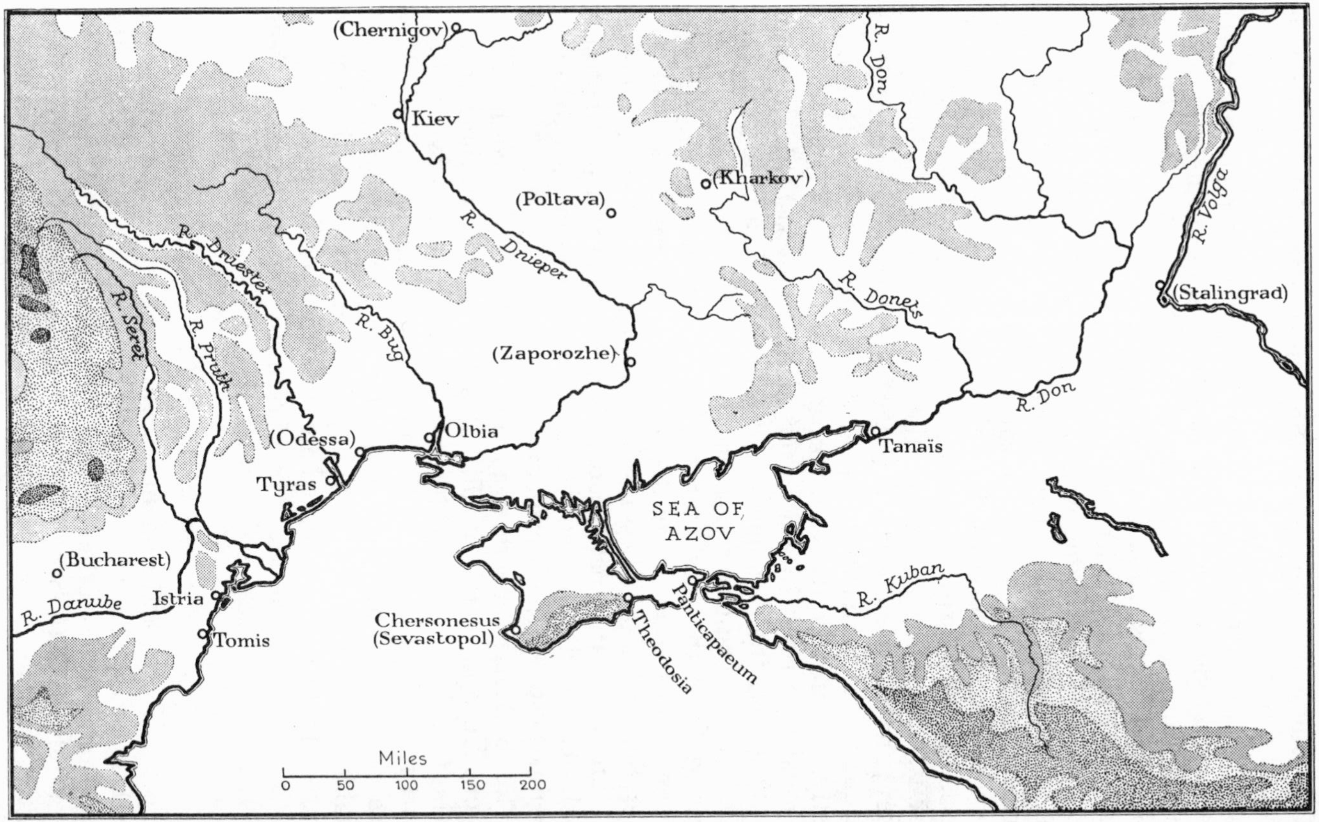

SOUTH RUSSIA AND MOLDAVIA

(Stalingrad)

R. Volga

R. Don

R. Donets

R. Don

R. Kuban

Tanaïs

(Kharkov)

SEA OF
AZOV

Panticapaeum

Theodosia

(Poltava)

R. Dnieper

(Zaporozhe)

Olbia

Chersonesus
(Sevastopol)

(Chernigov)

Kiev

R. Bug

Odessa

Tyras

Miles

0   50   100   150   200

R. Dniester

R. Pruth

Tomis

R. Seret

Istria

(Bucharest)

R. Danube

was not exploited in ancient times. The deposits of coal and iron in the Ukraine and the Don basin lay untouched; the hemp and honey, furs and pelts, which Genoese and Hansards in the Middle Ages imported to the Mediterranean and Baltic countries, had not yet become staple articles of commerce; and the wool of the south Russian steppes had a poor reputation among the Greeks.[1]

But its other assets were highly prized in the ancient world. The Black Sea, though poor in animal life in its open waters, contains important fishery-grounds at the mouths of its chief rivers, and the Sea of Azov is also well stocked. In addition to the usual Mediterranean species, the tunny and the mackerel, the giant sturgeon formed part of the catch,[2] though it was valued for its flesh rather than for its roe. But the most substantial treasure of Scythia lay in its wheatfields. The 'black earth' of the Ukrainian and Moldavian plains is exceptionally rich in the ingredients for cereal plants. In view of the hard winters, the sowing must be deferred until spring, and the ploughing has to be performed while the soil is still damp and sticky from a recent thaw, so that strong teams of horses are required for haulage. But horses have always been plentiful in the east European plain; and given a generous supply of spring rain, which as a rule falls plenteously,[3] a good harvest will follow with little additional labour. The surplus grain, moreover, can easily be moved by river to the Black Sea ports, where in ancient times ready buyers were to be found for the markets of Greece and the Aegean area. Finally, Scythia was the terminal zone of a gold-route from the Ural or the Altai.[4]

But the approach to Scythia from the Mediterranean is not easy. The entrance to the Black Sea is double-locked by the tortuous straits of the Dardanelles and Bosporus, where the current, under the stimulus of frequent north-easterly winds,

[1] The Scythians used hemp as a material for smoke-baths (Herodotus, iv. 75); they did not export it for cordage. Aristotle (*De animalium generatione* v. 3, p. 783*a* 14) commented on the hardness of Scythian wool.

[2] Herodotus, iv. 53. 3.

[3] The total annual rainfall does not exceed 12–18 inches, but a large proportion of it falls in spring. The conditions of climate are not unlike those of central Canada and the wheat-belt of U.S.A.

[4] On the provenience of the gold which was traded at the Black Sea ports see G. F. Hudson, *Europe and China*, ch. 1. The supplies were intermittent; but finds in south Russian tombs suggest a 'boom' in the fourth century B.C. (Rostovtzeff, *Iranians and Greeks in Southern Russia*, ch. iv). The same source of bullion maintained the gold coinage of Byzantium and, when conveyed to Italy by the Genoese or Venetians, permitted the resumption of gold coinage in western Europe.

may flow at a rate of six knots (p. 294) and shoot with disconcerting force off the numerous headlands.[1] Within the Black Sea northerly winds blow through most of the summer, so that in ancient days the season for entering it from the Aegean was restricted to a few weeks of spring, and a risk of autumn fogs would hasten the visitors' return.

The coast of Scythia was relatively easy of access. The sandbars with which the rivers have since fringed it had not yet become a serious obstruction in ancient times; and a current of warm water from the Mediterranean, which ascends the Dardanelles and Bosporus in an undertow and sets towards the Dnieper estuary, preserves the western ports from being icebound for more than one month.[2] The harbours of western Scythia were mostly situated on the high and firm western banks of the river mouths; and on parts of the Crimean coast erosion ports of the Mediterranean type gave adequate shelter for small craft.

But to the settlement of Greek immigrants in Scythia the climate was a serious deterrent. Greek writers could not agree about the Scythian summer, for while Herodotus called it cool and continuously wet,[3] and Aristotle damp and hot,[4] it was left to Strabo to describe it correctly as torrid.[5] But all were united in decrying the Scythian winter. According to Herodotus this season lasted eight months, and the cold was 'unendurable';[6] and Strabo related how Mithridates' cavalry crossed the Sea of Azov on ice.[7] In point of fact, the frost in southern Russia does not usually last more than seventy-five days, and it is less intense than in the north and centre, but it is accompanied by violent blizzards and blinding snowstorms which sweep unchecked over the bare plains.

The Black Sea in ancient times also had a bad reputation as a haunt of pirates. A good base for corsairs was furnished by the

[1] The story of the Symplegades or Clashing Rocks at the Bosporus entrance (Pindar, *Pythia* iv. 369–70) may be an inversion of a real danger to navigation: the rocks do not come to the ships, but the ships may go to the rocks.

[2] Thirty days at Odessa, as against a hundred at Rostov-on-Don. A. R. Burn's identification of Pindar's Symplegades or Clashing Rocks, which nearly wrecked the good ship Argo (Apollonius Rhodius, iv. 924 ff.), with ice-floes in the Black Sea (*Minoans, Philistines and Greeks*, pp. 191–3) would hardly suit the conditions on the Argonauts' track.

[3] iv. 28. 2–3.

[4] *Problemata* 938a 38–9.

[5] p. 307.

[6] iv. 28. 1–2.

[7] p. 73.

deep coves of the Sevastopol area in the Crimea,[1] and an even
better one by the highly indented sub-Caucasian seaboard.[2]

The interior of Scythia for the most part makes easy travelling.
Though the coastal regions were formerly streaked with forests,[3]
these nowhere formed an impenetrable curtain. The open plains
become veritable quagmires after the spring thaw, and in summer
they are swept by dust-storms; yet in the course of centuries they
have been the avenue by which countless invaders from Asia,
from Scythians and Sarmatians to Tatars, have made their way
into Europe. For voyages up country the rivers give excellent
conditions in the summer season. The fulsome language with
which Herodotus described the pure and sweet waters of the
Dnieper, and the rich meadows that lined it,[4] has found echoes
among modern travellers.

But progress up the rivers of south-western Russia is eventually
barred by waterfalls, due to a ridge of granite which resists
erosion and forms as it were a step in the beds of the streams. In
particular, the Zaporozhe falls on the Dnieper tend to isolate its
Kiev reach from the seaboard.[5] The chief barrier, however,
between the south Russian plain and its hinterland in ancient
times was the deep and continuous stretch of woodland extending
northward from latitude 50°. The felling of this immense forest
was hardly begun before the thirteenth century, when the Tatar
invasion drove the people of the southern plain to seek refuge in
clearances within the covert.[6] Herodotus' statement, that from
a point eleven days by boat up the Dnieper the land lay mostly
desolate, may therefore have held true of his own time.[7] Another
serious obstacle to the penetration of the inland consisted in the
vast marshes of White Russia and eastern Poland, where the
flatness of the land retards the run-off of rains and snows, and
a hard pan in the subsoil prevents their absorption. Before
the clearance of the forest this waterlogged area probably was
even more extensive, and we therefore need not reject absolutely

[1] Strabo (p. 308) describes the Crimean pirates as a thing of the past. But in the
days of Claudius the coast still harboured wreckers (Tacitus, *Annals* xii. 17. 4).

[2] Strabo, p. 495; Arrian, *Periplus Ponti Euxini*, ch. 15.

[3] Herodotus, iv. 18. 1; Theophrastus, *Historia Plantarum* iv. 5. 3; Dio Chrysostom, 36. 3 (forest near Olbia).

[4] iv. 53.

[5] A regular connexion between Kiev and the Black Sea and Bosporus was first
established in the ninth century by Varangians from the north working down river.

[6] In this emergency Moscow, as a refuge town within the forest belt, displaced
Kiev as the Russian capital.

[7] iv. 18. 2.

Herodotus' statement that the Scythian rivers had their origin in 'lakes',[1] though the lakes would be shallow meres rather than deep basins. Thus the geographical conditions indicated that Scythia would be late in coming within the ambit of the Mediterranean world, that its seaboard would eventually be studded with trading settlements, but that its hinterland should remain outside the sphere of ancient commerce and civilization.

The natural wealth of Russia gave rise to two prehistoric civilizations, of which one was based on the copper-mines of the Kuban valley (at the northern foot of the Caucasus),[2] and the other, the 'Tripolye' culture, on the wheatlands of the Ukraine.[3] By 2000 B.C. these civilizations had made contact with the Early Cycladic culture of the Aegean area; but it is doubtful whether they came into direct relation with that of Minoan Crete,[4] and the evidence for regular trade activities between Greece and the Black Sea in the days of the Achaean ascendancy is of the slenderest.[5] A permanent connexion between the Greek lands and Scythia was not established until the days of Greek colonization in the eighth and seventh centuries B.C.

Of the Greek settlements in Scythia, the more westerly ones of Tyras and Olbia were essentially trading-stations which bought wheat from the Scythian landlords and paid for it with Greek ceramic and metal ware. Both cities were built at river-mouths, so as to facilitate delivery of the grain. Tyras stood on the site of modern Akkerman, inside the 'liman' or shallow-water gulf into which the Dniester discharges.[6] Olbia was originally founded on a cramped site on the island (now a peninsula) of Berezan, at the joint effluence of the Dnieper and the Bug,[7] but was later transferred to a site on the Bug 'liman'. On this more roomy platform Olbia tapped the traffic of both rivers; by the Dnieper route it established extensive connexions with the hinterland.[8]

---

[1] iv. 51, 54, 57.

[2] Rostovtzeff, *Iranians and Greeks*, ch. 2.

[3] Childe, *Dawn of European Civilisation*, ch. xi.　　　　[4] Ibid., pp. 55–63.

[5] Cary and Warmington, *The Ancient Explorers*, p. 26. The siege of Troy has been represented as an attempt by the Achaeans to remove a wayside control of an early Aegean trade-route to the Black Sea (W. W. Leaf, *Homer and History*, ch. 6). But the archaeological evidence accords better with the view that it was a mere Viking adventure in quest of booty (M. Nilsson, *Homer and Mycenae*, p. 113).

[6] E. H. Minns, *Scythians and Greeks*, p. 445.

[7] E. v. Stern, *Klio*, 1909, pp. 139–52.

[8] Minns, pp. 453–4. Odessa, the modern counterpart of Olbia, was not founded until 1794. Its natural harbourage gives it indifferent shelter. Nikolaiev and Cherson (the later Genoese station) presumably lay too far up the Dniester for the early Greek colonists.

In the Crimea the Greeks discovered a Mediterranean oasis amid a strange continent. Here the submerged mountain chain that once linked the Caucasus with the Balkan range (p. 7) reappears in a ridge which rises to nearly 5,000 feet at its southern edge and makes its last dive to the Black Sea in cliffs of 500–700 feet. Within the mountain zone jagged limestone buttresses set amid ravines and deep sea-inlets reproduced a type of scenery familiar to the Greeks and gave them protection against marauders from the hinterland. At the western end of the mountain chain Greek settlers moved by a typical progression from the outer and indifferent harbour of Fanary Bay to the more sheltered inlet of Quarantine Bay. To afford security against raiders from the inland a wall was subsequently built (probably not until Roman times) across the western tip of the Crimea along the Chernaya ravine to Balaklava.[1] The land thus enclosed, though now bare, was formerly covered with vineyards; but the vines had to be covered over in winter.[2] The city of Chersonesus which was built along Quarantine Bay lacked opportunities on its semi-isolated site for inland trade, but it could offer a real 'home from home' to Greek immigrants.

The Riviera under the southern edge of the Crimean mountains has no good harbour and is too narrow to accommodate any large settlement. But its continuation in the Kertch peninsula, where the mountains slope more gently to the sea, and a rebate in the coast offers better shelter to shipping, invites closer habitation. Here the Greeks built a town named Theodosia, from which the grain of Kertch and the northern Crimea was exported to Athens in the fifth and fourth centuries.[3] But Theodosia was little more than an outpost of Panticapaeum (modern Kertch city), which stood on a commanding ridge (now known as 'Mithridates' armchair') above the Straits of Kertch and lay close to the best grain-fields of the Crimea.[4] Under a dynasty of native but phil-Hellene rulers, the Spartocids,[5] it became the seat of a small but long-lived empire which collected the grain crops on either side of the Straits and the merchandise from the Don valley. The gorgeous gold coinage of Panticapaeum shows

[1] Rostovtzeff, *Cambr. Anc. Hist.* xi, p. 96.
[2] Strabo, p. 308; Minns, op. cit., pp. 495 ff.; K. Neumann, *Die Hellenen im Skythenlande*, pp. 379–402.
[3] Strabo, p. 309; Minns, p. 556. Under the name of Kaffa, this site became a Genoese station in the Middle Ages.
[4] Strabo, p. 309; Minns, pp. 562–6.
[5] On this dynasty see Rostovtzeff, *Cambr. Anc. Hist.* viii, ch. 18.

that by 350 B.C. it had become the receiving-point of the bullion from the Ural or Siberian mines.[1]

The Sea of Azov, which now carries a large share of the grain-traffic, had little attraction for the Greeks, apart from its fisheries. Its extreme shallowness (previous to the advent of the modern dredger) made it unsuitable for the larger merchant vessels, which had to hire a pilot to avoid being grounded,[2] and the surrounding country-side was as yet untilled. The Greek town of Tanaïs at the mouth of the Don was the natural terminal point for any transcontinental trade between Scythia and central Asia; but its somewhat remote inland position[3] made its existence as a colony precarious, and it never attained an importance comparable to that of Panticapaeum.

In the days of the 'Pax Tatarica' (thirteenth to fifteenth centuries) a trade route from the Sea of Azov ascended the Don valley to the vicinity of Stalingrad, and after crossing the Volga near this site branched off into two tracks across the Kirghiz steppe, of which one dipped down towards Bactria and India, while the other kept straight on past the southern rim of the Altai mountains towards Mongolia and China. The second of these routes was probably pursued as far as the Altai range by a Greek traveller of the seventh or sixth century named Aristeas.[4] According to Aristeas the road went on to the outer sea by way of the 'Hyperborean' country. If his 'Hyperboreans' are not a mere product of his fancy, they may be identified with the Chinese.[5] It was no doubt by this route that some of the Mediterranean exports to the Far East (textiles and glass) were conveyed.[6] But Herodotus' haziness about Aristeas, and the general ignorance of the Greeks about the Volga (which they mostly ignored) and the Caspian Sea (which geographers intermediate between Herodotus and Ptolemy mistook for an inlet of the Northern Ocean), indicate that such trade as passed through

[1] Head, *Historia Numorum* (2nd ed.), p. 280.

[2] Polybius, iv. 40. 8.

[3] Minns, pp. 566–9. Presumably as the result of a change in the river's course, the town was transferred from the Don valley to a high cliff on the right bank.

[4] Herodotus, iv. 13. His story is accepted by How and Wells (commentary ad loc.) and by Hudson (*Europe and China*, ch. 1). Aristeas' route was re-opened in the thirteenth century by John Carpini and served during the Pax Tatarica to convey the costlier forms of merchandise to and from central Asia.

[5] Hudson, loc. cit.

[6] On the ancient China trade see C. Seligman, *Antiquity*, 1937, pp. 5–30. The glassware found in the Far East was apparently of Egyptian workmanship, but the northerly latitude in which it was discovered (in Mongolia and Korea) suggests that it went by the Siberian rather than by the Tibetan or Indian Ocean route.

Siberia was not confided to Greek hands. Similarly we may infer from Herodotus' ignorance of the great bend in the lower Dnieper, and of the falls near Zaporozhe,[1] that Greek traders did not get through to Kiev; and the paucity of Greek finds beyond Kiev confirms this view. The forests and marshes of inland Russia remained for the Greeks a wonderland of towering 'Rhipaean Mountains' and everlasting snow.

The export of grain from Scythia to the Aegean area, which was not seriously affected by the competition of Egypt in the Hellenistic period,[2] fell off in the days of Roman rule, when the Greek world tended to revert to a self-contained economy. But Scythian wheat was sent to the Roman military stations on the lower Danube and in Asia Minor.[3] The western end of the Scythian plain, moreover, had a strategic interest for the Romans, as a gate of entry into the Balkan peninsula and also (by way of the easy passes of the eastern Carpathians) into Dacia. A fleet was therefore set to patrol the river Seret, and two military roads were built, from the last Danube bend (near Galati) and from Tyras, to make an outer line of defence across the Moldavian plain and to connect the Black Sea stations with Transylvania.[4]

Stray finds of Hadrianic coins as far afield as Chernigov and Poltava[5] might suggest a renewed advance of Mediterranean traders under the Roman peace. But the important transcontinental traffic which was opened up in the third century and is betokened by copious finds of Late Roman coins on the Swedish island of Gothland (p. 286) should probably be credited, not to Greeks or Romans, but to the Goths who migrated from the Baltic to south Russia after A.D. 200.[6]

---

[1] Of the lower course of the Dnieper Herodotus merely said that it flowed south for forty days (iv. 53. 4).

[2] Rostovtzeff, *Hellenistic World*, ii, pp. 1249–52.

[3] F. Oertel, *Cambr. Anc. Hist.* xii, p. 244.

[4] Parvan, *Dacia*, pp. 192–3.

[5] Rostovtzeff, *Iranians and Greeks*, p. 215.

[6] Id., *Roman Empire*, p. 531; A. Alföldi, *Cambr. Anc. Hist.* xii, pp. 161–2. The amber found near Kiev may also have been brought by the Goths. (This seems more credible than that it was of local origin, as suggested by Minns, op. cit., p. 7.)

BIBLIOGRAPHY

A. ANCIENT SOURCES

1. GEOGRAPHICAL WORKS

(a) Greek

Two complete geographical treatises by ancient Greek writers survive: (i) The Γεωγραφικά of Strabo, which is a descriptive survey of the countries known to the Greeks and Romans at the time of Augustus and Tiberius, comprising seventeen books. Much of Strabo's information was at second hand, and not all of it was up to date; and the author, being a Homeric 'fundamentalist', digressed into many unprofitable disquisitions on the infallibility of Homer's geography. For these reasons his books on Greece are particularly disappointing. But as a piece of descriptive geography Strabo's work is no mean achievement—indeed his books on Italy, Spain, and Gaul deserve honourable mention for their range of knowledge and their geographic insight; and as a source of geographic information it is by far the most important of those at our disposal.

(ii) The Γεωγραφικὴ Ὑφήγησις of P. Claudius Ptolemaeus (Ptolemy), written c. A.D. 150. This work is devoted exclusively to mathematical geography and map-construction, and six of its eight books consist of tables of latitude and longitude. Apart from the topographic details which it provides, it is only of occasional value to the historical geographer.

Some shorter Greek works of a geographical character have been preserved in whole or in part. The more valuable of these, consisting mostly of περίπλοι or descriptions of the Mediterranean and other coasts frequented by Greek navigators, are collected in volume I of C. Müller's *Geographici Graeci Minores* (Paris, 1855). Particular importance attaches to the fragments of Hecataeus' Γῆς Περίοδος, the earliest extant description of the world as known to Greek travellers (c. 500 B.C.), and to the Περίπλους τῆς Ἐρυθρᾶς Θαλάσσης, a handbook of sailing-directions for the Red Sea and the Indian Ocean (c. A.D. 60). The most up-to-date text of Hecataeus' fragments is in F. Jacoby's *Fragmente der Griechischen Historiker*, i, pp. 16–47 (Berlin, 1923). Recent texts of the Περίπλους τῆς Ἐρυθρᾶς Θαλάσσης have been provided by J. I. H. Frisk (*Le Périple de la Mer Érythrée*, Gothenburg, 1927) and by W. H. Schoff (*The Periplus of the Erythraean Sea*, Longmans Green, 1912). Schoff's identifications are in some cases disputable, but his commentary on the text is copious and generally well informed.

(b) Roman

The loss of Agrippa's *Descriptio Orbis*, a commentary on his map of the world, is our worst misfortune in the field of ancient geography. The value of its miscellaneous information may be gathered from many quotations in the *Naturalis Historia* of Pliny the Elder. Of the surviving Roman road-books, the *Antonine Itinerary* (ed. G. Parthey and M. Pinder, 1848), a work mainly of the early third century A.D., provides us with the skeleton of our Roman road-maps.

2. HISTORICAL WORKS

(a) Greek

Herodotus, who might claim to be the 'Father of Geography' as well as the 'Father of History', created a tradition of interest in the geographical background of history which lived on in other major historians such as Thucydides and Theopompus, Polybius, and Posidonius. Herodotus is, along with Strabo, our chief source for the geography of ancient Egypt and Scythia. Much geographical information is disseminated in the writings of other Greek historians, notably of Diodorus, who at least had the merit of covering almost the entire range of the Greek world.

(b) *Roman*

Of the extant Roman historians, Caesar had an appreciation of geography which extended beyond the details of his campaigns. Sallust and Livy give good descriptions of particular sites, but do not supply the general geographic background of their histories. Tacitus might be called the most ungeographical, as Mommsen has dubbed him the most unmilitary, of Roman historical authors.

B. MODERN WORKS

(The following list of books and articles makes no attempt at completeness. It is limited to works which the present author has found useful.)

(a) BOOKS ON ANCIENT GEOGRAPHERS

H. BERGER, *Geschichte der wissenschaftlichen Erdkunde der Griechen* (2nd ed., Leipzig, 1903).
SIR E. H. BUNBURY, *History of Ancient Geography* (2 vols., Murray, 1879).
H. F. TOZER, *History of Ancient Geography* (2nd ed., by M. Cary, Cambridge University Press, 1935).
E. H. WARMINGTON, *Greek Geography* (Dent, 1934).

(b) DESCRIPTIVE GEOGRAPHIES

1. *The Mediterranean Area and Adjunct Countries*

M. P. CHARLESWORTH, *Trade-Routes and Commerce of the Roman Empire* (2nd ed., Cambridge University Press, 1926).
T. FISCHER, *Mittelmeerbilder* (Leipzig, 1913).
E. LUDWIG, *The Mediterranean* (Hamish Hamilton, 1942).
ELIZABETH MONROE, *The Mediterranean in Politics* (Clarendon Press, 1938).
SIR J. L. MYRES, *Mediterranean Civilization* (Cambridge University Press, 1943).
M. I. NEWBIGIN, *The Mediterranean Lands* (Christophers, 1924).
—— *South Europe* (Methuen, 1932).
A. PHILIPPSON, *Das Mittelmeergebiet* (Leipzig, 1904).
ELLEN C. SEMPLE, *The Geography of the Mediterranean Region. Its Relation to Ancient History* (Constable, 1932).
SIR A. E. ZIMMERN, *The Greek Commonwealth* (5th ed., Clarendon Press, 1931), part i.

2. *Greece*

(a) *General*

S. CASSON, *Ancient Greece* (Clarendon Press, 1922).
V. EHRENBERG, *Aspects of the Ancient World* (Blackwell, Oxford, 1946), ch. 3.
E. A. GARDNER, *Greece and the Aegean* (Harrap, 1938).
O. MAULL, *Griechisches Mittelmeergebiet* (Breslau, 1922).

316 BIBLIOGRAPHY

SIR J. L. MYRES, *Greek Lands and the Greek People* (Clarendon Press, 1910).
C. NEUMANN and J. PARTSCH, *Physikalische Geographie von Griechenland* (Breslau, 1885).
A. STRUCK, *Griechische Landeskunde* (Frankfurt, 1912).

(*b*) *Regional:* (i) *Northern Greece*

N. G. L. HAMMOND, *Annual of the British School at Athens*, vol. xxxi (1931–2), pp. 131–79. On the North Greek Highland.
W. M. LEAKE, *Travels in Northern Greece* (4 vols., 1838 ff.).
A. PHILIPPSON, *Thessalien und Epirus* (Berlin, 1897).
F. STÄHLIN, *Das hellenische Thessalien* (Stuttgart, 1924).
W. J. WOODHOUSE, *Aetolia* (Clarendon Press, 1897).

(*b*) (ii) *Peloponnesus*

E. CURTIUS, *Peloponnesos* (Gotha, 1851).
W. M. LEAKE, *Travels in the Morea* (3 vols., 1846 ff.).
A. PHILIPPSON, *Der Peloponnes* (Berlin, 1892).

(*b*) (iii) *The Aegean Area*

F. GEYER, *Topographie und Geographie der Insel Euboia* (Berlin, 1903).
A. PHILIPPSON, *Die griechische Inselwelt* (Gotha, 1901).
H. F. TOZER, *The Isles of the Aegean* (Clarendon Press, 1890).

3. *Italy*

T. ASHBY, *The Roman Campagna in Classical Times* (Benn, 1927).
G. BAGNANI, *The Roman Campagna and its Treasures* (Methuen, 1929).
H. NISSEN, *Italische Landeskunde* (2 vols.; Berlin, 1883 ff.).

4. *Sardinia*

E. S. BOUCHIER, *Sardinia in Ancient Times* (Oxford, Blackwell, 1917).

5. *Asia. General*

D. G. HOGARTH, *The Nearer East* (Heinemann, 1902).
E. HUNTINGTON, *The Pulse of Asia* (Houghton Mifflin, Boston and New York, 1907).
R. W. LYDE, *The Continent of Asia* (Macmillan, 1933).
L. D. STAMP, *Asia* (3rd ed.; Methuen, 1936).

6. *Asia Minor*

A. PHILIPPSON, *Reisen und Forschungen im westlichen Kleinasien* (Petermann's *Mitteilungen*, Ergänzungsbände 167, 172, 177, 180).
SIR W. M. RAMSAY, *Historical Geography of Asia Minor* (Murray, 1890).

7. *Syria*

E. HUNTINGTON, *Palestine* (Houghton Mifflin, Boston and New York, 1911).
C. F. KENT, *Biblical Geography and History* (Smith Elder, 1911).
G. A. SMITH, *The Historical Geography of the Holy Land* (25th ed., Hodder and Stoughton, 1931).

8. *Arabia*

CHRISTINA GRANT, *The Syrian Desert* (A. and C. Black, 1937).
D. G. HOGARTH, *The Penetration of Arabia* (Lawrence and Bullen, 1904).

BIBLIOGRAPHY 317

9. *Mesopotamia*
Sir W. Willcocks, *The Irrigation of Mesopotamia* (2nd ed., Spon, 1917).

10. *Persia*
Sir P. Sykes, *History of Persia*, vol. i (3rd ed., Macmillan, 1930).

11. *Afghanistan*
Sir G. Macmunn, *Afghanistan* (Bell, 1929).
Sir P. Sykes, *History of Afghanistan*, vol. i (Macmillan, 1940).

12. *India*
Sir T. Holdich, *India* (Heinemann, 1904).
—— *The Gates of India* (Macmillan, 1910).
E. H. Warmington, *The Commerce between the Roman Empire and India*, pt. i, chs. 1 and 2 (Cambridge University Press, 1928).

13. *Cyrenaica*
J. W. Gregory, *Geographical Journal*, vol. xlvii (1916), pp. 323–39.

14. *North-West Africa*
J. Carcopino, *Le Maroc Antique* (6th ed., Paris, 1943).
W. Fitzgerald, *Africa* (3rd ed., Methuen, 1910).
S. Gsell, *Histoire ancienne de l'Afrique du Nord*, vol. i (Hachette, 1913).

15. *Europe. General*
R. W. Lyde, *The European Continent* (4th ed., Macmillan, 1930).
J. Partsch, *Central Europe* (Heinemann, 1903).

16. *Spain*
A. Schulten, *Numantia*, vol. i, pp. 149–78 (Munich, 1914).

17. *France*
C. Jullian, *Histoire de la Gaule*, vol. i (Paris, 1943).
Hilda Ormsby, *France* (Methuen, 1931).
P. Vidal de la Blache, *Tableau Géographique de la France* (E. Lavisse, *Histoire de la France*, vol. i; Paris, 1903).

18. *Belgium*
F. Cumont, *Comment la Belgique fut romanisée* (2nd ed., Brussels, 1929).

19. *Holland*
A. Byvanck, *Nederland in den romeinschen tijd*, vol. ii (Utrecht, 1945).

20. *Britain*
R. G. Collingwood and J. N. L. Myres, *Roman Britain and the English Settlements*, chs. i and ii (2nd ed., Clarendon Press, 1937).
Sir H. J. Mackinder, *Britain and the British Seas* (2nd ed., Clarendon Press, 1930).
L. D. Stamp and S. H. Beaver, *The British Isles* (3rd ed., Longmans Green, 1941).

21. *Switzerland*
F. Stähelin, *Die Schweiz in römischer Zeit* (2nd ed., Basle, 1927).

22. The Balkan Lands

S. Casson, *Macedonia, Thrace, and Illyria* (Clarendon Press, 1926).
J. Cvijić, *La Péninsule balkanique* (Paris, 1918).
A. Struck, *Makedonische Fahrten* (C. Patsch, *Zur Kunde der Balkanhalbinsel*, Heft 4; Vienna and Leipzig, 1907).

23. Russia

Sir E. H. Minns, *Scythians and Greeks* (Cambridge University Press, 1913).
K. Neumann, *Die Hellenen im Skythenlande* (Berlin, 1855).

24. The Mediterranean and other coasts

The *Sailing Directions* of the British Admiralty, in the following books: *The Mediterranean Pilot*, and the *Atlantic, Black Sea, Indian Ocean, Persian Gulf* and *Red Sea* Pilots.

C. MAPS

(a) Survey maps

A list of the principal modern survey maps, on a scale ranging from 1:50,000 to 1:500,000, but mostly 1:50,000 or 1:63,360 (1 inch to a mile), will be found in A. R. Hinks, *Maps and Survey* (3rd ed., Cambridge University Press, 1933).
Attention may also be drawn to:
E. Curtius and J. A. Kaupert, *Karten von Attika* (1:25,000);
A. Philippson, *Das westliche Kleinasien* (1:300,000).
For the Mediterranean and other seas, see the *British Admiralty Charts*.

(b) Medium-scale maps

Murray's Handy Classical Maps. General editor, G. B. Grundy.
> Sixteen sheets in 11 volumes. Scale from 1:633,600 upward; coloured contours.
> Besides the maps of Greece (2 sheets, 1:633,600) and Italy (2 sheets, 1:1,200,000), special attention may be drawn to the map of Asia Minor (1 sheet, 1:2,500,000), by J. G. C. Anderson.

H. Kiepert, *Formae Orbis Antiqui.*
> Thirty-six sheets, with shadow-relief and light brown colouring; scale mostly 1:2,000,000 or 1:2,500,000; Italy 1:400,000 and 1:600,000; Greece, ranging from 1:600,000 to 1:1,200,000.

Roman Britain (Ordnance Survey, Southampton; 2nd ed., 1928).
> One sheet; coloured contours; scale 1:c. 1,000,000 (16 miles to an inch). This map contains many additions and corrections based on aerial surveys.

INDEX

(Exclusively modern names are given in italics)

INDEX